Seeds of Power

Seeds of Power

Explorations in Ottoman Environmental History

edited by

Onur İnal and Yavuz Köse

Copyright © 2019
The White Horse Press,
The Old Vicarage, Winwick, Cambridgeshire, PE28 5PN, UK

Set in 11 point Adobe Garamond Pro

British Library Cataloguing in Publication Data
A catalogue record for this book is available from the British Library

ISBN   978-1-874267-99-7 (HB) 978-1-912186-81-5 (PB)

CONTENTS

Contents

FOREWORD: OTTOMAN AND NATURE

Alan Mikhail

'The camel', wrote George Perkins Marsh, 'displays no inconsiderable sagacity'.[1] Marsh – naturalist, diplomat, philologist – is most famous for his 1864 treatise on humans and the environment entitled *Man and Nature*. About a decade before this work, though, Marsh penned a less well-known book on the suitability, mostly for military purposes, of the introduction of the camel to the United States. He writes that this topic has 'long since engaged my attention', and his conclusion, as might be guessed from the above quote, was that the camel would do well and prove of great utility in the United States.[2] He thus encouraged its importation and acclimatisation efforts.

Marsh was only able to reach this recommendation thanks to his time in the Ottoman Empire. In the 1850s, he spent five years as the United States ambassador to the Ottoman Empire, a period that allowed him to explore the history of camel domestication and the animal's behavior and physiology.[3]

Ungulates aside, the larger question of how Marsh's years in the Ottoman Empire shaped his thinking about the environment and humanity's relationships to it – how this experience influenced one of the foundational figures of environmental history, a 'prophet' as one of his biographers calls him, as well as his monumental text – has yet to be written. It is indeed a major lacuna in Marsh's biography and presents quite the gift to Ottomanists: one of the intellectual forefathers of the American school of environmental history and the conservation movement spent half a decade in the empire. When the story of Marsh and the Ottoman Empire is written, it will, one assumes, go a long way in showing the surprising influence of the empire on the formation of the field of environmental history and on the origins of the conservation movement.

---

1. George P. Marsh, *The Camel: His Organization, Habits and Uses, Considered with Reference to His Introduction into the United States* (Boston: Gould and Lincoln; New York: Sheldon, Blakeman, & Co.; Cincinnati: George S. Blanchard, 1856), p. 100.

2. Ibid., p. 5. See also Andrew Isenberg, '"A Land of Hardship and Distress": Camels, North American Deserts, and the Limits of Conquest', *Global Environment* 12, 1, Special Issue 'Deserts in Environmental History' (2019)

3. For a useful discussion of Marsh's years in the Ottoman Empire, see David Lowenthal, *George Perkins Marsh, Prophet of Conservation* (Seattle: University of Washington Press, 2000), pp. 109–34.

As we wait for this account, thankfully we have the present book. It does precisely what one might want that other book to do – it shows some of the importance of the Ottoman Empire for environmental history. However, it does much more than that as well. It points to the utility and potential of environmental history for the study of the Ottoman Empire. The essays in this book explore the myriad ways one of the world's largest and most durable empires, the longest-lasting in the history of the Muslim world, influenced how humanity lived with, in, through and against nature. This book, indeed, provides a holistic and robust treatment of the environmental history of the Ottoman Empire and will prove of enormous value for Ottoman and environmental historians, of course, but also historians of early modernity and the nineteenth century', empire and the history of science, and historians of the Middle East and Islam.

In their introduction, the editors tell us that the following chapters offer 'new answers to old questions'. That they do. They propose intriguing and novel explanations of both the emergence of the empire and its end. They explain something of the history of the imperial capital and its resource base. They expand our understanding of land management and the agrarian economy. They tell histories of important crops such as grapes, rice and figs. They enlist nonhuman actors as shapers of the Ottoman past. They inflect the social history of the empire with an ecological sensibility. From these essays, we gain new perspective on the history of capitalism, parliamentary government, demography and science.

In addition to the old questions, this volume also offers new answers to several relatively new ones. That is, it takes up some of the leads of the burgeoning field of Ottoman environmental history and suggests critical ways to take them forward. For example, the chapters that follow urge us to understand the relationships between humans and nonhumans beyond questions of just property and capital, as has been the norm to date. We come to see livestock playing crucial social and even familial functions in Ottoman Anatolia. These chapters, furthermore, both nuance and appraise how historians have so far viewed the role of the Little Ice Age in the empire. They also show how, when considered in different geographies, questions of infrastructure, disease, city-country relations and environmental improvement tell different stories from those we currently have. In these and many other ways, this volume both convincingly and productively pushes the historiography of Ottoman environmental history onto new terrain.

Foreword: Ottoman and Nature

The most significant collective contribution of these pieces is their argument for the specificities of a particular Ottoman environmental sensibility. What were the contours of such an Ottoman sensibility? The two legs on which it stood were stewardship and connection. The Ottomans valued the careful stewardship of the resources, labour and lands under their control. They preserved and carefully harvested their precious forests. Their land regime pumped tax revenue into the coffers of the state but also put a premium on avoiding the over-exhaustion of soils. At the same time, the Ottomans, and all those living in the empire, understood the ecological connections forged by imperial rule. Animals and humans were bound together not only through modes of production and labour, but also through their intertwined affective lives in hills and villages throughout the empire. Ideas about nature travelled, thanks to the translation of texts and as part of the use and understanding of specific natural resources. Such ecological linkages helped address deficiencies around the empire, but they also sometimes had negative consequences. Sweet water was meant to be used by the collective, but could also be monopolised by the few to coerce others. Regions relying on foodstuffs from other parts of the empire necessarily faced vulnerabilities in their food supplies. Above all, as the editors tell us, 'Ottoman power was predicated on the interconnections'. This, then, is the key to understanding what was specific about Ottoman environmental history – that the sprawling empire balanced and braided together its ecological resources and deficiencies to rule effectively.

FIGURES, MAPS AND TABLES

Figures and Maps

Chapter Two

Chapter Four

Chapter Five

Chapter Seven

Figures, Maps and Tables

Chapter Eight

Chapter Nine

Tables

Chapter Two

Chapter Four

Chapter Nine

GUIDE TO SPELLING AND PRONUNCIATION OF TURKISH WORDS

Spelling

All Ottoman Turkish and Arabic words and phrases have been spelled using the modern Turkish alphabet to make the text easy to the reader. Some words that have entered the Oxford English Dictionary are an exception to this, such as *janissary* instead of *yeniçeri*. All diacritics have been omitted in the interest of simplicity, with a few exceptions in original quotes, author names and book titles. All translations from non-English sources have been made by the authors.

Pronunciation

C, c = pronounced like the 'j' in justice
Ç, ç = pronounced like the 'ch' in change
Ğ, ğ = soft 'g' (hardly pronounced), likens to 'gh' as in weight
I, ı = a dotless 'i', pronounced like the 'i' in cousin
İ, i = a dotted 'i', pronounced like the 'ee' in see, but shorter
Ö, ö = pronounced like the 'i' in bird, the German 'ö', or the 'eu' in French word seulement
Ş, ş = pronounced like the 'sh' in shine
Ü, ü = pronounced like the 'u' in shine, or the German 'ü'

Notes on dates and place names

Dates
The dates in Ottoman primary sources have been given according to the Islamic *hicri* or the Ottoman *maliye* calendar, as they appear in the original document. The equivalent Gregorian dates have been given in brackets for each document.

Place names
Place names in the present day Balkans, Anatolia and Egypt are mostly different from their Ottoman labels. To avoid confusion for modern readers, however, places have been called according to the general international usage. For example, Salonica has been preferred to Thessaloniki, Izmir to Smyrna (and İzmir) and Nicosia to Lefkoşa. In a few exceptions where Ottoman names are used, Anglicised forms are given in brackets.

ACKNOWLEDGEMENTS

This books owes its origins to the 'Environmental History of the Ottoman Empire and Turkey' workshop that took place in Hamburg in the autumn of 2017, where the earlier versions of the essays in the book were presented. We thank all participants in the meeting. We owe grateful acknowledgement to the Deutsche Forschungsgemeinschaft (German Research Foundation, DFG), the Asien-Afrika-Institut (AAI) of the University of Hamburg and the European Society for Environmental History (ESEH) for their financial support to the workshop. Without their support, neither the workshop nor this volume could have existed. Personal thanks are especially due to the authors, who, despite their busy schedules, diligently prepared the essays, welcomed our critique and revised and re-revised their texts. Finally, Sarah Johnson of The White Horse Press deserves a special acknowledgement for her warm encouragement, advice and tireless copy-editing work.

BIOGRAPHIES

Elias Kolovos is Associate Professor of Ottoman History at the Department of History and Archaeology of the University of Crete, Greece. He holds a Ph.D. from the Aristotle University of Salonica. He is an elected member of the Board of the International Association for Ottoman Economic and Social History. As a visiting scholar, he has taught at the École Pratique des Hautes Études (Paris), Boğaziçi University (Istanbul) and at the Program of Hellenic Studies, Princeton University. He participates in research projects at the Institute for Mediterranean Studies, FORTH and at the École Francaise d'Athènes. He has written, edited and co-edited ten books and over forty papers in Greek and international publications and journals. His research interests include the Mediterranean economic history, the history of the insular worlds, the history of the frontiers, rural and environmental history and the spatial history and legacies of the Ottoman Empire.

Phokion Kotzageorgis completed his graduate and postgraduate studies in the School of History and Archaeology of the Aristotle University of Salonika. Since 2002 he has been working there as a Lecturer in Early Modern Greek History and from 2009 as an Assistant Professor with tenure. He has researched and published on the economic and social history of Greek lands under Ottoman rule, Ottoman urban history, monastic economy in Ottoman Greece and Ottoman environmental history.

Mehmet Kuru received his B.A. from Galatasaray University (2007) and his M.A. from Sabancı University (2009). He obtained his Ph.D. degree from the University of Toronto (2017) with a dissertation titled 'Locating an Ottoman Port City in the Early Modern Mediterranean: Izmir 1580-1780'. He teaches at Sabancı University. His research interests include urban economics, history of commerce and environmental history. Kuru is currently working on a book project mainly based on his dissertation which analyses the economic and ecological factors that triggered the institutional transformation of the Ottoman Empire during the sixteenth and seventeenth centuries.

Styliani N. Lepida completed her postgraduate studies at the Modern and Contemporary History Department of the Aristotle University of Salonika and received her master's degree from the Balkan and Turkish History Program, with a specialisation in Turkish History. Currently, she is a Ph.D. student in

Biographies

the Department of Turkish and Middle Eastern Studies of the University of Cyprus in Nicosia, where she conducts research on seventeenth century Cyprus.

Suraiya Faroqhi studied in Hamburg/Germany (Dr. Phil.), Istanbul and Bloomington (Indiana University, MA for Teachers). Before becoming a professor at the Ludwig Maximilians Universität in Munich (1988–2007), she had a lengthy career at the Middle East Technical University in Ankara, from instructor to full professor (1971–1987). After retirement from Munich in 2007, she became a professor of history at Istanbul Bilgi University, where she still teaches part-time as an emerita. As of September 2017, she is a full-time professor at the newly founded İbn Haldun University in Kayaşehir/Istanbul. She works on Ottoman social history, with a focus on artisan production, the use of objects as historical sources and urban consumption, recent publications being: *A Cultural History of the Ottomans: The Imperial Elite and its Artefacts* (London: I.B. Tauris, 2016) and *Artisans of Empire: Crafts and Craftspeople under the Ottomans* (London: I.B. Tauris, 2009, paperback edition 2012).

Onur İnal is a post-doctoral researcher at the University of Vienna. He received his Ph.D. from the History Department of the University of Arizona in 2015. He is the regional representative for Turkey of the European Society for Environmental History (ESEH) and the founder of Network for the Environmental History of Turkey (NEHT). His research focuses on the urban and environmental histories of the late Ottoman Empire and early Republican Turkey. His articles have appeared in journals such as the *Journal of World History, Journal of Ottoman Studies, Journal of Urban History* and *Environment and History*.

Semih Çelik obtained his Ph.D. from the European University Institute in Florence in 2017. Among other subjects, he has worked extensively on the environmental history of and famines in nineteenth-century Ottoman Anatolia, history of charity and humanitarianism and labour history. His current post-doctoral project at Koç University in Istanbul concerns the evolution of human-animal relationships in the Ottoman Empire throughout the long nineteenth century and agricultural productivity during the same period.

K. Mehmet Kentel is an urban and environmental historian of the late Ottoman Empire, and the Research Projects Manager at Istanbul Research Institute. He received his Ph.D. from the University of Washington in 2018 with his doctoral dissertation, 'Assembling "Cosmopolitan" Pera: An Infrastructural History of Late Ottoman Istanbul'.

Biographies

Mohamed Gamal-Eldin is a Ph.D. candidate in the Urban Systems-History track as part of a dual doctoral programme at the New Jersey Institute of Technology and Rutgers University-Newark. His dissertation research is at the intersection of environment, infrastructure, health and the built environment in the cities of Port Said, Ismailiyya and Suez.

Chris Gratien is Assistant Professor of History at University of Virginia. He held previous postdoctoral positions at the Harvard Academy for International and Area Studies and the Agrarian Studies program at Yale University. His research focuses on the social and environmental history of the late Ottoman Empire and the modern Middle East. He is author of a number of articles, including 'The Ottoman Quagmire: Malaria, Swamps, and Settlement in the Late Ottoman Mediterranean' (*IJMES*, 2017) and 'The Sick Mandate of Europe: Local and Global Humanitarianism in French Cilicia, 1918-1922' (*JOTSA*, 2016). He is also co-creator and producer of Ottoman History Podcast.

Yavuz Köse is Professor of Turcology at the University of Vienna. His research is focused on the social, economic and consumption history of the Ottoman Empire and Turkey. In particular, he is interested in the effects of modernisation and globalisation in the late Ottoman Empire. Another major topic Köse is engaged with is the emergence and development of tourism in the Ottoman Empire and modern Turkey. Among his latest publications are 'The Confusion of the Agha: A Short History of Chocolate in the Ottoman Empire (17th–20th Century)', *Food & History* **12** (1) (2015): 153–174; (ed.) *Osmanen in Hamburg – eine Beziehungsgeschichte zur Zeit des Ersten Weltkrieges* (Hamburg: Hamburg University Press, 2015); (ed.) *Junge Perspektiven der Türkeiforschung in Deutschland* Bd. II (with Burcu Doğramacı, Kerem Öktem and Tobias Völker; Berlin: Springer VS Verlag); (ed.) *Wunder der erschaffenen Dinge: Osmanische Manuskripte in Hamburger Sammlungen. Wonders of Creation: Ottoman Manuscripts from Hamburg Collections* (manuscript cultures 9) (with Janina Karolewski; Hamburg, 2018 (2nd edition)).

Selçuk Dursun is an environmental historian affiliated with the History Department of the Middle East Technical University (METU). He studied history at METU and the University of Texas-Austin before completing his Ph.D. at Sabancı University (Istanbul) in 2007. Dursun wrote his dissertation on the history of Ottoman forestry. In his own research, he has tried to illustrate the convergence of economic, administrative, political, legal and environmental processes in the context of forestry and forest administration of the Ottoman Empire and Turkey. His current research focuses on the environmental (ecological) history of the Ottoman Empire, the Balkans and the Middle East with a particular emphasis on the commons and the use and management of natural resources, like forests and fisheries. He was a fellow of the Europe in the Middle East–the Middle East in Europe (EUME) programme at the Wissenschaftskolleg zu Berlin and an associated fellow of the Leibniz Zentrum Moderner Orient (ZMO) during the 2008/09 Academic Year. His research on Ottoman environmental and economic history has been published in journals including *The History of the Family* and *New Perspectives on Turkey*. His latest article on the Ottoman and Turkish environmentalism appeared in the edited volume, *Environmentalism in Central and Southeastern Europe: Historical Perspectives* (Lexington Books, 2017).

Introduction

THE OTTOMAN ENVIRONMENTS REVISITED

Onur İnal and Yavuz Köse

The Ottoman Empire was one of the greatest world empires in the early modern period. Established by the Ottoman Turks, a small band of warriors, as a tiny principality in North-western Anatolia at the turn of the fourteenth century, it brought large areas under its control within less than three centuries. The rapidly expanding Ottoman Empire, on one hand, asserted control over diverse ethnicities, religions and cultures; on the other, it tried to understand and engage with nature in different forms and sought various ways of coping with disturbances and natural and man-induced disasters such as earthquakes, floods, fires, droughts, famines, food shortages, locust attacks, epidemics and epizootics. Effective strategies and techniques were developed for the *Ottomanization* not only of peoples and cultures, but also of topographically, geographically and ecologically diverse territories. The Ottomans, as they crossed rivers, mountains, deserts and seas, mutually interacted with the peoples, animals, plants and pathogens of the lands they encountered. They endeavoured to understand and harness, or to use David Blackbourn's definition, 'conquer', nature through technology and culture for their own ends.[1] In this respect, the Ottomans are remarkable not just for their political and military success but also for their desire and ability to understand, adapt, modify and manage different environments.

At its height in the second half of the seventeenth century, the Ottoman Empire stretched from the gates of Vienna in the west to the Caucasus Mountains in the east and from the tip of Arabian Peninsula in the south to the Ukrainian steppes in the north, covering an area of 3.81 million square kilometres.[2] This vast world empire encompassed an enormous diversity of natural environments, from the snow-covered mountains of Eastern Anatolia

---

1. Blackbourn 2006.
2. McCarthy 2014, p. 199.

and sweltering deserts of Libya to the primeval forests of Montenegro and fertile river deltas of Mesopotamia. The vegetation in Ottoman lands varied greatly from region to region, depending on the topography, climate and soil type. The Rhodopes and the Pirin Mountains in the Balkans and the Pontic Mountains in Northern Anatolia contained the best preserved forests in the region, providing timber for the imperial shipyards but also a variety of forest products such as firewood, charcoal, wax, honey, resin, game meat, animal skins and edible and medicinal plants.[3] Bushy *maquis* was found everywhere close to the Mediterranean coast and consisted of evergreen, drought-resistant woody plants and shrubs. Prairies and steppes, on the other hand, dominated the majority of Anatolia, the Middle East and North Africa.

The Ottoman Empire was an agrarian empire, in which the majority of population lived in the countryside and had constant contact with the soil.[4] In its exceptionally diverse and environmentally heterogeneous habitat, one could find a variety of agricultural crops. Cereals such as wheat, barley, rye and oat were cultivated in every corner of the empire because bread was a major staple of the Ottoman diet. In addition, aquatic crops such as rice and sugar cane; pulses such as pea, chickpea, lentil, bean and horse bean; vegetables; fruits; seeds; herbs and spices were widely available across the empire. Crop species in Ottoman lands became more diversified with the arrival of new plants from the Columbian Exchange, such as corn, tobacco, tomatoes, potatoes, peppers, beans, sunflowers and pumpkins.[5]

The Ottoman Empire had a wide variety of feral and domesticated animals. Millions of sheep, goat and cattle roamed over the vast prairies in the Balkans, Anatolia, Egypt and Syria and were the main source of livelihoods for both urban and rural people. They provided raw material for weavers and tanners, fertilised the soil through dung, and filled stomachs with meat, milk and other dairy products. Moreover, in the absence of paved roads and wheeled traffic, beasts of burden such as buffaloes, oxen, horses, donkeys, mules and camels were important means to convey merchandise, conduct pilgrimages, conquer or explore new lands. Donkeys and mules were mostly used for the transportation of goods, while horses rarely served as pack animals. Camels,

---

3. On forests, see Dursun 2007; on timber, see Mikhail 2013a.
4. İnalcık and Quataert 1994.
5. Stoianovich and Haupt 1962; Andrews 1993; Artan 2000, p. 112; Trépanier 2014; Bilgin 2016.

however, were preferred haul animal, simply because they could go long distances with little water and food and greater loads than other haul animals.[6]

The Ottoman Empire was surrounded by the world's richest bodies of water – the Black Sea, the Marmara Sea and the Mediterranean, but also major rivers such as the Tigris and Euphrates in the Fertile Crescent, the Nile in Egypt and the Danube in the Balkans – which included a variety of fish and seafood including mussels, oysters and shrimps.[7] The Ottoman rivers and lakes were sources of energy, too: they provided transportation, powered mills and watered farmlands. In short, the Ottoman Empire was more than a human-made assemblage; it was a living organism comprising humans, animals, plants, landforms, gems and germs. Both humans and non-humans (or 'more-than-humans') formed and transformed this living organism for more than six centuries. Thus, analysing its history requires an examination not only of Ottoman human society but also of the complex interactions between humans and their natural environment.

The prevalent historiography attributes Ottoman success primarily to the empire's military strength and centralised bureaucracy, with power emanating from the sultan and his household. Looking from an environmental historical viewpoint, however, it can be suggested that the Ottoman Empire's ability to control, manipulate and mobilise its financial, natural and human resources was a key to its sustenance and longevity. In other words, Ottoman power was predicated on interconnections among economy, society and nature as much as on military and political force. From the slowly turning wheels of watermills in Syria to the planters of citrus trees in Palestine and from the *fellah*s picking cotton along the Nile Valley to nomads milking goats and sheep in the Taurus Mountains in Anatolia, each and every human and non-human actor represented the seeds of Ottoman power, the power that allowed the Ottoman Empire to maintain control over large territories for a long period of time.

Ottoman Environmental History: A New Sub-Discipline with Deep Roots

Ottoman environmental history is a relatively new sub-discipline with deep roots. Even though the Ottoman Empire has only recently appeared on the radar of historians taking an environmental historical vantage point, its great

---

6.   For camels as haul animals in the Ottoman Empire, see Faroqhi 1982; Tuchscherer 2010, Mikhail 2014, p. 64.

7.   For the first – and hitherto most comprehensive – study of fish and fisheries in Istanbul and the Ottoman Empire, see Deveciyan 2006.

geographic, climatic and ecological diversity has long inspired researchers from different disciplines and sub-disciplines.[8] Over the past decades, researchers have engaged with various aspects of Ottoman environments and dealt with themes and issues pertaining to the Ottoman peasantry, agricultural production and the productivity of the land, tenurial relationships, urban-rural interactions, epidemics, natural disasters and the effects of government policies with environmental consequences.[9] Valuable information about environmental conditions and the enormously complex relationships among the empire's residents, animals, plants, pathogens, geographies, cultures and ideas can be found in the existing literature on Ottoman environments. However, the overwhelming majority of these studies have employed the lenses of, for example, military, political, economic, social, fiscal or agricultural history, but not environmental history.

Environmental history as a perspective, or a way of thinking about human-environment relations in the past, is a relatively new phenomenon in Ottoman studies. The environmental 'turn' touched Ottoman historians a very short time ago. Young researchers in Europe and North America have carried out excellent pioneering research about the Ottoman Empire. Alan Mikhail, perhaps the most prolific Ottoman environmental historian, has mainly written about early modern Egypt.[10] Sam White has researched the impact of the so-called 'Little Ice Age' on Ottoman lands, as well as pandemics and panzootics in early modern Ottoman Empire.[11] Except for some peripheral studies, natural disasters in the Ottoman Empire and responses to them at state, communal, and individual levels long remained under-researched. This lacuna has recently been filled by Yaron Ayalon.[12]

The last few years have seen an unprecedented level of interest in inter-disciplinary and cross-disciplinary studies. As a result, environmental historical

---

8. For an extended discussion of the field, see İnal 2010.

9. For some economic, social, fiscal and agricultural historical studies that refer to Ottoman environments, see Hütteroth 2006; McGowan 1981; McNeill 1992; Güran 1988; Toksöz 2010; Quataert 1980; idem 1981; Faroqhi 2010; İslamoğlu-İnan 1994.

10. Mikhail 2011; idem 2014; idem 2017. See also his edited volume on the environmental histories of the Middle East and North Africa, idem 2013b.

11. White 2010; idem 2011; idem 2017. Historians of disease, medicine and public health have more or less used the methodological framework of environmental history. Birsen Bulmuş has explored the long geopolitical history of plague and the interplay between disease, national sovereignty and quarantine (see Bulmuş 2012). Nükhet Varlık has dealt with correlations between epidemics, population changes and the natural environment in the Ottoman Empire (see Varlık 2013; idem 2015).

12. Ayalon 2014; idem 2011.

studies that speak to histories of science, technology, transportation, migration, consumption, tourism, public health and agriculture have appeared. For example, Michael Christopher Low has analysed the interconnections between Ottoman modernisation, technology and public health in the Hijaz in the late nineteenth and early twentieth centuries.[13] Camille Cole and Faisal Husain have researched imperial projects on the Tigris and Euphrates rivers in Ottoman Iraq from an enviro-technical point of view.[14] Chris Gratien has investigated the relationship between migration, settlement, disease and environment in Southern Anatolian littoral.[15] Alexandar Shopov has explored urban agriculture in the early modern Ottoman Empire, with a special focus on Istanbul.[16]

This edited volume is the first collective effort to take an original look at the Ottoman Empire through the lens of environmental history. It builds on, and aims to go beyond, previous efforts and casts light on applying environmental perspectives to historical processes and events in the long history of the Ottoman Empire that are somehow associated with 'nature' or 'the environment'. It is obvious that getting an environmental history of such a remarkably diverse ecological realm between the covers of a single book is not an easy task. This book, therefore, does not aim or purport to integrate everything about Ottoman environmental history. It simply aspires to illustrate major questions and interpretative insights that have become central to the field. Thus, it is no more than a modest attempt to raise questions and seek new answers to old questions about the ways Ottomans interacted with their natural environment through time.

The Ottoman 'Eco-System': A Jigsaw Puzzle

The Ottoman Empire needed a well-structured administration to utilise and manage its human and non-human resources in a sustainable manner. As the Ottoman Empire took control over diverse places, peoples and ecologies, the imperial administration was increasingly involved in and developed strategies for the provisioning of cities, armies and navies, drawing supplies from ever more distant sources and at times at greater costs. White has termed the Ottoman logistical project of food and good procurement a sort of 'imperial ecology', 'which operated on a far larger scale than anything else in Europe at the time,

---

13. Low 2015.
14. Cole 2016; Husain 2014; idem 2016.
15. Gratien 2017.
16. Shopov (forthcoming).

and encompassed a wide range of goods from wheat to salt and saltpeter'.[17] Mikhail, highlighting 'sets of relationships among resources, peoples, ideas, animals, and places in which all the elements of the system are connected to and depended upon one another', has recently described the Ottoman Empire as an 'eco-system'.[18] The idea of the Ottoman Empire as an ecosystem' he wrote, 'foregrounds how the smallest and largest of imperial actors were connected through means of trade, administration, and mutual reliance'.[19] Indeed, viewing the Ottoman Empire as an ecosystem, a series of ecological relationships, helps us to see how the Ottoman state and society interacted with other living organisms and non-living components of the environment. Stressing the interconnections between state, residents, animals, plants and natural resources, this book's chapters adopt a similar perspective and treat the Ottoman Empire as an 'ecological system'. The chapters that follow further explore ideas, actors, but also internal and external factors that formed, transformed and had an impact on the Ottoman terrestrial and marine ecological system, which was one of the richest in Eurasia and comprised a large number of crop species, non-crop plants, weeds, mammals, reptiles, invertebrates, insects, fungi, bacteria and parasites, but also non-living substances such as air, water, energy and soil minerals.

The book is organised into four parts, grouping chapters around four major topics: 1) Climate and Landscapes; 2) Resources and Energies; 3) Technologies and Infrastructures; and 4) Ideas and Actors. Chapters in each of these parts use different perspectives to make *explorations* in the environmental history of the Ottoman Empire. The chapters in the first part, 'Climate and Landscapes', deal with the interplay between climate change and transformations in Ottoman landscapes during the early modern period. In the opening chapter, Elias Kolovos and Phokion Kotzageorgis examine the impact of the 'Little Ice Age' climate fluctuations on Ottoman Greek lands. The Little Ice Age, which had an overwhelming impact on living creatures of every kind, manifested itself in the Ottoman Empire as freezing winters and wet summers and caused heavy snow and rainfall and inundations. The failure of crops during the Little Ice Age contributed to the political, economic and social crises in Anatolia in the sixteenth and seventeenth centuries. Ottoman historians have recently explored

---

17. White 2017, p. 93.
18. Mikhail 2017, p. 199. The term ecosystem was first used in 1935 by Arthur G. Tansley, an ecologist, to define 'the whole system (in the sense of physics) including not only the organism-complex, but also the whole complex of physical factors forming what we call the environment of the biome – the habitat factors in the widest sense'. (Tansley 1935)
19. Mikhail 2013b, p. 9.

The Ottoman Environments Revisited

from a historical-climatological point of view the interrelations among harsh climatic conditions, unpredictable weather, unravelling imperial provisioning and settlement system, and the *Celali* revolts which broke out in the 1590s. Existing studies suggest that the Little Ice Age and its environmental stress played a major role in the breakdown of Ottoman provisioning systems and the outbreak of the *Celali* revolts and subsequent political crises. Kolovos and Kotzageorgis challenge such sweeping generalisations with regard to the impact of Little Ice Age on the Ottoman Empire and draw attention to the importance of regional case studies that use local archives and microclimatic data. In their in-depth case study on Salonica and Crete, they demonstrate that the Little Ice Age was not as devastating as in the Anatolian plateau, simply because the geography, geomorphology, microclimate, demography and vegetation in these places were very different.

Early modern climatic fluctuations and their impact on Ottoman lands also form the subject of Mehmet Kuru's paper on Anatolia during the reign of Süleyman I (r. 1520–1566) Examining the long-term aridity index and climatic conditions, Kuru explains how the shifts in climatic conditions, fiscal population and agricultural production were interconnected at the height of the Ottoman Empire in the sixteenth century. 'Magnificent', the sobriquet given to Süleyman I by his contemporaries in Europe, metaphorically stands for the favourable climatic conditions in the period he investigates. Kuru claims, unlike in the late sixteenth and early seventeenth centuries, when extreme weather conditions characterised by freezing winters and wet summers were prevalent, the empire experienced a relatively long and exceptionally stable climatic interval era favouring population increase and agricultural expansion in Anatolia. In this extended period of 'magnificent' climate, the Ottoman state could rapidly compensate for the hardships of internal disturbances thanks to an increased abundance of agricultural products. Conversely, the *Celali* revolts at the turn of the seventeenth century were from place to place inescapable and dramatically uncontrollable. Climatic variability, and especially the irregularity of precipitation, made the situation worse.

In the last quarter of the eighteenth century, the Italian archaeologist and numismatist Domenico Sestini visited Istanbul and left an invaluable record of the vineyards on the shores of the Bosporus. Sestini's work is treasure trove for an environmental historian wishing to venture into socio-ecological aspects of viticulture in Ottoman Istanbul because he did not solely document the vineyards in and around the city, but also provided glimpses of the geomorphology, climate and ecology of the Bosporus with regard to grape growing and winemaking. In her article, Suraiya Faroqhi, through a close reading of Sestini's account, unearths interesting information with regard to viniculture and viticulture that Ottoman sources do not tell, such as differing opinions on and practices of grape cultivation, individuals involved in planting and harvesting, wine making and wine consumption, as well as wages and profits. Faroqhi concludes that the vineyards on the Bosporus 'have disappeared without a trace': presumably there existed a number of prosperous non-Muslim consumers in Istanbul who stopped drinking the mediocre wine produced in the environs of the city and opted for 'better wines from western Anatolia or even southern Thrace'.

As grapes retreated from the shores of the Bosporus, they expanded on the rich alluvial plains of Western Anatolia a couple of decades later and changed the course of the region's history. 'Resources and energies', the second part of the book, opens with a chapter that explores how we might consider figs and grapes as historical actors in nineteenth century Western Anatolia. Actually, the grape had been cultivated in the region for millennia, but it was in the second half of the nineteenth century that it became a major commercial crop. In this period, the grape in the form of the dried raisin, together with its companion, the fig, was the principal export item of the region, attracting foreign capital investment and technology, promoting trade, creating employment in the urban and rural, and bringing the countryside and city together. Every autumn, raisin and fig-laden camels arrived in the warehouses of Izmir. There, they were cleaned, sorted and packed, before being shipped to Western European and North American markets. Onur İnal argues that figs and raisins had a profound impact on economic and social life in Western Anatolia and transformed the region's human and natural landscape irreversibly. 'The story of fig and grape', he suggests, 'reveals a great deal about social and economic life in a major Ottoman port-city in the nineteenth century, but also illustrates the ways in which city and country interacted'.

In Ottoman realms, animals were almost everywhere, and they are central to understanding the Ottoman society. Up to the end of the Ottoman Empire, together with human beings, they constituted the principal sources of energy. In the second half of the nineteenth century, while camels plied between Izmir and its hinterlands, carrying sacks of dried figs and raisins, buffaloes transported timber from the deep forests in the Kocaeli district (*sancak*) in North-western Anatolia to the nearest docks for shipment to Istanbul. In his article, Semih Çelik focuses on the effect of the increasing demand of timber upon *kereste-keşan* (woodcutter) villagers and their animals, to show 'how the relationship between animals, human beings and nature was altered in relation to the development of politics of natural resource and labour'. Çelik notes that social and economic life of the villages in the Kocaeli district revolved around felling and transporting the wood to the shores of the Sea of Marmara. 'The need to breed cattle (buffaloes particularly) for dragging and transporting wood and timber', he suggests, 'tied the lives of animals, rivers, trees and human beings tightly'. In the chapter, he concludes that, because 'the fate of the animal and human beings were interwoven', any change to the human-animal relationship could be detrimental to the lives of both humans and animals.

In her chapter, Styliani N. Lepida enters a territory that has long awaited exploration by the environmental historians of the Ottoman Empire. She addresses the management of water in Cyprus, the third largest Mediterranean island after Sicily and Sardinia, during the seventeenth century. The island experienced a stable, favourable climate with enough precipitation during the Venetian period in the sixteenth century. However, shortly after it came under Ottoman rule in 1571, things changed for the worse and the island suffered from the effects of drought. Cyprus was surrounded by bodies of seawater, yet had limited sources of fresh water. The Ottoman administration sought ways to manage available water by building, preserving and improving water infrastructure such as watermills, wells and reservoirs. Through the study of travellers' accounts, Ottoman court documents and legal transactions, Lepida illustrates how the issue of water management was intertwined with other political, social and economic issues and involved 'almost all layers of the Cypriot social pyramid, bringing together various members of Ottoman society'. In this respect, her study covers much more than what its title implies.

Water, when examined through the lens of environmental history, has the capacity to bring the histories of, among other factors, labour, consumption, health and technology together. This is evident in two chapters in the third part of the book, 'Technologies and Infrastructures'. K. Mehmet Kentel's study focuses on the debates about and development of the Terkos waterworks, designed to supply the 'cosmopolitan' Pera (*Beyoğlu*) district of Istanbul with water. Kentel details the concerted effort of the Pera community, experts and urban administrators to bring potable water from Lake Terkos in the northern periphery of the city in the late nineteenth century. At the beginning of his study he points out the potential of water 'to provide a critical lens to explore the ways in which modern urban spaces have been shaped with the interaction of a wide variety of human and nonhuman actors, located not only at the heart of the urban centres but rather dispersed along a set of "uneven geographies"'.

Indeed, as he traces the ninety-kilometre-long pipes between Lake Terkos and the city centre, he reveals that they not only transported the Terkos water, but also ideas about the natural environment, thereby bringing the city to the periphery and vice versa. The construction of the Terkos waterworks helped the city to establish a new relation to nature. '[W]ith the start of the construction of the Terkos waterworks', Kentel notes, 'the material relations, expert knowledge, will to modernisation and ideology of progress, which was shaping Pera's urban space, had poured into the rural periphery'. In this respect, it brought about 'a set of messy and unequal relations between the various human and nonhuman actors involved, from Terkos to Pera'.

Egypt was the biggest and one of the most important Ottoman provinces. It was a source of revenue for the sultan and a major supplier of grain, cotton, sugar and other foodstuffs to the Ottoman Empire. Moreover, its geostrategic location between the Indian Ocean and the Mediterranean was of utmost importance to the Ottomans. Ottoman environmental historians have so far dealt with the Nile Valley and Delta as they were the most vital areas for Egypt.[20] In his paper, Mohamed Gamal-Eldin focuses on the intertwined issues of urban planning, population growth, engineering, sanitation and diseases in Ismailia and Port Said, the cities that came into existence with the opening of the Suez Canal in 1869. Gamal-Eldin describes the two cities as 'spaces on the margin' because their histories were overshadowed by large and prominent cities located on the Nile River and Delta such as Cairo and Alexandria. The decision to build two new towns on the Suez Canal and change the natural environment, however, was not without its discomforts and unwanted results. The increase in water in the already swampy environments of Ismailia and Port Said created stagnant pools, providing the perfect home for the larvae of malaria-carrying *Anopheles* mosquitoes to reproduce. In his chapter, Gamal-Eldin argues that decisions of urban development, canalisation projects and colonialism triggered the malarial outbreak in Ismailia and Port Said. Through the use of travelogues, reports, medical journals and visual archival data, he sketches the policies, practices and technologies developed to cope with the malaria situation in both cities in the late nineteenth and early twentieth centuries.

The fourth and last part of the book contains studies of persons, institutions, ideas, thoughts and regulations that shaped environmental thought and environmental decision-making in the Ottoman Empire and early Republican Turkey. In his chapter, Chris Gratien traces the political ecology of rice, exploring 'how rice prompted reflection on the differentiation and organisa-

---

20. See Mikhail 2011; Mitchell 2002.

tion of imperial, provincial and agricultural space as well as on the Ottoman government's responsibilities towards its citizens' in the late Ottoman Empire. Gratien shows how rice, an important staple of the Ottoman diet, occupied the political agenda probably more than any other agricultural product in 1910. In late winter that year, *Meclis-i Mebusan*, the lower house of the Ottoman parliament held heated debates over whether rice cultivation contributed to the spread of malaria or not. Whereas the critics of rice viewed rice paddies as a threat to public health, defenders of rice saw economic benefit in cultivating rice. The rice debates culminated in the creation of the Rice Cultivation Law (*Pirinç Ziraatı Kanunnamesi*). The law spelled out how rice should be cultivated so as not to aggravate malaria. Furthermore, it set the legal foundations of combatting malaria in early Republican Turkey.

Yavuz Köse in his article explores the traces Alexander von Humboldt (1769–1859) – the 'proto environmentalist' – left in the late Ottoman Empire and early Republican period. Even though Humboldt in his lifetime was already a legend and a much acclaimed scientist-traveller, and in 1869 almost the whole world was celebrating his centennial, there are surprisingly few Ottoman sources that mention him. It was only in 1932 that a certain Mustafa Niyazi [Erenbilge] published a short biography of Humboldt. Mustafa Niyazi (1887/88–1947), a soldier and geography teacher, was also the author of probably the first geography publication on Anatolia (published around 1922). Köse, after presenting the Ottoman and early Republican sources which allude to Humboldt, examines and discusses the Humboldt biography in close connection with Mustafa Niyazi's work on Anatolia. He suggests that, 'it is not Humboldt the cosmopolitan environmentalist but Humboldt the scientific traveller and discoverer who serves as a good role model and argues for the importance of geography in school education'. The incentive was to encourage Turkish youth to get know and love their new homeland.

The final chapter, by Selçuk Dursun, sheds light on the hitherto under-researched topic of forest commons, a special type of forests in the Ottoman Empire that encompassed both the *cibal-i mubaha* (unenclosed forests on the mountains) and the *baltalıks* (village coppices), and the chapter explains how forest commons intersect with environmental, legal and social issues. Because forest commons were not within the boundaries of the property regime until the last period of the Ottoman Empire, rural residents benefited from them in various ways. However, 'the privatisation of the use of forests', as Dursun argues, 'eventually entailed an absolute loss of poor peasants' right to use forests and woodlands'. In other words, state-led privatisation and commercialisation deprived villagers of a substantial means of livelihood and cut their ties with nature.

The environmental history of the Ottoman Empire resembles a jigsaw puzzle of thousands of pieces, comprising seas, lakes, rivers, mountains, forests, steppes, deserts, towns, villages, people and animals. Some pieces are there, but many are still missing; some are fairly clear, but some have to be reconstructed. It is, therefore, the task of Ottoman environmental historians to attempt to piece together the various parts of the picture. The contributors to this book have done their bit. Every chapter tells a story and adds another piece to the puzzle of the environmental history of the Ottoman Empire. The puzzle will acquire greater coherence and meaning when more pieces are fitted together.

REFERENCES

Andrews, Jean. 1993. 'Diffusion of Mesoamerican Food Complex to Southeastern Europe'. *Geographical Review* **83**: 194–204.

Artan, Tülay. 2000. 'Aspects of the Ottoman Elite's Food Consumption: Looking for "Staples", "Luxuries", and "Delicacies" in a Changing Century'. In Donald Quataert (ed.), *Consumption Studies and the History of the Ottoman Empire, 1550–1922* (New York: State University of New York Press), pp. 107–200.

Ayalon, Yaron. 2011. 'Ottoman Urban Privacy in Light of Disaster Recovery'. *International Journal of Middle East Studies* **43**: 513–28.

—— . 2014. *Natural Disasters in the Ottoman Empire: Plague, Famine, and Other Misfortunes.* Cambridge: Cambridge University Press.

Bilgin, Arif. 2016. 'From Artichoke to Corn: New Fruits and Vegetables in the Istanbul Market'. In Elif Akçetin and Suraiya Faroqhi (eds), *Living the Good Life: Consumption in the Qing and Ottoman Empires of the Eighteenth Century* (Leiden: Brill), pp. 257–82.

Blackbourn, David. 2006. *The Conquest of Nature: Water, Landscape, and the Making of Modern Germany.* New York: W.W. Norton.

Bulmuş, Birsen. 2012. *Plague, Quarantines and Geopolitics in the Ottoman Empire.* Edinburgh: Edinburgh University Press.

Cole, Camille. 2016. 'Precarious Empires: A Social and Environmental History of Steam Navigation on the Tigris'. *Journal of Social History* **50** (1): 74–101.

Deveciyan, Karekin. 2006 [1915]. *Türkiye'de Balık ve Balıkçılık.* Istanbul: Aras.

Dursun, Selçuk. 2007. 'Forest and the State: History of Forestry and Forest Administration in the Ottoman Empire'. Ph.D. Diss., Istanbul: Sabancı University.

Faroqhi, Suraiya. 1982. 'Camels, Wagons, and the Ottoman State in the Sixteenth and Seventeenth Centuries'. *International Journal of Middle East Studies* **14** (2): 523–39.

—— . (ed.). 2010. *Animals and People in the Ottoman Empire.* Istanbul: Eren.

Gratien, Chris. 2017. 'The Ottoman Quagmire: Malaria, Swamps, and Settlement in the Late Ottoman Mediterranean'. *International Journal of Middle East Studies* 49 (4): 583–604.

Güran, Tevfik. 1988. *19. Yüzyıl Osmanlı Tarımı Üzerine Araştırmalar*. Istanbul: Eren Yayıncılık.

Husain, Faisal. 2014. 'In the Bellies of the Marshes: Water and Power in the Countryside of Ottoman Baghdad'. *Environmental History* 19: 638–64.

——. 2016. 'Changes in the Euphrates River: Ecology and Politics in a Rural Ottoman Periphery, 1687–1702'. *Journal of Interdisciplinary History* 47 (1): 1–25.

Hütteroth, Wolf-Dieter. 2006. 'Ecology of the Ottoman Lands'. In Suraiya Faroqhi (ed.), *Cambridge History of Turkey, Volume 3: The Late Ottoman Empire (1603–1839)* (Cambridge: Cambridge University Press), pp. 18–43.

İnal, Onur. 2010. 'Environmental History as an Emerging Field in Ottoman Studies: An Historiographical Overview'. *Journal of Ottoman Studies* 38: 1–26.

——. 2015. 'A Port and Its Hinterland: An Environmental History of Ottoman Izmir in the Late Ottoman Period'. Ph.D. Diss., Tucson: University of Arizona.

İnalcık, Halil and Donald Quataert (eds). 1994. *An Economic and Social History of the Ottoman Empire, 1300–1914*. Cambridge: Cambridge University Press.

İslamoğlu-İnan, Huri. 1994. *State and Peasant in the Ottoman Empire: Agrarian Power Relations and Regional Economic Development in Ottoman Anatolia during the Sixteenth Century*. Leiden: Brill.

Low, Michael Christopher. 2015. 'Ottoman Infrastructures of the Saudi Hydro-State: The Technopolitics of Pilgrimage and Potable Water in the Hijaz'. *Comparative Studies in Society and History* 57 (4): 942–74.

McCarthy, Justin. 2014. *The Ottoman Turks: An Introductory History to 1923*. London: Routledge.

McGowan, Bruce. 1981. *Economic Life in the Ottoman Empire: Taxation, Trade, and the Struggle for Land, 1600–1800*. Cambridge: Cambridge University Press.

McNeill, John R. 1992. *The Mountains of the Mediterranean World*. Cambridge; New York: Cambridge University Press.

Mikhail, Alan. 2011. *Nature and Empire in Ottoman Egypt: An Environmental History*. New York: Cambridge University Press.

——. 2013a. 'Anatolian Timber and Egyptian Grain: Things that Made the Ottoman Empire'. In Paula Findlen (ed.), *Early Modern Things: Objects and Their Histories, 1500–1800* (New York: Routledge), 274–93.

——. (ed.). 2013b. *Water on Sand: Environmental Histories of the Middle East and North Africa*. New York: Oxford University Press.

——. 2014. *The Animal in Ottoman Egypt*. New York: Oxford University Press.

——. 2017. *Under Osman's Tree: The Ottoman Empire, Egypt, and Environmental History*. Chicago: University of Chicago Press.

Mitchell, Timothy. 2002. *Rule of Experts: Egypt, Techno-Politics, Modernity*. Berkeley: University of California Press.

14

Quataert, Donald. 1980. 'The Commercialization of Agriculture in Ottoman Turkey, 1800–1914'. *International Journal of Turkish Studies* 1 (2): 38–55.

——. 1981. 'Agricultural Trends and Government Policy in Ottoman Anatolia, 1800–1914'. *Asian and African Studies* 15: 69–84.

Shopov, Alexandar. [forthcoming]. 'Urban Agriculture in Early Modern Istanbul'. In Shirin Hamadeh and Çiğdem Kafesçioğlu (eds), *Early Modern Istanbul*. Leiden: Brill.

Stoianovich Traian and Georges C. Haupt. 1962. 'Le maïs arrive dans les Balkans'. *Annales (Économies, Sociétés, Civilisations)* 17 (1): 84–89.

Tansley, Arthur. 1935. *Elements of Plant Biology*. London.

Toksöz, Meltem. 2010. *Nomads, Migrants and Cotton in the Eastern Mediterranean: The Making of the Adana-Mersin Region 1850–1908*. Leiden: Brill.

Trépanier, Nicolas. 2014. *Foodways and Daily Life in Medieval Anatolia. A New Social History*. Austin: University of Texas Press.

Tuchscherer, Michel. 2010. 'Some Reflections on the Place of the Camel in the Economy and Society of Ottoman Egypt'. In Suraiya Faroqhi (ed.), *Animals and People in the Ottoman Empire* (Istanbul: Eren), pp. 171–85.

Varlık, Nükhet. 2013. 'From "Bête Noire" to "le Mal de Constantinople": Plagues, Medicine, and the Early Modern Ottoman State'. *Journal of World History* 24 (4): 741–70

——. 2015. *Plague and Empire in the Early Modern Mediterranean World: The Ottoman Experience, 1347–1600*. Cambridge: Cambridge University Press.

White, Sam. 2010. 'Rethinking Disease in Ottoman Society'. *International Journal of Middle East Studies* 42: 549–67.

——. 2011. *The Climate of Rebellion in the Early Modern Ottoman Empire*. Cambridge University Press.

——. 2017. 'A Model Disaster: From the Great Ottoman Panzootic to the Cattle Plagues of Early Modern Europe'. In Nükhet Varlık (ed.), *Plague and Contagion in the Islamic Mediterranean* (Kalamazoo: Arc Humanities Press), pp. 91–116.

PART 1

Climate and Landscapes

Chapter 1

SEARCHING FOR THE 'LITTLE ICE AGE' EFFECTS IN THE OTTOMAN GREEK LANDS: THE CASES OF SALONICA AND CRETE[1]

Elias Kolovos and Phokion Kotzageorgis

The 'Little Ice Age' was a crucial period of climate change for early modern Europe roughly between the 1550s and the 1850s.[2] In the Mediterranean, climate change produced increased precipitation and snow in higher altitudes during the cold months and opposite phenomena of intense droughts during the warm months. According to Faruk Tabak, who described the post-sixteenth-century era as the 'autumn' of the Mediterranean, when the centre of the world economy left the Inner Sea for the north of Europe, settlement in the Mediterranean moved during these centuries, as a result of climate change, from the plains up to the hills and the mountains.[3] More recently, Sam White has extensively studied the outbreak of the Little Ice Age in the Ottoman Eastern Mediterranean, focusing especially on the great drought of the 1590s.[4] White made a strong argument in favour of a connection between climate change and social unrest, i.e., the *Celali* rebellions in Ottoman Anatolia, which resulted

---

1. The authors would like to thank Adam Izdebski and Kostis Smyrlis for their valuable comments on this chapter.
2. For the term, its use in science and its conventional definition as 'the sixteenth-mid-nineteenth century period during which European climate was most strongly impacted', see Mann 2002. Michael Mann estimates the overall dropping of temperatures in the Northern Hemisphere at about 0.6°C between the fifteenth and the nineteenth centuries. For research on the 'Little Ice Age' and the term itself, see also Ogilvie and Jónsson 2001. For a general overview of the study of the role of climate in history, see Le Roy Ladurie 1959 (for the 'Little Ice Age', see especially pp. 4–5).
3. Tabak 2008, pp. 22–35.
4. White 2011, pp. 126–39 for the 'Little Ice Age', in particular, and pp. 140–62 for the big drought of the 1590s in the Eastern Mediterranean.

in a 'big flight' (*büyük kaçgun*) of the population from the countryside of the Anatolian plateau.[5] In his argument, he collated very attractively and challengingly the onset of the Ottoman Little Ice Age, with its effects of long drought, famine and epidemics, with the new millennium according to the Islamic calendar (starting in 1591/92), the 'Long War' in Hungary (1591–1606) and the *Celali* rebellions (ca. 1590–1610). He argued that this eventually 'swelled into a crisis of terrible proportions' for the Ottoman Empire as a whole.[6] In this paper, we would like to investigate the evidence concerning the effects of climate change in the Ottoman Greek lands, where no major rebellions, like those of the *Celalis*, broke out in the late sixteenth century,[7] and where there is not evidence of any major population movement similar to 'the great flight' in Anatolia. Moreover, the evidence White uses to expand his argument to the Balkans and the Eastern Mediterranean is not entirely compelling. For example, referring to a sultanic order related to a famine in Dubrovnik in 1564, which requested support of grain from such places as Chios, Rhodes, Limnos, Kos, Lesbos, Tarhanyat, Sığacık and Seferihisar, he mentions also a famine in Salonica in the same year. Nevertheless, White has misread the *mühimme defteri* (register of important affairs) 6/266, which shows that Salonica provided grains to Anatolia, an indicator of surplus.[8] Finally, in his chapter for the 'Great Drought' of the 1590s, White does not actually provide an adequate sample of evidence for the Balkans.[9]

Our case-studies in this paper will be the peninsula of Halkidiki, near Salonica,[10] which came under Ottoman rule in the late fourteenth century and again after 1420 and 1430; and the island of Crete, which passed from the Venetians to the Ottomans, after a long war in the mid-seventeenth century. Case-studying the effects of the Ottoman Little Ice Age might show that White's argument needs to be restricted spatially and that it is premature to paint an

---

5. The Great Flight (*büyük kaçgun*) refers to the mass migration of Anatolian peasants during the course of the *Celali* rebellions (Akdağ 1964). For the *Celali* rebellions, see also Akdağ 1963; Griswold 1983; Özel 2012.

6. White 2011, p. 140.

7. The revolts, which broke out in the Greek peninsula before and mainly after the Battle of Lepanto (1571) and occasionally lasted into the first decade of the 17th century had political-cum-fiscal connotations and could not have been connected with environmental issues. For these revolts, see Katsiardi-Hering 2009.

8. Compare Sam White 2011, p. 80; and Yıldırım 1995, p. 167 (no. 266).

9. In this chapter, as far as the Greek lands are concerned, White mentions only a famine in the Peloponnese in 1590 (?), with a reference to Mühimme Defteri 5ᶻ (sic)/373.

10. Based on our previous research. See Kolovos and Kotzageorgis 2015.

image of 'catastrophe' for the entire Ottoman Empire in the seventeenth century. It is certain that there is a need for more in-depth regional case-studies that use local archival sources and microclimatic data. Only in this way can a precise interpretation of the impact of Little Ice Age on the Ottoman Empire be made from an environmental point-of-view. This study is just a step in that direction. It aims to help us acquire a better understanding of the Little Ice Age's effects in the Ottoman provinces at a more regional and local levels and pave the way for future studies.

To the south-east of the city of Salonica, the large peninsula of Halkidiki covers an area of 2,918 square kilometres. The Halkidiki Peninsula is surrounded by the Aegean Sea, which penetrates deeply between its three minor peninsulas, known as the three prongs, with a total coastline of almost 500 kilometres. The central part of the peninsula of Halkidiki is dominated by the massif of Mount Holomondas (1,165 metres), but the highest mountain of the peninsula is Mount Athos, which peaks at 2,030 metres, one of the tallest mountains in Greece. In general, Halkidiki comprises mountains, plains, hills and plateaus, all adjoining to the Aegean Sea. Its fertile lands are limited, situated mainly along the coastlines.[11] Halkidiki lacks vast plains and its altitude is low. Therefore, one should not expect to observe such a strong impact of climate change on cultures and yields, population decrease and social unrest in Halkidiki, as in the majority of the Anatolian plateau, which lies at an altitude between 1,000–2,000 metres.

According to evidence drawn from tax surveys (*tahrir defterleri*), settlement in Halkidiki expanded during the sixteenth century. This is explained in the context of the large demographic increase that occurred during the first half of the sixteenth century all around Europe and the Mediterranean,[12] following the very considerable losses in the aftermath of the 'Black Death': *grosso modo* estimates for the population of Halkidiki vary between 19–30,000 people for 1519, 27–44,000 for 1527 and 29–47,000 people for 1568, with a maximum density of fifteen inhabitants per square kilometre for the same date.[13] Moreover, two of the smaller peninsulas of Halkidiki, those of Kassandra and Sithonia, which had no organised settlements from the fourteenth century, were resettled during the second half of the sixteenth century.[14]

---

11. See Tsigarida and Xydopoulos 2015, p. 37; Bellier et al. 1986.
12. For the demographic increase in the entire Mediterranean area, see Braudel 1995, vol. 1, p. 402.
13. See in detail Tables 1–5 in Kolovos and Kotzageorgis 2015, pp. 130–33.
14. Ibid., pp. 134–37.

The Kassandra Peninsula, in particular, was resettled at the initiative of a high-ranking Ottoman official, Gazanfer Ağa (d. 1603), the chief white eunuch at the Topkapı Palace (*kapu ağası*). The peninsula was granted to him in 1588 by Sultan Murad III (r. 1574–1595) with full ownership (*temlik*), according to a document granting tax immunity (*suret-i muafname-i cezire-i Kesendire*). Gazanfer Ağa was a few years later to convert the holding into a pious foundation (*vakıf*).[15] The expansion of settlement might also have had an environmental impact on the newly settled areas. The hilly region in the north-west part of the Kassandra Peninsula is currently cultivated with large tracts of cereals, separated by areas of pine forest. Travellers' narratives from the nineteenth century[16] show that the areas of pine forest were probably larger, and co-existed with areas of cultivated land and *maquis*. Nevertheless, the situation was very different in the fourteenth century, when, according to Byzantine records, not pine forests but oak forests existed and most of the arable land was used for stockbreeding. The disappearance of oak forests between the fourteenth century and the modern era has also been noted of the territory to the south-west of the Ormylia and Vourvourou districts on the Sithonia Peninsula.[17] The replacement of oaks by quickly spreading pine-trees was a frequent phenomenon from at least the early Middle Ages on, in places that used to be cultivated and were later abandoned.[18]

On the other hand, evidence from the Ottoman poll-tax registers (*cizye defterleri*) indicates a decrease in the population of Halkidiki in the first half of the seventeenth century. This correlates with the general downward trend in population growth in the Ottoman Empire at the time. In 1568 the Christian tax households in Halkidiki comprised a total of 10,106. In 1620–21, the sum of the poll-tax households (*cizyehane*), recorded in the two 'poll-tax provinces' (*cizye vilayetleri*) of Siderokavsia (*Sidrekapsi*) near Salonica and Siderokavsia near Gynaikokastro (*Avrethisar*), was only 5,759. More comparable data can be used from the registers of 1620–21 and 1642, when the poll-tax households in the tax province of Siderokavsia nearby Salonica (*vilayet-i Sidrekapsı tetimme-i Selanik*) decreased from 2,675 to 1,890. Two years later, 1,824 poll-tax households were counted in the same tax province.[19] The significant contraction of population observed in the above-mentioned data is to a certain extent fictitious. Comparative research on many regions in the Balkans (Bulgarian lands, Greek

---

15. Ibid., p. 135.
16. See in detail Bellier et al. 1986, pp. 112–13.
17. Ibid.
18. Izdebski 2013.
19. See in detail Kolovos and Kotzageorgis 2015, p. 141.

peninsula) and Hungary shows that in seventeenth century poll-tax registers, non-Muslim tax-payers were under-recorded, for various reasons, by 25 to fifty per cent on average.[20] Taking into account this point, there is no evidence of an extreme demographic contraction in Halkidiki, like in the case of the Anatolian plateau around 1600, nor a 'big flight' from the countryside. Moreover, the settlement network of this particular area remained more or less stable during the seventeenth century. The only comparable data to see how many villages disappeared is the list we have created of the recorded villages in the tax register of 1568 and another list from the *avarız* (extraordinary tax) register of 1722.[21] The first lists 122 villages, while the second lists 105 (fourteen per cent decrease). To the last number we have to add another six villages, which had been transformed into *çiftlik*s (big farms) by the end of the seventeenth century, without losing their inhabitants; therefore, the final decrease in the settlements' list was only nine per cent. Thus, the deserted settlements of the seventeenth century were not many, as in the Anatolian plateau,[22] and most were abandoned as a result of settlement regrouping.[23] A recent study on the north Aegean Sea area showed increasing humidity during the Little Ice Age – the sea surface temperature peaked around 1600, supporting the concept of a wet Little Ice Age in this part of the Mediterranean.[24] This element differentiates the Halkidiki case from that of Anatolia and explains, to a certain extent, the different demographic trends observed in them, i.e. the 'catastrophe' of Anatolia and the less significant change in Halkidiki.

The final years of both the sixteenth and the seventeenth centuries are considered to be, in general, two of the crucial phases of crisis during the long Little Ice Age. The major characteristics of the Little Ice Age during these phases were: a) instability in temperatures and b) unpredictability of the weather as a whole.[25] In the cases of Anatolia and the Middle East in general, the most visible characteristics of the climate during these particular years were very cold and wet winters and, in sharp contrast, summer droughts.[26] Severe droughts reduced grain and other crops especially, making survival and agriculture almost impossible. As a result, it was widespread during the Little Ice Age for peasants

---

20. For the relevant bibliography, see Kotzageorgis 2008, pp. 32–23.
21. Compare TT 723, pp. 2–399 and KK 2869, pp. 2–23, 81–115.
22. Quoted from Özel 2015.
23. Kolovos and Kotzageorgis 2015, pp. 141–42.
24. Gogou et al. 2016, p. 216.
25. Mann 2002; Mészáros and Serlegi 2010, p. 214.
26. White 2011, pp. 126–39.

to turn into pastoralists. On a micro-level, this would mean that peasants left their fields uncultivated; these fields were consequently transformed to pastures or, if not used, into pine scrub, forests or malarial swamps.[27]

In the case of Halkidiki, our existing sources from the seventeenth and eighteenth centuries actually indicate a significant presence of pasture.[28] These sources are also substantiated by recent palynological research in Halkidiki, which shows clear evidence of grazing-induced environmental changes in Ottoman times. Moreover, the pollen indicators *Chenopodiaceae, Plantago, Caryophyllaceae, Asteraceae, Ranunculus acris* type, and *Cichoriaceae* reached their maximum at the turn of the eighteenth century.[29] Several sources show the presence of village pastures and, in some cases, their mortgaging when the communities were in debts. The village pasture (*yaylak*) of Palaiochorion, for example, was rented (*icar*), in 1640, by the village community to the Athonite monastery of Xeropotamou for 38 years, in order to settle a debt of the village community to the monks.[30] In Western Halkidiki, in 1620, the monks of Aghios Pavlos agreed with a *yürük* (nomad or semi-nomad) of the region

---

27. Tabak 2008, pp. 22–23.

28. Our sources for these centuries mainly consist of documents, Greek or Ottoman, currently housed in the Athonite archives of the monasteries of Xeropotamou and Agiou Pavlou. The Athonite monasteries had extensive land properties in Halkidiki peninsula and thus most of the documents refer to various areas of the whole peninsula. These sources were complemented with Ottoman tax registers of cizye or avarız type, deposited in the Prime Ministry Ottoman Archives (*Başbakanlık Osmanlı Arşivleri*, BOA). These are: Maliyeden Müdevver (MAD) nos. 1209 (1642), 4609 (1692), 3461 (1697), 14947 (1710). Kâmil Kepeci Collection (KK) no. 2869 (1722).

29. Panajiotidis 2015, pp. 317–18 and diagram pp. 320–22.

30. Holy Monastery of Xeropotamou (Μονή Ξηροποτάμου [*Moni Xeropotamou*, MX]), Ottoman documents, folder D, doc. no. 96. The relevant document reads as following: 'Mahmiye-i Selanik muzafatından kasaba-ı Sidrekapsı'ya tabi cezire-i Aynaroz'da vaki İkşiropotam nam manastır ahalisinin reisleri olan Nikita ve Papa Kostandyo ve Liğori nam rahipler taraflarından ... Mihal bakkal nam zimmi meclis-i şer'-i hatır-ı lazımül-evkirde yine kasaba-ı mezbureye tabi Palihor nam karye sakin doğancı taifesinden Todori ve Dimitri İvrasta ve Yova ve Yovan İvrasta ve Yova Panayot ve reayadan Nikola semerci ve İskarlo ve Asteryo Martin ve Yova Martin ve İstoyko Meluş ve sairleri mahzarlarında bilvekale takrir-i kelam ve bast-ı meram edip: zimmiyun-ı merkumunün zimmetlerinde manastır-ı merkum malından bundan akdem ikraz olunmuş yirmi bin fıdda ve rayiç filvakt akçe hakk-ı şerileri olup lakin zimmiyun-ı merkumunden meblağ-ı mezburu edaya iktidarları olmağın karye-i mezbure hududu dahilinde vaki Vrestiça demekle maruf ve müştehar olmağla tahdid ve tavsıftan müstagni olan yaylaklarını here sene beş yüz akçe icare ile tarih-i kitaptan otuz sekiz sene tamamına değin manastır-ı merkum ahalisine meblağ-ı masfur mukabelesinde icar edip ... ,'.

to graze his flocks into the pastures of the monastic farm (*metochion*).[31] This is indirect evidence that the once fertile and productive lands of the farm had been transformed into pasture lands at the turn of the seventeenth century.

However, sources from the same period also testify to the granting of titles for cultivation of arable lands. Let us just cite another document dated 1640, which deals with the sale of an arable field in the village of Polychrono in the peninsula of Kassandra to the monks of the same monastery of Xeropotamou.[32] In another case from 1686, the monks of the monastery of Aghios Pavlos bought arable lands (*tarla*) in the Sykia village in the Sithonia Peninsula.[33] Therefore, we cannot be sure if and in what degree there was really a gradual abandonment of arable fields, and, consequently, a decline of agriculture in favour of pastoralism, as was the case during the so-called 'seventeenth-century crisis'.[34]

In theory, the Little Ice Age should have contributed to a reversal of the earlier (i.e. Late Medieval) period of deforestation; however, the population flight from lowlands and plains to hills and mountains during the early modern centuries, as analysed by Tabak, appears to have created new pressures on forests.[35] Our sources offer indications of deforestation in Halkidiki as well. Forests were an essential element of the landscape of Halkidiki, covering the slopes of Mount Holomondas in the centre of the peninsula. Even the three smaller peninsulas in the south had forests: one of these was Sithonia, called by the Ottoman name '*Longoz*', after the medieval Slavic name *Loggoz*, meaning 'dense forest'. In our sources, we have not located any references to state or communal forests in Halkidiki; there is, however, some information on forests belonging to Athonite monasteries, which were struggling to protect them from trespassing pastoralists or lumberjacks. In 1591, for example, the monks of

---

31. Holy Monastery of Agiou Pavlou (*Μονή Αγίου Παύλου* [*Moni Agiou Pavlou*, MAP]), Ottoman documents, folder 2, doc. no. 61: 'mahruse-i Selanik'den Kelemerye nahiyesine tabı Üç nam karye kurbinde vakı Aya Pavlo manastırı metohı rahiblerinden Liğori İkşeno ve Manahiya İkşeno ve Mantoya İkşeno ve Kalınıko nam rahibler meclis-i şeri-i şerifde hamil el-kitab Turali dede ibn Veli nam kimesne muhzırında takrir-i kelam idüb mezbur Turali dede yedinden kendi malımdan rayıç filvakt beş bin akçe ahz ü kabz eyeledik ol mukabilede mezburun koyunları metohımız sınurında rai olunmağa icazet virdik ... '.
32. MAP, Ottoman documents, folder E, doc. no. 46: 'cezire-i Kesendre'de vaki ... ber vech-i tahminen beş muzurluk tarlasını İksiropotan manastırından rahiplerinden Papa Kaliniko ve Liğori nam rahiplere rayıç filvakt iki bin akçeye beyi edip ... '.
33. MX, Ottoman documents, folder 13, doc. no. S/14.
34. See White 2011, pp. 229–48.
35. For deforestation in early modern Europe, see Rácz 2010, pp. 26–27. For modern deforestation after 1800 see McNeill 1992, pp. 286 ff.

the monastery of Aghios Pavlos protested to the Sultan against their Christian neighbours, who had entered without permission into their forest in Sykia, in the peninsula of Sithonia. The reply of the Ottoman state was that, since the forest was not in common use, the trespassers should be impeded from entering it. The same protest by the monks of the monastery of Aghios Pavlos was repeated in 1620 and in 1759, a sign that villagers were constantly trespassing into the monastic forest.[36] In another case, from 1725, two Christian wood tar manufacturers (*katrancıs*) from Florina (in Western Macedonia, Greece) entered illegally into the forest of the Xeropotamou monastery in Sithonia and cut 1,000 pine trees in order to make wood tar; they finally had to negotiate a settlement with the monks to compensate the latter in cash.[37] As everywhere in the Mediterranean, timber was also important for shipbuilding. In 1624, a Muslim was in conflict with the monks of the Xeropotamou Monastery who requested compensation for the timber he had cut for the building of a ship.[38] The aforementioned examples show how the forests were being exploited in the period under study, both by their owners and trespassers. More generally, tree-felling for timber and overgrazing in forestlands (a phenomenon caused by the shortage of pastures and/or the rising numbers of animals) were likely more than usual in early modern Halkidiki. An excellent overview study, based on a detailed comparison of palynological evidence, for both Byzantine and early Ottoman economies, shows a deforestation period for the Macedonian highlands between 1500 and 1700, suggesting an intensive cutting of forests.[39]

Tree-felling for the mines and the furnaces in Ottoman *Sidrekapsi* (modern Stratoni) contributed also to the deforestation of Halkidiki.[40] According to the testimony of the Ottoman traveller Aşık Mehmed (1555/57–1698), who spent some time in the mining town, wood cutting on the mountains surrounding

---

36. MAP, Ottoman documents, folder 13, no. S/23; folder 6, no. 10; folder 13, no. 27.

37. MX, Ottoman documents, folder A, no. 36.

38. MX, Ottoman documents, folder A, no. 99: 'Mahmiye-i Selanik muzafatından cezire-i Longoz'da olup kat' eden Kızıl Ali ibn Ayvat nam kimesne meclis-i şer'-i şerif-i lazımül-teşrifte işbu sahıbül-kitab Aynoroz'da vaki İkşiropotam nam manastır ruhbanından Matyo Koca ve Malahya ve Yakim nam rahipler muvacehesinde ikrar ve itiraf edip: mezburun rahipler ile bir miktar odun ve navl-ı sefineye verilen yedi bin akçemi bu ana gelince dava va niza üzere eylemiştim hala odunları mezburun almayıp sabıka zabıt olan Ahmet Ağa'nın adamları ahz ve kabz eylediklerinden bizim dahi malumumuz olmağın elhaletühazihi canibeynden muslihûn tavassüt ile üç bin nakit rayıc filvakt akçeye sulh edip … '.

39. Izdebski et al. 2015.

40. For the Ottoman mines of *Sidrekapsi*, see Kolovos 2015.

Sidrekapsi was prohibited to the villagers, because it was used for the operation of the furnaces of the mines:

> The mountain is located to the south of the town of Sidrekapsi, which is a silver mine. It is a high and wide mountain … Big and small trees on this mountain are innumerable. These trees are under the protection of the miners. They are protected from the villagers, so that they use them for the operation of the mine.[41]

Evliya Çelebi (1611–1685?) confirms Aşık Mehmed almost a century later:

> Such big trees as the trees of the mountain of Sidrekapsi cannot be found in any other country. Maybe only in the mountains of Ravna, in the vilayet of Bosnia. But in the case of the trees of Sidrekapsi, nobody is allowed to cut them. This is because the mountain and the trees are the property of the state [*miri kuhistan ve dırahtistandır*] and are being used for the smelting of the silver ore. If someone cuts a tree, he pays a fine.[42]

There is some scattered evidence that the need for timber, both for the galleries of the mines and for the production of charcoal by the charcoalers (*kömürciyan*), distributed among 150 villages in the area of Salonica, had serious implications for the forest. We have detailed information about the timber used for the galleries of the mine during the first years of the eighteenth century: almost 7,500 trees fell in 1703, over 35,000 in 1706 and almost 20,000 in 1707. Moreover, in 1731, according to an Ottoman report, there were not enough trees around the village of Arnaia (*Larigkova*) for the production of charcoal; because of that, the villagers were ordered to offer their services as miners. In 1782, the villagers of a group of villages of Halkidiki reported to the director (*emin*) of the mines that the mountains in the vicinity of their villages had no more timber for the production of charcoal. After an inspection, which corroborated the report, the production of charcoal was imposed on other villages, which had enough forest.[43]

In the light of the above information, it is interesting to note the disappearance of the forest in the area of the village of Peristera, on the southern slopes of the Hortiatis Mountain, to the north-western extreme of the Halkidiki area, of which we have testimonies in the eleventh century, but no longer in

---

41. Âşık Mehmed 2007, vol. 2, p. 406.
42. 'Ve bu cebelde olan eşcarat-ı azimeler bir diyarda yokdur. İlla Bosna vilâyetinde Ravna dağlarında vardır. Ammâ bu Sidirkapsi dırahtların bir ferd-i âferîde aslâ kat' edemez, zîrâ gümüş ma'denin hal etmeğe mîrî kûhistân ve dırahtistândır. Bir kimesne bir dıraht kat' etse kat'-ı eydeyn edüp tecrîm ederler'. Evliya Çelebi 2003, vol. 8, p. 44.
43. For these data see in detail Altunbay 2010, pp. 56, 123, 129.

the nineteenth century.[44] Another forest of which we have testimonies in the fourteenth century, but no longer in the nineteenth century, at least for a part of it, is that of the Kalavros Mountain.[45] The deforestation in these two areas might be attributed to the production of charcoal for the needs of the mines of *Sidrekapsi.* The palynological research carried out recently in Halkidiki suggests that more generally the Ottoman period marked an interruption in the expansion of both pine and oak cover.[46] In conclusion, the function of Ottoman mines seems to have transformed the environment of the Western Halkidiki through the exploitation of both the subsoil and the forest. This exploitation seems to have been intensified from the second half of the nineteenth century on and until today: nowadays the former Ottoman mines are claimed for exploitation by Canadian mining companies, as elsewhere in the world.

Another indicator for our research on the effects of the Little Ice Age might be the cultivation of olive trees; olives are threatened by prolonged frost during winter, but they are well adapted to dry climates.[47] An expansion of olive cultivation (see below) has been observed in the case of Crete from the late sixteenth and the early seventeenth century onwards: prior to this, Crete was a 'vast vineyard'.[48] Vines are threatened more by summer heat, spring hoar frost and late summer rain.[49] On the other hand, olive cultivation seems to have declined during the late Medieval period in the Greek lands, maybe as a result of the Black Death demographic crisis.[50] A similar case might be that of Halkidiki, where fifteenth- and sixteenth-century Ottoman tax registers mention almost nowhere a systematic cultivation of olive trees.[51] Actually, we can corroborate this argument with data from the recent palynological research carried out in Halkidiki, showing a considerable retreat of olive cultivation in

---

44. Bellier et al. 1986, pp. 91–92, 114.

45. Ibid., pp. 90, 92, 114.

46. Panajiotidis 2015, pp. 318–19 and diagram on pp. 320–22.

47. Xoplaki et al. 2015, pp. 4–5.

48. Greene 2002, pp. 118–19. See also Cañellas-Boltà et al. 2018, p. 71 and figs 4–6, for a recent pollen study which has found out relatively low values of Olea pollen during the Venetian period in eastern Crete.

49. Xoplaki et al. 2015, pp. 4–5.

50. Ibid., p. 20.

51. From the rich material of the Ottoman tax registers of the 16th century we came across only three entries regarding olive trees and all of these were in monastic farmlands. See National Library of Cyril and Methodius (*Narodna Biblioteka Kiril i Metodij; NBKM*), Oriental Department, OAK 83/85, f. 16b; BOA, Tapu Tahrir Defterleri, no. 7, p. 634 and no. 723, p. 1052.

Halkidiki, parallel only to the early Byzantine centuries.[52] On the other hand, the Ottoman tax survey of 1764 for the peninsula of Mount Athos, counted around 35,000 olive trees there.[53] We are inclined to assume that this figure refers to an impressive increase in the cultivation of olive trees, similar to that of Crete, which we will discuss below. We do not, however, have comparable data from the sixteenth century, since Mount Athos then paid tax in a fixed lump sum (*maktu*) for the monasteries. Travellers like Aşık Mehmed, however, had noticed the increased olive cultivation on Mount Athos by the sixteenth century;[54] yet they did not make similar observations for the rest of the Halkidikian countryside. One final observation we can extract from our sources is that the olive trees in Halkidiki were present at all altitudes during the eighteenth century. For instance, in 1741 some inhabitants of the semi-mountainous village of Galatista, located at a 450-metre altitude, endowed to the monastery of Xeropotamou 25 olive trees.[55] However, the lack of olive oil on Mount Athos is attested in a letter sent from Athonites to another monk, who was travelling to the Aegean island of Lesbos.[56] In sum, since the Ottoman tax registers from the eighteenth century do not mention taxes on olive cultivation on a large scale, we argue that, although olive trees were not absent from the landscape of Halkidiki before then, the intensification of production was a phenomenon of the seventeenth and even the eighteenth century. Because previous research suggests a wet Little Ice Age in this part of the Northern Aegean, we might attribute the comeback of olives to the end of the Little Ice Age.

On the other hand, we have already mentioned that the island of Crete became an island of olive trees from the late sixteenth century onwards. Was this an effect of 'Little Ice Age' conditions? Crete is the fifth largest island in the Mediterranean Sea (it covers an area of 8,336 square kilometres), with an elongated shape from east to west. Crete has especially high mountains (Psiloritis: 2,456 metres; the White Mountains: 2,454 metres; the Dikti Mountains: 2,148 metres). Because of its diversified landscape, Dimos Tsantilis has recently described Crete as a 'continent in an island'.[57] The historical sources concern-

52. Panajiotidis 2015, pp. 318–19 and diagram on pp. 320–22.
53. Balta 1999, pp. 149, 151, 153.
54. Âşık Mehmed 2007, vol. 2, p. 250.
55. Gounaridis 1993, doc. nos 76, 79, 82, 84–88, and 90.
56. Anastasiadis 2002, p. 215 (no. 214). The monks of the monastery requested the monk to send them 700–800 *okka* (ca. 900–1,000 kg) of olive oil from Lesbos island, because it was in short supply in their lands (i.e. on Mount Athos).
57. Tsantilis 2015.

ing the climate of Crete during the sixteenth and seventeenth centuries have been studied by Jean Grove and Annalisa Conterio:[58] their findings indicate that we can locate more specifically in the sources the effects of the Little Ice Age in winter droughts, very severe winters with snowfalls and heavy rainfalls during summer.[59]

More specifically, the research by Grove and Conterio shows that drought years cluster in 1561–66 and 1600–07.[60] Between 1547 and 1645, twelve years of winter drought occurred: in 1625–26, the Duke of Candia reported to Venice that 'the countryside is becoming so exhausted by the continental south winds which prevail ... that where ... a very abundant harvest was hoped for ... it will be a very bad year ... '.[61] South winds were the cause of the most severe winter and spring droughts in Crete, as today, affected by the extension of southerly air masses from the Sahara Desert.

At the same time, between 1547 and 1648, eight very severe winters were recorded in Crete. In 1601–02, for example, continuous rain and extreme cold caused the death of a large number of animals, according to Venetian reports; many men amongst the crews of the galleys on guard duty in Crete also died because of 'the very bitter cold'. Another Venetian report, dated 1659, during the Cretan War, mentions a 'terrible winter ... with two months of continual rain and snow up to the coasts'. [62] Grove and Conterio conclude that 'winter in the sixteenth and seventeenth centuries with heavy and prolonged rain, and in extreme cases heavy snowfall at low levels, were characterized by snowfall in higher elevations which was more plentiful and longer lasting than it is today'.[63] A Venetian report dated 1625 listed 28 rivers 'with abundant water' on the island; in 1847, only five from the 28 were listed in another account as rivers. Today, only four of them have abundant water.[64] And there are many historical accounts referring to snow on the mountains of Crete all the year round. Zuanne (Giovanni) Papadopoli (1655–1740), who wrote *L'Occhio*, a nostalgic memoir of his native island Crete, at the end of the seventeenth century in Padova, noted that in the mid-seventeenth century the summit of Mount Ida (*Psiloritis*) was snow-covered for a whole year and rich people were using it in

---

58. Grove and Conterio 1995.

59. Ibid., p. 231 and Table 1 in pp. 232–35.

60. Ibid., p. 236.

61. Ibid., p. 238.

62. Ibid., p. 239.

63. Ibid.

64. Rackham and Moody 1996, pp. 41–43.

feasts for cool drinks, in order to show off.[65] The French botanist Joseph Pitton de Tournefort (1656–1708), who visited Mount Ida in July 1700, noted that snow was everywhere around him, in deep reserves.[66] According to an Ottoman *vakfiye* (endowment deed), dated 1794, issued for the construction of a large fountain (*sebilhane*) in Herakleio (Candia, Kandiye), the founder, Hacı İsmail Ağa son of Ali, of the Kalıpsız Family, provided funding every summer for the transportation of four loads of snow from the mountains of Crete to the city, in order to cool the water of the fountain during the extremely hot Cretan summer. Today, however, this would be impossible: the snow melts from the mountain peaks of Crete in May, or at latest early June, and returns in November. There are no reports of snow reserves on Psiloritis (i.e., reserves of snow collected in the winter months for use during the summer, like the '*kar kuyuları*' in western and southern Anatolia); this year (2018) there was a report of a snow reserve on the White Mountains, but it was a natural one.[67] On the other hand, Crete, located south in the Mediterranean basin, escaped the ice which devastated France and Italy in 1709; in the 1730s the island was exporting to Marseilles 1,600 tons of olive oil annually.[68] As Grove and Conterio have remarked, climatic anomalies did not always occur simultaneously in the eastern and western Mediterranean.[69]

Only more rarely are heavy summer rains mentioned in the sources on Crete of the sixteenth and seventeenth centuries: they do, however include interesting information. In 1576, for example, a Venetian report attributed to the 'very heavy and unusual rains' of that year 'in the months of June, July, and August', the ruin of the wine vintage.[70]

Did the cooler climate have an impact on the demography and agricultural production of Crete? Again, we cannot find any major catastrophic demographic effect in the case of Venetian and, after the mid-seventeenth century, Ottoman Crete. As in the case of Halkidiki, we can identify a demographic decrease when comparing the population data of the Ottoman registers

---

65. Vincent 2007.

66. 'De quelque côté que notre veue se portât, d'une hauteur à l'autre, il ne se présentoit que fondrieres & des abismes remplis de neige'. Tournefort 1717, vol. 1, p. 53.

67. On the other hand, this year (2018) is the warmest summer people have experienced in Crete in their lives; the same is true for the whole of Europe, as a result of global warming conditions.

68. Rackham and Moody 1996, p. 106.

69. Grove and Conterio 1995, pp. 242–43.

70. Ibid.

of 1650 and 1670, during the Cretan War, around twenty per cent (or less, since our data do not include the converts to Islam during these years, which were numerous according to the judicial registers).[71] On the other hand, as in the case of Halkidiki, and unlike the case of the Anatolian plateau around 1600, we cannot find evidence of a 'big flight' from the countryside. The settlement network of Crete remained more or less stable during the seventeenth century, despite the long war on the island between 1645 and 1669. Vineyards were still extensive in Crete in 1670, covering around 5,500 hectares. Olive trees numbered a total of 732,000 in 1670, all around the island.[72] By the end of the nineteenth century, the Cretan olives had reached seven million trees. Olive trees might have been better adapted to the drier summers of the 'Little Ice Age' than the vineyards.

Conclusion

In conclusion, even if we can see in our case studies of Halkidiki and Crete the effects of the Little Ice Age, we have to be careful in our evaluations before making general arguments. Yes, the impact of the Little Ice Age would have been felt in the Balkans and the islands of the Eastern Mediterranean as well. But it looks as if it was less devastating than on the Anatolian plateau, as is very reasonable actually, in terms of geography and geomorphology. More regional case-studies have to investigate this issue in the future and we hope that they will do, since environmental history is currently in the ascendant. Moreover, human activity during the Little Ice Age, as shown especially in the case of the Ottoman mines in Halkidiki, and more generally, but somewhat ambiguously, with the expansion of the cultivation of olive trees both in Halkidiki and Crete, constantly interacted with the environmental change. Environmental historians should not forget that human agency is probably the most crucial factor for environmental changes. Thus, we have to assess our climate change sources more elaborately in the future against social history sources, and vice-versa: environmental history has a lot to gain from a social history approach. Another important factor, in our view, for the nascent environmental historiography of the Ottoman Empire, is to ground ourselves firmly in the sources, before

---

71. The Christian *neferan* (male adults) in Crete were recorded as 33,834 in the Ottoman registers of 1650 and 27,496 in the Ottoman registers of 1670. Report from Giorgos Vidras, a Ph.D. candidate, who studies the Ottoman registers of Crete for his dissertation concerning the population and agriculture of Crete during the seventeenth century. For these registers and their data, see also Gülsoy 2004.

72. Ibid.

making unduly sweeping generalisations. Environmental history, like social history in general, needs to create for itself a detailed sample of sources and case studies, before attempting to write the history of the Ottoman Empire in environmental terms.

REFERENCES

Unpublished Primary Sources

Prime Ministry Ottoman Archives (*Başbakanlık Osmanlı Arşivleri, BOA*), Istanbul

Tapu Tahrir Defterleri (TT) nos. 7 (1478), 70 (1519), 403 (1527), 143 (1527), 167 (1530), 723 (1613, copy of 1568).

Maliyeden Müdevver (MAD) nos. 1209 (1642), 4609 (1692), 3461 (1697), 14947 (1710).

Kâmil Kepeci Collection (KK) no. 2869 (1722).

National Library of Cyril and Methodius (*Narodna Biblioteka Kiril i Metodij, NBKM*), Sofia Oriental Department, OAK 45/30 (ca.1445), 83/35 (ca. 1500).

Holy Monastery of Xeropotamou (Μονή Ξηροποτάμου *[Moni Xeropotamou, MX]*), Mount Athos.

The Ottoman Archive.

Holy Monastery of Agiou Pavlou (Μονή Αγίου Παύλου *[Moni Agiou Pavlou, MAP]*), Mount Athos.

The Ottoman Archive.

Published Primary Sources

Âşık Mehmed. 2007 [1577?]. *Menâzirü'l-Avâlim, vol. 2*. 3 vols. Ed. by Mahmut Ak (Ankara: Türk Tarih Kurumu).

Evliyâ Çelebi. 2003. *Evliyâ Çelebi Seyahatnâmesi, vol. 8*. 10 vols. Ed. by Seyit Ali Kahraman, Yücel Dağlı and Robert Dankoff (Istanbul: Yapı ve Kredi Bankası).

Tournefort, Joseph Pitton de. 1717. *Relation d'un voyage de Levant, vol. 1*. 3 vols. Paris: Imprimerie Royale.

Yıldırım, Hacı Osman et al. (eds). 1995. *6 Numaralı Mühimme Defteri (972 / 1564–1565). Özet-Transkripsiyon ve İndeks*. Ankara: TC Başbakanlık Devlet Arşivleri Genel Müdürlüğü, Osmanlı Arşivi Daire Başkanlığı.

Secondary Sources

Akdağ, Mustafa. 1963. *Celâli İsyanları (1550–1603)*. Ankara: Ankara University.

——. 1964. 'Celâli İsyanlarından Büyük Kaçgunluk'. *Tarih Araştırmaları Dergisi* 2: 1–49.

Altunbay, Mustafa. 2010. 'Osmanlı Döneminde Bir Maden İşletmesinin Tarihi Süreci: Sidrekapsı'. Ph.D. Diss., Istanbul: Istanbul University.

Anastasiadis, Vasilis. 2002. *Αρχείο της Ι. Μ. Χιλανδαρίου. Επιτομές μεταβυζαντινών εγγράφων [Archeio tēs Hi. M. Chilandariou: epitomes metabyzantinōn engraphōn]*. Athens: National Research Foundation – Institute for Byzantine Studies.

Balta, Evangelia. 1999. 'Landed Property of the Monasteries on the Athos Peninsula and its Taxation in 1764'. *Arab Historical Review for Ottoman Studies* **19–20**: 179–207.

Bellier, Paul et al. 1986. *Paysages de Macédoine: leurs caractères, leur évolution à travers les documents et les récits des voyageurs*. Paris: Centre de Recherche d'Histoire et Civilisation de Byzance-Collège de France.

Braudel, Fernand. 1995. *The Mediterranean and the Mediterranean World in the Age of Philip II, vol. 1*. 2 vols. Berkeley: University of California Press.

Cañellas-Boltà, Nuria et al. 2018. 'Human management and landscape changes at Palaikastro (Eastern Crete) from the Late Neolithic to the Early Minoan period', *Quaternary Science Reviews* **183**: 59–75.

Gogou, Alexandra et al. 2016. 'Climate variability and socio-environmental changes in the northern Aegean (NE Mediterranean) during the last 1500 years'. *Quaternary Science Reviews* **136**: 209–28.

Gounaridis, Paris. 1993. *Ἀθωνικὰ Σύμμεικτα 3. Ἀρχεῖο Ἱερᾶς Μονῆς Ξηροποτάμου. Ἐπιτομὲς μεταβυζαντινῶν ἐγγράφων [Archeio tīs Ι. Μ. Xīropotamou: epitomes metavyzantinōn eggrafōn]*. Athens: National Research Center.

Greene, Molly. 2002. *A Shared World. Christians and Muslims in the Early Modern Mediterranean*. Princeton: Princeton University Press.

Griswold, William. 1983. *The Great Anatolian Rebellion 1000–1020 (1591–1611)*. Berlin: Klaus Schwarz Verlag.

Grove, Jean M. and Annalisa Conterio. 1995. 'The Climate of Crete in the Sixteenth and Seventeenth Centuries'. *Climatic Change* **30** (2): 223–47.

Gülsoy, Ersin. 2004. *Girit'in Fethi ve Osmanlı İdaresinin Kurulması*. Istanbul: Tarih ve Tabiat Vakfı.

Izdebski, Adam. 2013. *A Rural Economy in Transition: Asia Minor from Late Antiquity into the Early Middle Ages*. Warsaw: University of Warsaw Press.

Izdebski, Adam et al. 2015. 'Exploring Byzantine and Ottoman economic history with the use of palynological data: a quantitative approach'. *Jahrbuch des Österreichisches Byzantinistik* **65**: 67–110.

Katsiardi-Hering, Olga. 2009. 'Von den Aufständen zu den Revolutionen christlicher Untertanen des osmanischen Reiches in Südosteuropa (ca. 1530–1821). Ein Typologisierungsversuch'. *Südost Forschungen* **68**: 96–137.

Kolovos, Elias and Phokion Kotzageorgis. 2015. 'Halkidiki in the Early Modern Period: Towards an Environmental History'. In Basil G. Gounaris (ed.), *Mines, Olives and Monasteries: Aspects of Halkidiki's Environmental History*. Salonica: Epikentro; Pharos Books 2015. pp. 123–61.

Kolovos, Elias. 2015. 'Mines and the Environment in Halkidiki: A Story from the Ottoman Past'. *Balkan Studies* **50**: 71–94.

'Little Ice Age' Effects

Kotzageorgis, Phokion. 2008. *Small Towns of the Greek Peninsula During the Early Modern Era. The Case of Xanthi (15th-17th c.)*. Xanthi: Holy Metropolis of Xanthi and Peritheorion.

Le Roy Ladurie, Emmanuel. 1959. 'Histoire et Climat'. *Annales, Economies, Sociétés, Civilisations* 14 (1) : 3–34.

Mann, Michael E. 2002. 'Little Ice Age'. In Ted Munn (ed.), *Encyclopedia of Global Environmental Change, vol. 1: The Earth System: Physical and Chemical Dimensions of Global Environmental Change*. 5 vols. Princeton: Princeton University Press. pp. 504–09.

McNeill, John R. 1992. *The Mountains of the Mediterranean World: Studies in Environment and History*. Cambridge: Cambridge University Press.

Mészáros, Orsolya and Gábor Serlegi. 2010. 'The Impact of Environmental Change on Medieval Settlement Structure in Transdanubia'. *Acta Archaeologica Academiae Scientiarum Hungaricae* 62: 199–219.

Ogilvie, Astrid E.J. and Trausti Jónsson (eds). 2001. *The Iceberg in the Mist: Northern Research in Pursuit of a 'Little Ice Age'*. Dordrecht : Springer Netherlands.

Özel, Oktay. 2012. 'The Reign of Violence: The *Celâlis*, c.1550–1700'. In Christine Woodhead (ed.), *The Ottoman World*. London and New York: Routledge. pp. 184–202.

——— . 2015. 'The Question of Abandoned Villages in Ottoman Anatolia (Seventeenth to Nineteenth Centuries)'. In Elias Kolovos (ed.), *Ottoman Rural Societies and Economies, Halcyon Days in Crete VIII, A Symposium Held in Rethymno, 13–15 January 2012*. Rethymno: Crete University Press. pp. 95–130.

Panajiotidis, Sampson. 2015. 'Palynological Investigation of the Tristinika Marsh in Halkidiki (North-Central Greece): A Vegetation History of the Last Three and One-Half Millenia'. In Basil G. Gounaris (ed.), *Mines, Olives and Monasteries: Aspects of Halkidiki's Environmental History*. Salonica: Epikentro; Pharos Books 2015. pp. 303–22.

Rackham, Oliver and Jennifer Moody. 1996. *The Making of the Cretan Landscape*. Manchester and New York: Manchester University Press.

Rácz, Lajos. 2010. 'The Price of Survival: Transformations in Environmental Conditions and Subsistence Systems in Hungary in the Age of Ottoman Occupation'. *Hungarian Studies* 24: 21–39.

Tabak, Faruk. 2008. *The Waning of the Mediterranean, 1550–1870: A Geohistorical Approach*. Baltimore: Johns Hopkins University Press.

Tsantilis, Dimos. 2015. *Crete, A Continent in an Island*. Trans. by Ben Petre. Heraklion: Natural History Museum of Crete, University of Crete.

Tsigarida, Elisavet (Bettina) and Ioannis Xydopoulos. 2015. 'Halkidiki: Landscape, Archaeology, and Ethnicity'. In Basil G. Gounaris (ed.), *Mines, Olives and Monasteries: Aspects of Halkidiki's Environmental History*. Salonica: Epikentro; Pharos Books 2015. pp. 35–69.

Vincent, Alfred (ed.). 2007. *Memories of Seventeenth-century Crete: L'Occio (Time of Leisure) by Zuanne Papadopoli, Critical Edition with English Translation, Introduction, Commentary and Glossary*. Venice: Hellenic Institute of Byzantine and Post-Byzantine Studies.

Elias Kolovos and Phokion Kotzageorgis

Xoplaki, Elena, et al. 2016. 'The Medieval Climate Anomaly and Byzantium: A Review of the Evidence on Climatic Fluctuations, Economic Performance and Societal Change'. *Quaternary Science Reviews. Special Issue: Mediterranean Holocene Climate, Environment and Human Societies* **136**: 229–52.

White, Sam. 2011. *The Climate of Rebellion in the Early Modern Ottoman Empire*. Cambridge: Cambridge University Press.

Chapter 2

A 'MAGNIFICENT' CLIMATE: DEMOGRAPHY, LAND AND LABOUR IN SIXTEENTH-CENTURY ANATOLIA

Mehmet Kuru

The late sixteenth and seventeenth centuries were times of political upheaval, social unrest and economic turmoil for the Ottoman Empire. A series of large-scale rebellions, known as *Celali*s, swept the countryside, causing incalculable destruction in Anatolia. Ottoman historians have concurred that the period of crises had a long-lasting impact on the social and economic structure of the empire, but they differ on the factors that prompted these revolts.[1] They have pointed out some major dynamics behind the crisis; two of these are population increase recorded in the sixteenth century and the severe climatic conditions that appeared in the last decade of the century.[2] Surprisingly, these two interrelated factors have always been analysed separately. While historians who focused on the sixteenth-century population growth mostly neglected contemporary climatic conditions, researchers who examined the impact of the 'Little Ice Age' on the *Celali* rebellions confined the timeline of their work to the relevant period with the assumption that the pre-existing climatic conditions constituted a stable ground zero. In this paper, I propose to reconsider the Anatolia-wide demographic growth of the sixteenth century – a widely accepted historical phenomenon – and aim to explore the relationship between the shifts in climatic conditions, fiscal population[3] and agricultural production that took place in this period. In relation to that, I argue that the temporary shift in climatic condi-

---

1. For a compact review, see Faroqhi 1994, pp. 411–636.

2. For the alternative perspectives on the basis of Celali rebellions, see Barkan 1953; Akdağ 1963; Cook 1972; İslamoğlu-İnan 1994, pp. 151–56; İnalcık 1980; Faroqhi 1987; idem 1995; Barkey 1994; Griswold 1983, Griswold 1993; White 2011.

3. I use the term 'fiscal population' to refer to sedentary tax-payers of the Ottoman Empire and this does not include the semi-nomadic pastoral tribes or tax-exempt groups.

tions enabled expansion of arable lands, growth of population and increase of taxable agricultural production during the sixteenth century. Allegorically, the reign of Süleyman I, the 'Magnificent' (r. 1520–1566), also had a 'magnificent' climate, with regard to its precipitation regime. On the other hand, it should be noted that I do not aim to put forward temporal climatic dynamics as the sole factor that shaped the sixteenth-century Ottoman Empire but rather am suggesting inclusion of this factor in the analysis alongside other economic, social and political determinants, in order to examine this period profoundly.

My research has three steps. Firstly, based on an analysis of *tahrir* (tax surveys) conducted in the sixteenth century, I argue that the Anatolia-wide demographic growth of this period was characterised by sharp regional discrepancies. While the Mediterranean coastal zones witnessed limited or no change in their fiscal population, both inner and south-eastern Anatolia experienced extraordinary demographic development over half a century. Secondly, by examining the long-term aridity index and climatic conditions, I conclude that the regions that experienced a marked population growth were mainly the semi-arid regions of Anatolia, whereas the somewhat humid regions on the Mediterranean remained relatively stable. Finally, I uncover the relationship between temporary climatic conditions observed in the sixteenth century and their impact on demographic structure and agricultural production. Recent dendrochronological research has revealed that Ottoman Anatolia experienced the wettest period of the second millennium between 1518 and 1587.[4] By means of an analysis of this data, I suggest that the vast inner semi-arid lands turned into well-watered areas and new fields were opened for agricultural production during the sixteenth century on account of this temporal climatic variance. Concomitantly, the fiscal population of these regions increased markedly.

Demographic Change in Sixteenth-Century Anatolia and Regional Climatic Discrepancy

In the case of sixteenth-century Anatolia, *tahrir defterleri* (tax registers) are essential sources for analysing the socio-economic transformation of the provinces.

---

4. For details on long-term precipitation patterns and the relevant discussion, see fig. 1. It must be mentioned that these dates do not point to an instant shift between the periods, rather they are the beginning and end of 70-year running means, which were created in order to capture a periodical comparison. For a brief review on research in dendroclimatology in the eastern Mediterranean, see Touchan et al. 2014. Several significant studies on tree-ring dendrochronology in Turkey are available, such as Touchan et al. 2005; Touchan et al. 2007; Heinrich 2013; Köse et al. 2011; Köse 2007.

A 'Magnificent' Climate

In order to capture the variations in regional fiscal populations, I compiled the figures extracted from the *tahrir* registers which have been previously published by several Ottoman historians. Such use of *tahrir* registers in statistical demographic studies undoubtedly has certain limitations, as various scholars have shown.[5] For example, as fiscally-oriented registers, they exclude several tax-exempt groups such as members of the military class. Secondly, the most accurate method of multiplying the recorded number of households in order to reach a figure for the total population remains a controversial issue among historians. Finally, regional survey methods in the Balkans, Anatolia and the Arab lands and frontiers may have differed, making any comparisons debatable.

However, I consider these legitimate criticisms to be less applicable to the case at hand. Firstly, it should be highlighted that the demographical statistics I employ here refer only to fiscal population. I do not attempt to uncover the actual population figures, but rather endeavour to discern general trends of fiscal population growth and decline observed throughout the century. My approach, therefore, is diachronic and vertical rather than synchronic and horizontal, establishing a time series rather than the validity of historical data against historical reality. Thus, my priority is to maintain consistency throughout the surveys analysed and my focus is on the relation between land and labour, rather than on one or the other. Basically, I compare and correlate the trends.

These *tahrir* registers contain two main categories that are useful for demographic studies: the enumeration of heads of *hane*s (households) and of *mücerred* (single landless adult males). Historians are largely in agreement about the 'household' as a category recorded in these registers. However, the term *mücerred* is more controversial. The tax registers, conducted at regular intervals, show significant variance in the number of *mücerred* listed for certain regions. Certain researchers propose alternative explanations on this issue.[6] With respect to the conflicting hypotheses, I prefer here to consider only the number of households – that is, the main tax-payers – and exclude the *mücerred*s from my analysis in order to avoid a potential statistical bias due to this highly contested category. The drawback of such a choice is the omission of this category for the assessment of macro aspects of demography, but I do not mean to underestimate the importance of the *mücerred*s in the context of social dislocation or even military transformation. However, my aim here is

---

5.   Ataman 1992; Faroqhi 1999, pp. 86–95; Lowry 1992; Coşgel 2004; idem 2006.

6.   Cook 1972, p. 27; Erder and Faroqhi 1979, p. 336; Özel 2016, pp. 114–15, especially see footnote 50.

38

Mehmet Kuru

not to arrive at a population estimate, but to illustrate the change in the fiscal population by percentile ratios.

Studies on the demographic structure of the sixteenth-century Ottoman Empire date back to the mid-twentieth century. In his monumental work, *The Mediterranean and the Mediterranean World in the Age of Philip II,* Fernand Braudel estimated that the total population of the entire Mediterranean region doubled between the years 1500 and 1600.[7] This projection was welcomed with great interest by Ottoman historians. For instance, Ömer Lütfü Barkan, a leading Ottoman historian, began to examine the Ottoman archives as early as the 1950s to test Braudel's predictions.[8] Since then, numerous researchers who have worked on sixteenth-century Ottoman tax registers have emphasised a shared demographic trajectory for the lands of Ottoman Empire.[9] However, neither demographers nor historians have noticed the discrepancies between regional demographic fluctuations.[10] And while Braudel was to a certain extent correct in claiming that there was a general demographic growth for this period, regional discrepancies were overlooked by subsequent researchers. In fact, the level of increase displays significant variations among Anatolian regions. While the Mediterranean coastal areas indicate limited change in regional fiscal populations, the interior and the south-eastern regions of Anatolia experienced a demographic explosion.

Map 1 below depicts demographic changes in the rural areas based on the fiscal registers surveyed for the periods 1520s–30s and 1570s–80s. While regions close to the Mediterranean did not display a remarkable demographic development, inner and south-eastern areas reveal an extraordinary growth over the course of approximately five decades. I should note that there are still significant gaps on the map, particularly in north-western Anatolia. Even though I culled data from almost the entirety of extant literature on *tahrir* registers, a complete demographic map of sixteenth-century Anatolia is not possible at this point, in the absence of studies on several districts.

---

7.   Braudel 1977, vol. 1, pp. 394–410.

8.   Barkan 1953; idem 1954.

9.   Cook 1972; Jennings 1976; Erder 1975; Faroqhi 1979–80. Several prominent works based on *tahrir* registers include Emecen 1989; Öz 1999; İslamoğlu-İnan 1994. A list of relevant titles can be found in the notes to the appendix.

10. Ronald C. Jennings was the only historian who pointed out the varying rate of growth for cities under different political, economic and geographic circumstances, but he did not have a large-scale sample to reach a more general conclusion in terms of regional demographic/fiscal variation at that time. See the previous note.

A *'Magnificent' Climate*

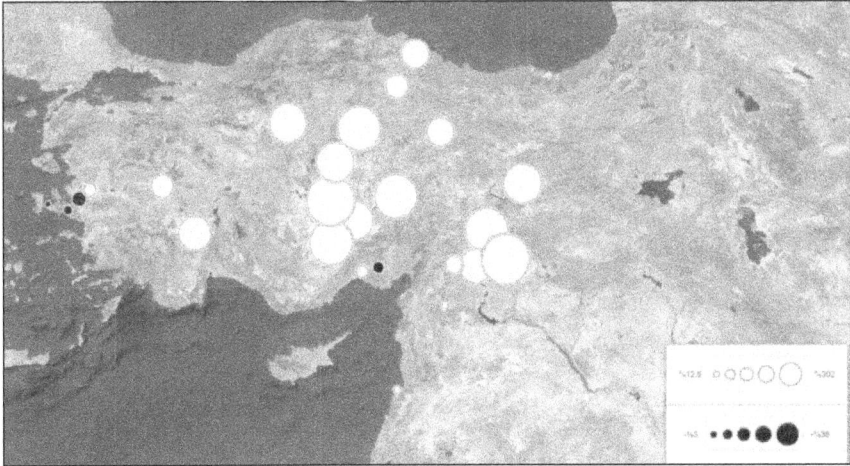

Map 1. Rural demographic change in sixteenth-century Anatolia between 1520s/30s and 1570s/80s. Based on the tahrir *registers.*[11]

In the coastal regions, while several districts were losing a certain number of their rural taxpayers, others showed only a slight population growth, as depicted in the map. In contrast, the zones of inner and South-eastern Anatolian followed a very different trajectory: in these regions, the level of increase in the population of taxpayers soared as high as 300 per cent. Therefore, it is unrealistic to claim that there was a homogeneous demographic pattern for Ottoman Anatolia as a whole.

This regional variation also points to a climatic differentiation between the coastal areas and inner regions. While the western and southern coasts of Anatolia are under the influence of Mediterranean climatic conditions, the interior is characterised mostly by a continental climate.[12] As the map below indicates, the precipitation regimes and aridity index for the Mediterranean and interior regions of Anatolia are completely different.

---

11. For further details, consult the figures tabulated for each centre in the appendix. The dates of the surveys, sources and the figures can be found there. An online version of the map is also available via the following link, see https://mehmetkuru.carto.com/viz/ef84ccb2-fb42–11e5–9a8c-0e98b61680bf/public_map

12. Mediterranean climate receives its name from the Mediterranean basin and is characterised by hot, dry summers and cool, wet winters and location between about 30° and 45° latitude north and south of the Equator and on the western sides of the continents. Humid continental climate is another major climate type of the Köppen classification that exhibits large seasonal temperature contrasts with hot summers and cold winters.

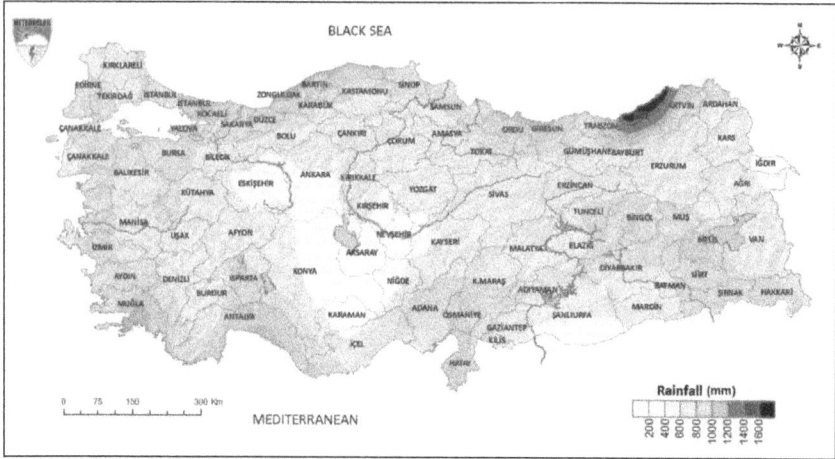

Map 2. Geographical distribution of average areal annual precipitation (1981–2010).[13]

In Map 2 above, the geographical distribution of the annual precipitation index is depicted for three decades from 1981 to 2010. However, it should be mentioned here that the average precipitation index of late twentieth-century Anatolia also intersects the average of the entire millennium.[14] In the sense of geographical distribution of precipitation, the map is also consistent with the long-term averages of the regional distribution.[15] Therefore, the evidence shows that the regions that observed extraordinary demographic growth in the sixteenth century are the driest areas of Anatolia. Aksaray, Konya, Niğde, Karaman and Urfa were regions that displayed the most aggressive demographic growth in this century, whereas Izmir, Aydın, Muğla, Antalya and Adana were relatively stable areas-the populations of which fluctuated in a narrow strip. Map 3 below displays the different ecologically homogeneous areas of Anatolia, as determined using drought index and elevation data, and provides a more nuanced perspective on regional differences that cut across similarities in vegetation and shared agricultural production patterns.

13. Map taken from Ulupınar et al. 2016, p. 3. http://www.mgm.gov.tr/FILES/arastirma/yagis-degerlendirme/2015alansal.pdf (accessed on 30 July 2018). Public domain image: Turkish Meteorological Service. For a detailed analysis of regional variation of climatic indices in Turkey, see Deniz, Toros and Incecik 2011.

14. For the relevant figure and the discussion, see fig. 1 below.

15. For long-term dendroclimatological analyses of Anatolia, see Dalfes et al. 2006. For a summary of this project, see Köse 2007, pp. 31–32.

A 'Magnificent' Climate

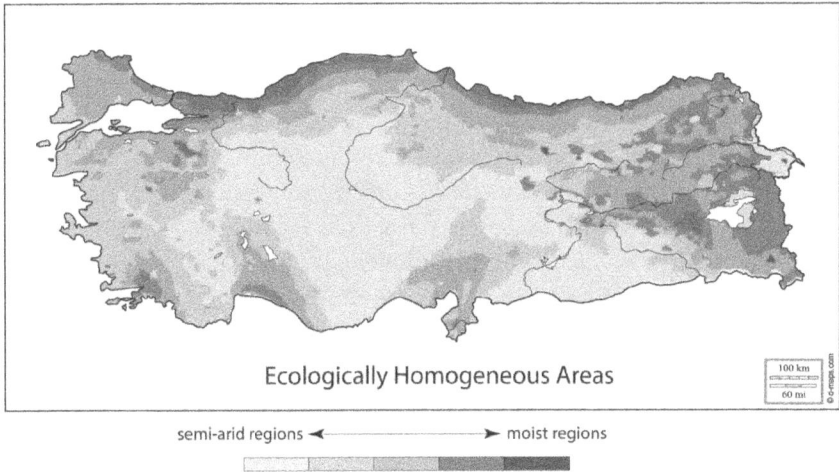

Ecologically Homogeneous Areas

100 km
60 mi

semi-arid regions ◄───────────► moist regions

The map shows the spectrum between semi-arid regions and moist regions based on shared vegetation patterns.

Map 3. Map of ecologically homogenous areas of Anatolia.[16]

As these maps indicate, there is a discernible intersection between semi-arid regions and those areas that observed significant demographic growth in sixteenth-century Anatolia, whereas those regions with higher precipitation averages were relatively stable in regard to the fiscal population for the same period. How can this variation between Anatolian regions be interpreted? Why did the semi-arid regions follow a more vigorous course of demographic development compared to those provinces under a Mediterranean climate? The high rate of increase of fiscal population, which doubled or even tripled for certain regions, could not have been based only on natural demographic growth. Tax surveys also reveal that several semi-nomadic pastoral groups became sedentary in these regions during the period in question. For instance, in most villages of

---

16.   This map is a simplified version of Yıldız et al. 2009, p. 20 (on the original map, lands are shaded in 37 different colours that correspond to vegetation classification). The most arid region (palest grey) is depicted in South-east Anatolia around the borderland of Syria and the wettest area (darkest grey) is shown in the north-east, around Artvin. Other shades display the various zones in between. It should be noted that the available ground and surface water resources influence the agricultural crops for specific regions through irrigation systems and accessible water resources. This map is simply based on drought index (total evapo-transpiration and precipitation regimes), and the impact of elevation.

the three Central Anatolian provinces of Bozok (Yozgat), Niğde and Kırşehir, growth was based largely on the settlement of pastoral tribes during this period.[17]

So, the question arises as to which dynamics were responsible for the demographic growth of settled taxpayers. Research conducted on different regions in Europe has argued for a direct relationship between climate change and fiscal population.[18] The impact of climatic fluctuations on agriculture is a determinant of demographic and even settlement patterns in pre-industrial societies.[19] Martin L. Parry's seminal monograph convincingly demonstrates how long-term climatic change can enable the expansion of new agricultural fields into agriculturally 'sensitive' lands.[20] Inspired by Parry's approach, the following part carefully analyses the climatic history of sixteenth-century Anatolia in order to understand pertinent factors behind its demographic variations.

A 'Magnificent' Climate: Age of Rainfall

Several studies have reconstructed the precipitation index and temperature dynamics over extended periods of time in Anatolia and the Near East, providing historians with valuable sets of data. In one of these reconstructions, seen in Figure 1, Ramzi Touchan and his colleagues developed a 900-year-long precipitation index by using tree-rings from South-western Anatolia, which roughly covers the Konya, Hamit (Isparta) and Teke (Antalya) regions. A seventy-year moving average is also included in order to demonstrate a periodical comparison.

---

17. Metin 2007, pp. 37–58. The growth rate in the number of settlements was enormous in these provinces. The number of villages seen on the 1530 survey was only five in Bozok, but had reached 629 in the 1574 survey. Similarly, Kırşehir had 10 villages in 1530, but this number was 752 in the following survey conducted in 1584. The number of villages increased from 275 to 455 in Niğde between 1518 and 1584. In his dissertation, Onur Usta also presents relevant arguments for the relation between settlement and mobility of nomads and taxation. Usta 2017.

18. Michaelowa 2001, pp. 201–17; Lee 1981, pp. 356–401.

19. For a review on relationships between climatic fluctuations on European agriculture, see Bourke 1984, pp. 269–314.

20. Parry 1978.

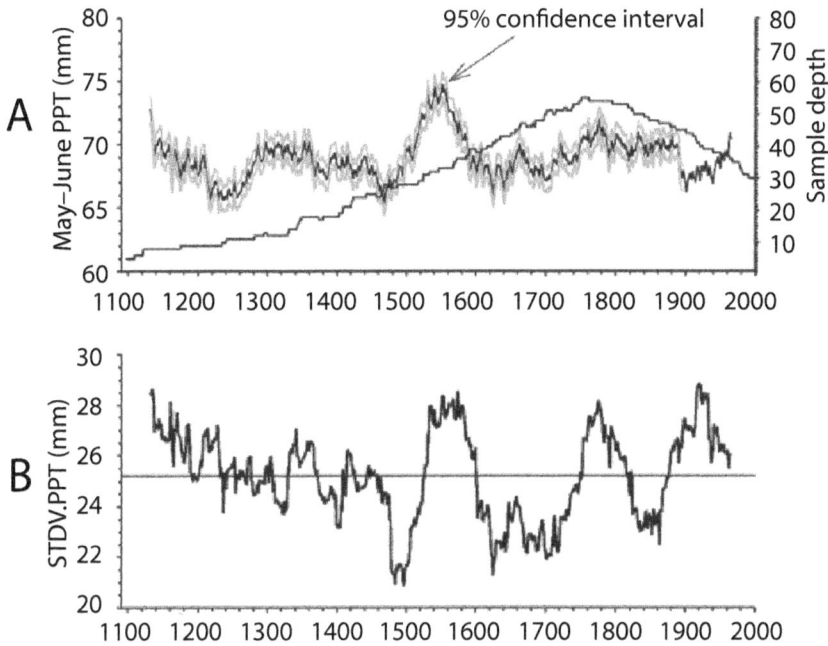

Figure 1. (A) Seventy-year running mean of reconstructed May–June precipitation for the period AD 1097–2000. (B) Seventy-year running standard deviation for the reconstruction.[21]

According to their findings, the seventy-year period in the May-June reconstruction that was identified to have the highest recorded precipitation occurred between 1518 and 1587. The periods of 1098–1168 and 1743–1812 are marked as the second and third wettest periods in the second millennium, respectively. In comparison, the periods of 1195–1264, 1434–1503 and 1591–1660 were the driest periods. This set of precipitation data depicts an interesting climatic landscape for early modern Anatolia. In the course of the sixteenth century, Anatolia experienced its wettest seventy-year period of the second millennium, falling in between two of the three driest. While this specific study focuses on May–June precipitation and covers only a limited area, other research and proxy data support the findings of this investigation for other seasons and for a larger region.[22] This extraordinary wet season can

21.   Touchan et al. 2007, p. 200. By permission of Cambridge University Press.
22.   Another work of research, based on 36 time series from 42 sites, was developed for Turkey, Syria, Lebanon and Greece, presenting a more comprehensive perspective for

be attested not only by the dendrochronological findings, but also by the sedimentary records of lakes in Anatolia. For instance, a high-water-lake interval with a low benthic diatom content found in Lake Çubuk confirms the high level of precipitation for the period of the sixteenth century in Anatolia.[23] Consequently, 'leaps' of driest-to-wettest and wettest-to-driest periods took place in the sixteenth century in terms of climatic conditions, with consideration to the previous and following periods.

The dendrochronological proxy data also indicates that the wettest year recorded in the last 900 years was 1565, and four very humid years in a row occurred during the years 1532–1535.[24] High precipitation was not the only characteristic of this period; there was also a high alternation in extremely wet and dry events, whereas the lowest standard deviations were associated with the driest periods.[25] This high standard deviation in the precipitation indices shows a high variability in consecutive years. This signifies a precarious situation for fields located along river basins, due to the risk of flooding, and thus could negatively impact annual crop yields. It is also possible that the high level of fluctuation of the annual crop could be caused by this climatic variability.

Another significant determinant of climatic conditions, and one of the key variables for agriculture, is temperature patterns. Considering the contemporary temperature dynamics, the climate reconstructions of Anatolia and the northern hemisphere shared a common long-term pattern. However, while the average temperature for the northern hemisphere had already begun to follow a decreasing trend about a hundred years earlier, in Anatolia, the decreasing trend of temperature after the warm medieval period began only in the early sixteenth century.[26] Thus, the average temperature of Anatolia was higher than the average of the entire northern hemisphere for the sixteenth century and it did not reach a similar cold threshold until the mid-seventeenth century.

---

the contemporary climatic conditions of the region and reproducing similar findings: cf. Touchan et al. 2005, pp. 84–87.

23. As a technical term, 'benthic diatom' refers to the unicellular, marine or freshwater algae found at the lowest level of a body of water such as ocean or a lake. In the studies on climate history, this kind of algae is examined in order to trace climatic fluctuations. For the research on Lake Çubuk, see Ocakoğlu et al. 2016, pp. 205–21. The same article also mentioned that lake margin trench stratigraphy (lake margin sands over alluvial gravels) also independently supports a higher lake level for this period.

24. Touchan et al. 2005, p. 88.

25. Ibid., p. 89; Touchan et al. 2007, p. 199.

26. See Heinrich et al. 2013, p. 1694. For another study referring to hemispherical temperatures, see Mann et al. 2008; Moberg et. al. 2005, pp. 613–17.

A 'Magnificent' Climate

Moreover, by about the middle of the sixteenth century, the temperature of Anatolia was the same as the mean of the second millennium temperature scores.

Apart from the findings of natural scientists, several clues can also be derived from the contemporary tax registers to grasp the drastic impact of temporal climatic shift. Salt production can be seen as a good historical measure of the impact of climatic shift because this industry as practised in Ottoman Anatolia, whether via salt lakes or from the Mediterranean coasts, was mainly dependent on high levels of evaporation due to the region's dry summers and reduced precipitation. Two of the most significant saltworks were located in Menemen, north of Izmir at the intersection between the Gediz River and the Gulf of Izmir; and in Koçhisar, alongside the Salt Lake (*Tuz Gölü*) in Central Anatolia.[27] Due to its relatively low cost, the technique of producing salt from seawater remained unchanged for centuries. Essentially, it involves transferring seawater to salt pans around river basins in the middle of the Anatolian winter and waiting for the water to evaporate during the dry summer months. The deposited salt was then collected and stored by workers during the first half of September. Even today, the level of production using this method varies depending on the summer weather and early autumnal rains. A high level of unseasonal rainfall tends to lower the amount of salt production.[28]

In the sixteenth century, the saltworks of Menemen was rented out as a tax-farm, the market value of which was determined by considering the average annual income of that asset. The revenue from this saltworks was recorded as 433,334 *akçe* in the 1531 survey, but dropped to 355,000 *akçe* in 1575.[29] The nominal loss of revenue was about seventeen per cent, but when we include the effect of inflation, it represents a decline of over 25 per cent in real value. The case of the Koçhisar saltworks is even more telling. The income from this saltworks established on the banks of the Salt Lake was 300,000 *akçe* in the 1522 survey, but had fallen almost by half (as low as 170,000 *akçe*) in the 1582 survey. The period between these two surveys coincides with the beginning and end of the wettest period of Anatolian climate in the second millennium and, as a result of this shift, salt production decreased by more than half relative to the old production levels, even after accounting for inflation. Furthermore, while the revenue from this saltworks constituted over nineteen per cent of the

27. These saltworks meet two thirds of Anatolia's salt demand even in modern-day Turkey.

28. Tıraş 2007.

29. Bakkal 1995, p. 264.

entire tax collected in the Aksaray district for the earlier period, this portion fell to nine per cent by 1582.[30]

This exceptional precipitation level and moderate temperature scores most likely had an unexpectedly positive impact on the semi-arid regions of Anatolia in the sixteenth century. These regions – depicted as pale grey fields in Map 2 – transformed into well-watered lands. Due to this significant climatic shift, these interior zones containing vast plains became the granaries of the Ottoman Empire.[31] Such extraordinary climatic conditions also influenced the crop cycle throughout Anatolia. Peasants were quite responsive to the climatic change, and adapted their crop cycle according to the new conditions. Thus, they did not limit themselves to the production of established crops, but instead began to cultivate alternative crops to replace the former ones. All these transformations can be traced through the contemporary tax registers.[32]

Expansion of Arable Lands and Land-Labour Ratio

Tahrir registers from the sixteenth century not only include the names of taxpayers but also the size of their lands, and the type and proportionate amount of taxes levied on their agricultural produce. Especially, the shift in the size of arable lands and its regional variance may provide us with an insight into the change in land-labour ratio underpinned by climatic and demographic fluctuation.

In order to follow general trends in land use and land-labour ratio, total arable lands liable to taxation can be calculated through those registers. The fixed term used in the registers to define the arable lands is çift, literally meaning 'pair' and referring to a piece of land that would be tilled by a pair of oxen in a year.[33] The size of a çift would vary depending on the fertility of the

---

30. Yörük 2005, p. 185.

31. These semi-arid regions are also in the lowest slope class of Anatolia, which means that they are the most suitable areas for agriculture, at least as far as slope is concerned. In the Konya region, 40% of the lands are classified as being under a 2% slope. Similarly, 26% of the land is under a 2% slope in the mid-Euphrates region, which includes Urfa and Adıyaman. These are the largest plains of Anatolia suitable for agricultural production. It should be noted that the average slope of land in Turkey is about 17%. Elibüyük and Yılmaz 2010.

32. The crop rotation will be discussed in detail from an ecological perspective in a prospective publication.

33. For these terms and detailed analysis of the customary dues with the same names: See İnalcık 1959; idem 1994, pp. 143–54; Cook 1972, pp. 67–71.

soil, so this size may be different in different regions of the empire. Considering this possible variance, I prefer not to convert the number of çifts into metric sizes but rather leave them as çift units to examine nominal change in a given category over time for a certain region. Furthermore, *nim* means half so the *nim-çift* is used to denote a half-farm. Finally, the last term, which is related to the taxable arable lands liable to taxation, is *bennak*. This term refers to arable land less than a half-farm and it is mostly interpreted by Ottomanists as one third of a farm. Apart from these, some other plots, named *zemin*, are recorded separately in these registers and, if these lands are cultivated by landless peasants, the cultivators have to pay a tax called ground rent, *resm-i zemin*. Thus, the registers enable us to calculate the approximate size of arable lands in the sixteenth century and land-labour ratio can be estimated by adding up the number of households in the calculation. I have picked three samples from various regions to investigate periodical change in terms of land-labour ratio. For the first instance, the following table depicts the figures of Urfa (Ruha), a prominent *sancak* (district) located in South-eastern Anatolia.

Table 1. Land–labour ratio changes in sixteenth-century Urfa (Ruha)[34]

Urfu (Ruha)			
	1518	1566	Change
Çift (Full Farm)	550.5[35]	2996[36]	445 %
Nim-Çift (Half Farm)	535	726	35 %
Bennak (1/3 Farm)	266	1306	391 %
Total Arable Lands (all converted into Çift)	905	3814	321 %
Total Number of Households	1334	5257	294 %
Land / Labour (Full farm/ Household)	0.67	0.72	7 %
Resm-i Zemin (akçe)	0	240 akçe	

As the figures reveal, the expansion of arable lands was enormous over half a century for the region of Urfa. Growth rates of farmland expansion

---

34. Figures are taken from Turan 2012, pp. 32, 73.
35. In the 1518 register, there is one 1.5 çift and eleven double-çift. Those are included in the full-çift as 23.5 full-çift.
36. In the 1566 register, there are 141 double-çift and 14 triple-çift. These are included in the full-çift as well.

reached over 300 per cent and that rate was even higher than the growth of fiscal population. As a result of this agricultural land expansion, land-labour ratio also increased from 0.67 farm per household to 0.72. Another crucial indicator is the share of full farms in total arable lands. In the relevant literature, it is generally accepted that full farms were split into smaller pieces as a consequence of huge population growth; however this prediction is not valid for south-eastern Anatolia. In Urfa, the share of full farms in total arable lands was around sixty per cent (550.5 / 905), but this share became 78 per cent (2996 /3814) in the following register. Briefly, it is possible to argue that the land-labour ratio increased in sixteenth-century Urfa, even if that region experienced one of the most aggressive population growths in relation to the other regions of Anatolia in this period.

Table 2. The change in land–labour ratio during the sixteenth-century in Çubuk.[37]

Çubuk (Ankara)			
	1523	1571	Change
Çift (Full Farm)	537	980	83 %
Nim-Çift (Half Farm)	1512	1718	14 %
Bennak (1/3 Farm)	602	5655	839 %
Total Arable Lands			
(all converted into Çift)	1494	3724	149 %
Total Number of Households	3425	8467	147 %
Land / Labour			
(Full farm/ Household)	0.43	0.44	2 %
Resm-i Zemin (akçe)	1690 akçe	16763 akçe	x 10 times

As for the second example, the figures for Çubuk, a district of inner Anatolia, are displayed in Table 2. The numbers show us that the arable lands expanded as much as the population growth in this region as well. The number of households advanced from 3,425 to 8,467 which means an increase of about 147 per cent for half a century but total arable lands also expanded at the same level in the meantime. Eventually, the land-labour ratio remained stable for this region at around 0.43 farm per household. The share of full farms decreased from 35 per cent (537/1494) to 26 per cent (980/3724) unlike the region of Urfa, even if the total number of full farms almost doubled. On the other hand, the tax collected from the *zemin* lands increased tenfold simultaneously.

---

37.   Figures are taken from Çınar and Gümüşçü 2002, pp. 119, 165–66.

This means the size of unattended lands, cultivated by peasants, soared, and it indicates that land use developed at a faster pace than population growth in this region, considering the use of these unattended lands.

Table 3. Land–labour ratio change during the sixteenth-century in Manisa.[38]

Manisa			
	1531	1575	Change
Çift (Full Farm)	430[39]	170[40]	–60 %
Nim-Çift (Half Farm)	422	642	52 %
Bennak (1/3 Farm)	704	1083	54 %
Total Arable Lands			
(all converted into Çift)	875	852	–3 %
Total Number of Households	1559	1914	22 %
Land / Labour			
(Full farm/ Household)	0.56	0.44	–21 %
Hariç Raiyyet (Full Farm)[41]	628	567	–10 %

The last sample is taken from Manisa, western Anatolia, to detect regional variation. The population growth is modest in this district vis-à-vis the previous examples and it was around 22 per cent in the period between two registrations. However, total arable lands retreated slightly, so the land-labour ratio decreased from 0.56 farm per household to 0.44. Along with this, the exploitation of unattended lands diminished in Manisa. Surprisingly, Manisa followed a reverse trajectory in terms of land-labour ratio, although the population growth was limited in relation to the interior zones which experienced a demographic boom. Furthermore, full farms were split in this region and the share of them was around 49 per cent among all arable lands in 1531, but this rate was as low as twenty per cent for the following period. Therefore, it can be suggested that the population pressure for the western front of Anatolia was unlike the others. To sum up, the expansion of arable lands and the land-labour ratio

38. Emecen 1989, p. 231. Emlak, one of the subdistricts of Manisa, is not included into calculation due to it being missing in the register of 1531.

39. One triple-farm, seven double-farms and nine 1.5 farms are included in the count of çift (full-farm).

40. One triple-farm and two double-farms were included in the çift count.

41. Emecen converts the ground rent (resm-i zemin) into the scale of full farms for comparison. I take these figures as provided.

varied from region to region and over time in accordance with the climatic and geographic conditions of the area. Unexpectedly, the agricultural fields of inner and south-eastern Anatolian regions, which can be defined as semi-arid areas, expanded significantly in order to meet extraordinary population growth of the regions but arable lands retreated in western Anatolia and the land-labour ratio diminished even with a limited population increase. Overall, the agricultural system of Anatolia displays discernible irregularity during this specific period when considered in relation to long-term regional ecological characteristics.

Conclusion

All the data presented above point to Ottoman Anatolia experiencing an exceptional climatic era, and implies that the patterns of agricultural production of the time stemmed from unexpectedly wet climatic conditions in contrast to preceding and following exceptionally dry ones. This temporarily wet climate of the sixteenth century enabled the Ottomans to open up new arable lands in the semi-arid regions of inner and south-eastern Anatolia. The extraordinary growth in fiscal populations in these regions stemmed not only from a natural population increase, but also from the sedentarisation of pastoral tribes, who subsequently began to take up farming. However, these climatic conditions did not have a similar positive impact on coastal Anatolia. The climate conditions of the Mediterranean zones temporarily approached those of a humid climate, and this had a restrictive impact on the region's established agricultural sectors, such as viticulture or cotton cultivation. The demography of the Mediterranean zones also remained relatively stable, in sharp contrast to developments in inner and south-eastern Anatolia and the land-labour ratio also decreased, unlike that in traditionally semi-arid regions.

The impact of this ecological and agricultural transformation on contemporary Ottoman military organisation is well beyond the scope of this research. However, it should be noted that the expansion of grain fields undoubtedly enabled the feeding of a larger army, either as an element of the Ottoman military organisation (*tımar* system) financed by taxes on agricultural production or as supplier of food staples for military expeditions.[42] Therefore, the climatic and agricultural transformations of the period were probably among the most significant factors in sustaining the continual military expeditions organised in the sixteenth century. In this period, taxes were collected in kind (*ayni*) rather

---

42. Güçer 1964.

than cash, and the extraordinary growth of the fiscal population in inner and south-eastern Anatolia entailed a rising supply of material for the imperial army.

Secondly, it should be mentioned that the sustainability of agricultural production and the abundance of food underpinned by the high level of precipitation probably worked to mollify any social discord in the Anatolia region. There are records of local uprisings and clashes connected to rivalries for the throne recorded during the reign of Süleyman I, indicating that the Empire during his reign was not as politically stable as is generally supposed. However, these incidents did not have a long-lasting impact or gain momentum in Anatolia.[43] Hence, the hardships of internal conflicts or local uprisings could be rapidly compensated for, thanks to the sustainability and bounty of crop production. In contrast, during the following period of the driest decades of the turn of the seventeenth-century, uprisings and political unrest such as that of the *Celali* revolts had destructive and long-lasting impacts.

The climatic conditions presented in this article were transient, and reversed at the end of the sixteenth century. The average precipitation dropped from the highest level of the millennium to one of its driest periods. A destructive drought hit the region in 1590s for five consecutive years, marking the irreversible end of this unusually wet period. Research based on tree rings suggests that this drought was the region's longest in the last 900 years. In addition, a stretch of intermittent dry periods lasted in Anatolia until the middle of the seventeenth century. In the late sixteenth and early seventeenth centuries, *Celali* revolts also spread throughout Anatolia and disrupted the social order. As a result, interior zones lost their fiscal population during the late sixteenth and early sixteenth centuries and regional population levels were pushed back to early sixteenth-century levels. Subsequently, the demographic cycle triggered by the exceptionally wet climatic conditions was closed in the following century.

Bibliography

Akdağ, Mustafa. 1963. *Celâlî İsyanları (1550–1603)*. Ankara: Ankara Üniversitesi Basımevi.

———. 1975. *Türk Halkının Dirlik ve Düzenlik Kavgası*. Istanbul: Bilgi Yayınları.

Arıkan, Zeki. 1988. *On Beşinci ve On Altıncı Yüzyıllarda Hamit Sancağı*. Izmir: Ege Üniversitesi Edebiyat Fakültesi Tarih Bölümü Yayınları.

Ataman, Bekir Kemal. 1992. 'Ottoman Demographic History (14th–17th Centuries). Some Considerations'. *Journal of the Economic and Social History of the Orient* 35 (2): 187–98.

---

43. For the contemporary conflicts taking place in Anatolia, see Turan 1961; Akdağ 1975.

52

Mehmet Kuru

Bakkal, Cevat. 1995. 'Menemen Kazası XV. – XVIII. Yüzyıllar'. Ph.D. Diss. Izmir: Ege University.

Barkan, Ömer Lütfü. 1953. 'Tarihî Demografi Araştırmaları ve Osmanlı Tarihi'. *Türkiyat Mecmuası* 10: 1–26.

Barkey, Karen. 1994. *Bandits and Bureaucrats: The Ottoman Route to State Centralization.* Ithaca and London: Cornell University Press.

Bilgili, Ali Sinan. 2001. *Osmanlı Döneminde Tarsus Sancağı ve Tarsus Türkmenleri: Sosyo-ekono-mik Tarih.* Ankara: Kültür Bakanlığı.

Bourke, Austin. 1984. 'The Impact of Climatic Fluctuations on Agriculture'. In Hermann Flohn and Roberto Fantechi (eds), *The Climate of Europe: Past, Present, and Future.* Dordrecht: D. Reidel Publishing Co. pp. 269–314.

Braudel, Fernand. 1977. *The Mediterranean and the Mediterranean World in the Age of Philip II, vol. 1.* 2 vols. Harper Collins.

Cook, Michael A. 1972. *Population Pressure in Rural Anatolia, 1450–1600.* New York: Oxford University Press.

Coşgel, Metin M. 2004. 'Ottoman Tax Registers (Tahrir Defterleri)'. *Historical Methods* 37 (2): 87–100

——. 2006. 'Agricultural Productivity in the Early Ottoman Empire'. *Research in Economic History* 24: 161–87.

Çakar, Enver. 2003. *XVI. Yüzyılda Haleb Sancağı, 1516–1566.* Elazığ: Fırat Üniversitesi.

——. 2012. *Doğu Akdeniz Sahilinde Bir Osmanlı Sancağı, Trablus (1516–1579).* Ankara: Türk Tarih Kurumu.

Çınar, Hüseyin and Osman Gümüşçü. 2002. *Osmanlı'dan Cumhuriyet'e Çubuk Kazası.* Ankara: Bilge Yayınları.

Dalfes, Nüzhet, et al. 2006. *Anadolu'nun İklim Tarihinin Son 500 Yılı: Dendroklimatoloji Yöntemleriyle Rökonstrüksiyonlar ve Uzay-Zaman Analizleri.* TÜBİTAK, YDABAG 102Y063 nolu proje.

Deniz, Ali, Hüseyin Toros and Selahattin Incecik. 2001. 'Spatial Variations of Climate Indices in Turkey'. *International Journal of Climatology* 31 (3): 394–403.

Elibüyük, Mesut and Erkan Yılmaz. 2010. 'Türkiye'nin Coğrafi Bölge ve Bölümlerine göre Yükselti Basamakları ve Eğim Grupları'. *Coğrafi Bilimler Dergisi* 8 (1): 27–55.

Emecen, Feridun Mustafa. 1989. *On Altıncı Asırda Manisa Kazâsı.* Ankara: Atatürk Kültür, Dil ve Tarih Yüksek Kurumu.

Erder, Leila and Suraiya Faroqhi. 1979. 'Population Rise and Fall in Anatolia 1550–1620'. *Middle Eastern Studies* 15 (3): 322–45.

Erder, Leila. 1975. 'The Measurement of Preindustrial Population Changes: The Ottoman Empire from the 15th to the 17th Century'. *Middle Eastern Studies* 11 (3): 284–301.

Faroqhi, Suraiya. 1979–80. 'Taxation and Urban Activities in Sixteenth-Century Anatolia'. *International Journal of Turkish Studies* 1 (1): 19–53.

——. 1987. 'Political Tensions in the Anatolian Countryside around 1600: An Attempt at Interpretation'. In Jean-Louis Bacqué-Grammont, Barbara Flemming, Macit Gökberk and İlber Ortaylı (eds), *Türkische Miszellen: Robert Anhegger Festschrift – Armağanı – Mélanges*. Istanbul: Divit. pp. 117–30.

——. 1994. 'Crisis and Change, 1590–1699'. In Halil İnalcık and Donald Quataert (eds), *An Economic and Social History of the Ottoman Empire*. Cambridge: Cambridge University Press. pp. 411–636.

——. 1995. 'Seeking Wisdom in China: An Attempt to Make Sense of the Celali Rebellions'. In Suraiya Faroqhi (ed.), *Coping with the State: Political Conflict and Crime in the Ottoman Empire*. Istanbul: Isis Press. pp. 99–121.

——. 1999. *Approaching Ottoman History: An Introduction to the Sources*. Cambridge: Cambridge University Press.

Gökçe, Turan. 2000. *XVI-XVII. Yüzyıllarda Lazıkiyye (Denizli) Kazası*. Ankara: Türk Tarih Kurumu.

Griswold, William J. 1983. *The Great Anatolian Rebellion, 1000–1020/1591–1611*. Berlin: Klaus Schwarz Verlag.

——. 1993. 'Climatic Change: A Possible Factor in the Social Unrest of Seventeenth Century Anatolia'. In Heath Lowry and Donald Quataert (eds), *Humanist and Scholar: Essays in Honor of Andreas Tietze*. Istanbul: Isis Press. pp. 37–57.

Güçer, Lütfi. 1964. *XVI-XVII. asırlarda Osmanlı İmparatorlugunda hububat meselesi ve hububattan alınan vergiler*. Istanbul: İstanbul Üniversitesi İktisat Fakültesi Yayınları.

Gümüşçü, Osman. 2001. *Tarihi Coğrafya açısından bir araştırma: XVI. Yüzyıl Larende (Karaman) kazasında yerleşme ve nüfus*. Ankara: Türk Tarih Kurumu.

Heinrich, Ingo, et al. 2013. 'Winter-to-Spring Temperature Dynamics in Turkey Derived from Tree Rings since AD 1125'. *Climate Dynamics* 41 (7–8): 1685–1701.

İnalcık, Halil. 1959. 'Osmanlılarda Raiyyet Rüsûmu'. *Belleten* 23 (92): 575–610.

——. 1980. 'Military and Fiscal Transformation in the Ottoman Empire, 1600–1700'. *Archivum Ottomanicum* 6: 283–337.

——. 1994. 'The Ottoman State: Economy and Society, 1300–1600'. In Halil İnalcık and Donald Quataert (eds), *An Economic and Social History of the Ottoman Empire*. Cambridge: Cambridge University Press. pp. 9–409.

İslamoğlu-İnan, Huri. 1994. *State and Peasant in the Ottoman Empire: Agrarian Power Relations and Regional Economic Development*. Leiden and New York: Brill.

Jennings, Ronald C. 1976. 'Urban Population in Anatolia in the Sixteenth Century: A Study of Kayseri, Karaman, Amasya, Trabzon, and Erzurum'. *International Journal of Middle East Studies* 7 (1): 21–57.

Karaca, Behset. 2002. *XV. ve XVI. Yüzyıllarda Teke Sancağı*. Isparta: Fakülte Kitabevi.

Köse, Nesibe. 2007. 'Batı Anadolu'da İklim Değişikliği ve Yıllık Halka Gelişimi.' Ph.D Diss., Istanbul: Istanbul University.

Köse, Nesibe, et al. 2011. 'Tree-Ring Reconstructions of May–June Precipitation for Western Anatolia'. *Quaternary Research* 75 (3): 438–50.

Kurt, Yılmaz. 1992. 'XV. Yüzyıl Adana Tarihi'. Ph.D. Diss., Ankara: Hacettepe University.

Kütükoğlu, Mübahat S. 2000. *XV ve XVI. Asırlarda İzmir Kazasının Sosyal ve Iktisâdî Yapısı.* Izmir: İzmir Büyükşehir Belediyesi Kültür Yayını.

——. 2010. *XVI. Asırda Çeşme Kazasının Sosyal ve İktisâdî Yapısı.* Ankara: Türk Tarih Kurumu.

Lee, Ronald. 1981. 'Short-Term Variation – Vital Rates, Prices and Weather'. In E. Wrigley and R. Schofield (ed.), *The Population History of England.* London: Edward Arnold. pp. 356 – 401.

Lowry, Heath W. 1992. 'The Ottoman Tahrir Defterleri as a Source for Social and Economic History: Pitfalls and Limitations'. In Heath W. Lowry (ed.), *Studies in Defterology: Ottoman Society in the Fifteenth and Sixteenth Centuries.* Istanbul: Isis Press. pp. 3–18.

Mann, Michael, et al. 2008. 'Proxy-based reconstruction of hemispheric and global surface temperature variations over the past two millennia'. *Proceedings of the National Academy of Sciences of the United States of America* **105** (36): 13252–257.

Mete, Zekai. 2004. 'XV. ve XVI. Yüzyıllarda Muğla ve Yöresi'. Ph.D. Diss., Istanbul: Istanbul University.

Metin, Rafet. 'XVI. Yüzyılda Orta Anadolu'da Nüfus ve Yerleşme'. Ph.D. Diss., Ankara: Gazi University.

Michaelowa, Axel. 2001 'The Impact of Short-Term Climate Change on British and French Agriculture and Population in the First Half the Eighteenth Century'. In Philip D. Jones, Astrid E.J. Ogilvie, Trevor D. Davies and Keith R. Briffa (eds), *History and Climate; Memories of The Future.* Dordrecht: Kluwer Academic/Plenum Publishers. pp. 201–17.

Moberg, Anders, et al. 2005. 'Highly Variable Northern Hemisphere Temperatures Reconstructed from Low- and High-Resolution Proxy Data'. *Nature* **433** (7026): 613–17.

Ocakoğlu Faruk, et al. 2016. 'A 2800-year multi-proxy sedimentary record of climate change from Lake Cubuk (Goynuk, Bolu, NW Anatolia)'. *The Holocene* **26** (2): 205–221.

Öz, Mehmet. 1999. *XV-XVI. Yüzyıllarda Canik Sancağı.* Ankara: Türk Tarih Kurumu.

Özdeğer, Mehtap. 2001. *15–16. Yüzyıl Arşiv Kaynaklarına Göre Uşak Kazasının Sosyal ve Ekonomik Tarihi.* Istanbul: Filiz Kitabevi.

Özdeğer, Hüseyin. 1982. *XVI. Yüzyıl Tahrir Defterlerine Göre Antep'in Sosyal ve Ekonomik Durumu.* Istanbul: Türk Dünyası Araştırmaları Yayınları.

Özel, Oktay. 2000. '17. Yüzyıl Osmanlı Demografi ve İskan Tarihi İçin Önemli Bir Kaynak: 'Mufassal" Avârız Defterleri'. In *XII. Türk Tarih Kongresi, Ankara, 12–16 Eylül 1994: Kongreye Sunulan Bildiriler, vol. 3.* 4 vols. Ankara: Türk Tarih Kurumu. pp. 735–44.

——. 2000. 'Avarız ve Cizye Defterleri.' In Halil İnalcık and Şevket Pamuk (eds), *Osmanlı Devleti'nde Bilgi ve İstatistik.* Ankara: Devlet İstatistik Enstitüsü. pp. 33–50.

——. 2004. 'Population Changes in Ottoman Anatolia during the 16th and 17th Centuries: The "Demographic Crisis" Reconsidered'. *International Journal of Middle East Studies* **36** (2): 183–205.

——. 2016. *The Collapse of Rural Order in Ottoman Anatolia: Amasya 1576–1643.* Leiden and Boston: Brill.

Parry, Martin L. 1978. *Climatic Change, Agriculture, and Settlement.* Folkestone: Dawson.

Solak, İbrahim. 2004. *XVI. Asırda Maraş Kazası, (1526–1563).* Ankara: Akçağ.

——. 2007. *XVI. Yüzyılda Zamantu Kazasının Sosyal ve İktisadi Yapısı*. Konya: Tablet.

Taşdemir, Mehmet. 1999. *XV. Asırda Adıyaman*. Ankara: Türk Tarih Kurumu.

Tıraş, Mehmet. 2007. 'Çamaltı Tuzlası'. *Eastern Geographical Review* 12 (18): 291–300.

Touchan, Ramzi, et al. 2014. 'Dendroclimatology in the Eastern Mediterranean'. *Radiocarbon* 56 (4): 61–68.

Touchan, Ramzi, et al. 2005. 'Reconstructions of Spring/Summer Precipitation for the Eastern Mediterranean from Tree-Ring Widths and Its Connection to Large-Scale Atmospheric Circulation'. *Climate Dynamics* 25 (1): 75–98.

Touchan, Ramzi, Ünal Akkemik, Malcolm K. Hughes and Neşat Erkan. 2007. 'May–June Precipitation Reconstruction of Southwestern Anatolia, Turkey during the Last 900 Years from Tree Rings'. *Quaternary Research* 68 (2): 196–202.

Turan, Ahmet Nezihi. 2012. *XVI. Yüzyılda Ruha (Urfa) Sancağı*. Ankara: Türk Tarih Kurumu.

Turan, Şerafettin. 1961. *Kanuni Süleyman Dönemi Taht Kavgaları*. Istanbul: Bilgi Yayınları.

Ulupınar, Yusuf, et al. 2016. *2015 Yılı Alansal Yağış Değerlendirmesi*. Ankara: Meteoroloji Genel Müdürlüğü.

Usta, Onur. 2017. 'In Pursuit of Herds or Land? Nomads, Peasants and Pastoral Economies in Anatolia from a Regional Perspective, 1600–1645'. Ph.D. Diss., University of Birmingham.

Ünal, Mehmet Ali. 1989. *XVI. Yüzyılda Harput Sancağı (1518–1566.)* Ankara: Türk Tarih Kurumu.

White, Sam. 2011. *The Climate of Rebellion in the Early Modern Ottoman Empire*. Cambridge: Cambridge University Press.

Yıldız, Hakan, et al. 2009. 'Rakım ve Kuraklık İndisi Değerlerine Göre Türkiye'nin Homojen Alanlarının Belirlenmesi'. *Tarla Bitkileri Merkez Araştırma Enstitüsü Dergisi* 18 (1–2): 17–21.

Yılmaz, Ali. 2009. *XVI. Yüzyılda Birecik Sancağı*. Istanbul: Kitaplık Yayınları.

Yörük, Doğan. 2005. *XVI. Yüzyılda Aksaray Sancağı, 1500–1584*. Konya: Tablet Kitabevi.

Mehmet Kuru

APPENDIX

Rural Demographic Change in Sixteenth Century Ottoman Anatolia

Districts/Provinces	1520s–30s Number of Households	1570s–80s Number of Households	Percentage Change
Manisa[1]	1542	2161	40 %
Menemen[2]	1370	1444	5 %
Aydın[3]	5747	6181	8 %
Çeşme[4]	3308	2676	–19 %
İzmir[5]	4100	2609	–36 %
Muğla[6]	5712	5872	2 %
Antalya[7]	8418	8178	–3 %
Tarsus[8]	8341	12245	47 %
Adana[9]	1147	779	–32 %
Aleppo[10]	26668	30761	15 %
Tripoli[11]	13728	11602	–15 %
Bozok (Yozgat)[12]	13785	42736	210 %
Kırşehir	9222	24346	160 %
Niğde	12596	39400	212 %
Çubuk (Ankara)[13]	3425	8467	147 %
Larende (Karaman)[14]	5322	12762	139 %
Rum (Tokat)[15]	5435	9731	132 %
Burdur[16]	12617	23125	83 %
Lazikiyye (Denizli)[17]	2699	5845	116 %
Canik (Samsun)[18]	11873	21041	77 %
Harput[19]	5333	11332	112 %
Birecik[20]	1753	3359	92 %
Maraş[21]	422	2227	428 %
Amasya[22]	9171	15754	72 %
Uşak[23]	2035	3450	70 %
Antep[24]	1639	2579	57 %
Aksaray[25]	3386	13625	302 %
Koçhisar	39	3239	
Zamantu (Kayseri)[26]	1802	5635	212 %
Adıyaman[27]	3410	10105	196 %
Urfa sancağı[28]	1334	5257	294 %
Ereğli (Konya)[29]	3342	6642	98 %

The Mediterranean regions rows are Manisa through Tripoli; Inner regions and Northern Regions rows are Bozok through Ereğli.

A 'Magnificent' Climate

Notes

1. Emecen 1989, p. 125.
2. Bakkal 1995, pp. 80–156.
3. Cook 1972, p. 84.
4. Kütükoğlu 2010, pp. 54-66.
5. Kütükoğlu 2000, p. 88.
6. Mete 2004, p. 229.
7. Karaca 2002, p. 158.
8. Bilgili 2001, pp. 342–4.
9. Kurt 1992, p. 98.
10. Çakar 2003, p. 153.
11. Çakar 2012, p. 245.
12. Metin, 2007, pp. 94–108. Following sancaks (Kırşehir and Niğde) are also extracted from this work.
13. Çınar and Gümüşçü 2002, pp. 103–6.
14. Gümüşçü 2001, p. 153.
15. İslamoğlu-İnan 1994, p. 175.
16. Arıkan 1988, pp. 75–6.
17. Gökçe 2000. pp. 307–12.
18. Öz 1999, p. 64.
19. Ünal 1989, p. 84.
20. Yılmaz 2009, pp. 78–168.
21. Solak 2004, pp. 51–117.
22. Özel 2016, p. 113.
23. Özdeğer 2001, p.128.
24. Özdeğer 1982. pp. 101–7.
25. Yörük 2005, p. 76. Statistics of Kuçhisar are also taken from the same work, p. 104.
26. Solak 2007, p. 212.
27. Taşdemir 1999, pp. 50–95. (Hısn-ı Mansur, Behisti, Kahta, Gerger are included in this statistic.
28. Turan 2012, p. 44.
29. Yörük 2005, p. 74.

Chapter 3

PRODUCING GRAPES AND WINE ON THE BOSPORUS IN THE EIGHTEENTH CENTURY: THE TESTIMONY OF DOMENICO SESTINI

Suraiya Faroqhi

In the world of the Roman Mediterranean, the three major crops were grain, olives and grapes: grains for bread and porridge, olives for oil and presumably for eating 'as is' and grapes mostly, though not exclusively, for wine. In the Ottoman Empire, this pattern changed, but in an unexpected fashion. While we might expect that in a Muslim polity, the cultivation of the vine declined or even disappeared, the contrary was true. Recent studies of olive consumption have shown that the practice of cooking in olive oil declined, once again becoming fashionable only in the twentieth and twenty-first centuries.[1]

As for the continued favour of grape cultivation even on the part of the pious Sultan Süleyman I (r. 1520–1566), a story relayed by the Habsburg ambassador Ogier Ghiselin de Busbecq (1522–1592) is of interest.[2] Busbecq visited the Ottoman lands in the mid-1500s, when Sultan Süleyman had forbidden the making of wine. If Busbecq's story is at least partly true, certain Greek peasants, to demonstrate the plight in which they found themselves after this prohibition, uprooted their vines just as the monarch passed near their locality. When the sultan asked the reason, the growers claimed that now the vineyards were of no further use; and they wanted to retrieve the vines for use as firewood. Busbecq recorded that the sultan did not accept this reasoning and told the peasants that table grapes were perfectly licit and even desirable. However, the story may be an invention of the author's, who wrote his book long after his return. Or else the sultan may not have known much about viticulture, as not all grapes useable for wine production will be desirable as table

---

1. Yılmaz 2010; Doğan 2008, pp. 231–42.
2. Busbequius 1994, pp. 304–05.

grapes. Furthermore, it is hard to assess whether *pekmez* (grape syrup), while permitted, was profitable to the growers of Anatolia and the Balkans, while the sugar content of many types of grapes may have been too low for preservation as raisins. After all, sections of the Rhine Valley in western Germany produce reputable wines, but no table grapes or raisins.

In the present paper however, we will focus on a much later period, namely the last quarter of the eighteenth century; for the Italian scholar Domenico Sestini (1750–1832) has left us a unique source on the cultivation of vineyards on the shores of the Bosporus in his time.[3] His text contains an incredible amount of information on viticulture and winemaking. Some of his information was probably erroneous but most of it likely true, and we will attempt to sort out which is which.

Why is this account worth studying? Firstly, interest in Ottoman consumption as a legitimate chapter of economic and social history, to say nothing of the ongoing nostalgia for 'authentic' Ottoman food, has provided motivation for the study of the fields and gardens cultivated by the sultans' subjects. Thus, Arif Bilgin has shown that in the 1700s, the inhabitants of Istanbul began to consume a larger variety of fruits and vegetables than had been available before that time.[4] When studying the natural environment, it is therefore important to trace the manner in which the needs of the Istanbul population for food and drink shaped the surroundings of the city. This is a new question, on which we have only limited research.[5] Ottoman historians have known for quite some time that gardens and vineyards were more likely to appear when a village grew into a small town, as fruits and vegetables were minor luxuries likely to attract people with more money to spend than peasants had at their disposal. Conversely, the expansion of any city turned gardens into real estate suitable for construction or even into public parks, as is common in present-day Istanbul.

In addition, modern means of transportation might make vineyards near a wine-consuming city like Paris unprofitable: subject to climatic variations, the vineyards near the French capital mostly produced wines of modest quality. In Provence and Languedoc, by contrast, the weather was more predictable; and thus in the nineteenth century, when moderately priced wines from the south

---

3.   Sestini 1785; idem 1786. While checking the original from time to time, I have mainly used the German translation, as my knowledge of viticulture and gardening terminology is limited in any language and non-existent where Italian is concerned.

4.   Bilgin 2017.

5.   For a very old attempt at mapping, see Faroqhi 1984, p. 80. The importance of the northwestern tip of Anatolia as a source of foodstuffs is notable.

could reach the modest urban consumer by rail, the wines of the Île de France no longer had a market.[6] As we will see, the florescence and disappearance of Istanbul's vineyards may conform to the same pattern.

How will we tell our story? After briefly introducing Domenico Sestini, we discuss the Bosporus vineyards as they appeared before the lifetime of this author. The first volume of Evliya Çelebi's (1611–1685?) great travelogue, entirely dedicated to Istanbul, is a major source, and Ottoman archival documents from the mid-1700s are helpful as well. After speculating a bit on the reasons why Sestini may have authored his treatise, we discuss his account of the biology of the vine and the skill of the Istanbul growers, who made use of its peculiarities to produce optimal fruits. We then proceed to Sestini's comments on the grape harvest and winemaking, and briefly discuss the reasons why the local wine apparently turned out much inferior to the grapes from which it derived. Sestini was not much concerned about the workpeople that he or his friends might have employed, since he saw the matter purely from the business point of view. We will, however, try to disentangle whatever information on the labour force the author has included in his account of investments and profits. As a coda, we focus on the gradual disappearance of the Bosporus vineyards in the nineteenth century, a major phenomenon, which to date has not attracted much attention. Yet the fading away of the Bosporus vineyards changed the world Sestini had known beyond recognition; and, intriguingly, this change occurred long before the refashioning of the Bosporus shores during the twentieth century.

The Life and Work of Domenico Sestini

Born in Florence, Sestini in his youth had become a monk – the sources differ on the order that he had joined – but he soon found out that he was unsuited to the monastic life.[7] As a first stage of his lengthy travels, the author, who continued to use the courtesy title of *abate* (abbot), spent time in southern Italy, becoming an expert on antique Greco-Roman coins and medals.[8] By a circuitous route, he proceeded from Italy to Istanbul, arriving in 1778, where

---

6.   Dion 1977, repr. 2010.

7.   Anonymous author, 1836–7, pp. 100–02. I have also used a second biography, by Luppi 1890, pp. 473–80. The text is accessible online: http://www.socnumit.org/doc/Numismatici/SESTINI_Domenico.pdf (accessed 25 Nov. 2016).

8.   Both in Italian and in French, in the eighteenth century the title *abate/abbé* was in use even for clerics without any ecclesiastical function.

he witnessed a major plague epidemic and described it in detail. Based on this report, which Sestini sent home to Florence, Peter Leopold of Habsburg, the current prince of Toscana, revised the sanitary regulations applicable in this principality. For some time, Sestini earned a living as tutor to the sons of the ambassador of the then Kingdom of Naples, accompanying the young men on their travels. Later he found other patrons among the princes of Wallachia and, most importantly for his studies, in Sir Robert Ainslie (1730–1812), the British ambassador to the Ottoman court. Particularly between 1782 and 1792, Sestini travelled all over the Ottoman Empire, returning to Istanbul but intermittently. During these years, Sestini apparently learned some Turkish: he could converse with members of the Ottoman elite, possibly with the help of an interpreter, for it is hard to judge the extent of his linguistic skills. In 1792, perhaps because the wars between England and Revolutionary France made it difficult to find patrons in Istanbul, he left the city for good.

Among his fellow scholars in Europe, Sestini owed his great reputation to his expertise on the numismatics of the ancient world; and for many years, he earned a living by collecting antique coins and medals for a variety of aristocratic patrons and by organising collections, both pre-existing and assembled by himself. After long travels in post-French Revolution and Napoleonic Europe, the new Grand Duchess of Tuscany, Napoleon Bonaparte's (1769–1821) sister Elisa Bonaparte (1777–1820), appointed him to a professorship, which allowed him to live in his hometown of Florence. Sestini managed to retain this position after the fall of Napoleon Bonaparte in 1815, authoring further numismatic studies. In addition, he published many of his travel accounts, some of which appeared in translations as well. Thus, as noted, the text occupying us here is available both in the Italian original and in a near-contemporary German translation.[9] Sestini's descriptions are so valuable because he was quite prepared to enter places most foreigners would have hesitated to go; after all, he often financed his studies by guiding less experienced travellers.

Back in Istanbul, this author gained access to Ottoman grandees and their gardens; and for our present purposes, it is most important that botany was one of his avocations. Sestini thus made a point of recording both the local and the new botanical names of the flowers, which ornamented the gardens of wealthy and prominent Ottomans.[10] In the late 1700s, the taxonomy of plants according to the system invented by Carl Linnaeus (1707–1778) was very popular among people with scientific interests, and certain Ottoman

---

9.   Sestini 1785; idem 1786.

10.   Sestini 1785, Section 3, p. 115; Karababa 2015.

dignitaries perhaps shared this curiosity. For whatever reason, some of these people apparently were quite ready to admit Sestini into their gardens.[11] In this context, we should view the author's interest in Istanbul's flora – and, to a lesser extent, in the fauna as well.

Vineyards on the Bosporus: Evliya Çelebi and Ottoman Official Records

What do we know about the Bosporus vineyards of the 1600s and earlier 1700s? The seventeenth-century courtier and traveller Evliya Çelebi was much interested in food and has left quite a bit of information on vineyards, grapes and even wine, although he always expressed his pious abhorrence of a drink forbidden to Muslims.[12] However, sentiment did not prevent him from recording the practices of both acknowledged and 'closet' wine bibbers. He wrote about people trying to get the best of both worlds as well, noting that certain inhabitants of the Ottoman capital boiled wine until it had reduced to one third of its original quantity (*müselles*), when they could reasonably assume that no alcohol remained, but apparently, the liquid continued to taste of wine. The traveller also recorded other fruit juices from which people might produce wine, with sour cherry juice being especially popular.[13] Perhaps these varieties permitted people to persuade themselves and others that they were not doing anything illegal. Grape juice enriched with cloves was also available; but as cloves were an exotic spice, this beverage probably was accessible only to the better off.[14]

When evaluating Evliya Çelebi's account, we must remember that, in his time, the term *bağ* included all kinds of orchards and even ordinary gardens, and did not necessarily denote vineyards. Even so, the author's discussion of the fruits produced in sites called *bağ* makes it clear that quite often, grapes were a major – if not the principal – product. If eighteenth-century practice can be any guide to what was customary in Evliya Çelebi's time, people planting vineyards also planted fruit trees and, during the first year of cultivation,

---

11. Anonymous author. 'Carl Linnaeus (1707–1778)': http://www.ucmp.berkeley.edu/history/linnaeus.html (accessed 25 Nov. 2016). Shopov and Han 2013 discuss the cultivation of fruits and vegetables within the Byzantine walls of sixteenth to eighteenth-century Istanbul (accessed on 17 Oct. 2018, I thank Halil Berktay for the reference).

12. Evliya Çelebi 2006, vol. 1, pp. 236, 263, 287, 355. For a superb guide to Evliya Çelebi's many references to food and drink, see Yerasimos 2011.

13. Yerasimos 2011, p. 252. The author warns her readers that it is often difficult to decide which beverages contain a significant degree of alcohol and which ones do not.

14. Evliya Çelebi 2006, vol. 1, p. 236.

even vegetables; this combination of crops ensured that the plantation would render maximum profits.

Evliya Çelebi also mentioned the names of certain varieties of grapes cultivated on the shores of the Bosporus. Thus, Üsküdar had a reputation for grapes known as *hora*, probably after the Greek word for village, and the same variety was available on the European shore of the Bosporus, in Rumelihisar.[15] However, as Marianna Yerasimos has pointed out, in the seventeenth century fresh seasonal fruit were quite expensive, a delicacy that ordinary people probably did not get to consume very often unless they had orchards of their own.[16] On the other hand, Domenico Sestini in the last quarter of the eighteenth century claimed that the consumption of fresh grapes in Istanbul was enormous; presumably he meant among the better off who were his principal contacts. Moreover, grapes were available on the market throughout the year, especially those brought in from the Bay of Izmit, perhaps sometimes preserved in mustard seed or olive oil. However, while both Busbecq and Ottoman office holders of the 1700s have recorded these methods of making grapes last, Sestini did not refer to them.[17] Likely, in the meantime, grapes had become more easily available, given Arif Bilgin's observations on the growing variety of fruits and vegetables sold in the Istanbul markets of the 1700s.[18]

The variety of grapes mentioned in Evliya Çelebi's work is somewhat limited. By contrast, Sestini knew many more types, of which he mentioned not only the Turkish names but also their Italian equivalents where applicable. His list included *yerli üzüm* (Greek: *topico*), a grape called *marizza* whose Turkish name is not given but which supposedly resembled the Florentine *uva trebinna*, a white grape with a purple design called *mor* in Turkish and *barbarossa* in Italian, *altın üzüm* similar to the Florentine *alratico* and other varieties including the *çavuş üzümü* (Italian: *uva moscadella*).[19] Sestini had no trouble finding the Italian equivalents of most of the Bosporus grapes; evidently there had been so much give-and-take over the centuries that there was by now but little difference between the two vine-growing cultures, both part of the same Mediterranean world.

15. Evliya Çelebi 2006, vol. 1, p. 236; Yerasimos 2011, p. 225. However, for Istanbul, Evliya Çelebi listed many more varieties of peaches than of grapes.
16. Yerasimos 2011, pp. 225–26.
17. Faroqhi 2018.
18. Bilgin 2017.
19. Sestini 1786, pp. 40–41.

Suraiya Faroqhi

We can glean incidental information on Bosporus and especially Üsküdar vineyards from an Ottoman official source preceding Sestini's observations by just a few decades, namely the *Vilayet Ahkâm Defterleri* (provincial registers of imperial rescripts) covering Istanbul. Beginning in the 1740s, this series recorded sultanic commands issued in response to requests from office-holders, and petitions from ordinary taxpayers living in the surroundings of Istanbul.[20] Typically, the texts relevant to gardens and vineyards concerned owners trying to avoid the traditional duty known as *resm-i bağ*, already recorded in sixteenth-century tax registers, which amounted to ten per cent.[21] Very often, the cultivators claimed that they had come to an agreement with a previous tax-taker permitting them to pay a lump sum (*maktu*) instead of the tithe, an arrangement advantageous to eighteenth-century villagers given frequent debasements of the currency. However, presumably for that very reason, the central administration often disallowed such claims.[22] Due to local conditions impossible to reconstruct today, the opposite also might happen; and people might complain that officials demanded lump sums even though they were prepared to pay the customary tithe.[23]

Other documents concerned different tax-takers disputing the revenue among themselves; in addition, we find – apparently illegal – attempts to tax grape products twice, first as juice and then as *pekmez*.[24] Incidentally, the villagers submitting this complaint tried to strengthen their case by pointing out that even if a certain tax document might mention a tithe on grape juice this demand was no longer valid, after the prohibition of wine making. We do not know whether the complainants referred to Sultan Süleyman's prohibition, whose consequences Busbecq had recorded, or else to a later command of the same kind. Seemingly, the registers available to the central administration did not refer to a separate tithe payable from *pekmez*; but the officials did not explicitly say that this due was illegal. Given the entrenched local power of many tax-takers, we therefore cannot tell whether this command, couched in ambiguous language, ended the practice of double tithing. Even so, in one way or another, wine production did continue, as we shall see.

---

20. For a selection: Kal'a et al., eds. 1997–98.
21. Kal'a et al., eds., vol. 2, p. 269.
22. Kal'a et al., eds., vol. 1, p. 139.
23. Kal'a et al., eds., vol. 1, p. 172. However, this complaint concerns Kartal, located on the Sea of Marmara and not on the Bosporus.
24. Kal'a et al., eds., vol. 2, p. 198.

Vineyards on the Bosporus: Why was Sestini so Interested?

Domenico Sestini provided details on grape-growing information because he wanted to show that a vineyard by the Bosporus could yield a respectable profit; and therefore he needed to assess all factors with a possible impact. Unfortunately, as the available biographies deal mainly with the author's achievements as a scholar, and do not say anything about his qualities in business, it is hard to say why Sestini became interested not only in the botanical, but in the economic and financial aspects of cultivating a vineyard.

Differently from many European visitors to Istanbul, when describing urban settings, Sestini quite often took an interest in people at work. He thus recorded a glass-producing atelier near the former Byzantine palace of Tekfur Sarayı, the skills of artisans cutting seals and ornaments out of agate, and the labours of the numerous workpeople employed by the coffee-roasting establishment (*tahmishane*). Apparently, the latter supplied a large part of the Istanbul population and, by the second half of the eighteenth century, coffee had become an article of everyday consumption.[25]

With respect to garden plants, Sestini noted that cultivators could make a good profit, about 500 piasters, from the sale of jasmine, recording in detail how the gardeners should plant and care for the bushes to obtain optimum quality, namely straight and long-lived plants.[26] Probably, the flowers of *gelsomino*/jasmine were not the main aim of cultivation, for people manufactured pipes (*çubuk*) out of long and regularly shaped stalks.

Visibly, the author was interested in the profits of horticulture in the broad sense of the term; but we do not know whether he or one of his friends actually got involved in this business. As travelling occupied so much of Sestini's time, moving back and forth between Istanbul and the Aegean islands, Anatolia, Syria and Iraq in the east and Wallachia in the north, it is difficult to imagine him cultivating his vines on the Bosporus. However, perhaps at one time he had played with the idea of retiring to a *bağ* near Istanbul; or else he was following the lead of the Physiocrats, French economists who were his exact contemporaries and believed in the absolute primacy of agriculture as a producer of value.[27]

---

25. Sestini 1784.
26. Sestini 1784, pp. 180–81, 190.
27. On the Physiocrats compare: http://www.economist.com/blogs/freeexchange/2013/10/economic-history-0 (accessed 27 Nov. 2016). However, to date I have not found any evidence linking Sestini with the Physiocrats.

Sestini begins with a discussion of the rocks bordering the Bosporus, for the earth available to gardeners is, after all, a product of the decomposition of surface minerals due to rain, wind, snow and frost; in the vicinity of the Bosporus, agriculturally usable lands contain clay and chalk. The author records that the resulting red and yellow earth is suitable for vineyards, while black earth, probably due to the disintegration of basalt, is good for fruit trees; but the sandy soil, also found in certain places, is altogether infertile. The author then discusses the prevailing winds and winter rains. His description of the winters shows that Sestini was a denizen of the Little Ice Age: for he comments on snow, hail and frost 'no different from any other place'.[28] Furthermore, he notes the dense fogs frequent in December and March, while observing that, in the summer, temperatures are not excessive. The author does not tell us what advantages or disadvantages soil and climate imply for the owner/cultivator of a vineyard. At the same time, he likely does not assume that under normal circumstances, the vines will be in any special danger.

Acquiring a piece of land is the next item on the agenda. Sestini introduces the local *dönüm*, defined as a square of forty paces. At the time of writing, even in France, the adoption of the metre as a standard measure of length was still over ten years in the future. However, people often regard the 'pace' of an adult as approximately equivalent to eighty centimetres. Thus, the growers working on the shores of the Bosporus must have used a *dönüm* of about 1,024 square metres, roughly equivalent to today's *dönüm* of 1,000 square metres.[29]

Sestini assumes that a grower would want to acquire ten *dönüm* for his vineyard, and he bases his calculations on a piece of real estate of just this size. He also assumes that the land at issue is available for purchase as something resembling freehold property; for while Turkish technical terms occur quite often, there is no mention of the *rakabe* or eminent domain belonging to the sultan (*has*), an assignee of peasant taxes (timar-holder, *sipahi*), or a pious foundation (*vakıf*). In reality, however, the prospective cultivator would have needed to acquire the permission of these persons or institutions by means of a special payment.

---

28. Sestini 1786, p. 25.
29. For today's *dönüm*, see: 1 dönüm = 0,01 ha, http://www.kacyapar.com/2015/02/1-donum-kac-hektar-eder-1-hektar-kac-donum/ (accessed 13 Jan. 2018). At the İzmir Akdeniz Akademisi meeting of 3 Dec. 2016 (Üzümün Akdeniz'deki Yolculuğu No. 5), where this paper was first presented, an engineer, who unfortunately did not give his name, told me that today, a 'pace' is equivalent to 80 cm. I cordially thank the anonymous provider of this information.

Producing Grapes and Wine on the Bosporus

In any case, Sestini assures his readers that any inhabitant of the Ottoman capital can possess a vineyard, 'Franks' included – but the author does
not discuss the difference between the 'Latin' inhabitants of Galata, subjects of
the sultan, and temporary sojourners including himself.[30] In another section
of his account, he simply notes what we also know from Ottoman documents,
namely that both Muslims and Greeks may own vineyards.[31] Only additional
investigations will show whether, around 1780, acquiring the land for a
Bosporus vineyard was as easy as Sestini believed. We may speculate that, at
this time, there was much uncultivated land in the area; and local tax-takers
preferred to encourage prospective cultivators, who would pay dues in years
to come. Whatever the truth of the matter, Sestini assumed that one *dönüm*
of uncultivated land suitable for conversion into a vineyard would cost ten
'Levantine' piasters. Presumably, by that term, he meant an Ottoman piaster
(*guruş*) as opposed to the Spanish, Dutch or Austrian varieties. Lands ready
to use as a field fetched double this price, and if preparations for a vineyard
had already taken place, the asking price would be around thirty piasters. As
a result, the prospective cultivator would need to spend 100–300 piasters on
the acquisition of the land, although Sestini remarked that if stones usable for
lime burning appeared when digging up the future vineyard, the owner might
realise a small profit from their sale.[32]

When making these calculations, Sestini and/or his friends seem to have
completely ignored the difficulties involved in transforming a field, which could
not normally be fully private property but might be available for rent from the
Ottoman exchequer, into a garden or vineyard; for the latter pieces of real estate
quite often were the property of the people that managed them.[33] Concerning
agricultural lands on the shores of the Sea of Marmara, a few kilometres away
from the Bosporus, a mid-eighteenth-century command by Sultan Mahmud
I (r. 1730–54) laid down the law. If local inhabitants had transformed fields
into gardens/vineyards without the permission of the tax-taker, this personage
could have the vines uprooted and the land returned to field agriculture within
three years of planting. If, however, this time-span had passed and the vines
had begun producing grapes, the tax-taker had to tolerate the new plantation

---

30.   Sestini 1786, p. 42.

31.   Faroqhi 1998.

32.   Sestini 1786, p. 27.

33.   For relevant cases, see Faroqhi 1980; and for a *bağ* explicitly described as *mülk*, see Kal'a
        et al., eds., vol. 1, p. 147.

and simply collect his tithe.[34] It is hard to tell why the author(s) of Sestini's computation thought that this matter did not need special consideration. Certainly, the author was a foreigner, but presumably, the people with whom he expected to negotiate the sale were locals, who should have known something of Ottoman law. Perhaps these people expected that the new vineyard would survive the critical first three years and then benefit from an amnesty, similar to that accorded by Mahmud I (r. 1730–1754).

An Excursion into Plant Biology: Preparing the Ground for a Bosporus Vineyard

Among other features, Sestini's text is so interesting because he mostly describes practices he has observed in the region of Istanbul, about which we otherwise know very little; and he clearly distinguishes them from those he had seen in Italy. Thus, he notes that crop-sharing arrangements (*mezzadria*), widespread in Italy at this time, did not exist on the shores of the Bosporus, so that the person cultivating a vineyard needed to find the daily wageworkers indispensable for cultivation.[35] In another context, he records that vineyards only receive fertiliser 'according to need', suggesting that the Italian practice of using the leaves left over from pruning would produce a good fertiliser.[36]

As for his informants, some of them were the Dalmatian subjects of the Republic of Venice, often unable to find employment at home and thus looking for work in Istanbul. The author noted that these gardeners usually had some rudiments of Italian, and commented on the oddity of hearing conversations in 'bad Italian' on the northern end of the Bosporus, near the shores of the Black Sea.[37] Other gardeners were Albanians and Greeks, with a few Turks and Armenians thrown in. At times, Sestini recorded differing opinions on vineyard cultivation, presumably current among rival workmen: some people felt that a certain kind of treatment increased productivity during the first years of the vine's existence, while others warned that as a result of the disruption involved, the plant might die off more quickly.[38] In this case, Sestini did not offer an opinion.

---

34. Ibid., pp. 305–06.
35. Sestini 1786, p. 28.
36. Ibid., p. 39.
37. Ibid., p. 29. The German translation only says 'Italian', leaving out the 'bad'.
38. Ibid., p. 32.

As for the locations of the Bosporus vineyards, the author pointed out that, even though the Anatolian side enjoyed a warmer microclimate, vineyards were more numerous on the European side. On the latter, the main locations were Ortaköy, Yeniköy, Tarabya, Büyükdere and Feneraki, the latter close to the place where the Bosporus joins the Black Sea. By contrast, on the Asiatic side, vintners had been active mostly near Kadıköy and Üsküdar, as Evliya Çelebi had already noted over a century earlier. Beyond Üsküdar, the vineyards only reached as far as Yuşa Tepesi, perhaps because, viniculture being quite labour-intensive, vineyards were mostly located in the vicinity of larger settlements. However, the latter were not very common on the northern section of the Anatolian coast.

Sestini observes that vineyards are always close to the water, facing either the rising or else the noonday sun. While noting that many vineyards are quite large, encompassing sixty to a hundred *dönüm*, we have seen that he makes his own calculations for a much more modest property of only ten *dönüm*.[39] Possibly the larger vineyards belonged to members of the Ottoman elite, but the author does not specify. He merely suggests that the holder/owner of land suitable for a vineyard should start working it between October and December, to draw maximum benefit from the fruit trees, which he will, of necessity plant along with his vines. On 1,600 square metres, he suggests planting 1,000 vines and thirty young fruit trees, the latter to encircle the vineyard and line the paths by which the gardener will approach his vines; in particular, a path should follow the fence all around the property.[40] In addition, the grower should protect his vines by planting dense bushes including, for instance, wild hazelnuts, to prevent grazing animals and human thieves from entering. Remarkably, the text does not say much about setting up scarecrows and hiring guards; only at the very end of the text is there a brief reference to a Slavonian guard, who is to receive one piaster for his trouble.[41] To clear the land of rocks and roots, the workers will dig two long ditches, using the earth excavated from the second to fill in the first; in the end, these filled-in ditches will cover the entire future vineyard. If necessary, some of them will also be left open, to permit surface water to run off.

---

39.   Ibid., p. 38.
40.   Ibid., pp. 27–37.
41.   Ibid., p. 46.

Suraiya Faroqhi

Harvesting Grapes and Making Wine

Ottoman documents do not tell us much about wine making; after all, Muslims were not supposed to have anything to do with it and the activities of non-Muslims very often escaped the radar of the sultan's bureaucracy. Therefore, accounts like that of Sestini, who apparently had good relations with certain Orthodox inhabitants of Istanbul, are of special value.

In Sestini's time, no Bosporus village could begin to harvest its grapes before the *çorbacı* in charge of the settlement had given his permission. This local office-holder was subordinate to the *bostancıbaşı*, a high palace official in charge of policing the Bosporus and who, after the 1800s, often reported to the sultan on the owners of villas near the waterfront.[42] Presumably, the *çorbacı* also had police duties; and the dues he received may have amounted to twenty para a year.[43] However, as Sestini claimed that the dues collected were substantial, and twenty para was a relatively small sum, it is also possible that the heading 'for the grape/wine harvest', which amounted to one piaster, did not refer to the workmen's pay, but rather to the dues collected by the *çorbacı*.[44] At the present state of our knowledge, we cannot be sure.

Towards the end of September, the villagers received permission to begin the harvest, with those located closer to the city receiving their permissions first.[45] Taking on the role of a profit-minded manager, Sestini somewhat sourly remarked that it was not the dates at which individual vineyards produced ripe grapes, but rather administrative convenience that determined the sequence of harvests. Orthodox vineyard owners celebrated the event with eating, drinking, dancing and singing. At this stage of his story, Sestini focused on non-Muslims exclusively, describing how people pressed the grape juice on the property and then conveyed it to the pub owners who took charge of the wine making process; he had heard a rumour that some Muslims sold their grape juice to non-Muslims. In addition, the author had observed the process of pressing

---

42. For a fine discussion, see Kaplan 2012.

43. I have not found valid information on the Istanbul exchange rate of *para* and *guruş* in the late 1700s. Pamuk 2000a, p. 94 has a conversion table, but it ends in 1688. Another table in the same publication records the exchange rate of Egyptian *para* to *akçe* (1: 2.8), see p. 175; but this information is not very relevant. Akyıldız 2007 has important general information, but no conversion table at all.

44. Sestini 1786, p. 46. On p. 43, the author recorded that most owners harvested their grapes with familial labour, and thus did not spend any money on this stage of vineyard management.

45. Ibid., pp. 43–46.

the grapes, boiling the juice and cleaning the vats; wild asparagus served as a means of cleansing the grape juice and the remnants in the vats served for the manufacture of spirits.

Interestingly, Sestini had learned that spirits as opposed to wine were very popular 'among Asians', by this term, he probably meant Anatolian non-Muslims. Thus, there seems to have been a change in consumption habits, as Fikret Yılmaz has found that in the late 1500s, wine was the alcoholic drink of choice and *rakı* not very popular.[46] As a fancier of wine, Sestini felt that the results of winemaking in the Bosporus villages were not particularly impressive: the alcohol content was low and the wine did not have much taste, tending to be on the sour side. In addition, the local wines did not keep well. We may wonder what elite non-Muslims did about their wine; perhaps they imported it, from the Principalities of Moldavia and Wallachia or even from Italy.

Wages and (Hypothetical) Profits

Unfortunately, Sestini's accounts are 'task-oriented' and record payments of lump sums for whatever jobs the owner wanted done. Often, they do not specify how many people were at work; nor, in most cases, does the author note the daily wages payable for different tasks. The accounts merely contain summary entries on the model of 'daily wages and other expenses, 9 piasters and 30 para'.[47] However, Sestini does record that planting vines was a job for three people; and the team received 1.5 piasters for every *dönüm* planted. By this calculation, a worker planting a *dönüm* with vines received 0.5 piasters. If only we knew for sure how long it took the team to plant a *dönüm*! We can however hypothesise that as two teams worked for five days on what was supposedly a ten-*dönüm* field, receiving fifteen piasters, six people received three piasters for a day's work, and the daily wage was half a piaster per person.[48] Presumably, different rates applied to other tasks

Sestini continued his account by describing, often in minute detail, the tasks necessary in every one of the five years covered by his calculations. While this is not the place for a further discussion of viticulture, the economic/financial aspect is worth a closer look. Some of the data are quite difficult to interpret: after recording the expenditure of 100 piasters for the purchase of ten *dönüm*

46. Yılmaz 2014, pp. 145–72.

47. Sestini 1786, p. 37.

48. Ibid., p. 30. Pamuk 2000b has wage data on Istanbul construction workers but not on agricultural labourers.

of hitherto unused land, the author entered five piasters as interest; however, given the scarcity of capital, it is hard to imagine that anybody would have lent out money at just five per cent. At the end of the first year, the author calculated the net expense as 182 piasters and eighteen paras, to which he added nine piasters and five paras as interest, so that once again, the latter should have been around five per cent. This low rate keeps reappearing until the fifth year, when for the first time, the vineyard supposedly produced a profit. If, however, we assume that the would-be cultivator would have to pay at least ten per cent, the going rate even if he had access to the low-interest loans granted by pious foundations, he would have needed to wait much longer for his investment in the vineyard to produce even a modest profit.[49]

Disappearing Vineyards

Of course, the most intriguing aspect of Sestini's account is the fact that the vineyards he described with such loving detail have disappeared without a trace. No indication remains that the Bosporus villages were ever a grape- and wine-producing territory beyond a few place names, such as the Üsküdar district of Bağlarbaşı (the beginning of the vineyards). Furthermore, the vineyards must have disappeared long before the expansion of the city in the second half of the twentieth century. After all, the Baedeker travel guide of 1914, which must have appeared just a few weeks or months before the beginning of the Great War, has a lot of recommendations on possible excursions near the Bosporus, mentioning all kinds of trees; but the author(s) say(s) nothing about vineyards.[50] Similarly, the American author Harrison Griswold Dwight (1875–1959), who began the research for his book on 'Constantinople' in 1907 but could only bring out the first edition in 1915, included a lengthy and somewhat romanticised chapter on gardens, in which he discussed numerous examples by the Bosporus, illustrated by copious photographs; but he too felt no need to include information on vineyards.[51] Nor does the travel guide published by John Murray in 1840 contain any references to vineyards on the Bosporus.[52]

---

49. Çizakça 2013.
50. Baedeker 1914.
51. Dwight 1926, pp. 227–64.
52. I am grateful to Yavuz Köse for the following references: Joanne and Isambert 1861, p. 393 mention vineyards, and so does Anonymous author (Meyers Reisebücher) 1902, p. 301: 'In der Umgebung von Jeniköi hübsche Spaziergänge durch Weinberge und Pinienwäldchen und dem Meer entlang nach Therapia (wohin auch hoch oben auf dem Berg ein Fußweg führt)'. My heartfelt thanks go to Ali Akkaya, librarian of the

Producing Grapes and Wine on the Bosporus

In order to document the disappearance of Istanbul's vineyards, we thus need to scan a sizeable number of nineteenth-century travelogues and tourist guides. Unfortunately, some of the texts that immediately come to mind are not very helpful. Thus the well-known scholar and diplomat Joseph von Hammer-Purgstall (1774–1856) in 1822 published a two-volume description of Istanbul and environs, whose copious footnotes include references to Sestini's work, but Hammer-Purgstall's interest was in buildings and in the poetry, both Ottoman and non-Ottoman, which they had inspired; as a result, the short chapter on natural phenomena does not contain any relevant information.[53] As for the Russian naturalist Pierre de Tchihatcheff (Pyotr Chikhachyov) (1808–1890), who did write a short chapter about vineyards for his book published in 1864, he has quite obviously derived his account from Sestini's work – although the Russian author, who wanted to attract a non-specialist public, did not include many footnotes.[54]

Perhaps the phylloxera epidemic that ravaged European vineyards during the late nineteenth century is at least partly responsible for the disappearance of the Bosporus grapes. However, even if that assumption should be true we would still need to explain why the owners did not reconstitute their vineyards with the help of resistant American vines, as happened in Italy, France and elsewhere. After all, in the late 1800s and early 1900s, Istanbul had a large Orthodox population; and, as Sestini's account shows, these people were particularly active as growers. Thus, the question is still open; and we can only hope to find further sources in the future.

Conclusion

While full of information not available elsewhere, Sestini's account leaves many questions unanswered. First of all: where and how had a former monk and prominent numismatist become interested in viticulture, beyond the concern with plant biology that was probably widespread among educated contemporaries? For whom did he write this text – for curious European aristocrats and people concerned with 'scientific agriculture/gardening'? In some cases, it is hard to find practical reasons for the interest of readers in this type of work. However,

---

Deutsches Archäologisches Institut/Istanbul for his help in tracking down further references.

53. Hammer-Purgstall 1822. Hammer-Purgstall dedicated his work to the Habsburg princess Marie Louise of Parma, who had briefly been Napoleon's second wife.

54. De Tchihatchef 1864, pp. 210–13.

Suraiya Faroqhi

as noted, a Berlin publisher brought out a German translation shortly after Sestini's work on vineyards had come out in Italy. Surely, not many people in the still very provincial Prussian capital had ever been near the Bosporus; but the esteem which the king had expressed for Sestini's scholarly achievements and the latter's lengthy visit to Berlin may have sparked a degree of interest.[55] Perhaps Sestini's patrons among the Wallachian nobility, many of whose members had spent time in Istanbul, were also among the readers of the original version, as envisaged by the author and his publishers.

On a more personal level, did Sestini perhaps, at some point in his life, plan to spend his retirement on the Bosporus, managing his vineyard like a Roman grandee of antiquity? Seemingly, the author's information was insufficient, especially when it came to acquiring the land on which to plant the vines, to say nothing of the rate of interest current in Istanbul. Perhaps Sestini gave up the idea when he realised the extent of these difficulties. Yet Sestini's voluminous correspondence, published and perhaps unpublished as well, may provide further information. At present, we just do not know.

Likely, a historian familiar with eighteenth-century viticulture will be able to mine this account for further information on the agricultural history of the Mediterranean. While the present author cannot lay claim to any such knowledge, even a non-specialist can say that, when it came to growing table grapes, Tuscany and the shores of the Bosporus were part of the same vine-growing civilisation. We may assume that in both places, there lived a number of consumers with money to pay for good-quality fruits and the leisure to develop a taste for fine grapes. However, when it came to wine, presumably the number of prosperous non-Muslims living in the Ottoman capital and interested in up-market qualities was limited; and this situation probably explains why, as Sestini was well aware, the vineyard owners of the Bosporus paid so little attention to quality.

Whatever the quality of the product, in Sestini's time, the Bosporus vineyards were thriving; but by the mid-twentieth century, they were gone. One might think that the emigration of the Greek inhabitants was the main reason for this change in land use; but population movement, certainly momentous, can only have been a contributing factor. After all, early twentieth-century travel guides barely mentioned the Bosporus vineyards and, at that time, the Greeks of Istanbul were still in place. Perhaps *mutatis mutandis*, the reasons resembled those that Roger Dion had identified for the Paris region in the nineteenth and

---

55. Biographical information from Luppi 1890: http://www.socnumit.org/doc/Numis-matici/SESTINI_Domenico.pdf (Accessed 29 Nov. 2016).

early twentieth centuries.[56] The Istanbul climate is too cool and rainy for table grapes or raisins; and the quality of the wine produced near the Bosporus was mediocre. Thus, similarly to what happened in northern France, once it became easy to supply Istanbul consumers with better wines from western Anatolia or even southern Thrace, interest in the local vineyards declined. It would be nice if we could draw a connection between modern transportation and the disappearance of the vineyards, or, expressed differently, changes in land use. However, at least to the knowledge of the present author, historians have not studied this phenomenon, and therefore, we can only 'suppose this supposition'.

Bibliography

Published Primary Sources

Anonymous author. 1836–7. 'Domenico Sestini'. *The Numismatic Journal* 2: 100–02. https://books.google.com.tr/books?id=YXZRAAAAcAAJ&pg=PA100&lpg=PA100&dq=domenico+sestini+biography

Anonymous author. 1914. *Meyers Reisebücher: Balkanstaaten und Konstantinopel Anatolische und Bagdadbahn*. Leipzig and Vienna: Bibliographisches Institut.

Baedeker, Karl. 1914. *Konstantinopel, Balkanstaaten, Kleinasien, Archipel, Cypern: Handbuch für Reisende*, 2nd edition. Leipzig and Vienna: Karl Baedeker.

Busbequius, Augerius Gislenius. 1994 [1589]. *Vier brieven over het gezantschap naar Turkije* [orig. *Legationis turcicae epistolae quattuor*]. Ed. by Zweder von Martels, trans. by Michel Goldsteen. Hilversum: Verloren.

De Tchihatchef, P[ierre]. 1864. *Le Bosphore de Constantinople avec perspectives des pays limitrophes*. Paris: Morgand.

Dwight, H[arrison] G[riswold]. 1926. *Constantinople: Settings and Traits*. New York, London: Harper & Brothers.

Evliya Çelebi. 2006. *Evliya Çelebi Seyahatnâmesi, Topkapı Sarayı Bağdat 304 Yazmasının Transkripsyonu –Dizini, vol. 1*. 4 vols. Seyit Ali Kahraman, Yücel Dağlı and Robert Dankoff (eds). Istanbul: Yapı ve Kredi Bankası.

Hammer-Purgstall, Joseph von. 1822. *Constantinopolis und der Bosporus, örtlich und geschichtlich beschrieben*, 4 vols., Budapest [Pesth]: Hartlebens Verlag.

Joanne, Adolphe and Émile Isambert. 1861. *Itinéraire descriptif, historique et archéologique de l'Orient*. Paris: Librairie de L. Hachette.

Kal'a, Ahmet et al. (eds). 1997–98. *İstanbul Tarım Tarihi*, 2 vols. Istanbul: İstanbul Büyükşehir Belediyesi.

---

56. Dion 2010.

Suraiya Faroqhi

Luppi, C[onstantino]. 1890. 'Domenico Sestini', under the heading *Società numismatica italiana: I Grandi Numismatici, Rivista Italiana di Numismatica (RIN)*, 473–80. www. socnumit.org/doc/Numismatici/SESTINI_Domenico.pdf (accessed 25 Nov. 2016).

Sestini, Domenico. 1784. *Lettere del Signor Abate Domenico Sestini scritte dalla Sicilia e dalla Turchia a diversi suoi amici, vol. 6.* 6 vols. Livorno. https://books.google.com.tr/ books?id=DOfGKXu4_zoC&pg=PP2&lpg=PP2&dq=abate+domenico+sestini (accessed 26 Nov. 2016).

——. 1785. *Opuscoli del signor abate Domenico Sestini. 1. Descrizione del littorale del Canale di Costantinopoli e della coltura delle vigne lungo le coste del medesimo.* Florence.

——. 1786. *Beschreibung des Kanals von Konstantinopel, des dasigen Wein-, Acker- und Garten-Baues und der Jagd der Türken.* Trans. by C.J. Jagemann. Hamburg.

——. 1798. *Voyage de Constantinople à Bassora, en 1781, par le Tigre et l'Euphrate, et retour à Constantinople, en 1782, par le désert et Alexandrie.* Paris: Dupuis.

Secondary Sources

Akyıldız, Ali. 2007. 'Para'. In *Türkiye Diyanet Vakfı İslâm Ansiklopedisi, vol. 34.* 44 vols. Istanbul: Türkiye Diyanet Vakfı. pp. 163–66.

Bilgin, Arif. 2017. 'From Artichoke to Corn: New Fruits and Vegetables in the Istanbul Market'. In Elif Akçetin and Suraiya Faroqhi (eds), *Living the Good Life: Consumption in the Qing and Ottoman Empires of the Eighteenth Century.* Leiden: Brill. pp. 257–82.

Çizakça, Murat. 2013. 'The Economy'. In Suraiya Faroqhi and Kate Fleet (eds), *The Ottoman Empire as a World Power, 1453–1603.* Cambridge, New York: Cambridge University Press. pp. 241–75.

Dion, Roger. 2010 [1959/1977]. *Histoire de la vigne et du vin en France, des origines au XIXe siècle.* Paris: CNRS Editions.

Doğan, Faruk. 2008. 'Osmanlı Devletinde Zeytinyağı Üretimi ve Tüketimi.' In Arif Bilgin and Özge Samancı (eds), *Türk Mutfağı.* Ankara: T.C. Kültür ve Turizm Bakanlığı. pp. 231–42.

Faroqhi, Suraiya. 1980. 'Land Transfer, Land Disputes and *askeri* Holdings in Ankara (1592–1600)'. In Robert Mantran (ed.), *Mémorial Ömer Lütfi Barkan.* Paris: Adrien Maisonneuve. pp. 87–99.

——. 1984. *Towns and Townsmen of Ottoman Anatolia, Trade, Crafts, and Food Production in an Urban Setting 1520–1650.* Cambridge: Cambridge University Press.

——. 1998. 'Migration into Eighteenth-Century "Greater Istanbul" as Reflected in the Kadi Registers of Eyüp'. *Turcica* **30**: 163–83.

——. 2018. 'Should it be Olives or Butter? Consuming Fatty Titbits in the Early Modern Ottoman Empire'. In Angela Jianu and Violeta Barbu (eds), *Earthly Delights: Economies and Cultures of Food in Ottoman and Danubian Europe, c. 1500–1900.* Leiden: Brill. pp. 33–49.

Kaplan, Ayşe. 2012. 'From Seasonal to Permanent: A Study on the Effects of Göç Tradition on the Bosphorus Shores 1791–1815'. MA Thesis, Istanbul: Istanbul Bilgi University.

Karababa, Eminegül. 2015. 'Marketing and Consuming Flowers in the Ottoman Empire'. *Journal of Historical Research in Marketing* 7 (2): 280–92.

Pamuk, Şevket. 2000a. *A Monetary History of the Ottoman Empire*. Cambridge: Cambridge University Press.

——. 2000b. *İstanbul ve Diğer Kentlerde 500 Yıllık Fiyatlar ve Ücretler. 1469–1998/500 Years of Prices and Wages in Istanbul and Other Cities*. Ankara: TC Başbakanlık Devlet İstatistik Enstitüsü.

Shopov, Aleksandar and Ayhan Han. (2013). 'Osmanlı İstanbul'unda Kent İçi Tarımsal Toprak Kullanımı ve Dönüşümleri'. *Toplumsal Tarih* **236**: 34–38.

Yerasimos, Marianna. 2011. *Evliya Çelebi Seyahatnâmesi'nde Yemek Kültürü: Yorumlar ve Sistematik Dizin*. Istanbul: Kitap Yayınevi.

Yılmaz, Fikret. 2010. '16. Yüzyılda Tarımsal Yapılarda Değişim ve Yağ Kullanımı'. *Tarih ve Toplum* **10**: 23–42.

——. 2014. 'What about a Bit of Fun? Wine, Crime and Entertainment in Sixteenth-Century Western Anatolia'. In Suraiya Faroqhi and Arzu Öztürkmen (eds), *Celebration, Entertainment and Theater in the Ottoman World*. Calcutta, London, New York: Seagull Books. pp. 145–72.

Web Sources

Anonymous author. Undated. 'Carl Linnaeus (1707–1778)'. www.ucmp.berkeley.edu/history/linnaeus.html (accessed 25 Nov. 2016).

'C.W.' 2013. 'Economic History: Who Were the Physiocrats? Economics' First Systematic Thinkers'. www.economist.com/blogs/freeexchange/2013/10/economic-history-0 (accessed 27 Nov. 2016).

PART 2

Resources and Energies

Chapter 4

FRUITS OF EMPIRE: FIGS, RAISINS AND TRANSFORMATION OF WESTERN ANATOLIA IN THE LATE NINETEENTH CENTURY[1]

Onur İnal

Ottoman port-cities, because of their privileged position at the interface of two or more distinct economic systems, cultures and environments, have long fascinated historians. In their studies, they have primarily dealt with the processes and developments that linked these cities to the centres of global economy.[2] On the other hand, historians have also studied Ottoman port-cities within the framework of city-country relations for quite some time.[3] They have, however, focused principally on the ways cities exercised influence over the countryside and often viewed transformations in the hinterlands as results of impact of the city on the country. Historical interplay between port-cities and their hinterlands has remained a rather neglected aspect of Ottoman history. This paper aims to fill a gap in our understanding of the complex relationship between port-cities and hinterlands in the Ottoman Empire and give an environmental perspective on the subject through the study of *interactions* between Izmir and Western Anatolia in the nineteenth century.

The rapid ecological, economic and social transformation of Izmir and its surrounding area in the late Ottoman period, roughly the decades between

---

1. This chapter was originally published in *Environment and History* (Fast Track, 2018).

2. For a theoretical and methodological framework on Ottoman port-cities and their role in the integration of the Ottoman Empire into the expanding world-economy, see Kasaba, Keyder and Tabak 1986, pp. 121–35; Reimer 1991, pp. 135–56; Keyder, Özveren and Quataert 1993, pp. 519–57; and Eldem, Goffman and Masters 1999, especially 'Istanbul' and 'Izmir' chapters.

3. For studies on city-country relations within the Ottoman context, see Kurmuş 1977; Kasaba 1988; Frangakis-Syrett 1993, pp. 411–34; Toksöz 2004, pp. 71–90; idem 2010.

the 1840s and 1890s, is the main focus of this paper. In this period, Izmir, by extending access to and control over the natural resources in its immediate hinterland, grew most rapidly in external trade and became the major link connecting the empire to Europe and the rest of the world. Settlers, migrants, and investors helped shape and reshape this urban environment by exploiting the natural resources and geographic assets available in Western Anatolia to create a hub of transportation of people and goods both inward to urban markets and outward to connect the hinterland markets to the global economy. By the end of the nineteenth century, Izmir eclipsed all other Ottoman ports in trade and, after Istanbul, became the quintessential example of Ottoman port-cities that connected the East and the West and facilitated the movement of people, goods and ideas.

Figs and raisins take a starring role in this research because these two crops had a profound impact on economic and social life in Western Anatolia and played a remarkable role in shaping the region's human and natural landscape. In the period under investigation, the expansion of fig and grape growing was an integral part of the process of Western Anatolia's integration into the market economy and is demonstrated by the railroad lines, stations, warehouses, entrepôts and processing and packing units that multiplied during this period. Figs and grapes attracted foreign capital investment and technology, promoted trade and tied the countryside and city together. The expansion of fig and grape cultivation, furthermore, stimulated the movement of people across the region by creating seasonal employment for thousands of urban and rural residents. Figs and grapes transformed valleys, marshlands and hilltops into the physical basis for Izmir's growth and development in the second half of the nineteenth century. Thus, it is my contention in this study that tracing the story of figs and grapes not only reveals a great deal about social and economic life in a major Ottoman port-city in the nineteenth century, but also illustrates the ways in which city and country interacted.

Fig and Grape Growing in Western Anatolia: A Long History

The fig and the grape have a history as old as that of humankind. Both fruits are indigenous to the Mediterranean basin and have been cultivated in the region from the earliest historical times. Anciently, the fig symbolised fertility and reproduction and, for example, we are told that Adam and Eve 'sewed fig leaves together and made coverings for themselves'.[4] The Greeks learned to

---

4.   Kohlenberger 2004, p. 3.

cultivate the plant from the Carians, calling it *Ficus carica*, and introduced it into Italy, Morocco and Spain. The Ruminal fig tree, or the *Ficus Ruminalis*, was a fig tree renowned for its association with Remus and his twin brother Romulus, the main characters of Rome's foundation myth; and was venerated for centuries as the 'reputed oldest sacred tree in Rome'.[5]

The grape has also been cultivated across the Mediterranean from the earliest historical times. The primary use of the grape is to make wine. Humans have made wine for about 7,000 years and Anatolia was one of the first places on earth where viticulture and wine-making began.[6] The Egyptians and Phoenicians made wine from grapes around 3,000 BC. The Chinese traded it along the Silk Road. The Greeks began to make wine about 2,000 BC and spread it throughout the Mediterranean. To the Greeks, wine was so important that it had its own god, Dionysus. And because wine comes from it, the grape symbolised fertility and sacrifice. Like the Greeks, the Romans had a god of wine, Bacchus.[7] Archaeological and historical evidence suggest that the beginning of viticulture in Western Anatolia occurred in the Early Bronze Age, about 2,500 BC, in Troy and Kumkale near Çanakkale.[8]

The fig and the grape played a significant role in Western Anatolia's economy and culture throughout Ottoman history. The Ottomans continued the Greek and Roman methods of fig and grape growing. The fig grew anywhere within a distance of 100–150 miles from the sea, but predominantly on hillsides in the Büyük Menderes valley, where 'climatic conditions, soil, and conformation of terrain appear to be especially favourable for fig production'.[9] There, hot summers with maximum temperatures ranging up to 40–45° C allowed the growing of thin-skinned and fine-textured figs, which were highly esteemed in the market. Whereas hot and dry winds coming from the north in July hastened fruit maturity, westerly winds in August brought some humidity and prevented the figs from overheating or too rapid drying.[10] The calcareous soil, rich in iron, furthermore, helped this district to become 'the garden of the fig'.[11] In other words, microclimatic conditions in this part of Western Anatolia were well adapted to the requirements of the fig.

---

5.   Mazzoni 2016, p. 93; Zoch 2012, p. 9; Hunt 2016, pp. 100–120.

6.   Gökbayrak and Söylemezoğlu 2010, pp. 465–72.

7.   'Grapes', in Cumo 2013, p. 473.

8.   Gökbayrak and Söylemezoğlu 2010, p. 465.

9.   Ravndal 1926, p. 103.

10. Condit 1947, p. 83.

11. Hamparzum 1908, p. 4.

84

The largest fig gardens were on southern slopes of the Aydın Mountains around the towns of Aydın, Nazilli and Sultanhisar. According to one commentator, the best quality of fig came from the town of İncirliova, which literally means 'the valley of figs' in Turkish.¹² Western Anatolia's temperate climate and rich soil rendered it an ideal region for growing grapes, too. With the transformation of Izmir into a busy port, the Gediz valley in particular became the centre of viticulture, where farmers grew grapes and produced raisins for local and export markets.¹³

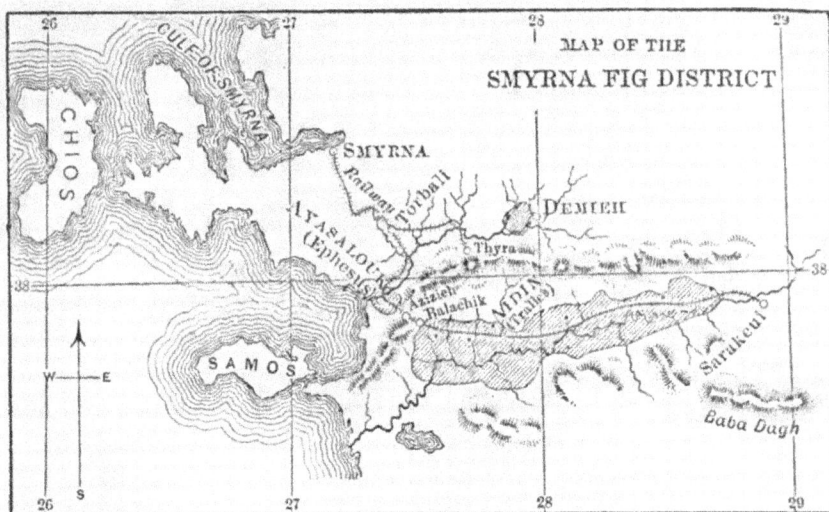

*Map 1. The fig districts in Western Anatolia. From 'The Smyrna Fig Harvest', Harper's Monthly Magazine **80** (1 Dec. 1889): 287.*

Dried figs and raisins, which were imported to Western and Northern Europe in Medieval times, were a significant item of elite consumption. Like other foods that could not be produced locally, figs and raisins were an expensive import, which the majority of consumers hardly knew 'except at Christmas time'.¹⁴ Figs and raisins remained luxury food items, at least until the eighteenth century, when they were seasonally available in local markets. There is no reliable information about when dried figs and raisins from West-

12. 'The Smyrna Fig Trade', *Journal of the Society of Arts* 54 (1906): 634.
13. Issawi 1980, p. 264.
14. Richard Witherby, 'Report on Dried Fruits', *Journal of the Society of Arts* 21 (1873): 585.

ern Anatolia penetrated European markets; however, sources testify that the English were given special permission to import figs and raisins from Western Anatolia in the late seventeenth century, 'ostensibly for the use of the King of England', even though Ottoman governments prohibited the export of these items.[15] Smyrna figs and raisins began to be widely consumed in Europe and North America in the second half of the eighteenth century. Between 1784 and 1790, an average of 7,400 tons of raisins were sent to Britain alone.[16] Among the recipes of an English cookbook published in 1792, there was a recipe for 'Smyrna raisin wine'.[17] From London or Liverpool, raisins also found their way to the United States. In 1785, a Boston merchant advertised that he had 'a few casks of Smyrna raisin for sale'.[18] In the 1780s, the 'Smyrna fig' was also listed amongst the 'goods imported into the port of London'.[19]

From the seventeenth to the early nineteenth centuries, Izmir was a significant transit port for Ottoman exports and imports, but not a gateway city in the strict sense of the term.[20] It was the leading export and import centre of the empire and was connected to many other ports across the Mediterranean through maritime trade routes, yet its relation to its surrounding hinterlands remained weak due to certain social, economic and environmental limitations. Despite American and Western European interest in consuming figs and raisins from Western Anatolia, therefore, the production and trade of these crops in the region was on a limited scale in the early modern period. Figs and raisins became a matter of real importance in the city's exports from the mid-nineteenth century on, when agriculture and trade prospered, transport and marketing infrastructures were improved, and business and labour networks became established. Fig and grape growing was a high priority for farmers in Western Anatolia in the second half of the nineteenth century, a time period that corresponds to the widespread consumption of dried figs and raisins in American and Western European cities.

---

15. Wood 1935, p. 98.

16. Issawi 1980, pp. 264–65.

17. Collingwood and Woolams 1792, p. 338.

18. Gordon 1931, p. 41.

19. 'Goods imported into the Port of London from Tuesday Dec. 13th, to Tuesday the 20th of Dec. 1785'. *The Times* (22 Dec. 1785): 4; 'Goods imported into the Port of London from Tuesday Jan. 17th, to Tuesday the 24th of Jan.' *The Times* (30 Jan. 1786): 4.

20. For a recent discussion on the role of Izmir as a 'gateway city', see İnal 2018.

The Expansion of Fig and Vine Growing in Western Anatolia

The opening up of Western Anatolia to international markets and the expansion and diversification of trade networks was a process that started in the eighteenth century. In the early to mid-nineteenth century, cereals and cotton furnished the impetus for the expansion of agriculture and became the major agent of economic and ecological change throughout the region. The repeal of the Corn Laws in 1846 opened up new fields to cultivation and channelled the cereals produced in farmlands surrounding Izmir to European markets. Another event, the Crimean War in 1853–56, also had a great impact on the expansion of cereal cultivation in the region. During the war, demand for cereals from the Ottoman Empire increased incredibly because the war interrupted Russian grain shipments to Europe and the cheapest and the most efficient way to feed the soldiers of Allied armies fighting in the Crimean peninsula was to import grain from the Ottoman Empire.[21] Cotton production, on the other hand, spread rapidly across the region concomitantly with the disruption of the Atlantic trade during the American Civil War in the 1860s. In these years, Western Anatolia – in Izmir and its vicinity – was one of the regions where the Ottoman government and British merchants made efforts to regenerate cotton cultivation. These efforts proved successful and cotton became the predominant cash crop, stamping a unique character upon the economic and environmental life of Western Anatolia.[22]

In the second half of the nineteenth century, the Western Anatolian countryside saw a gradual and cautious shift from cereals and cotton towards fig and grape growing. The expansion of fig and grape growing complemented and overlapped with the intensification of human settlement and land use through cereal growing and expansion of land reclamation and commercial agriculture through cotton cultivation. The emergence of figs and raisins as a commercial crop dramatically altered the social, economic, and ecological landscape of Western Anatolia. The last decades of the nineteenth century witnessed fig trees and vines being commercially grown almost everywhere in the region, from the edge of the Mediterranean to the hilltops. In this period, social and economic life in many Western Anatolian cities and towns revolved around the fig and the grape. It would not be an exaggeration to say that what the banana meant for tropical lands was denoted for Western Anatolia by the fig and the grape.

---

21. Owen 1981, p. 111. For more on the extension of cereal cultivation in Western Anatolia in the mid-nineteenth century, see İnal 2015, pp. 133–43.

22. For the impact of the American Civil War on cotton production in Western Anatolia, see Kurmuş 1977, pp. 88–95; idem 1987, pp. 160–69; İnal 2015, pp. 144–56.

Fruits of Empire

The expansion of fig and vine growing across the region and the commodification of dried figs and raisins were closely related to three overlapping processes that altered the context in which the city and country interacted economically, socially and ecologically in the second half of the nineteenth century.

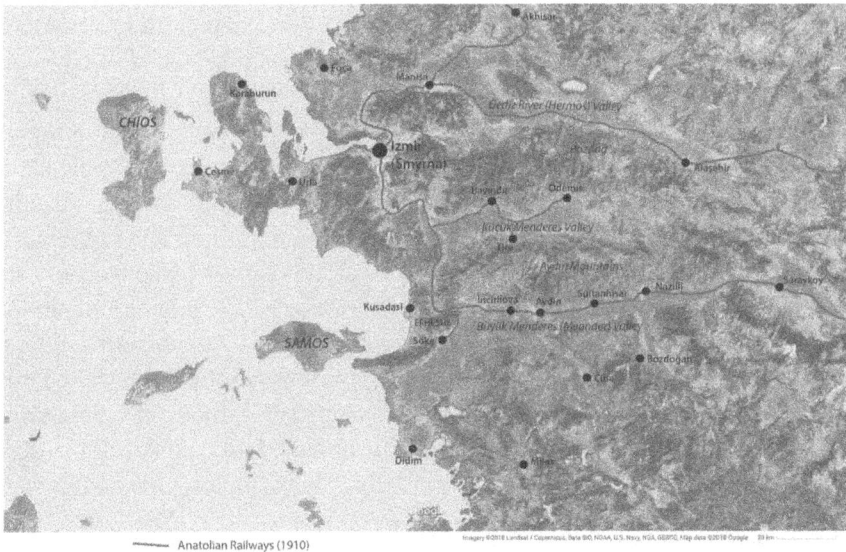

Anatolian Railways (1910)

Map 2. Western Anatolia showing railway routes in 1910.

The first one is demographic processes related to changes in the size, composition and distribution of population in the Western Anatolian countryside. From the mid-nineteenth century onwards, there was a steady growth of population due to natural increase and the improvement in sanitary conditions. Furthermore, migrants and refugees escaping from wars and conflicts in the Morea, Crimea, Caucasia and elsewhere, as well as the sedentarisation of nomadic and semi-nomadic groups, added to the population of Western Anatolia. The number of people involved in agricultural activity increased, while the expanding manufacturing and industrial sector in Izmir created employment opportunities for urban populations. In other words, dramatic changes in agricultural practices and land use in the rural area and the expansion of manufacturing and industrial sectors in the city were closely related to each other and were the consequence of a steady growth of population in the city and country.

The most significant outcome of population growth in rural areas was the opening of new lands to cultivation and consequently an increase in agricultural production. In the years of opening up, roughly the period stretching from the 1840s to 1880s, a great effort was made to extend the area under cultivation by clearing, cleaning and reclaiming the land on the edge of towns, villages, pastures and forests to create fertile and productive farmland. The cultivation of fig and vine played a significant role in this 'opening-up' and allowed rural inhabitants of Western Anatolia to extend the range of their agricultural activities. Western Anatolians cleared rocky terrain and forests on the hillsides in order to plant fig trees and vines in this period. They preferred to reclaim hilly land because a considerable percentage of abandoned land was found in highlands and remote areas. Fig producers gave close attention to the hills and mountains because production was directly related to the number of trees planted per acre and the yield on hillsides was higher than in lowlands. While in mountainous areas as many as a hundred fig trees per acre could be planted, the number was eighty in the valleys and 64 in the fields.[23] Hillsides were also better suited for the cultivation of vines. As Gwynne Harris Heap (1817–1887), the American consul in Istanbul, noted: 'The best results are obtained from vineyards planted in good soils on the hillsides, the next being those situated on undulating tablelands, and afterwards from those planted in the valley.'[24] As long as the settlers did not cut forests reserved exclusively for the shipyard or for imperial hunting, the Ottoman government did not take any action against agricultural clearing within its borders.[25] Because the timber from Western Anatolia was not suitable for shipbuilding, there was no restriction on fig and vine growers penetrating forest areas within reach of rural settlements.

In the lack of archival and statistical data, it is not easy to get a complete picture of land reclamation and deforestation in Western Anatolia.[26] There is some information, for example, in the accounts of European travellers regarding the ongoing land reclamation activities and deforestation in the Western Anatolian hills in the second half of the nineteenth century. Such information, if not taken completely at face value, is valuable and can help us to understand

---

23. Djevad Sami Bey 1928, p. 17.

24. Heap 1884, p. 727.

25. Dursun 2007, p. 38.

26. The Ottoman Archives include records on fig and raisin exports to Europe and the United States through the port of Izmir. However, such reports do not give us any clue about the correlation between land reclamation, deforestation and fig and vine cultivation in Western Anatolia.

human impacts on landscapes.[27] For example, 'as you proceed the mountain rises more and more abruptly from the plain, which is fertile and well culti-vated', wrote Henry John Van Lennep (1815–1889), who travelled from Izmir to the interior in 1870, and added, 'vineyards, mulberry plantations, and fields of grain, extend to the distant hills'.[28] Some two decades after Van Lennep's visit, William Cochran remarked the following: 'About six years ago the hills behind the village of Bournabat, a few miles out of Smyrna, were covered with jungle, and useless, they are now, to a considerable extent, clothed with vines, belonging, in every instance, to families who were once the poorest peasants.'[29] Cochran's notes on reclamation give further detail about the expansion of viniculture in the region:

> Each person makes a selection on those hills, and during his leisure hours, after his usual employment, clears away the bush, which sells for firewood at a remunerative price. When the land is free, it is planted with vines, the same routine being repeated season after season until the vineyard is as large as he and his family can manage. As the planted areas are successively completed, a government officer measures the land occupied, and the peasant pays at the rate of one medjid per doloon – a doloon being forty square paces – when he becomes the proprietor, and in a surprisingly short time little independent revenues of £30 to £50 a year are realized.[30]

The second process that altered interactions between Izmir and Western Anatolia was the regulation of land reclamation and use by a series of imperial laws and edicts. In the mid-nineteenth century, the density of human settlement and activity reached a level at which competition for fertile agricultural lands and other natural resources intensified. This situation naturally led to some ambi-guities with regard to property acquisition. In 1856, the French historian and journalist Abdolonyme Ubicini (1818–1884) made interesting observations on how rural residents in the Ottoman Empire acquired property rights over land:

---

27. European observers' descriptions, both textual and visual, of Western Anatolia testify to the extent of land reclamation and deforestation. However, because they intentionally dispraised Ottoman lands in their value judgments to facilitate European governments' political, economic and cultural involvement with the Ottoman Empire and blatantly distorted and misrepresented what they witnessed in Ottoman lands, such accounts should be read very critically and the information they provide should not be taken for granted.

28. Van Lennep 1870, vol. 2, p. 303.

29. Cochran 1887, pp. 217–18.

30. Ibid., p. 218. By 'doloon' the author refers to 'dönüm', or 'dunam', a unit of land area equal to 1,000 square metres.

Onur İnal

The waste and unenclosed lands (*adiyet* or *mouaet*), which had not been included in the partition at the time of the conquest, or such as through the neglect of the occupants had been suffered to lie fallow, became the property of any individual, Musulman, or otherwise, who, to borrow the expression of the law, *restored their soul to them*. So, also whoever plants a tree in a waste spot becomes the owner of that tree, and of five feet of ground all around it.[31]

In this state of uncertainty and confusion, the Ottoman government found it necessary to regulate poorly or vaguely defined property rights and to redraw the boundaries of pastures, forests and common grazing lands by a number of imperial laws and edicts in order to prevent conflicts among settlers. Among the legal steps taken, the 1858 Land Code was the most important one with respect to the economic and ecological transformation of Western Anatolia. From an agroecological perspective it started a new period when human impact on the environment accelerated and intensified because it redefined property relations that 'radically altered the allocation of land as a source'.[32] The new Code reiterated the right of individuals to claim *mevat arazi* (abandoned lands), if they brought them under cultivation or planted them with trees within three years.[33] In the aftermath of the 1858 Land Code the pace of reclamation throughout the Ottoman Empire grew impressively; seventy per cent of cultivable lands in the empire became *mülk* (private property) in the decade following the Code, while *miri* (public) lands were reduced to a mere five per cent.[34] In the process of land reclamation, the increased labour force needed for the performance of a variety of tasks such as watering, ploughing and planting, was largely drawn from migrants and refugees, as well as newly settled nomads. In this respect, the Code was supportive of the government's efforts to maximise its agricultural revenues through settlement and reclamation.[35]

By the 1858 Land Code, the land in Western Anatolia was divided into smaller plots and titles were granted to individuals with the intention of creating a denser peasant population. The majority of small-scale land-holding peasants in the region were Greeks.[36] Although there are no definitive statistics regarding the number of small proprietors in Western Anatolia, we can deduce from consular reports that the number of small proprietors increased with

---

31. Ubicini 1856, vol. 1, p. 258.
32. İslamoğlu 2000, p. 34.
33. Tabak 2008, p. 211.
34. Pamuk 1987, p. 91.
35. Dursun 2007, p. 38.
36. Anagnostopoulou 1988, pp. 199–204, quoted in Themopoulou 2002, p. 89.

respect to the growth of agricultural population in the region following the 1858 Land Code. For example, Robert William Cumberbatch (1821–1876), the British consul in Smyrna, reported in 1870 that in Aydın province the cultivable land in the vicinity of towns and villages was 'generally divided into very small tenements, which the proprietors cultivate on their own account'.[37] In short, the Code, by allowing individual ownership in land, encouraged rural residents to reclaim and till the uncultivated land and reveal the commercial potential of the region.

The 1858 Land Code was very important with respect to vine and fig cultivation, because it provided some sort of motivation for rural residents to extend the boundaries of agricultural areas beyond the traditional fig and grape growing districts along the Gediz, Küçük Menderes and Büyük Menderes rivers. Donald Quataert has argued that twenty per cent of all vineyards in the Ottoman Empire were in the vicinity of Izmir in the 1870s and they produced 50,000 tons of raisins, half of which were exported with the other half destined for the domestic market.[38] He has further estimated that the number of vine-yards in Aydın province had risen tenfold by the 1870s.[39] According to another estimate, in 1882 the land under vine in the province was over 350,000 acres.[40] The transformation of pastures and forests into fig orchards in the last decades of the nineteenth century was also remarkable. According to one observer, the area under fig cultivation in Western Anatolia more than doubled within twenty years from 1870 to 1890.[41] An estimate suggests that there were 'about fifteen to eighteen thousand orchards, representing about a million and a half of fig trees'.[42] Even though these figures give an idea about the intensity of fig and vine growing, in the absence of reliable statistics it is still hard to make a precise estimate of the total area covered with fig orchards and vineyards.

The third process that significantly contributed to the ongoing processes of land reclamation and rehabilitation in Western Anatolia was the formation of capital and commercial networks. The nineteenth century was a period of economic and commercial boom in Western Europe, when European merchants sought new ways to penetrate Ottoman lands to sell low-priced

37. 'Consul Cumberbatch to Earl Granville', 4 Nov. 1870, *Accounts and Papers*, vol. 68 (1871), p. 847.
38. Quataert 1981, p. 72.
39. Idem 1973, p. 217.
40. 'Trade and Commerce of Smyrna', *Journal of the Society of Arts* 30 (1882): 915.
41. 'The Smyrna Fig Harvest', *Harper's New Monthly Magazine* 80 (1889): 287.
42. Hamparzum 1908, p. 18.

manufactures, especially English cotton goods, and to buy agricultural goods and raw materials that were high in demand in European markets. As in other Eastern Mediterranean ports, British merchants were very active in Izmir and they became the driving force behind the city's integration with the Western Anatolian countryside. Their operational scope increased with the dissolution of the Levant Company in 1825, an event that allowed British merchants to act independently in Ottoman territories. However, what really caused an increase in scale and networking of the operations of British merchants in Western Anatolia was the Anglo-Ottoman Trade Convention in 1838.

The Convention, known also as the Baltalimanı Treaty, abolished state monopolies on a variety of goods and opened the doors of the Ottoman Empire to British merchants. The Anglo-Trade Convention was a prelude to attracting foreign commercial capital and investment and promoting the export-led growth of Western Anatolia. Even though the Ottoman government signed similar conventions with other European merchants, with the French at the end of 1838, the Hanseatic cities and Sardinia in 1839, the Netherlands, Belgium, Prussia, Spain, Sweden and Norway in 1840, and Denmark and Tuscany in 1841, British merchants took the lion's share of the region's imports and exports and remained the most influential of the European merchants in Izmir and its surroundings until the turn of the twentieth century.[43]

In the years following the Anglo-Ottoman Trade Convention of 1838, foreign merchants who set up businesses in Izmir also obtained better access to the city's surrounding hinterlands. Impressed by the opportunities Western Anatolia offered for the fig and grape business and aware of the increasing demand for these crops in European and North American markets, these far-sighted tradespeople spread their commercial and trading networks across the region. The number of foreign companies, agents and sub-agents specialising in transporting dried fruits to European markets grew in tandem with the expansion of fig and grape growing in the region. They formed partnerships, alliances and agreements with other foreign and local merchants, intermediaries and producers. In short, the 1838 Anglo-Ottoman Trade Convention was an important event in relation to the expansion of fig and grape growing in Western Anatolia and the building up of a symbiotic relationship between city and countryside. The Convention was a game changer in terms of creating an opportunity for not only British and other foreign merchants, but also wholesalers, agents, intermediaries, producers and all the other individuals who profited from the production and trade of figs and raisins.

43. Tengirşenk 1940, pp. 290–93; Geyikdağı 2011, pp. 23–24.

Fruits of Empire

Finally, the second half of the nineteenth century saw, as the major infrastructural project in Western Anatolia, the creation of a railroad network of hundreds of miles. When completed in 1866, the Izmir-Aydın and the Izmir-Kasaba (Turgutlu) railroads, the main lines of a larger network, altered urban and rural residents' relation with their environments and promoted the interchange between city and country. These two lines made it possible to move raw materials, agricultural products, foodstuffs, textiles, manufactured goods and so on over vast distances and at cheaper costs. The Western Anatolian railroad network continued to expand in the following years, stretching from Izmir to the interior. Within less than three decades, with eastward and north-ward extensions, the whole length of these two main lines and their branches covered a vast area, as far as Soma in the north and Afyonkarahisar in the east.

The railroads served as a major catalyst for the cultivation and export of figs and grapes in Western Anatolia in the last decades of the nineteenth century. It is no surprise that the principal fig and vine-growing districts were located along the railway lines between Izmir and the interior, because in the nineteenth century railroads were mainly built where commercial prospects were most rewarding. The railroads in Western Anatolia were no exception to this. Cities and towns along the Izmir–Aydın railway line and its extensions such as Nazilli, Bozdoğan, Söke, Karacasu, Çine, Ödemiş and Bayındır became the principal fig growing districts, while grape growing was commercially important in settlements along the Izmir–Kasaba line and its extensions such as Alaşehir, Manisa and Akhisar. 'From the heart of the town a railway starts', reported a European observer in 1890, 'running south to Ephesus and east-wards to Sarakeui [Sarayköy], and the traffic of the line depends largely on the fruit harvest', confirming the increasing importance of fig and vine growing in previously untapped areas along the railroad lines.[44]

The expansion of fig and vine growing in Western Anatolia increased the value of fig orchards and vineyards along the railroad lines and some foreign merchants hoped to make fortunes, not only through commercial agriculture but also through land speculation. The Ottoman government, aware of the increased interest of foreign merchants, investors and speculators in fig orchards and vineyards, began selling the *miri arazi* (public lands) in the vicinity of the railroad lines to these people. In 1880, the average price of arable land near market towns was £6 per acre and in thinly populated parts less than £1. The same amount of land with vineyards on it could be bought and sold for £10

44. 'The Smyrna Fig Harvest', p. 287.

and with orchards for at least £16.[45] About three decades later, the value of land more than tripled and was no less than £18 to £20 per acre.[46] Firmin Rougon, the French consul in Izmir, reported in 1885 that 1,000 to 1,500 acres of land suitable for the cultivation of vineyards was on sale in the vicinity of the Izmir-Aydın railroad line.[47]

Western Anatolian railroads, in short, traversed hundreds of miles along the fertile river valleys and served to tap the enormous potential of the region, bringing in figs and raisins. Railroads, nevertheless, did not eliminate the role of camel caravans in Western Anatolia. After the opening of the railways, camel caravans continued to exist and function mostly as 'feeders to the railway'.[48] For example, one commentator reported the arrival of camels loaded with figs in 1882 with the following words: 'Though the Aiden [Aydın] railway now transports great quantities, camels are still employed in their transportation'; he added, 'the consignees in Smyrna who have made advances to the growers during the year, dispose of the day's market supply, in an ordinary year 800 to 1,000 camels-loads of 400 lbs each'.[49]

From Nature to Market

In the second half of the nineteenth century, the growth of urban and rural population, the formation of urban-rural commercial networks, the regulation of land reclamation and use, and the construction of railroads all together encouraged fig and vine cultivation on a more organised and commercial basis. Izmir became indisputably the centre of the dried fruit trade in the Ottoman Empire and the number of individuals and companies involved in the fig and raisin business increased considerably. Commissioners, trade agents, dealers and moneylenders made the city the base for their commercial operations in Western Anatolia. As the production and trade of figs and grapes grew, the operations related to their picking, processing, packing and delivery expanded and diversified, providing employment for innumerable urban and rural residents.

---

45. 'Tenure and Produce of Land in Smyrna' *Journal of the Society of Arts* **28** (1880): 919.

46. Hamparzum 1908, p. 3.

47. Rougon 1892, p. 28.

48. Kurmuş 1977, p. 104.

49. Jeanne C. Carr, 'Concerning Figs', *The Pacific Rural Press*, 4 Mar. 1882.

Fig and raisin networks penetrated from Izmir to into the interior, with many entrepreneurs, merchants, artisans, local actors and middlemen involved.[50]

Figs and grapes promoted the transformation of the natural environment into a commodified landscape, contributed to the already-increasing interaction between the city and country and connected residents in either space to each other. What is so impressive about these crops, which shaped the Western Anatolian landscape in the nineteenth century, is not only their quantity, but also their quality and diversity. Both fruits were highly sought after for their flavour and shape. The fig produced in Western Anatolia had two major varieties. 'Bardacık',[51] or 'hurda', was a small fig with a thin skin that was largely consumed fresh locally, while 'lob', or 'sarı lob', or 'eleme', was a large fig mainly exported because it preserved its flavour and quality after drying.[52] Hurda figs were carried in 'yellow bags of ordinary sacking', while goat-hair bags were used for the transport of the lob figs.[53] The American botanist Gulian Pickering Rixford (1838–1930) described the lob fig as 'the sweetest and most luscious fig for consumption fresh and unequaled as a dried fruit'.[54] It was also called 'Calimyrna', or 'California Smyrna', because it was introduced to California and proved satisfactory in the 1880s.[55] The three varieties of raisins produced in the region, on the other hand, were *sultanas*, *rosakias* (red raisins), and black raisins.[56] Some sources also mention the production of Corinthian raisins, also known as *currants*, in the Foça district.[57] The seedless sultana raisins constituted more than ninety per cent of the entire production in Western Anatolia. Locals consumed only a small portion of the sultana raisins fresh or used them in bakeries; the rest of the produce was shipped to Britain, Austria, Hungary and Germany.[58] Rosakias and black raisins were very suitable for winemaking

---

50. For example, quite a number of businesses, occupations and professions are listed in trade catalogues and trade registries such as *Indicateur Commerciales, Annuaire Oriental du Commerce de l'industrie*, and *Indicateur des Professions Commerciales & Industrielle de Smyrne, de l'Anatolie* published in Izmir in the 1890s.

51. This name is a combination of two Turkish words; *bardak* (pitcher) and *cık* (tiny). The shape of the fig resembles that of a small pitcher.

52. 'The Smyrna Fig Harvest', 292; Hamparzum 1908, p. 3; Ravndal 1926, p. 103.

53. 'The Smyrna Fig Harvest', 292.

54. Rixford 1918, p. 35.

55. Condit 1947, p. 71; Howard 1900, p. 80.

56. Ravndal 1926, p. 104.

57. 'The Production of Smyrna Raisins', *Journal of the Society of Arts* 31 (1883): 1035–36.

58. Rougon 1892, p. 79.

and were therefore chiefly exported to France.[59] The best quality rosakias and black raisins were grown in Karaburun, followed by the second quality grown at Urla and Foça, and the third at Çeşme.[60]

Figure 1. Fig competition in Izmir. Image courtesy of Uğur Yeğin.

In nineteenth-century Western Anatolia, fig and grape shaped the region's social and economic landscape. The two crops were so important that, besides the four calendar-based seasons marked by changes in weather and climate, there were 'fig and grape seasons' that were based on local ecological, economic and social realities. During these seasons, farmers, labourers, merchants, dealers, agents, wholesalers and other men involved in the production and trade of the fig and raisin became bonded together around these crops. The fig season began with the ripening of figs in early summer and ended with the shipment of the last boxes of dried figs from the port of Izmir to Western Europe and North America in autumn. When figs ripened, wilted and partly dehydrated on the trees, they shrivelled and dropped to the ground. Before the harvest began, *bekçi*s (watchers) were hired and stationed in fig gardens to keep guard

---

59.   Ibid.; 'The Production of Smyrna Raisins', 1036; and Bauer 1933, p. 40.

60.   Ravndal 1926, p. 104.

day and night and secure the trees from pilferers.[61] The fig harvest took place between late August and early November and generally lasted about six weeks.[62] Inhabitants of the neighbouring villages or labourers were hired specifically for picking figs from the ground and then gathering, drying and sacking them crowded fig gardens. Men, women and children worked from sunrise to sunset; they gathered figs and piled them into baskets.[63] The fig harvest was a time of intense labour and a good opportunity to earn an income. An agricultural worker earned an average of fourteen cents a day, but during the time of harvest this amount could increase to a half a dollar.[64] Once the harvest was complete, the next process was fig drying, a process that lasted about a week in the hot September sun. The process of drying figs was an effective way to keep them fresh. After figs had been dipped in boiling salt solution, composed of three ounces of salt to one gallon of water, they were spread on wooden trays or mats and placed in the sun to dry. After a week or ten days, they were left in the shade for further curing.[65] When finally dried, figs were divided into first, second and third qualities and become ready to be moved.[66]

Once packed into bags, figs were handed over to *deveci*s, or camel drivers. Whether they had a quasi-intermediary role between the producer and purchaser or not is not clear, but it is clear that they were not just carriers of the product and their functions '[were] much wider than their name would suggest'.[67] A *deveci* was, indeed, more than a camel driver and his duty was not complete 'till a sale has been actually effected, the money received, and the figs

61. 'The Smyrna Fig Harvest', 289. Fig orchards were 'surrounded by walls, five to six feet high, made of dirt and covered on top with brush and thorny branches to keep out marauders during the harvest season' (Roeding 1903, p. 23).

62. 'Cultivation of the Fig in Turkey', *Journal of the Society of Arts* 29 (1880): 100; Heap 1884, p. 739; and Ravndal 1926, p. 103.

63. 'The Smyrna Fig Harvest', 289; 'Der Feigencultur- und Feigenhandel Smyrna's', *Österreichische Monatsschrift für den Orient* (1881): 14.

64. 'The Smyrna Fig Harvest', 290. Another account shows that there was not much change in daily wages over the years. According to this account from 1900, during the harvest season the women received four piasters (about sixteen dollar cents) and men eight piasters (about 32 dollar cents) per day, working twelve hours and boarding themselves (Roeding 1903, p. 31).

65. Djevad Sami Bey 1928, p, 18.

66. 'Cultivation of the Fig in Turkey', 100; 'Der Feigencultur- und Feigenhandel Smyrna's', 15.

67. 'The Smyrna Fig Harvest', 291.

handed over to the purchaser'.[68] *Deveci*s accompanied the camels as far as the nearest rail station, where the figs were 'put in the freight cars and conveyed to Smyrna'. There, the figs were loaded again on camels and sent to the fig market. At the market, they were purchased by the representatives of fig packing companies.[69] *Deveci*s, together with merchants, trade agents, moneylenders and other middlemen, were a part of a complex network of people involved in the purchase, transport and sale of figs and raisins.

The grape season coincided with the fig season and the methods of gathering, drying and sacking of grapes were simple and similar to figs. In the mid-summer, once collected, grapes were arranged on trays or spread on mats and left in the sun to dry. After nine to twelve days, the grapes needed to be turned over and kept in the sun three or four more days.[70] Oil was sprinkled on them 'to prevent evaporation of the moisture, and also to give the fruit, when packed and shipped, a better chance of preservation'.[71] Grapes, once dried into raisins, were ready to be marketed. From the vineyards, *deveci*s took over and brought the raisins to the nearest rail station in sacks. Special care was taken with these gunny bags and they were never packed on top of one another. In the wagons, there were shelves constructed for the figs and raisins, 'so there [was] absolutely no danger of pressure or jolting'.[72] Every year towards the end of July, before other varieties, sultanas appeared in the market. Rosakias and black raisins from Urla, Foça and Çeşme followed sultanas in the middle of September. Finally, the Karaburun rosakias and black raisins arrived at the end of September or the beginning of October. In other words, the three varieties of raisins arrived in the market 'in an inverse order to their quality'.[73]

Figs and raisins became a centrepiece of the city's economy and the leading export item of Western Anatolia by the 1870s (Table 1).[74] Heap recorded the arrival of 54,000 camel-loads of figs, each camel carrying four hundred pounds,

---

68. Ibid.

69. William Stewart Emmett, 'Value of exports from the consular district of Smyrna to the United States during the four quarters of the year ended June' (15 Jan. 1890) *Fruit Culture in Foreign Countries. Reports from the Consuls of the United States on Fruit Culture in their Several Districts, in Answer to a Circular from the Department of State* (Washington DC: Government Printing Office, 1890), p. 738.

70. Djevad Sami Bey 1928, p, 20.

71. Witherby 1873, 585.

72. 'The Fig Industry of Smyrna', *Journal of the Society of Arts* 57 (1908): 753.

73. 'The Production of Smyrna Raisins', 1036.

74. Quataert 1981, pp. 71–72.

in October 1882. 'Fifteen years before that time', he said, 'not more than half that amount was recorded for the whole season'.[75] Heap noted that in 1881, in one night only, 'no fewer than 195,000 barrels, cases, bags, boxes, drums, and baskets of figs and raisins' were shipped from Izmir.[76] Heap's calculation seems to be realistic, because the French consul had noted the 1861 crop as 23,000 loads and 1862 as 35,000.[77] The value of figs exported from Izmir quadrupled in four decades and exceeded 30,000 tons, i.e., 140,000 loads, per annum in 1908.[78] More strikingly, the increase in fig prices by seventy per cent between 1891 and 1908 made fig growing a profitable enterprise in Western Anatolia.[79]

Table 1. Annual average quantity of fig exports from Izmir (1876–1908)

YEARS	EXPORTS (tons)
1876 – 1880	8,642
1881 – 1885	12,370
1886 – 1890	--
1891 – 1895	--
1896 – 1900	13,982
1901 – 1905	21,107
1906 – 1908	30,450

Source: Quataert, 'Ottoman Reform and Agriculture in Anatolia', 301.

Raisin production in Western Anatolia, despite fluctuations, rose steadily in the second half of the nineteenth century and, according to the reports of US consuls in Izmir, reached its climax in 1884 with 95,000 tons of raisins (Table 2). Firmin Rougon, the French consul in Izmir, calculated that the amount of raisin exports from September 1885 to August 1886 exceeded 33,000 tons and from September 1886 to August 1887 40,500 tons.[80] Gustav Eisen claimed that the Western Anatolian region was in second place in Europe in the world's raisin production in 1889 and supplied about 38 per cent of raisins in the world

75. Heap 1884, p. 738.
76. Ibid., p. 739.
77. Issawi 1980, p. 261.
78. Quataert 1981, p. 72.
79. Quataert 1973, pp. 300–1.
80. Rougon 1892, p. 80.

Onur İnal

Table 2. Raisin exports from Izmir (1844–1884)

YEAR HARVESTED	PRODUCTION (tons) (Eisen)	PRODUCTION (tons) (Kasaba)
1844	6,000 to 8,000	
1845		7,433
1846		2,843
1847		3,565
1848		2,357
1849		2,630
1850		2,117
1851		4,312
1852		8,058
1853		15,049
1854		13,984
1855		7,899
1856		4,607
1857		5,614
1858		4,821
1859		11,828
1860		6,510
1861		11,249
1862		6,870
1863		9,491
1864		7,455
1865		8,181
1866		4,825
1867		4,888
1868	19,000	13,150
1869		9,804
1870		27,534
1871	48,000	27,860
1872	31,000	39,981
1873		38,812
1874		31,497
1875		40,438
1876	27,000	45,925
1877		
1878		
1879	75,000	
1880		
1881	49,000	
1882		
1883		
1884	95,000	

Source: Eisen, *The Raisin Industry*, pp. 176–77, and Kasaba, *The Ottoman Empire*, p. 126

Fruits of Empire

markets.[81] In that year, as Rougon calculated, raisin exports reached 56,000 tons.[82] Britain had the largest share of raisin exports from Izmir, followed by Austria, Germany and France. Black raisins from Karaburun and Urla were especially favoured in the markets in Britain and its colonies.[83] These small grapes contained a large proportion of saccharine, and therefore were 'much valued by British wine-makers'.[84] The production of wine from black raisins of Western Anatolia was very popular in France during the years when phylloxera disease decimated the French grape crop. The value of black raisins exported into France was 642,000 Francs in 1873; the figure increased to 11,041,560 Francs in 1879 and 14,486,840 Francs in 1880.[85]

Packing for the Market

In nineteenth-century Western Anatolia, figs and raisins meant a lot to urban and rural residents and were the evidence of an emerging city-hinterland symbiosis, a mutually reinforcing economic, social and environmental development. 'So intimate was the connection with the rural hinterland', as Roger Owen has stated, 'that it is certainly wrong to think of the city as belonging to a different economic and political order'.[86] The fortunes of the fig or raisin merchant, wholesaler and dealer were tightly linked with the fortunes of farmers and producers. There was a mutual interdependence between the merchant who sold the Smyrna figs and raisins to Europe and the wage labourer who worked in the orchards and vineyards. Figs and raisins were so vital to the city's trade and prosperity that the arrival of the first figs from the country was always celebrated as a popular festival, in which fig-laden camels were 'followed by a throng of shouting people to the fruit market'.[87] This excitement was due to the fact that 'a large number of poor families in Smyrna obtain their total

---

81. Eisen 1890, p. 177.

82. Rougon 1892, p. 78.

83. Witherby 1873, p. 586.

84. Ibid.

85. 'Smyrna raisins', *Journal of the Society of Arts* 1554 (1882): 964.

86. Owen 1981, p. 45.

87. 'Smyrna Figs', *The Times* (3 Oct. 1888): 4. The 'fig festival' was celebrated for about five decades from the 1880s to the 1930s. It was held near the Alsancak Train Station in the last week of August every year. For more information on the festival, see Ziya 1928, pp. 48–49; Atilla 2002, p. 139; and Anaç 2014, pp. 118–27.

Figure 2. Sorting the figs, Izmir. Image courtesy of Uğur Yeğin.

livelihood during the fig season'.[88] Fig packing and processing was perhaps the best industry in which to find seasonal employment and one could make 'enough money in the three to four months' packing season to live throughout the winter'.[89] Male labourers in the fruit-packing industry earned ten to twenty piastres in return for ten hours of work per day, while females were paid about a half of the amount paid to males. The wages were not high; even so, labourers in the fig-packing industry in the city earned double what their fellows in the rural districts did.[90]

After purchase, the figs were brought to factories or packing establishments owned by the shipping and packing companies and emptied out on the floor in a square heap. There, labourers of both sexes, but mostly women and children, who specialised in stringing figs, were employed (Figure 2). For example, some 1,500 labourers were employed in the 'Camel Brand' factories

---

88. Ibid.

89. 'The Fig Industry of Smyrna', *Journal of the Society of Arts* **57** (1909): 754.

90. S. Stab, 'Labour and Wages in the Province of Smyrna', *Journal of the Society of Arts* **33** (1885): 637.

Fruits of Empire

Figure 3. Sorting the figs, Izmir. Image courtesy of Uğur Yeğin.

Figure 4. Ottoman men packing the figs in boxes, Izmir. Image courtesy of Uğur Yeğin.

of Aram Hamparzum in 1908.[91] In the factories, fig workers flattened each fig with their fingers 'to render it soft, and give it the required oblong form'.[92] On the heap was a row of low baskets, which were used to separate the figs of first and second quality (Figure 3). The undersized, tough, or spotted figs, which were at least ten per cent, were thrown in a separate heap for domestic consumption.[93] The figs were then laid on long benches occupied by the practised packers. They packed the figs swiftly and dexterously in boxes that lay in front of them (Figure 4).[94]

Fig packing, however, was not new to the second half of the nineteenth century. European travellers had observed the business of fig and raisin packing much earlier.[95] For example, Godfrey Levinge had noted in 1839 the arrival of 'strings of loaded camels', which were 'piled with figs.' The camels deposited their loads in the courtyards of merchants' houses, he observed, adding, 'where a number of women and children, who are squatted round the heaps, proceeded to pick the figs from the branches and leaves; then they pack them into drums, sprinkling each separate layer with sea water'.[96] What was new to the 1870s and 1880s was that the old-fashioned style of 'drum' packing was replaced by a newer mode of packing figs in rows and layers explained above. This mode, called 'pulled' packing, was preferred by merchants because it gave each fig a larger appearance and improved the chance of marketing in Europe.[97] When the packing was completed, finally, the boxes were again passed on to the women, who 'complete the process by placing laurel leaves between the upper rows before the final nailing down and polishing off by the carpenter.'[98]

The manner of packing raisins also had to meet the requirements of purchasers or consumers. The best quality rosakias were packed in wooden boxes of thirty pounds, except for Russia, where they were delivered in barrels of 250 pounds each. The cheaper sultana raisins were sent to Austria in boxes of twelve pounds and to Britain of 22 pounds. They were sent to Germany and the Netherlands in cases of thirty and sixty pounds. Black raisins, on the other

---

91.   Hamparzum 1908, p. 15.

92.   'Cultivation of the Fig in Turkey', 100.

93.   Ibid., pp. 100–01.

94.   Ibid., p. 101.

95.   MacFarlane 1829, pp. 64–65; Madden 1829, vol. 1, pp. 147–48.

96.   Levinge 1839, pp. 218–19.

97.   Witherby 1873, 586.

98.   Ibid.

hand, were exported in large barrels of 370 pounds each.[99] For both sellers and buyers, it was important to assure that the merchandise was weighted precisely. Scale-making developed as a new line of manufacturing and there were eleven scale-makers in the city in 1895.[100] Their profits depended on those of the fig and raisin market every year.

Consumer preferences in Europe also played a role in the variety of raisin produced in the region. In the second half of the nineteenth century, there was a 'decided trend toward the producing of sultanas' because of the increased demand in Europe for the seedless type of raisins.[101] In the years 1900–1904, with an annual average of 34,700 tons, sultana raisins constituted seventy per cent of the total raisin exports from Izmir. This figure increased to 43,500 tons and 86 per cent in the years 1906–1910.[102] It is also important to note that not all grapes were dried and marketed as raisins. Grapes were also eaten fresh or used to make *şıra* (grape juice), *pekmez* (grape molasses), wine and distilled liquors such as *rakı*. There were at least twenty distilleries, thirty wine and liqueur makers and eighteen bottling facilities in Izmir in the 1890s, all belonging to non-Muslims.[103]

The promotional role of displaying products was important in a market in which Smyrna figs and raisins competed with other varieties produced across the Mediterranean. Aware of the important role the box of figs or raisins might play in grabbing the attention of the prospective buyers, merchants and marketers introduced new packing ideas and concepts. For example, Aram Hamparzum, an Armenian merchant, was the first to do away with labelling the boxes with marking ink, 'which by the slightest contact with moisture, not only soiled the hands but dirted the box to such an extent that it was no more presentable' and to introduce 'stenciling', a more modern style of marking the

99. Heap 1884, p. 731.
100. *Indicateur des Professions Commerciales & Industrielle de Smyrne, de l'Anatolie etc.* 1895, p. 110.
101. Bauer 1933, pp. 41–42.
102. Ibid.
103. *Indicateur des Professions Commerciales & Industrielle de Smyrne, de l'Anatolie etc.* 1893, p. 345; *Indicateur des Professions Commerciales & Industrielle de Smyrne, de l'Anatolie etc.* 1895, pp. 111–12. The production and consumption of alcohol was banned for Muslims in the Ottoman Empire. Non-Muslims, however, were tolerated and given permission to produce everything from wine to *rakı* and consume them at home or in *meyhanes* (taverns), to which Muslims also went, despite the prohibitions, as we know from the fact that they were repeatedly punished for doing so.

lid with a red hot stamp.[104] Hamparzum later improved on the style of boxes and ordered his 'Skeleton cases' to be manufactured 'to close on all sides without any gap whatever', making sure their contents were 'well protected against dust and dirt during the voyage'.[105] The manufacture of boxes and packing cases for figs and raisins required expertise. *Kutuculuk* (box-making) emerged as a new line of business in the centre of Izmir. Nine manufacturers are listed under the name 'cardboard boxes and timber for dried fruits' in the commercial almanac of 1893.[106] Later, box-makers became organised under the umbrella of the Fig and Raisin Box-Makers Artisan and Workers Association (Üzüm ve İncir Kutucu Esnaf ve Amele Cemiyeti).[107]

Figs and grapes transformed the Western Anatolian landscape and became the mainstay of thousands of urban and rural residents in the second half of the nineteenth century. Producers in the country shifted from cereals and cotton towards figs and raisins and this shift manifested itself in the diversity of urban occupations. As the examples above show, manufacturers oriented their business around figs and raisins and became much more depended on by producers and farmers in the countryside than ever before.

Conclusion

The decades from the 1840s to the 1890s saw major social, economic and ecological changes in Western Anatolia. In this period, the amount of land under cultivation expanded rapidly, agricultural output increased and the region transformed into an export-oriented agrarian economy, which benefited from growing trade with Western Europe. As a result, Izmir, a city that once turned its back on its surrounding hinterlands, found itself at the heart of an agricultural boom. The city experienced a phenomenal commercial growth, a growth making it a major outlet for the agricultural produce of Western Anatolia.

In this paper, using environmental history as a methodological tool, I have tried to provide a new interpretation of Izmir's growth and prosperity in tandem with Western Anatolia in the late nineteenth century. I have analysed complex sets of relationships among urban and rural residents, resources, animals, places and technologies to reconstruct not only the process of Western

---

104. Hamparzum 1908, p. 11.

105. Ibid.

106. *Indicateur des Professions Commerciales & Industrielle de Smyrne, de l'Anatolie etc.* 1893, p. 273.

107. Özgün 2014, p. 229.

Fruits of Empire

Anatolia's integration into the market economy, but also the city's integration with the Western Anatolian countryside through the stories of figs and raisins. I have drawn attention to how the increased interaction between human and natural actors within the city and its surrounding country in the late nineteenth century created an interdependent space, in which urban and rural people shared the products and commodities they produced and consumed; and suggested that figs and raisins were significant – yet previously overlooked – historical actors that figured prominently in the connected tales of city and countryside in nineteenth century Western Anatolia.

From an environmental point of view, figs and raisins were, indeed, the two commodities that linked rural people with urban residents. These two crops contributed to the remarkable growth of Izmir and transformed the social, economic and environmental landscape of Western Anatolia. It would not be an exaggeration to claim that no other crop has influenced and dominated Izmir and its hinterlands as much as figs and raisins in the late nineteenth century. The two crops, furthermore, left not only an imprint that shaped the urban and rural landscape in Western Anatolia in late Ottoman Empire, but a legacy that also contributed to the foundations for a national economic and social order in the Turkish Republic. Co-operative unions formed in Izmir in 1915 for the sales of figs and raisins, and then also cotton and olive oil, evolved into an umbrella-organisation called the TARİŞ in early republican period. The TARİŞ has since functioned as a state-owned – and only recently as an autonomous – enterprise to look out for the interests of dozens of cooperatives and thousands of fig and raisin producers in Western Anatolia. Figs and raisins have continued to be Western Anatolia's most important export to the present day.

Bibliography

Unpublished Primary Sources

Accounts and Papers of the House of Commons, London

Published Primary Sources

Harper's New Monthly Magazine.
Journal of the Society of Arts
Österreichische Monatsschrift für den Orient
The Pacific Rural Press
The Times (London)

Cochran, William. 1887. *Pen and Pencil in Asia Minor; or Notes from the Levant*. London: S. Low, Marston, Searle & Rivington.

Eisen, Gustave. 1890. *The Raisin Industry*. San Francisco: HS Crocker and Co.

Fruit Culture in Foreign Countries. Reports from the Consuls of the United States on Fruit Culture in their Several Districts, in Answer to a Circular from the Department of State. Washington DC: Government Printing Office, 1890.

Hamparzum, Aram. 1908. *Something Interesting About Smyrna Figs*. New York: Hills Brother Co.

Heap, Gwynne Harris. 1884. 'Fruit Culture in Turkey'. *United States Consular Reports* 41 (5): 726–40.

Howard, Leland Ossian. 1900. 'Smyrna Fig Culture in the United States', in *U.S. Department of Agriculture Yearbook*. Washington DC. pp. 79–106.

Indicateur des Professions Commerciales & Industrielle de Smyrne, de l'Anatolie etc. 1895. Izmir.

Indicateur des Professions Commerciales & Industrielle de Smyrne, de l'Anatolie etc. 1893. Izmir.

Levinge, Godfrey. 1839. *The Traveler in the East*. London.

MacFarlane, Charles. 1829. *Constantinople in 1828, A Residence of Sixteen Months in the Turkish Capital and Provinces*. London: Saunders and Otley.

Madden, Richard Robert. 1829. *Travels in Turkey, Egypt, Nubia, and Palestine, vol. 1*, 2 vols. London: Colburne.

Rixford, Gulian Pickering. 1918. *Smyrna Fig Culture*. Washington, DC: US Dept. of Agriculture.

Roeding, George Christian. *1903. The Smyrna Fig: At Home and Abroad: A Treatise on Practical Fig*. Fresno, CA.

Rougon, Firmin. 1892. *Smyrne: Situation Commerciale et Économique*. Paris: Berger Levrault.

Ubicini, Abdolonyme. 1856. *Letters on Turkey, vol. 1*, 2 vols. London: John Murray.

Van Lennep, Henry John. 1870. *Travels in Little Known Parts of Asia Minor, vol. 2*, 2 vols. New York: Van Lennep, 1870.

Secondary Sources

Anaç, Hilmi. 2014. 'Unutulan İncir Bayramları Üzerine'. In Naim Özdamar (ed.), *Aydın'ın Balı İncir*. Aydın: İncirliova Ziraat Odası Yayını. pp. 118–27.

Anagnostopoulou, Sia. 1988. Μικρά Ασία 19ος αι.-1919 οι ελληνορθόδοξες κοινότητες [*Mikrá Asía, 19os ai.-1919: oi ellênorthódoxes koinótêtes: apó to Millét tôn Rômiôn sto ellênikó éthnos*]. Athens: Ellenika Grammata.

Atilla, A. Nedim. 2002. İzmir Demiryolları. Izmir: İzmir Büyükşehir Belediyesi Kent Kitaplığı.

Bauer, Walter. 1933. *Foreign Production, Trade, and Government Aid in the Raisin and Currant Industry*. Berkeley, CA: University of California.

Cumo, Christopher. (ed.) 2013. *Encyclopedia of Cultivated Plants: From Acacia to Zinnia, vol. 2*, 3 vols. Santa Barbara, CA: ABC-CLIO.

Fruits of Empire

Collingwood, Francis and John Woolams. 1792. *The Universal Cook and City and Country Housekeeper.* London: R. Noble.

Condit, Ira Judson. 1947. *The Fig.* Waltham, MA: Chronica Botanica.

Djevad Sami Bey. 1928 'The Smyrna Fig and Raisin Industry'. *Levant Trade Review* **16** (1): 17–21.

Dursun, Selçuk. 2007. 'Forest and the State: History of Forestry and Forest in the Ottoman Empire'. Ph.D. Diss., Istanbul: Sabancı University.

Eldem, Edhem, Daniel Goffman and Bruce Masters (eds). 1999. *The Ottoman City between East and West: Aleppo, Izmir, and Istanbul.* Cambridge: Cambridge University Press.

Frangakis-Syrett, Elena. 1993. 'Patras'. *Review* **16**: 411–34.

Geyikdağı, V. Necla. 2011. *Foreign Investment in the Ottoman Empire.* London: I.B. Tauris.

Gökbayrak, Zeliha and Gökhan Söylemezoğlu. 2010. 'Grapevine throughout the History of Anatolia'. *International Journal of Botany* **6** (4): 465–72.

Gordon, Leland J. 1931. *American Relations with Turkey, 1830–1930: An Economic Interpretation.* Philadelphia: University of Pennsylvania Press.

Hunt, Alisa. 2016. *Reviving Roman Religion: Sacred Trees in the Roman World.* Cambridge: Cambridge University Press.

İnal, Onur. 2015. 'A Port and Its Hinterland: An Environmental History of Izmir in the Late Ottoman Period'. Ph.D. Diss., Tucson: University of Arizona.

———. 2018. 'The Making of an Eastern Mediterranean Gateway City: Izmir in the Nineteenth Century'. *Journal of Urban History*: 1–18. doi: 10.1177/0096.

İslamoğlu, Huri. 2000. 'Property as a Contested Domain: A Reevaluation of the Ottoman Land Code of 1858'. In Roger Owen (ed.), *New Perspectives on Property and Land in the Middle East.* Cambridge, MA: Center for Middle Eastern Studies of Harvard University. pp. 3–63.

Issawi, Charles. 1980. *The Economic History of Turkey, 1800–1914.* Chicago: University of Chicago Press.

Kasaba, Reşat, Çağlar Keyder and Faruk Tabak. 1986. 'Eastern Mediterranean Port Cities and Their Bourgeoisies: Merchants, Political Projects, and Nation-States'. *Review* **10** (1): 121–35.

Kasaba, Reşat. 1988. *The Ottoman Empire and the World Economy: The Nineteenth Century.* Albany, NY: State University of New York Press.

Keyder, Çağlar, Y. Eyüp Özveren and Donald Quataert. 1993. 'Port-Cities in the Ottoman Empire. Some Theoretical and Historical Perspectives'. *Review* **16** (4): 519–57.

Kohlenberger, John R. (ed.) 2004. *The Contemporary Bible.* Oxford: Oxford University Press.

Kurmuş, Orhan. 1977. *Emperyalizmin Türkiye'ye Girişi,* 2nd ed. Istanbul: Bilim Yayınları.

———. 1987. 'The Cotton Famine and its Effects on the Ottoman Empire'. In Huri İslamoğlu-İnan (ed.), *The Ottoman Empire and the World-Economy.* Cambridge: Cambridge University Press. pp. 160–69.

Mazzoni, Cristina. 2016. *She-Wolf: The Story of a Roman Icon.* Cambridge: Cambridge University Press.

Owen, Roger. 1981. *The Middle East in the World Economy, 1800–1914*. London: Methuen.

Özgün, Cihan. 2014. *Bereketli Topraklarda Üretmek ve Paylaşmak: İzmir ve Çevresinde Ticari Tarım (1844–1914)*. Izmir: İzmir Büyükşehir Belediyesi.

Pamuk, Şevket. 1987. *The Ottoman Empire and European Capitalism, 1820–1913: Trade, Investment, and Production*. Cambridge: Cambridge University Press.

Quataert, Donald. 1973. 'Ottoman Reform and Agriculture in Anatolia'. Ph.D. Diss., Los Angeles: University of California.

———. 1981. 'Agricultural Trends and Government Policy in Ottoman Anatolia, 1800–1914'. *Asian and African Studies* 15: 69–84.

Ravndal, Gabriel Bie. 1926. *Turkey: A Commercial and Industrial Handbook*. Washington DC: Government Print Office.

Reimer, Michael. 1991. 'Ottoman-Arab Seaports in the Nineteenth Century: Social Change in Alexandria, Beirut, Tunis'. In Reşat Kasaba (ed.), *Cities in the World-System*. New York: Greenwood Press. pp. 135–56.

Tabak, Faruk. 2008. *The Waning of the Mediterranean, 1550–1870*. Baltimore: John Hopkins University Press.

Tengirşenk, Yusuf Kemal. 1940. 'Tanzimat Dönemi'nde Osmanlı Devleti'nin Harici Ticari Siyaseti'. In Ahmed Hamid Ongunsu (ed.), *Tanzimat I*. Istanbul: Maarif Matbaası. pp. 289–320.

Themopoulou, Emilia. 2002. 'The Urbanisation of an Asia Minor City. The Example of Smyrna'. In Paschalis Kitromilides et al. (eds), Σμύρνη: η Μητρόπολη του Μικρασιατικού Ελληνισμού [Smyrnē: hē mētropolē tou mikrasiatikou Hellēnismou] = *Smyrna: Metropolis of the Asia Minor Greeks*. Athens: Ephesos, 2002. pp. 41–91.

Toksöz, Meltem. 2004. 'Ottoman Mersin: The Making of an Eastern Mediterranean Port-town'. *New Perspectives on Turkey* 31: 71–90.

———. 2010. *Nomads, Migrants and Cotton in the Eastern Mediterranean: The Making of the Adana-Mersin Region, 1850–1908*. Leiden: Brill.

Wood, Alfred C. 1935. *A History of the Levant Company*. London: Oxford University Press.

Ziya, Mehmet. 1928. *İncir*. Izmir: Bilgi Matbaacılık.

Zoch, Paul A. 2012. *Ancient Rome: An Introductory History*. Norman: University of Oklahoma Press.

Chapter 5

'IT'S A BAD FATE TO BE BORN NEAR A FOREST': FOREST, PEOPLE AND BUFFALOES IN MID-NINETEENTH CENTURY NORTH-WESTERN ANATOLIA

Semih Çelik

Introduction

Historians of the Middle East, and of the Ottoman Empire in particular, have long scrutinised the relationship between actors, networks and structures in their quests to answer historical questions. Whereas attention has long been devoted to human actors, and institutions and structures produced by them, historians have recently expanded their scholarly interest towards non-human actors such as animals, plants, mountains, rivers and all other components of nature. The roles of geography, climate and non-human actors have gained equal significance in answering questions regarding the past cultural and economic lives of Ottoman communities.[1] Despite their contributions to an emerging historiographical trend in Ottoman history, scholars have usually tended to reproduce narratives that considered non-human actors within property relations that served the interests of their owners.[2] While it is mostly true that environmental resources were of important property value, pre-industrial (and even industrial) societies developed a mixed valuation process whereby social, cultural and economic lives of a community were determined by not only a market economy, but also an emotional economy of intimacy between various

---

1. For thorough reconsideration of the historiography see Mikhail 2012; İnal 2018.
2. This is especially true for animals as they were of important exchange value throughout centuries. See examples in Faroqhi 2010.

human and non-human actors and eco-religious values[3] that blended religious and ecological valuation processes.[4] Therefore, the relationship between human and non-human actors within a pre-industrial context requires going beyond the market and taxation-oriented discourses of the archival material the Ottoman institutions produced.

As an attempt at going beyond limitations of the literature and the archival sources, in this article, I would like to focus on a development that took place in North-western Anatolian villages, particularly in the Kocaeli district (*sancak*). Briefly, this article scrutinises the reactions of *kerestekeşan* (woodcutter)[5] villagers to the increasing demand for timber, requiring enormous amounts of human and animal labour, particularly that of buffaloes in the 1850s. Doing so, I would like to demonstrate how the relationship between animals, human beings and nature was altered in relation to the development of politics of natural resource and labour management in the middle of the nineteenth century, in a particular part of the Empire. Despite their seemingly insignificant characteristics and minor importance, these developments firstly had longer-term consequences, and secondly marked the agency of Ottoman peasants in the shaping of Ottoman state's policies towards natural 'resources' and towards the environment in general. Furthermore, and more importantly,

---

3. Beinart 2000, pp. 269–302.

4. Callon and Çalışkan (2009, pp. 369–98 and 2010, pp. 1–32) offer a new trait in researching 'economy' as a consequence of processes of 'economisation' that, to put it briefly, referred to the 'broader movements that bring the economic into being'. Those movements contain not only 'rational' valuation processes suggested by classical economic theories, but also encompass concrete emotional, textual, technical and moral elements that determined economy's organisation. For an empirical example of such a study, see Çalışkan 2010.

5. The *kerestekeşan* system refers to a centuries-old practice of forced mobilisation of mountain and forest villagers for the felling and transportation of timber to meet the needs of Ottoman public institutions, mostly for the Imperial dockyards. In exchange for the corvée, the villagers were exempted from the certain extraordinary taxes and, by the first half of the nineteenth century, the tree trunks were bought by the state from the village representatives, however with a symbolic price. Each village had a previously set amount of timber due to be brought to the nearest docks. Those who could not meet the demand had to pay for the remaining part. The system remained more or less unchanged, though with local variations according to the local geographic and climatic requirements, until the mid-nineteenth century. The literature on the *kerestekeşan* system is yet to develop. The few accounts that seek to explain it do not refer to the corvée: see Baş 2016, pp. 152–53. Suraiya Faroqhi, on the other hand, has pointed to the forced aspect of the labour provided in serving the state, expecially in mines, without explicitly referring to the *kerestekeşan* system (Faroqhi 2009, pp. 53–54).

the reactions of the villagers suggest conclusions that fit into a larger discussion on the transformation of energies that determined the direction industrialising economies had taken throughout the nineteenth century. According to Edward Anthony Wrigley, transformation of energy sources from an agriculture-based organic economy to a mineral-based economy marked the passage of Britain to an industrial economy. This required a 'disturbance' in the relationship between humans and non-humans.[6] Similarly, Alan Mikhail's account of animal-human relationships at the turn of the nineteenth century in Egypt suggests the advent of a quest for a new energy regime. An important period of change, 1790–1830, marked the passage from an animal-based labour force to one based on human labour.[7] The case of the buffalo of *kerestekeşan* villagers in North-western Anatolia, however, suggests that necessary energy for construction projects was, almost until the last quarter of the nineteenth century, extracted through the intense relationship between humans and non-humans. Whereas in Egypt the role of cattle diminished due to a 'top-down' process of waves of epizootics and revaluation of land and human labour over that of animals, in the North-western Anatolian case, a relatively bottom-up process persisted of getting rid of buffalo to survive against the state's insistence on keeping corvée based on buffalo and human labour. Despite efforts of the *kerestekeş* villagers the corvée system survived the century and continued into the early decades of the next.

The story in the following pages took place in the sub-districts and villages of Kocaeli district of the empire, albeit not limited to that area. The district was famous, with its forests defined as a sea of forest (*ağaç denizi*). The sixteenth-century geographer Aşık Mehmed (1555/57–1698) stated that 'even if the whole world had come together, it would be impossible to cut all its trees down till the end of time'.[8] The forests provided the raw material for the shipbuilding industry of the workshops in Gemlik and Izmit sub-districts, as

---

6. Wrigley 2016.

7. Mikhail 2013a. Also, for a long-term and larger scale analysis of changes in animal labour in the Middle East, see Bulliet 2012.

8. '… ve bu nehrün havalisi ağaç denizi dimekle ma'ruf cebel-i dûr ü dirâz ve gayza ve bî-şe-zardur ki eşcar-ı kûhisin kat' içün halk-ı âlem içtima itse inkıta'-ı ezmana dek itmamı müyesser değüldür' (Âşık Mehmed 2007, vol. 3, p. 263). The famous Ottoman traveller Evliya Çelebi states that the sun did not penetrate under the trees, and those who were not used to such darkness became easy prey for wild beasts (Evliya Çelebi 1993, vol. 2, pp. 741–42).

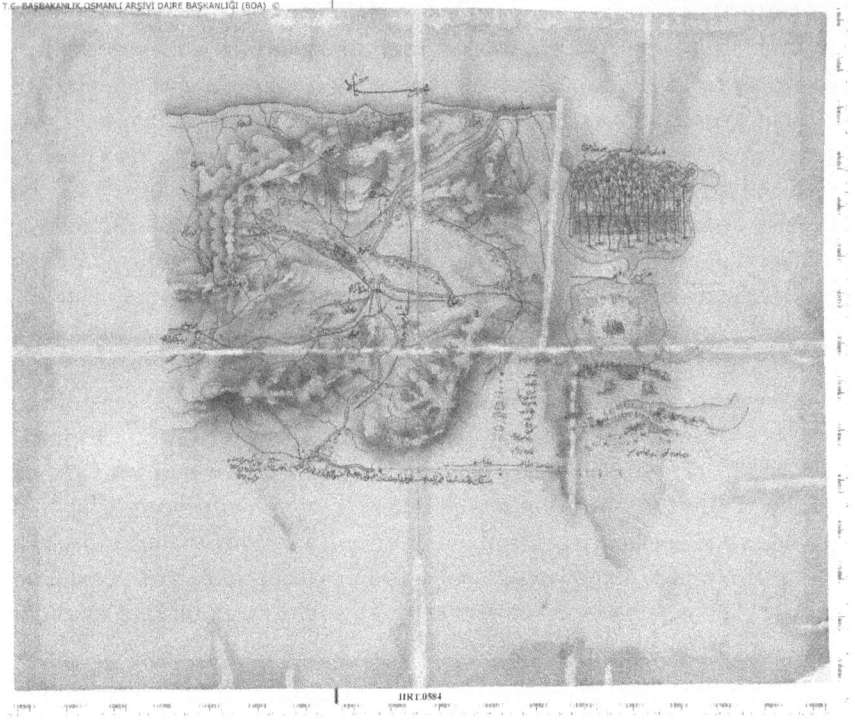

Map 1. The Kocaeli district in the late Ottoman period, 1884 (Source BOA, HRT.h 584; public domain), Note the detail on the upper right corner that depicts the Harmantepe fortress, almost lost among dense trees. Today, almost no trees remain around the fortress.

well as the imperial dockyards in Istanbul for centuries.[9] The advent of wood also made the district a source for the charcoal that warmed the capital city. If one defining aspect of the landscape and the economy of the district was its dense forests,[10] the other one was the Sakarya River that fed the valleys, making agriculture possible (Map 1). Equally important was the role of the river in transportation. Whereas administrative division and borders of the Kocaeli

9.   According to Tuncay Zorlu, Ottomans had relatively better access to timber. However, the amount of forest in Kocaeli province dramatically decreased from that needed to build ten galleys to the amount for seven galleys by the end of the seventeenth century, due to heavy clearance during the sixteenth and seventeenth centuries. See Zorlu 2008, pp. 3–4, 17.

10. Baş 2016; Narin 2011.

district changed many times over the three decades under scrutiny here, the forest economy defined the administrative relationship between the coastal town centres and the mountainous hinterland. To put it differently, in managing natural resources, the Naval Council in Istanbul had more responsibility and authority than the local councils of sub-districts in the Kocaeli district. For the Naval Council, natural resources and labour pool mattered more than administrative borders.

Therefore, for centuries, the social and economic life of the district and its vicinities was formed around woodcutting and its transportation to the nearest docks. The need to breed cattle (buffaloes particularly) for dragging and transporting wood and timber tied the lives of animals, rivers, trees and human beings tightly together.[11] However, this forest and buffalo-oriented economy had to be controlled and manipulated by the Ottoman administrators in order to achieve large-scale ship and infrastructure building projects with the least cost and in the quickest way possible. The *kerestekeşan* system that required forest villages to provide the necessary human and animal power to cut trees down and transport them to the nearest docks in exchange with exemption from certain extraordinary taxes, was established from time immemorial (*kadimden*). This system seems to have worked with only minor problems until the early to mid-nineteenth century,[12] when large-scale projects of ship and infrastructure building required clearance of large areas of forests and mass mobilisation of human and animal power. Peasants who were forced to work as woodcutters and transporters reacted to these developments in various ways, challenging

---

11. The history of buffaloes among other bovines in North-western Anatolia needs further research. However, archaeological research suggests that buffaloes were rather rare in central and western Anatolia in comparison to the Arabian Peninsula, until the fifteenth and sixteenth centuries. Buffalo was a breed whose breeding Ottoman administrators promoted and they were among the most valued cattle by the nineteenth century. See Hongo 1997. Xavier de Planhol argues that the culture of using bovines as beasts of burden was as common in the west of Kurdistan as in the east by the seventeenth century (De Planhol 1969, p. 317). Compare with Faroqhi 2010, p. 12, Mikhail 2013b and Tabak 2008, p. 26.

12. Zorlu claims that, by the late eighteenth century onwards, the Ottoman Empire had developed well-organised timber management and was rich in skilled human power for the felling and transportation of timber. This was due to change by the second half of the nineteenth century. Zorlu 2008, pp. 15–18. Zorlu's study nowhere mentions the cattle or buffaloes that were of such crucial importance for the felling and transportation of timber.

the political economy of forest and natural resource 'management' behind such policies.[13]

The actors within this story are human beings and buffaloes forced to work by the Ottoman state. Despite similar cases in the past, those who were bound by the system after the 1826 abolition of the janissaries, who held major roles in the organisation of the *kerestekeşan* system, had more space to challenge it. Adding to local climatic and demographic changes, overexploitation of trees, human and animal labour became an issue of conflict between the Ottoman state and the villagers in and around the district. The reflection of this conflict in official correspondence makes it possible to reconstruct the story of exploitation and resistance. However, textual narration of events and ideas in the official documents from the period reflects the bias of Ottoman state. Documents concerning the *kerestekeşan* system, especially from the 1830s onwards, employ a discourse that justifies overexploitation of both forests and animal and human labour on the basis of the prosperity of the empire. Building of naval ships and later roads were necessary for the wellbeing of the empire. However, when put together aside with (a few) other sources, the discourses and actions of *kerestekeş* villagers become more visible. Conflict and resistance can be read between the lines.

Cutting Woods, Prospering the Empire – A Non-Reacted Venture?

The 1830s and 1840s witnessed a significant increase in requests for raw wood and timber from the North-western Anatolian forests by the imperial dockyards, mainly for the building of two royal vessels, and further due to the need for construction projects.[14] The idea of 'improvement' (*nafia*) became institutionalised throughout roughly the decades between the 1830s and 1860s

---

13. Compare with Dursun 2007.
14. See Prime Ministry Ottoman Archives (*Başbakanlık Osmanlı Arşivleri, BOA*), ŞD.d. 1–4 (1869). As the economy was in transition, new infrastructure such as roads and railroads, and new production facilities, were needed. As early as 1846, a textile factory was built in Hereke, in the vicinity of Kocaeli. Construction of the building required considerable amounts of timber to be brought from the nearby forests. See BOA, A.MKT 174/30 (19 Rebiülevvel 1265 [12 Feb. 1849]). Similarly, timber for the construction of macadamised (*şose*) roads in Izmir was to be provided by the Kocaeli *kerestekeş* villagers. See BOA, BEO.AYN.d. 1718–78 (I am most thankful to Sinan Kaya of Koç University/29 Mayıs University for sharing the information and the source.) Such projects required a great deal of the labour of the *kerestekeşan* to the extent that the officials at the imperial dockyards were alarmed by the exploitation of forests for purposes other than the needs of the dockyards. See BOA, ŞD.d. 1–4 (1869).

and required extraction of raw materials from previously unexploited natural sources. This meant modifying the landscape and vegetation cover in most cases. Furthermore, natural resource extraction needed the mobilisation of vast amounts of human and animal labour, therefore altering the social landscape too. Ottoman administrators in Istanbul and the provinces considered these actions vital; however they were not always received positively by the affected local populations. Whereas it can be claimed that such responses were out of pure economic interest, I suggest that 'economic' in the mid-nineteenth-century context should be taken as a larger phenomenon, signifying a set of relationships determined by various actors in and out of market mechanisms. Ottoman peasants bound by the *kerestekeşan* system were affected by climatic, political and local economic developments. As the system was based on the availability of three important factors – human and animal labour, and trees for timber – functioning and sustainability of the system depended on ensuring a complex economy built on interrelations between animals, human beings and forests. On the ground, however, the scene was not as favourable as the Ottoman state wished to see.

The 1830s and 1840s were marked by hitherto unseen drought and famines, which, eventually led to epizootics. Numbers of cattle (as well as human beings) in western and central Anatolia during and after the drought and famines decreased dramatically.[15] However, numbers of buffalo, a breed that was of crucial value in that part of the empire, seem to have held up better. Charles MacFarlane (1799–1858) noted in 1847 that during his trip around a village in Susurluk, he had seen buffaloes in excellent condition, despite the heavy drought prevailing around the region. However, the peasants did not want to put the buffalo to work as a reaction to the taxation policy introduced by the *Tanzimat* reforms:[16]

> We saw an unusual quantity of cattle, and the oxen and buffaloes (both are used for the plough and for draught) seemed all in excellent condition. Yet the house of a farmer at which we stopped, and every other house in the village, were half in ruins; and the Greeks were wringing their hands and tearing their hair, and vowing that they would plough and sow no more …

Whereas such reactions as foot dragging and abstaining from work rose from an ideology based on economic rationality, economy was much larger in the minds of the peasants than the notion degraded to market relations that pre-

---

15.   Erler 2010.
16.   MacFarlane 1850, pp. 242–43.

vailed throughout the nineteenth century. Unlike most accounts of Ottoman peasantry, peasants in Ottoman Anatolia were active in responding to the development of a new political-economy of natural resource extraction and taxation, which had potentially destructive effects in the lives of the villagers.[17] This was equally true for peasants elsewhere, who employed various tactics in order to cope with and react to the changes that altered the relative 'balance' between humans, animals and other components of the environment.[18] Their reaction may not have stopped the 'destruction' of the balance by the central authorities; however, by expressing their discontent and disagreement, common men and women helped to create a sensitivity towards issues arising around the alteration of natural habitat. This was resonant in Istanbul in the ways some reforms were pursued. One significant example was the building of four-wheeled oxen carts and proper roads for them, not only because technical and economic developments demanded this, but because the two-wheeled oxen cart was tormenting and painful for the oxen. On the other hand, it can be claimed that such reaction on the peasants' side became the basis of what is coined as 'environmentalism of the poor'.[19]

Such comments may be speculative and 'anachronistic'; however peasants of villages that were supposed to provide timber for the imperial dockyards started to challenge the corvée style employment of the human and animal labour from the late 1830s onwards. Villages and at times whole sub-districts of the Kocaeli district asked for their exemption from the system with the claim that they lacked the necessary amount of buffaloes.[20] In 1844, villages that were destined to transport the tree-trunks brought down from the mountains refused to fulfil their 'ages old' mission.[21] Cart owners (*arabacı*) in other villages, on the other hand, were not strong enough to carry the burden of such a task. The state had to find other solutions, like using the Sakarya River to transport the trunks. Furthermore, in places with dry and unusual climate, buffaloes were weak and

---

17. For a theoretical and empirical reflection on Ottoman subaltern tactics for coping with the empire, see Erdoğan 2000.

18. By the late seventeenth century, woodcutters and transporters in Venice slowed down work, or abstained from doing certain work, in order to react to the overexploitation of the forest and their labour. See Appuhn 2009, pp. 172–73.

19. Armiero 2008.

20. BOA, A.MKT.NZD 360/84 (26 Muharrem 1278 [3 Aug. 1861]); BOA, A.MKT.NZD 385/45 (14 Cemazeyilahir 1278 [17 Dec. 1861]); BOA, A.MKT.UM 502/59 (25 Rebiülevvel 1278 [30 Sept. 1861]); BOA, A.MKT.UM 523/35 (6 Cemazeyilahir 1278 [9 Dec. 1861]).

21. BOA, A. MKT 135/7 (15 Recep 1264 [17 June 1848]).

'It's a Bad Fate to be Born Near a Forest'

smaller in size. This was expressed collectively or individually through petitions. Either way, petitions submitted to the administration in Istanbul claimed that the *kerestekeşan* system was harmful to both animals and human beings. They referred to a system sustained by 'traditional' agricultural production, practised by means of an alliance between farmers and their buffaloes. A shared burden of farming the arid land connected both humans and animals intimately,[22] in a way that the administrators in Istanbul would not be able to comprehend.

The peasants' demands, voiced in the form of petitions, were partially heard, though. The first solution to the peasants' request to quit the system was to provide buffaloes for them to work in the fields and to transport the timber. This seemed to be a feasible and applicable solution despite the large number of buffaloes to be transported to the villages in question. In early-1830s, *kerestekeş* villages in the Kocaeli district held around 10,000 pairs of buffalo, whereas in around ten years this figure went down to 2,000 pairs. The Ottoman state admitted that this obstructed the functioning of the *kerestekeşan* system and required immediate action. A lack of written correspondence makes it impossible to follow the story of the buffalo promised to the peasants. However, the fact that peasants still claimed a lack of buffaloes at their disposal and the figures that the administrators give allows us to reflect that the problem was not by any means solved. In four *kerestekeş* sub-districts in Kocaeli district, Ada, Apsoni, Sarıçayır and Hendek, only 56 pairs of buffalo remained.[23] There were problems of financing, as compensating for the loss of 8,000 pairs of buffalo required massive amounts of money. Local authorities warned the state that even 1,000 pairs required sums that local timber custodians would not be able to collect. Central authorities were expected to intervene.

The central administration acknowledged the dimensions of the problem, yet it did not iron it out. Peasants in Kocaeli continued to complain that there were not enough buffaloes to satisfy the requests of the imperial dockyards; moreover, the remaining few were weak. If the buffalo were to be employed in felling trees and carrying timber from the mountains, it would be impossible to till the fields. Therefore, state policy to force peasants to spare their cattle for carrying timber was destructive for both the buffaloes and human beings. Beyond textual representations of their misery under the *kerestekeşan* system,

---

22. MacFarlane describes the relationship between the *kerestekeşan* villagers and the buffaloes as 'most amicable.' Compared to the 'sullen, fierce, fiery-eyed, diabolical-looking animals' in the Campagna of Rome and in the Kingdom of Naples, those buffaloes were 'docile and tame' (MacFarlane 1850, p. 103).

23. BOA, A.MKT.UM 393/87 (9 Recep 1276 [1 Feb. 1860]).

villagers decided to send representatives to Istanbul to discuss their state. Ten senior representatives (*ihtiyar adem*) were sent by the villages of a town near the border with Ankara district, which had recently been forced to provide labour for timber. The old men tried to convince the authorities in Istanbul that the villages were not historically part of the *kerestekeşan* system, that the land they lived on was unfavourable and arid, and that the only animals they held were a few donkeys, which were mostly rented. Furthermore, the men expressed that they had already been asked to fell trees and transport them to the some-hundreds-of-miles-away docks in 1844, and had then been successful in convincing the state about the harms that would create for humans and animals, even if the latter could be found. However, in 1861, they were not as lucky. The villagers were supposed to fell the trees and transport the timber midway to the docks, and inhabitants of the closest village were to continue the troublesome journey.[24]

The reasons for peasants' resistance to continued timber felling and transportation were hidden in the details of how the operation was actually carried on. We do not know much about the length of the journey between the village, the mountain and the nearest wharf in the Kocaeli district. In India, by the first decade of the nineteenth century, buffaloes had to travel between three to twenty days in order to transport timber from forests. At times around twenty per cent of the animals perished while dragging a large tree.[25] In the absence of proper roads in Ottoman north-western Anatolia, buffalo had to suffer even more. Ottoman administrators in Istanbul considered a total of fourteen hours of time-distance between the mountain and the docks manageable. Villagers in *kerestekeş* towns did not agree with that. Mountain roads were usually rocky and steep, therefore prone to accidents. Accidents that resulted in injuries and sometimes death were common, and human beings and buffalo had shared the same fate.[26] Individuals whose buffalo perished while carrying timber asked

---

24. BOA, A.MKT.UM 502–59 (1862).

25. Peluso 1992, p. 41.

26. In 1853, Kozoğlu Ahmed, a man from the Elmacık village in Kocaeli/Izmit district, requested compensation as his buffaloes perished during transportation of the tree-trunks for the construction of an imperial galleon. See BOA, A.MKT.NZD 83/43 (13 Şevval 1269 [20 July 1853]). It was usually trees that fell on animals or the villagers that created health issues. A man from a village in Kastamonu (not too far from Kocaeli) got his and his buffalo's leg broken this way in 1850. See BOA, A.MKT. NZD 15/14 (10 Zilkade 1266 [17 Sept. 1850]). Even in cases where oxen-carts were used to transport tree-trunks, injuries and deaths were not uncommon. One such case took place in a village near Gemlik in 1861. The brakes of an oxen-cart loosened and the buffalo pulling

Figure 1. Kerestekeş buffaloes dragging timber from the mountains of Sinop in Northern Anatolia, c. 1930s. Source: KA Dergi 1:1 [2015]. Public domain image.

for a compensation for the buffalo (*manda bahası*). Similarly, men who lost the ability to walk, or work, requested support from the state. Administrators responded negatively to the villagers' requests as they were paid for the trees they brought, or further inquiry was requested in order to find out whether the claim was right.[27]

The condition of the roads in the provinces made life harder for the villagers and the buffalo. Although the Ottoman state acknowledged the need to ameliorate the condition of the roads and especially the bridges so that buffalo carts could travel more easily, construction of macadamised (*şose*) roads had to wait for around a quarter of a century. In any case, using buffalo carts was almost a fantasy in the absence of proper roads. Most of the time, trunks and timber were dragged, causing injuries and deforming the timber.[28] Completing a journey between the villages, the forest and the wharf was not always the end

it crushed the man walking in front to death. See BOA, MVL 620/66 (26 Cemazeyilahir 1278 [29 Dec.1861]).

27. BBOA, A.MKT.NZD 218/59 (29 Recep 1273 [25 Mar. 1857]).

28. BOA, A.MKT 135/7 (15 Recep 1264 [17 June 1848]).

of the story. Trees were expected to be of a certain quality and in order to receive provisions, a villager had to take the tree to the workshop near the wharf, where its quality was checked. Sometimes the villager went home empty-handed as the tree he had brought was not considered useful. In such cases, the buffalo and the villager had probably to make an extra round to earn at least their survival. Until the mid-1840s, tree-trunks were expected to fit the requirements of the catalogue provided by the imperial dockyards. Trunks larger or smaller than the expected size and proportions were not paid for. In 1846, a commission made up of representatives from the *kerestekeş* sub-districts of Kocaeli and an official from the Imperial Arsenal decided that at least tree-trunks that had bigger proportions should be paid the normal price, while those lacking in size and proportion should lose ten per cent of the total value.[29] Despite minor improvements in the system, between the mid-1830s and the mid-1840s, the buffalo population in the Kocaeli region decreased by around eighty per cent, presumably due to the heavy conditions under which they were put to work.

Of course, the historical context of the 1840s exacerbated the reaction by peasants. It was a decade in which the warming of the weather since the beginning of the century reached a peak.[30] Summers were exceptionally warm and droughts were more common than ever. Discourses that described 'climate change' were widespread. Since the 1830s, the increasing difficulty in tilling the land and securing a successful harvest made Ottoman peasants in Anatolia shy away from agriculture and migrate to urban centres where they would be employed in service sectors, and mostly as domestic workers.[31] In March 1843, in a coffeehouse in the Üsküdar district of Istanbul, a certain Mustafa Reis from Değirmendere/Izmit complained that due to the failure of harvests, he did not have any income to pay his taxes. Although he had wanted to continue farming, there was nobody left in the village to continue agriculture except for women and old men.[32] This was confirmed by comments from the countryside. However, for the purposes of this article, it is more important to see how the lives of buffalo and human beings were intertwined. In one village, two old men complained in a petition that the young men had left the village for urban towns, and the policy of the state to employ their buffalo in timber transporta-

---

29.   BOA, İ.MVL 95/1965 (12 Cemaziyelevvel 1263 [28 Apr. 1847]).

30.   For an analysis of 'climate change' in light of contemporary discourses and factual sources from the first half of the century, see Çelik 2017.

31.   See id. [forthcoming].

32.   Kırlı 2009, p. 389 [entry 1049]. Also see Kokdaş and Araz 2018.

tion made it impossible to continue farming as they were too weak to plough their fields without their fellow *sons or buffalo* – giving the two equal value.[33]

That this was an issue of utmost importance, with consequences on an economy that surpassed material needs, was observed by contemporary observers too. MacFarlane had talked to peasants in the region and recorded their commentary on the issue:[34]

> 'The forest', said they 'is our friend, giving us fuel and light; but the forest is also our enemy, for they cut great trees there for the Padishah's ships and they take our oxen to drag them towards the coast. To-day there is a demand upon us for twenty pair of oxen, to drag a giant tree! We have not twenty yoke left in the village: we could not do the thing even if we left our fields all untilled, and the time for the tillage is at hand. We cannot do it, but we shall suffer from it! ... Yes, it is a bad fate to be born near a forest.

Yes, it was a bad fate. However, villagers who were 'born near a forest' kept on struggling against that fate. Whereas the state still considered demands to be exempt from the *kerestekeşan* system legitimate, there was no real solution and response to the demands. The state rejected almost all exemption requests. As individual and village level petitioning did not work, more collective solutions were sought. A petition signed by the whole town of Kocaeli was submitted in 1851.[35]

A galleon in the mid-seventeenth century required nearly 2,000 trees to be cut down. It took around a century for such a tree to grow.[36] In the 1830s, alongside smaller vessels, the state had taken on the building of two imperial galleons, which most probably required more than 4,000 trees of different qualities to be cut. To be precise, in 1847, the state requested 7,794 trees to be cut down by the *kerestekeşan* of Kocaeli.[37] If Tuncay Zorlu's estimations are correct, around two thirds of the whole forest cover in the Kocaeli district was expected to be cleared.[38] Similar to the expression of MacFarlane's peasants, the collective petition reflected more systemic concern going beyond the immediate requirements of the agrarian economy. The peasants warned the state of possible negative outcomes of such a vast destruction of the nearby forests.

---

33. BOA, DV 4–19 (1848).
34. MacFarlane 1850, pp. 149–50.
35. BOA, A.MKT.UM 48/22 (Rebiülahir 1267 [5 Feb. 1851]).
36. Baş 2016, p. 164. Also see Zorlu 2013, p. 90.
37. BOA, İ.MVL 95/1965 (12 Cemaziyelevvel 1263 [28 Apr. 1847]).
38. Zorlu 2013, p. 90.

Their concern was that absence of forests in the area would decrease rainfall and have negative effects on the climate, therefore on agriculture.[39] Furthermore, mobilisation of buffaloes and men of nearby villages would trigger a crisis of agricultural production. Therefore, the *kerestekeşan* system, and the clearance of forests in such an intense way, were considered as unsustainable and ecologically harmful.[40] It was probably no coincidence that the inhabitants of Kocaeli submitted the petition a year after the Ottoman state had recognised that the forests on the nearby Ahu Mountain (Ahudağı – modern Uludağ) were overexploited and no 'useful' trees remained on it.[41]

Selling Buffaloes – Freezing the Capital

In the late 1840s, negotiations between the state and the *kerestekeş* villages were still in progress. In the sub-district of Izmit, 'ancient' *kerestekeş* villages had only a bunch of buffaloes left. However, this time the reason was not the overexploitation of the animals. Besides trying to warn the state against the climatic and economic consequences of the *kerestekeşan* system through petitions, peasants in and around Kocaeli had generated some solutions to the problem. Since the state had not actually responded positively to demands for exemption from the system, peasants in villages that were part of the *kerestekeşan* system started selling their buffaloes to the inhabitants of non-*kerestekeş* villages. In return, they either bought oxen or bought no cattle at all.[42] This is significant in many ways. First of all, it demonstrates that peasants had not given up negotiating the conditions of the system with the state, and they were more or less aware that they had the power and leverage to do so. Secondly, the 'invention' of a

---

39. BOA, A.MKT 135/7 (15 Recep 1264 [17 June 1848]). A petition submitted by inhabitants of Edincik district in Bursa employs a similar discourse. See BOA, A.MKT 69/58 (17 Rebiülevvel 1263 [5 Mar. 1847]). Compare with BOA, C.ML 66/3027 (11 Cemaziyelevvel 1257 [1 July 1841]), a petition from 1841 submitted by kerestekeş inhabitants of four villages in Silistre/Ahyolu in Rumelia. Whereas the arguments in the first two petitions are based on a socio-ecological consciousness, the latter reflects a more political, rights-based approach as the villagers demand their release from the *kerestekeşan* system since the Tanzimat Edict had abolished all corvée.

40. An implicitly similar example can be seen in the forced-miners' reactions to the exploitation of nearby silver ore mines in Halkidiki. See, Kolovos 2015, p. 91. See also the article by Elias Kolovos and Phokion Kotzageorgis in this volume.

41. BOA, MVL 325/7 (5 Cemaziyelevvel 1266 [19 March 1850]).

42. BOA, MVL 7/34 (26 Ramazan 1262 [17 Sept. 1846]; BOA, A.MKT.MHM 181/47 (26 Ramazan 1276 [17 Apr. 1860]); BOA, A.MKT 55/74 (6 Zilhicce 1262 [25 Nov. 1846]).

tactic to use that power is telling of the 'unconventional' the socio-ecological thinking of peasants. Selling buffaloes was economically 'irrational' as buffalo were valued much more than cows or oxen, and were more resilient to conditions unfavourable to other cattle. Furthermore buffalo had more strength; therefore, they made life easier for the farmers. Of course, the state authorities in Istanbul did not understand why and how peasants sold their buffaloes. To them, Ottoman peasants were 'rational' actors and buying oxen in place of buffalo was incomprehensible:[43]

> Those people are *kerestekeşan* from time immemorial. And they have been cutting and transporting wood with a price that they had collectively set, and applied with no exceptions. So why do they sell animals in their possession to others and get rid of them? There has to be a reason behind it ...

On the other hand, the administration seems to have realised the 'trick' and they immediately forbade the selling of buffalo in the district. Those who had buffalo were no longer allowed to take them to market.[44]

Despite the Ottoman state's attempts at preventing peasants in Kocaeli from selling their buffalo, peasants seem to have successfully gotten 'rid' of the burden their cattle put on them. Although their 'protest' against the *kerestekeşan* system did not bring it to an end, the 'protest' caused enough trouble in Istanbul that the state recognised whom it was dealing with. '[E]ven the dust of charcoal was dear', wrote Ahmed Cevdet Pasha (1822–1895) in 1857, underscoring that the charcoal famine that hit the capital in that year, an occurrence largely due to the charcoal producers' selling off their buffaloes. Hacı Hüsam Efendi (1797–1872), the mayor of Istanbul, paid for what happened and was dismissed. However, this did not prevent the complaints of the inhabitants that the rulers were not capable of managing so crucial and basic an issue, let alone ruling a whole empire.[45] Although without such a detailed record as the 1857 case, in 1848 MacFarlane echoed Ahmed Cevdet Pasha's account, that there was not enough charcoal in the city even to heat up the heathens in private

---

43. '... ahali-i merkumenin mine'l kadīm kereste-keş olduğu ve kat ve tenzil eyledikleri kerestenin kendi rızalarıyla kararlaştırılmış olan fiyat vechle ücret-i kat ve nakliyesi ... tamamen ita kılınmakda bulunduğu halde ellerinde bulunan hayvanatı bu suretle ahire füruht ve def etmesi ... elbette bir sebebe mebni olmak lazım geleceğinden ...'. See BOA, A.MKT.UM 393–87 (9 Recep 1276 [1 Feb. 1860]).

44. BOA, MVL 7/34 (26 Ramazan 1262 [17 Sept. 1846].

45. Ahmet Cevdet Paşa, 1991, pp. 46–48. For the archival evidence of the correlation between selling buffaloes and coal famine, see BOA, A.MKT.MHM 123/73 (20 Cemaziyelevvel 1274 [6 Jan. 1858]).

residences, and charcoal beggars emerged due to the famine.[46] The Ottoman administration was well aware of the fact that selling buffaloes might result in serious crisis, hence the effort to prevent *kerestekeş* villagers from doing so. On the other hand, Ahmed Cevdet Pasha's awareness of the reasons for the famine suggests that there were other officials out there to inform the state in 1848. It also implies that selling buffalo was a frequently deployed tactic when the system made it a bad fate to be born near a forest.

The struggle between the state and the buffalo-owner *kerestekeşan* did not stop there. Although in fragments, archival sources tell us that the system carried on, but so did the reactions. We know through Ahmed Cevdet Pasha's account that it was so in 1857. About five years after him, a report written by Donald Sandison (1795–1868), the British consul in Bursa, refers to the exact same problem of the *kerestekeşan* system that overexploited animal labour to the extent that it made various cattle types in the region extinct. The Bursa district lacked enough oxen and buffalo to increase agricultural production.[47]

All the efforts to force the state to improve the conditions under which humans and buffalo worked, if not to totally abolish the work, seem to have made the state reconsider the condition of the buffalo as well as of the men. In 1865, a decision was taken by the Grand Imperial Council (*Meclis-i Vala*) to determine the amount of trees to be felled and transported in proportion to the buffaloes owned by the villagers in a sub-district. That this was the 'success' of the actions of the *kerestekeş* villagers was indirectly admitted by the council:[48]

> [the number of trees to be cut and transported] will be determined in accord-ance with the ability and potential of each village and town, and the amount of animals they possessed ... Unless so, they will be mistreated; *complaints and disturbance will be endless.* Eventually transportation of timber will be delayed.

However, the sub-district of Bursa was relatively lucky as, in 1869, a decision to keep the villagers of Bursa exempt from the system came from Istanbul. In a petition praising the decision, the inhabitants thanked the sultan releasing the

---

46. MacFarlane 1850, p. 169.

47. The National Archives, London (TNA), FO 78/1686, 'Report on the Trade of the District of Brussa for the year 1861', pp. 55–58.

48. Emphasis added. 'kereste-i mezkurenin hayvanat-ı mevcudeye nisbetle tevzi'i yoluna gidilmese ... ashab-ı hayvanat hakkında ... haml-giran ve bi-adil olarak bi'l-vücud mağduriyetlerini ve envai seda ve sızıldının vukuuyla beraber kereste-i matluba ve mürettebenin teehir-i tenzilini müstelzem olacağı ...'. See BOA, MVL 702/74 (20 Zilkade 1281 [16 Apr. 1865]).

weight of a system that turned them into beasts of burden/'horses' (*bargiran*).[49] In Kocaeli on the other hand, forests were about to share the same fate as those on the Ahu Mountain in Bursa.

Conclusion

The case of *keresteke*ş villagers and their buffaloes in north-western Anatolia in the middle of the nineteenth century demonstrates that the fates of the animals and human beings were interwoven. In an agrarian context, not only economic structures, but also social and cultural life, were highly dependent on the 'complex interaction between humans and non-humans; insects, viruses, animals, or other incipient agencies'.[50] A glance at how this interaction takes place at the local level may give us clues about how a particular system actually worked. At a time of dramatic economic, social and climatic change, assumptions regarding incorporation of the Ottoman economy into globalising capitalism through changing trade relations will not mean much without understanding local reactions and responses to these developments. During the 1830–1860 period, the Ottoman state tried to make the ends meet that reforms and trade relations deemed necessary, requiring the exploitation of its human and natural resources to an extent theretofore unseen. That, of course, needed a shift in how nature and its components were perceived. Throughout the period, the state employed all means to commodify commons that formerly provided the survival of communities too far away from the reach of the market structures. It tried to tax and formalise the informally exchanged products that did not previously fit into official market mechanisms. If one takes official correspondence at face value, Ottoman institutions may depict a relatively smooth adaptation of the Ottoman peasant into the realities that the new official ideology required. Exploitation of natural resources, as the buffalo labour case here suggests, depended on collaboration between the state and the local population. However, mobilising locals that perceived the new political economy of natural resource extraction as harmful to the human and animal communities living in the vicinity was not that easy.

In the story of felling and transportation of timber from the forests in the Kocaeli district to the nearby docks, the lives of buffaloes were negotiated as a key agent in guaranteeing the survival and future wellbeing of the communities in the district. I claim that the buffalo case in Kocaeli represents the

49.   BOA, İ.DH 603/42016 (28 Şaban 1286 [3 Dec. 1869]).
50.   Çalışkan 2010, p. 8.

'cattle complex' of the Ottoman Anatolian communities. Although archival resources within our reach do not tell much about the cultural significance of buffalo in the lives of communities in the north-western Anatolian provinces, from narrative sources it is possible to derive that buffalo, and cattle in general, were almost sacred for forest and mountain communities. In the 1840s, Derviş Paşa (1811/12–1896) and Mehmed Hursid Paşa's (1813?–1878) comments in the *Seyāhatnāme-i hudūd* give explicit examples of how the lives of many village communities were determined by their buffalo in the south-eastern provinces of Anatolia.[51] Until the 1880s, the *tahtacı* communities in the south-western Anatolian mountains demonstrated 'conservationist' characteristics that tried to keep a balance between the tree and animal population in areas where they operated and resided.[52] In communities with predominant oleiculture in western Anatolia, even in the mid-twentieth century, the olive tree was perceived as a factor of production, whereas livestock held more non-market value for they transmitted social messages based on kinship or religious codes.[53] We cannot be entirely sure if the same holds true for the *kerestekeş* communities in the Kocaeli district; however it is obvious that the *kerestekeş* villagers in Kocaeli district sold their buffalo particularly to villagers outside of the *kerestekeşan* system not for the profit, but more to free themselves and the buffalo from the increasing burdens of the system. The Ottoman state rightfully coined this act as 'irrational'.

The buffalo in mid-nineteenth century north-western Anatolia held economic, as well as non-economic value. To use Çalışkan and Callon's conceptualisation, 'economisation' of the buffalo by the state into commodities in

---

51. Mehmed Hurşîd Paşa 1997.

52. Bent 1891 p. 272. More about the *tahtacı* communities can be found in Roux 1970, pp. 39–40; Dursun 2007, p. 41; McNeill 1992, pp. 93, 122; Gökalp 1980. *Tahtacı* communities in south-eastern Turkey employed mules to drag tree-trunks in the 1970s. They maintained the same attitude toward the forest and their beasts of burden. A 1979 documentary by Süha Arın documented lives and ideas of members of one such community. Discourses that the forest is a 'treasure' and a 'burden' at the same time still prevailed around 130 years after MacFarlane's peasants' comments: 'There is no need for someone to tell us if there is a fire in the forest. We tend forest fires with an inner love towards the forest, with no personal interest at all … For me, the forest is a treasure … Yet, I cannot enjoy any of the forest-rights, workers' rights, even if I am willing to. ('Orman yangınlarında bize yangın var diye söylenmesine hiç lüzum yok. Bir menfaate dayanarak değil, içimizden ormana karşı gelen bir sevgiye dayanarak orman yangınlarına gideriz … Orman benim için hazine … Ama ben sahip olmak istiyorum da, ormanın hiçbir haklarından, işçi haklarından, ben yararlanamam'.) (Arın 1979).

53. Gökalp 1980, pp. 157–67.

the market and 'machines' that had existed merely for exploitation, did not take place easily and without reaction. In an agrarian economy where production and exchange relations were determined by the at times intimate and 'irrational' interaction between human beings, animals and other components of nature,[54] the peasants under consideration here resisted the forced economisation of their cattle for more than three decades. The struggle was taken on by different actors within the changing political institutionalisation, as in 1918, when Hasan Fehmi Efendi (1867–1933), the Member of Parliament for the Sinop district criticised the economic condition of the *kerestekeşan* of the Sinop and Bolu districts:[55]

> In the district that I am elected to represent and its vicinities, this natural wealth [forests] has up to this very day and hour appeared to be a reason for disaster [*mucib-i felaket*] for the *kerestekeşan* villagers … Timber is brought down to the docks from 8–10 hours away, without carts, without any proper instrument, but dragged … Do you know how many days it took a pair of buffaloes to drag the timber, a year before the war [1913]? My guess is at least 5–6 days … Roads under such terrible conditions, such barren territory, stones and rocks, would every two rounds destroy the shoes of the buffalo … And is it only a pair of buffaloes and one human being [doing that]? A pair of buffaloes and a boy of 10–15 years accompanying them. [Do you know] how much money they would make, a pair of buffaloes and a kid, spending 6 days dragging the timber, and paying for their own provisions?

---

54. Çalışkan 2010. Also see Hribal 2003, p. 436.

55. 'Benim doğrudan doğruya dâire-i intihâbiyyem bulunan Sinop ve mülhakatında o servet-i tabîiyye-i Memleket, kerestekeş olan – kereste tüccarı değil – köylü için bu güne kadar ve bu saata kadar şekli, mûcib-i felâkettir … Beyefendiler, sekiz, on saat mesafeden, hem araba ile değil, vesait, yolu yok, sürüklemek suretivle kereste iskeleye iner … Muharebeden 1 sene evveli bir çift manda ile … bugün dağdan kereste acaba kaç günde inerdi? Bendeniz diyoram ki 5, 6 günde koşum kereste iskeleye inerdi … öyle fena yollar, öyle arızalı arazî, taşlar ve saire dolayısıyla, yâni her seferinde değilse de iki seferinde bir çift nal, mandanın ayağından gider … Sade bir çift manda ile acaba bir tek kişi mi? Bir çift manda, yanıbaşında da 10, 15 yaşında bir çocuk, beraber giderdi. Bunları 6 günde, bir çift mandanın ve çocuğun yiyeceği, tamamiyle kendisine ait olmak üzere iskeleye indirirse, kaç kuruş bir menfaat temin etmiş olur?' *Meclis-i Mebusan Zabıt Ceridesi (MMZC)*, Devre 3, Cilt 3, Sene 4, 79. İnikad (31 Mart 1334 [31 Mar. 1918]), p. 552 All references to the parliamentary proceedings are taken from the minutes of the Ottoman parliament, published by the Press of the Grand National Assembly of Turkey (Türkiye Büyük Millet Meclisi; TBMM) in 1985 and available through the TBMM website. See https://www.tbmm.gov.tr/kutuphane/tutanak_sorgu.html The TBMM transliteration differs in some cases from standard spelling and transliteration practices in modern Turkish, and the original transliterations have been modified to conform to the style guidelines of this volume. Translations of the minutes are my own.

130

Hasan Fehmi Efendi continued the discussion juxtaposing destroyed shoes (*çarık*) of the kid with the buffalo shoes (*nal*).[56] Destruction of both shoes trying to drag timber for the building projects of the Ottoman state symbolises how much the *kerestekeşan* system tied the lives of humans and animals together even as late as 1918. The process of detachment of lives of human beings and their buffalo in that part of Anatolia took more than a century, and the significance of cattle and buffalo in the lives of Anatolian villagers remained until the introduction of mechanised agriculture during the 1950s, which accelerated during 1970s with rapid urbanisation.

Bibliography

Unpublished Primary Sources

Prime Ministry Ottoman Archives (*Başbakanlık Osmanlı Arşivi, BOA*), Istanbul

Bab-ı Âlî Evrâk Odası Ayniyât Defterleri (BEO.AYN.d.) 1718–78

Cevdet Maliye (C.ML) 3027

Deâvî Nezâreti Defterleri (DV) 4–19

Haritalar (HRT.h) 584

İrade Dahiliye (İ.DH) 603–42016

İrade Meclis-i Vala (İ.MVL) 95–1965

Meclis-i Vala Evrakı (MVL) 620–66, 325–7, 7–34, 702–74

Sadâret Mektubî Kalemi Evrakı (A.MKT) 174–30, 69–58, 135–5, 55–74, 135–7,

Sadâret Mühimme Kalemi Evrakı (A.MKT.MHM) 181–47, 123–73

Sadâret Mühimme Kalemi Umum Vilayet Evrakı (A.MKT.UM) 502–59, 523–35, 393–87, 502–59, 48–22

Sadâret Mühimme Kalemi Nezaret ve Devâir Evrakı (A.MKT.NZD) 218–59, 360–84, 385–45, 83–43, 15–14

Şûrâ-yı Devlet Defterleri (ŞD.d) 1–4

The National Archives of the United Kingdom (TNA), London

Foreign Office (FO) 78/1686, 55–8.

Published Primary Sources

Ahmet Cevdet Paşa. 1991 [1933]. *Tezakir 21–39 (vol. 2)*. Ed. by Cavid Baysun. Ankara, Türk Tarih Kurumu.

Âşık Mehmed. 2007 [1577?]. *Menâzirü'l-Avâlim*. 3 vols. Ed. by Mahmut Ak. Ankara: Türk Tarih Kurumu.

---

56. Meclis-i Mebusan 1991 [1918], p. 553.

'It's a Bad Fate to be Born Near a Forest'

Evliya Çelebi. 1993. *Evliya Çelebi Seyahatnamesi, vol. 2.* 10 vols. Istanbul: Üçdal Neşriyat.

MacFarlane, Charles. 1850. *Turkey and Its Destiny: The Result of Journeys Made in 1847 and 1848 to Examine into the State of that Country.* Philadelphia: Lea and Blanchard.

Meclis-i Mebusan. 1991 [1918]. *Meclis-i Mebusan Zabıt Ceridesi, vol. 2/98.* Ankara: TBMM Kütüphanesi.

Mehmed Hurşid [Paşa]. 1997 [1877]. *Seyâhatnâme-i hudûd.* Ed. by Alâattin Eser. Istanbul: Simurg Yayınları.

Secondary Sources

Appuhn, Karl. 2009. *A Forest on the Sea: Environmental Expertise in Renaissance Venice.* Baltimore: John Hopkins University Press.

Armiero, Marco. 2008. 'Seeing Like a Protestor: Nature, Power, and Environmental Struggles'. *Left History* 59: 59–76.

Baş, Yaşar. 2016. 'Kocaeli'den İstanbul'a Kereste Nakli, Tersane ve Tophane'de Kullanımı'. *Studies of the Ottoman Domain* 6: 149–71.

Beinart, William. 2000. 'African History and Environmental History'. *African Affairs* 99: 269–302.

Bent, Theodore. 1891. 'The Yourouks of Asia Minor'. *The Journal of the Anthropological Institute of Great Britain and Ireland* 20: 269–76.

Bulliet, Richard W. 2012. 'History and Animal Energy in the Arid Zone'. In Alan Mikhail (ed.), *Water on Sand: Environmental Histories of the Middle East and North Africa.* New York: Oxford University Press. pp. 51–70.

Callon, Michel and Koray Çalışkan. 2009. 'Economization Part 1: Shifting Attention from the Economy towards Processes of Economization'. *Economy and Society* 38: 369–98.

——. 2010. 'Economization, Part 2: Research Programme for the Study of Markets'. *Economy and Society* 39: 1–32.

Çalışkan, Koray. 2010. *Market Threads: How Cotton Farmers and Traders Create a Global Commodity.* Princeton: Princeton University Press.

Çelik, Semih. 2017. 'Scarcity and Misery at the Time of "Abundance Beyond Imagination": Climate Change, Famines and Empire-Building in Ottoman Anatolia (c. 1800–1850)'. Ph.D. Diss. Florence: European University Institute.

——. Forthcoming. '"No Work for Anyone in this Country of Misery": Famine and Labour Relations in mid-Nineteenth Century Anatolia'. In M. Erdem Kabadayı and Leda Papastefanaki (eds), *Working in Greece and Turkey: A Comparative Labour History from Empires to Nation States 1840–1940.* New York: Berghahn.

De Planhol, Xavier. 1969. 'Le boeuf porteur dans le Proche-Orient et l'Afrique du Nord'. *Journal of the Economic and Social History of the Orient* 12: 298–321.

Dursun, Selçuk. 2007. 'Forest and the State: History of Forestry and Forest Transformation in the Ottoman Empire'. Ph.D. Diss. Istanbul: Sabancı University.

Erdoğan, Necmi. 2000. 'Devleti "İdare" Etmek: Maduniyet ve Düzenbazlık'. *Toplum ve Bilim* 83: 32–47.

Erler, Mehmet Yavuz. 2010. 'Animals During Disasters'. In Suraiya Faroqhi (ed.), *Animals and People in the Ottoman Empire*. Istanbul: Eren. pp. 333–52.

Faroqhi, Suraiya. 2009. *Artisans of Empire. Crafts and Craftspeople under the Ottomans.* London: I.B. Tauris.

——. 2010. 'Introduction'. In Suraiya Faroqhi (ed.), *Animals and People in the Ottoman Empire*. Istanbul: Eren. pp. 11–54.

Gökalp, Altan. 1980. *Tetes Rouges et Bouches Noires. Une confrérie tribale de l'Ouest anatolien.* Paris, Societe d'Ethnographie.

Hongo, Hitomi. 1997. 'Patterns of Animal Husbandry, Environment, and Ethnicity In Central Anatolia In The Ottoman Empire Period: Faunal Remains From Islamic Layers at Kaman-Kalehöyük'. *Japan Review* 8: 275–307.

Hribal, Jason. 2003. '"Animals Are Part of the Working Class": A Challenge to Labor History'. *Labor History* 44: 435–53.

İnal, Onur. 2018. 'Ottoman and Turkish Environmental History: An Overview of the Field'. *Environment and History* 24: 297–99.

Kırlı, Cengiz. 2009. *Sultan ve Kamuoyu. Osmanlı Modernleşme Sürecinde Havadis Jurnalleri.* Istanbul: Türkiye İş Bankası Kültür Yayınları.

Kokdaş, İrfan and Yahya Araz. 2018. 'İstanbul'da Ev İçi Hizmetlerinde İstihdâm Edilen Kuzeybatı Anadolulu Kız Çocuklarının Göç Ağları Üzerine Bir Değerlendirme (1845–1911)'. *Tarih İncelemeleri Dergisi* 33: 41–68.

Kolovos, Elias. 2015. 'Mines and the Environment in Halkidiki: A Story from the Ottoman Past'. *Balkan Studies* 50: 71–94.

McNeill, John R. 1992. *The Mountains of the Mediterranean World. An Environmental History.* Cambridge: Cambridge University Press.

Mikhail, Alan, 2012. 'Introduction – Middle East Environmental History: The Fallow between Two Fields'. In Alan Mikhail (ed.), *Water on Sand: Environmental Histories of the Middle East and North Africa*. New York: Oxford University Press. pp. 1–26.

——. 2013a. *The Animal in Ottoman Egypt*. New York: Oxford University Press.

——. 2013b. 'Unleashing the Beast: Animals, Energy, and the Economy of Labor in Ottoman Egypt'. *The American Historical Review* 118: 317–48.

Narin, Resül. 2011. 'Osmanlı Devleti Zamanında Kocaeli Ormanları'. *Belleten* 77: 769–81.

Peluso, Nancy Lee. 1992. *Rich Forests, Poor People: Resource Control and Resistance in Java.* Berkeley: University of California Press.

Roux, Jean-Paul. 1970. *Les Traditions des Nomades de la Turquie Meridionale. Contribution a l'etude des representations religieuses des societes turques d'apres les enquetes effectuees chez les Yörük et les Tahtaci par J.-P. R. et K. Özbayri.* Paris: Adrien Maisonneuve.

Tabak, Faruk. 2008. *The Waning of the Mediterranean, 1550–1870.* Baltimore: The Johns Hopkins University Press.

Wrigley, Edward Anthony. 2016. *The Path to Sustained Growth: England's Transition from an Organic Economy to an Industrial Revolution.* Cambridge: Cambridge University Press.

Zorlu, Tuncay. 2008. *Innovation and Empire in Turkey: Sultan Selim III and the Modernization of the Ottoman Navy*. London: I.B. Tauris.

——. 2013. 'Osmanlı Deniz Teknolojisinden Bazı Sayfalar'. *Hendese – Bilim Teknoloji ve Düşünce Dergisi* 2: 82–95.

Audiovisual Material

Arın, Süha. 1979. *Tahtacı Fatma [Fatma of the Forest]*. Istanbul: MTV Film Televizyon.

Chapter 6

WATER MANAGEMENT ISSUES IN AN OTTOMAN PROVINCE:
THE CASE OF CYPRUS IN THE SEVENTEENTH CENTURY

Styliani N. Lepida

In an attempt to approach the historical reality of a given place and time, the everyday life of the people of a region, their culture and the way in which their cohabitation was organised, it is sensible to turn our attention to an indicator capable of directing us or of providing us with information about all of these. *Water* could well be such an indicator. The case through which I approach water as an indicator of historical reality and as a source of data and information is Cyprus in the seventeenth century, a period during which the island was under Ottoman rule. This article, drawing on travellers' accounts and Ottoman and European archival documents, takes Cyprus as a case-study to illustrate the vital importance of water to an Ottoman province. In this article, I approach the water from a purely historical perspective, with the ultimate goal that this effort could be a small step in the ever-increasing effort of historians to deal with environmental issues. At this point, however, let me make clear that the article is limited to rain and spring water. It does not include the study of sea-water, despite the fact that Cyprus as an island could be examined historically in this light, too.[1]

---

1.   Historical studies on Cyprus mostly focus on economic and social issues and developments. The effects of the environment on Cypriot society have so far been only peripherally treated in Ottoman studies. See Panzac 2009; Bostan 2003; Kolovos 2007, pp. 49–122; idem 2006; idem 2017; idem 2018.

Water Scarcity Factors

The climate of Cyprus, given its geomorphological features of an insular and not continental piece of land, as well as its geographical location as part of the Mediterranean, is characterised mainly by abundant sunshine and low rainfall, long, hot and dry summers and mild winters – the typical characteristics of the Mediterranean climate.[2] This intense Mediterranean identity, along with strongly marked seasonal and regional features, has significantly affected many fields of the economy and society. The majority of recorded descriptions by travellers who visited Cyprus during the seventeenth century confirm the essentially Mediterranean character of the island's climate and reveal the greatest natural threat the island faced and is arguably still facing: drought.[3] Despite the risks involved in using literary sources such as travellers' accounts, this article presents some testimonies from literary sources that could potentially give a different or more detailed image from the one encountered in administrative documents.

One observes, however, that there is a difference between the references of late sixteenth-century travellers and those of the seventeenth century. In the writings of most travellers who visited the island in the sixteenth century, water is described as abundant. For example, Gio. Sozomeno, a Cypriot nobleman, as well as Paolo Paruta (1540–1598), a Venetian historian, both referring to the siege of Nicosia by the Ottomans in 1570, spoke of a city in which water was abundant.[4] Étienne de Lusignan (1537–1590) painted a similar picture of Nicosia in his *Chorografia* in 1573.[5] According to Tommaso Porcacchi Castilione's (1530–1585) description in 1576, there were water-demanding crops in the countryside, such as cotton and sugar, the cities were full of gardens and there were thousands of water sources.[6] In 1599, Johannes Cotovicus, also known as Jan van Cootwijk (d.1629), described a well-watered countryside and praised the plentitude of water in the urban centres of the island, through references to Kouklia and Nicosia respectively.[7]

The image of water abundance is overturned in seventeenth-century travel books, which, in the majority, present a picture of water scarcity and drought. William Lithgow (1582–1645), who toured the island during the

---

2. Braudel 1972, vol. 1, pp. 259–67.

3. Cobham 1908, p. 199; Archimandrite Kyprianos 1902 [1788], p. 458.

4. Cobham 1908, pp. 82, 100.

5. Ibid., p. 120; Lusignano di Cipro 1573.

6. Cobham, pp. 164–66.

7. Ibid., pp. 193–95.

first two decades of the seventeenth century, referring to one of his routes to Nicosia, mentioned that he was struggling because of high temperatures and lack of water.[8] An imperial order (*suret-i ferman*) of Sultan Murad IV (r. 1623–1640) dated 1634 mentions that the island of Cyprus was once again struck by drought and some Orthodox monks of the Kykkos Monastery asked the sultan's permission to make religious processions for rain, using the image of the Virgin Mary.[9]

A remarkable geomorphological feature of Cyprus is the absence of large and permanent flowing rivers. Water sources in the island's territory are confined to torrents or springs, such as two springs in Nicosia, one called Pigadia (Πηγάδια, meaning 'Wells' in Greek) and the other Glyko Nero (Γλυκό Νερό, meaning 'Sweet Water' in Greek),[10] and in the seventeenth century these were the main sources for the water supply of the island. However, these water sources were reduced due to prolonged summer heat or drought.[11] Sieur de Stochove, a French nobleman from Bruges, visited Cyprus in 1630 and noted that the island had no rivers, but only a few springs and torrents that dried out during the summer months.[12] Similarly, John Heyman (1667–1737), a Dutch professor, who visited Cyprus in the first years of the eighteenth century, wrote that the island did not have a regular river but only several lakes, ponds and swamps.[13] Along with the above, one more geomorphological characteristic of the island, which increased the lack of water, is the absence of high mountains and consequently of snow-fed rivers or creeks. The mountains of Cyprus, which do not exceed 2,000 metres in altitude, were unable to conserve enough snow to feed rivers by melting in the summer months. Moreover, the amount of water that accumulated thanks to winter rainfall was not enough to supply the island sufficiently because it evaporated due to the high summer temperatures.

The hot climate of Cyprus, as noted by contemporary observers, was one of the factors that contributed to the scarcity of water and made the management of available water even more difficult, especially during the summer

---

8. There is no indication of exactly which year Lithgow visited Cyprus and whether it was just one trip or more, but Cobham, who studied and published his travel text, places his visit to the island between the years 1609 and 1621. Cobham, pp. 202–03.

9. Theocharides 1993, pp. 100–01.

10. Cobham 1908, p. 119.

11. Ibid., pp. 184, 200–01, 236, 240–41.

12. Ibid., p. 216.

13. Ibid., pp. 246–47.

period.[14] Rainfall was minimal during the warm periods but sometimes during the whole year. Heyman gave the following information:

> Sometimes no rain falls for a long time; and it appears from history that the inhabitants were once obliged to quit it, no rain falling in the space of seventeen years. And in the time of Constantine the Great it was visited with a drought of six and thirty years. It does not indeed want fountains and wells, but the water in all is thick and turbid. These, however, frequently fail, so that in the heats of summer no verdure is to be seen in the whole country, which seems parched and arid.[15]

The hot season ran from May/June to September/October, culminating in the summer months (June-August). The nobleman Giovanni Antonio Soderini, who visited Cyprus in 1671, wrote, in a letter to his son, that the island's hot climate during the summer months was unbearable and that it lasted until October and even November.[16] The saltpans in the vicinity of Larnaca, known also as *Tuzla* or *Salines*, began to lose their waters in June due to rapid evaporation and were completely dried up by mid-August, turning into salt.[17]

Given the above information, questions arise regarding the quality of available water on the island. The existing information, so far, is minimal and somewhat contradictory. Some talk about plenty and clean water, especially in Nicosia[18], even during the troubled period of the siege of Cyprus in 1570–71, but others mention the poor water quality.[19] At this point, we should take into account that the above data relate to different regions of Cyprus and different periods of time, across which environmental circumstances might have differed.

Socio-Economic Burden of Water Scarcity

The lack of water in Cyprus during the seventeenth century is evidenced by impacts on many areas, particularly on society, administration and economy.[20]

---

14. Ibid., pp. 202–03. Antonis Hadjikyriacou interprets the effects of drought on the island in the seventeenth century as a symptom of the Little Ice Age, and not as a permanent feature of the climate of the island. See Hadjikyriacou 2011, pp. 55–59.

15. Cobham 1908, p. 247. Stochove also mentions this incident. See Ibid., p. 216.

16. State Archives of Venice (*Archivio di Stato di Venezia*), Civico Museo Correr, Ms. Cicogna, file number 999bis, p. 4.

17. Cobham 1908, pp. 165, 202–03.

18. Ibid., pp. 100, 119–21, 165, 193, 195.

19. Ibid., pp. 122, 247.

20. Ursinus 1999, pp. 265–72.

Agricultural production is, undoubtedly, the first sector that could provide evidence about the impact of water shortage, both in terms of crop species and productivity. In addition, I suggest that the type of agricultural production in Cyprus was also determined by the insufficiency of water. Crops that required relatively less water, such as grain, barley, grapes, olives, fruit trees and carobs, flourished on the island during the seventeenth century and formed the basis of its agricultural production. But we also come across the following paradox: in the sixteenth century, evidence suggests that the island also abounded in crops with high water requirements, such as sugar and cotton.[21] At the same time, the urban landscape was dominated by a large number of gardens, especially in Nicosia, the capital of the province.[22] Data on the island's crops in the sixteenth century show that cotton cultivation was widespread in the majority of Cypriot villages.[23] Sugar was also important for the island's budget during the same century (in the regions of Paphos and Limassol). However, there is evidence that sugar production, which demanded water for both its cultivation and processing, showed some variation in yields.[24] Irrigation was used to preserve and protect these crops from the heat.[25] Further research remains to be conducted regarding the extent to which the production, and consequently, the market price of these products were affected by water scarcity.[26]

---

21. Ibid., pp. 174, 185; Jennings 1999, pp. 443–62; Both cotton and sugar have flourished in the Cypriot territory since the Venetian period, despite the fact that sugar production began to decline during the 17th century for economic reasons concerning changes in sugar trade in the Mediterranean and not because of change in environmental conditions on the island. See Hadjikyriacou 2011, pp. 40–48.

22. Cobham 1908, pp. 217, 233.

23. Jennings 1990, p. 471; Jennings 1993, pp. 325–29; Dündar 1998, pp. 231–32.

24. Sahillioğlu 1967, pp. 11–12, 21, 27; Dündar 2010, pp. 1038, 1043–44; Jennings 1993, pp. 321–23; Constantini 2009, pp. 133–34.

25. Cobham 1908, pp. 122, 199.

26. Ronald C. Jennings identifies this gap in the Ottoman sources and the explanatory weakness thus created, citing the following: 'Inadequate data prevents a definitive study of prices in Cyprus. Any generalization must be attempted with great caution. There is virtually no information about seasonal effects on food prices. There is too little data to coordinate prices with the even sparser data on good or bad harvests or with disasters like plagues and the swarming of locusts'. Jennings 1993, p. 313. For prices and products, see Jennings 1993, especially the chapter 'The Economy as Seen through Ottoman Sources', pp. 311–41. See also Jennings 2009. For a general view on agricultural product and process, see Barkan 1975, pp. 3–28; Sunar 1987, pp. 65–68; Faroqhi 1999, pp. 251–63; Tvedt 2010, pp. 143–66.

Another field directly related to agricultural production was taxation. A possible decline in agricultural production would signify, at the same time, a drop in tax revenues for the central and provincial administration, since rural tax-payers in particular would not be able to fulfil their tax obligations. A petition (*arz*) Hassan Pasha, the treasurer (*defterdar*) of Cyprus, wrote to the Sublime Port, includes the statement of the collector of the island's poll-tax (*cizye*) for the year of 1648:

> Some of the poor *reayas* have died, some have scattered and left Cyprus, while others have returned to the religion of Islam. The above-mentioned *reayas* were scattered again because their forces were not sufficient (to pay) the poll-tax, because for a few years, at the will of the supreme Allah, they did not collect the wheat and the barley they had produced, being oppressed by the drought and the overpricing and the crowd of locusts. That is why the fund was found to be in deficit.[27]

Moreover the report that Mustafa Efendi, the judge (*kadı*) of Nicosia, sent on the same issue reveals that the *cizye* was not collected from the 10,000 registered *hanes* (taxable units), but from 15,052 *hanes*, adding an extra burden on the taxpayers.[28]

Another equally important effect was famine, which seems to have accompanied every major natural disaster, like locust attacks, in Cyprus during the period under investigation.[29] Archimandrite Kyprianos (1735–1803?) reports that in the 1620s the island had suffered from the natural scourges of drought and locust attacks to such an extent that not only were agricultural crops destroyed, but the population began to decline on the island since many residents chose to flee as a means of salvation.[30] Flight as a means of dealing with environmental and economic conditions was a phenomenon quite common in seventeenth century Ottoman territory.[31] In the 1640s, it seems that again the island suffered from water scarcity. The extended drought period, coupled with locust attacks in the area, was largely responsible for the decline in agricultural output, which in turn led to overpricing of goods, economic hardship and famine.[32]

---

27. National Library of Cyril and Methodius (*Narodna Biblioteka Kiril i Metodij, NBKM*), F.275A, a.e. 797, I., p. 1; Theocharides 1987, p. 219.
28. NBKM, F.275A, a.e. 797, I., p. 2; Theocharides 1987, pp. 220–21.
29. Hadjianastasis 2004, pp. 168–70.
30. Archimandrite Kyprianos 1902, p. 458.
31. Hütteroth 2006, pp. 32–37; Faroqhi 1994, pp. 411–636.
32. Theocharides 1993, p. 211; White 2011, pp. 140–62.

Styliani Lepida

In times of drought, water scarcity was associated with food deficiency, especially bread.[33] In addition, bread production was based on the function of watermills, which required a sufficient quantity of water. In 1661, a Venetian document, a report the Franciscan missionary priest Giovanni Battista da Todi sent to *Propaganda Fide* concerning the socio-religious conditions on the island, water shortage and the consequent famine are described as major problems of Cyprus.[34]

Managing the Available Water

The scarcity of water, along with the warm climate, seemed to be an important incentive for constructing water-saving structures, but also for maintaining existing ones. Such structures, in seventeenth-century Cyprus, were aqueducts, tanks, wells and canals of rain or spring water, where water was stored so as to be available for everyday use but also during periods of drought.[35] Many court documents (mainly *hüccet*s) reveal that such water-related constructions or assets, along with the sale of land, were often sold as integral part of agricultural production and everyday life on the island. Indicatively, in such a document dated 1612, a non-Muslim sold a field along with an irrigation channel for 2,000 *akçe*.[36] A similar document dating from 1644 records the sale of water-wells and tanks.[37]

The water saved by these means was intended either to meet the daily needs of the island's residents or to water farmlands and gardens.[38] Irrigation and the distribution of water to cities or the countryside was carried out by using surface or underground irrigation canals, while the pumping of water from the wells was done with large wheels, driven by beasts of burden, usually horses or oxen.[39] Domestic animals, especially horses and cattle, played an important role in the rural economy and the daily routine of Ottoman countryside's residents. They not only participated in agricultural and food production, but in many cases also replaced human labour.[40] The water pumped from the wells

---

33. Cobham 1908, p. 247.
34. Tsirpanlis 1973, p. 165; Pieraccini, 2013, pp. 46–47.
35. Theocharides 1993, pp. 12–13, 120–21; Cobham 1908, p. 109.
36. Theocharides 1993, pp. 64–65.
37. Ibid., pp. 120–21.
38. Cobham 1908, pp. 200–1.
39. Ibid., pp. 122, 199; İslamoğlu-İnan 1987, p. 117; and Asdrahas 1988, pp. 101–122.
40. Mikhail 2014, pp. 19–22.

was firstly disposed into tanks and then piped to fountains in cities.[41] Fountains as a means of water supply were widespread in Ottoman lands.[42] The fountains and the toponyms of Cyprus, which are recorded in travellers' accounts, testify the importance of water in the cultural and social life of the island. For example, Cornelis Van Bruyn (1652–1727) referred to a fountain dedicated to the mythical ancient goddess Aphrodite in the area of Kithrea, as well as to another one close to it, named *Kefalovryso*, meaning spring-head in Greek.[43]

Apart from irrigation, water was used to power watermills to help grind cereals and other plant products into flour or crush sugar canes to make into sugar.[44] Watermills were used in the agricultural production in many places of the Ottoman countryside, such as in Anatolia and the Balkans,[45] as well as in Cyprus during the sixteenth and seventeenth centuries.[46]

At the time of the conquest of the island by the Ottomans, more than a third of the villages had watermills. Many of these watermills were founded during the Venetian period. Ronald C. Jennings noted that the villages in the southern and central part of the island had a greater number of watermills than those in other areas. Specifically, in Karpasia and the areas west of Limassol, such as Episkopi and Kolossi, where water resources were more efficient,[47] there were large watermills and the villages of these areas paid large amounts of tax for the watermills. Nevertheless the largest amount of watermill tax (*resm-i asiyab*) was paid by the village of Agios Andronikos in the northern part of the island. The village paid 5,000 *akçe* as watermill tax, making almost forty per cent of all rural taxes paid by that village.[48]

The duration of the period of operation of the watermills was determined on a seasonal basis according to the payment of taxes for a certain period. Watermills in Ottoman provinces functioned on an annual, semi-annual or a monthly basis. Jennings, based on his observations on irregularly paid taxes, which were most probably due to water shortages during the extended sum-

41.   Cobham 1908, pp. 122, 192, 199–201.

42.   Çokuğraş 2012, pp. 624–25.

43.   Cobham 1908, p. 237.

44.   Ibid., p. 174.

45.   Mutafçieva 1988, p. 57; İslamoğlu-İnan 1987, p. 154

46.   Faroqhi 1977, p. 183.

47.   Hadjikyriacou 2011, pp. 50–54.

48.   Jennings 2009, pp. 114–15.

mer and lack of rivers capable of feeding watermills constantly, speculated that the watermills in Cyprus were in operation for three or six months in a year.[49]

Regarding the ownership status of watermills, it should be noted that they could be a private or even property of a pious foundation (*vakıf*).[50] *Vakıf*s were often involved in the management and maintenance of water resources such as wells and fountains.[51] A judicial document (*hüccet*) from 1587 refers to interesting parameters regarding the whole process of buying and selling watermills. A Muslim resident had purchased a watermill from the monks of the Kykkos Monastery for the sum of 4,000 *akçe*. He claimed to have deposited the amount to the public treasury, so he sold anew the watermill to the monks at the same price. However, in the meantime the watermill was registered in the imperial cadastre as a pious foundation, so the sale was not considered valid and was cancelled. Furthermore it was proven that the abovementioned Mehmed had not, as he claimed, deposited the money from the watermill's purchase in the public treasury. For this reason, it was decided that the mill should be sold by the state.[52] The Ottoman state was involved in the purchase and sale of water structures, even though some travellers asserted the contrary. For example, Cotovicus, who visited the island in 1598 noted that local Ottoman authorities did not display any particular interest in the maintenance of water management constructions, tanks and canals.[53] Cotovicus's assessment, however, should not be taken granted because it does not come from systematic records but from the author's subjective judgment.

Recent studies have shown that the Ottoman authorities identified water shortage as a serious problem and acknowledged water management as a matter of priority. Netice Yıldız, through her study of the Ottoman pious foundations in Cyprus, argued that the Ottoman authorities, from the time of conquest in 1571, identified water shortage as a serious problem and acknowledged water management as a matter of priority. The Ottoman authorities tried to solve the problem by setting up water *vakıf*s. Eventually, two aqueducts were constructed in Cyprus in the seventeenth century, the first in Famagusta in 1609 and the latter in Lefka in 1690.[54] Much more attention was given to

---

49. Ibid., p. 116.
50. Faroqhi 1977, pp. 183–84.
51. Stournaras 2009, pp. 172–76.
52. Theocharides 1993, pp. 18–19.
53. Cobham 1908, p. 192.
54. Yıldız 2009, pp. 140–43; idem 1996, pp. 93–106; Dinç and Çelik 2012, pp. 37–59.

water *vakıfs* construction in Cyprus from the eighteenth century onwards.[55] In 1696 the representatives of an Orthodox monastery applied to the governor of Cyprus and asked for permission to build a cistern for their daily needs. Interestingly, the permission, which was eventually issued, included specific guidelines for the erection of the cistern, such as the point where it would be built, its distance from the monastery, and even its dimensions of six metres in length, five metres in width and four metres in depth.[56]

Water-related transactions often caused disagreements between the parties involved. In a court document (*kadı sicili*) dating from 1651, a resident of the district (*kaza*) of Paphos filed a lawsuit against Nikiforos (d. 1676?), the Archbishop of Cyprus, blaming him for selling a watermill for the sum of 10,000 *akçe*. The resident claimed that he had owned the watermill through donation. Eventually, there was a compromise, and the resident withdrew his claim after Nikiforos forwarded him the money he had gained through the sale.[57]

In cases where property or possession of watermills was not clear or someone deliberately acted against another in order to take advantage of water management, disputes arose, which sometimes resulted in litigation. For example, in 1675 a Muslim resident claimed a watermill as his own, which, in fact, belonged to a monastery. The watermill had been donated to the monastery by a Christian resident. The court of justice examined this case and eventually approved the monastery's proprietorship of the watermill.[58]

The Ottoman authorities had the obligation to intervene whenever a property problem occurred. However, managing a valuable commodity like water could cause controversy between the local authorities and the inhabitants. In such cases, the issue was communicated to the Sublime Porte. In 1634, an imperial order was issued by the sultan, following the request of Cypriot monks to be given permission to pray for rain. The order, which was addressed to the *beylerbeyi* (governor) of Cyprus and the *kadı* of Lefka, reported that the monks of Kykkos Monastery sent a request to the Sublime Porte explaining that, due to the drought, they went out praying according to their religious ritual. However, they were hindered by some local government officials who were opposed to the prayers and asked to receive extra money. Thus, the sultan

---

55. Yıldız 2009, pp. 140–43.
56. Theocharides 1993, pp. 276–77.
57. Ibid., pp. 128–29.
58. Ibid., pp. 154–55.

ordered an investigation to be carried out and, if the monks were right, decreed that they should be allowed to do so in accordance with their religious ritual.[59]

According to another document from 1698, the abbot of the Agios Georgios Monastery, which belonged to the *kaza* of Pentageia in the north-western part of the island, filed a lawsuit against a Muslim resident of the same region, named Hussein. The monastery claimed that Hussein cut the water's flow in order to irrigate his field, even though it had the right over the water that flowed from the channel known as *Kritikos* (Cretan). Hussein said that the monks could drink from the water of that channel but they did not have the right to use it for irrigation. However some Muslim witnesses testified that the channel's water belonged to the monastery. The court accepted the testimony and the case was closed. [60]

The vitalness of water in agricultural production and in day-to-day activities of the inhabitants of the island made it, as shown in the above cases, often a 'bone of contention'. Of course, there were also cases of personal dispute over this issue. However, the requirement on the part of local authorities to collect taxes from agricultural production, coupled with water scarcity that affected that production's yields, was the cause of such disputes.

Apart from disagreements, incidents of unfair pressure are also recorded. Such cases were solved in the court under the supervision of the *kadı*; however, under certain circumstances, senior officials of the administration could intervene as well. According to a sixteenth-century letter (*mektub*) of the governor of Cyprus to the *kadı* of Paphos, a non-Muslim resident of the area of Lefka was being harassed by some other residents of the same village regarding the possession of a water mill, which he had held hereditarily for over thirty years. The governor ordered an investigation to be carried out by the Ottoman court. The *kadı* investigated the case and confirmed that the watermill was legally owned by the non-Muslim resident. [61]

Transactions and Monetary Values of Water Assets

In land sale/transfer documents, land property often appears to be sold along with assets related to water management, such as irrigation channels, wells, tanks and watermills. In 1612, a transaction took place between two Christians concerning the sale of a two-acre piece of land, in which there was a well, five

---

59.   Ibid., pp. 100–01.

60.   Ibid., pp. 296–97.

61.   Ibid., pp. 4–5.

almond trees and a pear tree. The above were sold to a non-Muslim citizen for the sum of 2,000 *akçe*.[62] The field's transfer was made under the *sipahi's* (assignee of provincial taxes) authorisation and the buyers paid an extra sum of 1,600 *akçe* to receive the right to property (*tapu* fee).[63] In a judicial document (*hüccet*) of 1695, which records a sale made by non-Muslims to non-Muslims, a well and a water tank are included among other assets.[64] Wells were fairly common assets in seventeenth-century transactions since they were among the most essential means of water management. In most cases wells were contained in the sales of property of land, houses or gardens. In 1621, for example, two non-Muslims sold to a Muslim resident of the Morphou region a land property, which also included three houses and a ruined well, for the sum of 3,030 *akçe*. Under the permission of the *sipahi*, they also sold him a cultivated field of twelve acres, but, before that, they had already paid 1,000 *akçe* as a *tapu* fee.[65] In a similar case in 1657, a *ziamet*-holder (large fief holder) sold to the non-Muslim inhabitants of Nicosia for the total amount of 96 *riyali kuruş* a part of his property, which, as well as a house, a shed (or cottage), an orchard of two acres, eighteen olive trees, seventy mulberry trees and three apricot trees, also included a well.[66]

In Ottoman court documents from seventeenth-century Cyprus, we often encounter cases, in which plots of land are sold together with water related assets. Watermills in particular used to be inextricably linked to agricultural lands. In the middle of the seventeenth century, a watermill was valued around 10,000 to 15,000 *akçe* and could be sold whole or in part. In 1649, the abbot of the Kykkos Monastery sold to a non-Muslim named Loizos half of a watermill for the sum of 6,500 *akçe*. The watermill was co-owned by the Kykkos Monastery and Loizos. However, because of proven debts, the monastery was forced to sell its share.[67] Another category of transactions involving the aquatic element is also interesting. Apart from the water management constructions mentioned above, one could also sell or buy the right to use water, usually for watering farmlands. In Ottoman court documents from Cyprus there are cases where someone could sell or buy the use of running water for specific days and hours.

---

62. The *akçe* was the most widespread silver coin in the Ottoman Empire.

63. Theocharides 1993, pp. 64–65.

64. Ibid., pp. 270–71.

65. Ibid., pp. 90–91.

66. Ibid., pp. 134–35. *Riyali piasters* or *riyali kuruş*, were silver coins of Spanish origin. Liata 1996, pp. 197–99; Gerber 1982, p. 309.

67. Theocharides 1993, pp. 124–25.

Typically, the water received or transferred was spent every fifteen days, from morning or noon to sunset.[68]

Water management, apparently, required particular organisation in terms of availability for irrigation needs, where the quantities of water required were large. Low rainfall, combined with the need of some crops for water, especially during the summer months, forced residents to organise the supply of water using the above-mentioned methods. In one such case, in 1655, a Muslim resident of Nicosia sold to a non-Muslim resident of the same city, for the amount of 6,000 *akçe*, the right to use the running water in the nearby village of Kato Chrysida, from noon to sunset every fifteen days.[69] In the same area, a similar transaction took place in 1689. This time, a Muslim sold to a non-Muslim an orchard of four acres, located in the village of Kato Chrysida, for the sum of 400 *esedi kuruş*. The orchard included trees and running water every other Monday.[70] In 1693, a Muslim resident sold to a non-Muslim resident of the Agios Andronikos village the right to use his share of the water flowing from the channel. The water flowed from sunrise to sunset every other Tuesday.[71] Here is one more case: a document dating from 1699 records a transaction of water-related assets between non-Muslims in the Paphos district, which included the right to hold running water. Along with the water, uncultivated fields with olive trees and fruit trees were sold for the sum of 80 *esedi kuruş*.[72] As already illustrated, what sold was the right to use the source of running water for specific days or even hours.

Water-Related Property Issues

Through the study of water management transactions, some other aspects of the water management issues can also be illuminated. The necessity of water as well as its widespread and multipurpose use are the two basic factors that extended the already wide range of people involved in water management transactions. In Ottoman court documents from Cyprus, one observes that a variety of people used and managed the available water in various ways and

68. Ibid., pp. 224–25, 252–53.

69. Ibid., pp. 130–31.

70. *Esedi piastres* or *esedi kuruş* were silver piasters of Dutch origin. See Gerber 1982, pp. 309–11; Pamuk 2000, pp. 99, 144, 162–63, 175–76; Liata 1996, pp. 197–202; Theocharides 1993, pp. 224–25.

71. Theocharides 1993, pp. 252–53.

72. Ibid., pp. 308–9.

for different purposes. As I have listed in several cases above, the presence of ordinary people, both Muslims and non-Muslims, usually residents of rural areas, who used water and related assets to cultivate fields or to meet life's needs, is very common in judicial Ottoman documents.

Ottoman officers and representatives of foreign states also participated in water-related transactions, an indication of the extent of the property of people holding such offices. In 1644, the chief of janissaries (*yeniçeri ağası*) via his representative, sold to a group of non-Muslim residents a part of his property consisting of a house with three wells, trees and water-tanks for the sum of 37,000 *akçe*.[73] In 1684, the Venetian Consul in Cyprus sold to the governor of the island, a part of his property of a total value of 2,250 *kuruş*.[74] In addition, he transferred to the governor of Cyprus (*beylerbey*) the right to take over a 1,500-acre field along with running water located at the boundaries of the village of Lakatamia, a seventy-acre field in the same village and a 1,600-acre field in the area of Strovolos for the sum of 400 *esedi kuruş*.[75] In 1686, the governor of Cyprus sold to a non-Muslim resident part of his property, including three wells and three water-tanks, with a total value of 3,000 *akçe*. Furthermore he sold a field of 1,500 acres with running water within the boundaries of the Lakatamia village for the amount of 500 *esedi kuruş*, a seventy-acre field in the same village and a 1,060-acre field in the village of Strovolos.[76] It is probable that these two documents are connected and this is rather a case of re-trading on the same property.

Orthodox Christian monks are another category of people involved in water-related transactions. Monks also participated in various ways in the issues concerning water management in Cyprus. They not only participated in transactions but also, as I have shown above, were the ones who took action in every possible way during periods of drought. Their transactions mainly aimed at meeting the needs of the monastery or maintaining its property. Monks as representatives of monasteries were involved in water-related transactions. In 1585, the abbot of Kykkos Monastery and some monks sold to a Muslim resident a watermill that belonged to the monastery, together with uncultivated

---

73. Ibid., pp. 120–21.

74. The *kuruş or piastre*, was a silver coin. During the seventeenth century its value fluctuated between 80 and 150 *akçe*. There were different types and names of *kuruş* (*riyali kuruş, esedi kuruş*, etc). Liata 1996, 106–08, 197–99; Gerber 1982, pp. 309–14.

75. Theocharides 1993, pp. 174–75.

76. Ibid., pp. 188–89.

lands, two apricot trees, running water and a stone building, all for the sum of 4,000 *akçe*.[77]

In 1606, some artillery soldiers of the Paphos Fortress, sold to a monk of the Kykkos Monastery the right to own running water and uncultivated fields in the village of Sindi in the *kaza* of Paphos, for the sum of 52 *altun*.[78] Both the running water and the fields were formerly owned by a monk.[79] In some cases transactions were carried out exclusively among the monks. In 1699, a monk sold to the abbot of the Kykkos Monastery an orchard, together with trees and running water, located within the boundaries of the district of Paphos, for the sum of 4,000 *akçe*.[80]

Conclusion

As I have presented through travellers' descriptions and European and Ottoman archival documents, there are several indicators of water scarcity in seventeenth-century Cyprus. The island, due to its geographic location and climate, was exposed to long periods of heat and drought and lacked abundant quantities of water. The scarcity of water affected the Cypriots' daily lives considerably. Agricultural production and taxation, demography and social cohesion were some of the sectors affected by water scarcity. Existing water sources defined the boundaries not only of arable land but also of inhabited areas and also prescribed the variety and type of crops.

The means of water management in the period under investigation were mainly structures designed for the storage of rainwater and its disposal on arable land. Water-related assets, which functioned as an integral part of the agricultural sector, defining the boundaries of arable land, also had a decisive role in the daily life of the island's residents. Water and its means of management were of great significance when it came to the transactions between the inhabitants of the island, mainly accompanying real estate transactions, whether agricultural land or houses. Furthermore, water management involved almost

---

77. Ibid., pp. 12–13.

78. The *altun* was a gold coin that had been circulated in the Ottoman Empire since the Mehmet II's era. During the sixteenth century, one *altun* was roughly equivalent to 55 to 70 *akçe*, but in the late sixteenth and seventeenth centuries, given the fluctuations in the coin currencies, the ratio of an *altun* ranged from 120 to 370 *akçe*. Sahillioğlu 1964, p. 228; Liata 1996, pp. 84, 191–93.

79. Theocharides 1993, pp. 50–51.

80. Ibid., p. 303.

all layers of the Cypriot social pyramid, bringing together various members of Ottoman society.

A historical study that focuses on issues such as water management eventually opens a range of other issues, with which these interact indirectly or directly, causing interesting interpretations on a macro-, meso-, or micro-level analysis. Through the study of water, one can traverse an interesting path, which starts from its environmental identity and leads to the shaping of a multifaceted historical identity, consisting of economic, administrative, social and cultural aspects. Through this path, a historian can consider water as a natural resource, as a common asset, as a biotic necessity and, on the other hand, as a field of political and economic administration, as a social *conditio sine qua non* and as a cultural asset.[81] This article has sought to partially raise the issue of water management, through the case of seventeenth-century Cyprus, where water played a key role in determining the 'precarious lives'[82] of the island's people.

Bibliography

Unpublished primary sources

State Archives of Venice (*Archivio di Stato di Venezia*), Venice

    Civico Museo Correr

National Library of Cyril and Methodius (*Narodna Biblioteka Kiril i Metodij, NBKM*), Sofia

Published primary sources

Archimandrite Kyprianos. 1902 [1788]. *Ιστορία χρονολογική της νήσου Κύπρου ερανισθείσα εκ διαφόρων ιστορικών και συντεθείσα απλή φράσει υπό του, της Αγιωτάτης Αρχιεπισκοπής Αρχιμανδρίτου Κυπριανού αρχομένη από του κατακλυσμού μέχρι του παρόντος, εν η προσετέθη, και η περί της Αυτονομίας της Ιεράς Εκκλησίας των Κυπρίων Έκθεσις του Αοιδήμου Αρχιεπισκόπου Κυρίου Φιλοθέου άμα και περί ενδόξων Ανδρών και Αγίων Κυπρίων* [*Istoría chronologikí tis nísou Kýprou eranistheísa ek diáforon istorikón kai syntetheísa aplí frásei ypó tou, tis Agiotátis Archiepiskopís Archimandrítou Kyprianoú archoméni apó tou kataklysmoú méchri tou paróntos, en i prosetéthi, kai i perí tis Aftonomías tis Ierás Ekklisías ton Kypríon Ékthesis tou Aoidímou Archiepiskópou Kyríou Filothéou áma kai perí endóxon Andrón kai Agíon Kypríon*]. Nicosia: Evagoras.

---

81. The Islamic law (*sharia*) recognised as a fundamental the right of access to water for both humans and animals (*shafa*) and for crops (*shirb*). Hughes 2001 [1885], p. 579; Zargar 2014, pp. 112–23; Hillenbrand 2009, pp. 27–56.

82. Fernand Braudel used this term to characterise the life conditions of the people who lived in the Mediterranean islands, including Cyprus, especially in the second half of the 16th century. See Braudel 1972, vol. 1, p. 151.

Styliani Lepida

Cobham, Claude Delaval. 1908. *Excerpta Cypria, Materials for a History of Cyprus*. Cambridge: Cambridge University Press.

Duteil-Loizidou, Anna Pouradier. 1995. *Consulat de France à Larnaca (1660-1696): documents inédits pour servir à l'histoire de Chypre, vol. 2*. Nicosia: Cyprus Research Centre.

Hughes, Thomas Patrick. 2001 [1885]. *A Dictionary of Islam, being A Cyclopaedia of the Doctrines, Rites, Ceremonies, and Customs, together with the Technical and Theological Terms, of the Muhammadan Religion*. London: W.H. Allen and Co.

Lusignano, Steffano. 1573. *Chorograffia et Breve Historia Universale dell' Isola de Cipro principiando al tempo di Noe per in fino al 1572 per il R.P. Lettore Fr. Steffano Lusignano di Cipro dell'Ordine de Predicatori*. Bologna.

Theocharides, Ioannis P. 1993. *Οθωμανικά έγγραφα 1572-1839, τόμ. 1 [Othomanika Eggrafa 1572-1839, vol. 1]*. Nicosia: Kykkos Monastery Research Centre.

Tsirpanlis, Zacharias. 1973. *Ζαχαρίας Ν. Τσιρπανλής, Ανέκδοτα έγγραφα από τα αρχεία του Βατικανού, Λευκωσία: Κέντρο Επιστημονικών Ερευνών [Anékdota éngrafa apó ta archeía tou Vatikanoú 1625-1667]*. Nicosia: Cyprus Research Centre.

Secondary sources

Asdrahas, Spiros I. 1988. *Οικονομία και Νοοτροπίες [Oikonomía kai Nootropíes]*. Athens: Hermes.

Barkan, Ömer Lütfi. 1975. 'The Price Revolution of the Sixteenth Century: A Turning Point in the Economic History of the Near East'. *International Journal of Middle East Studies* 6 (1): 3–28.

Bostan, İdris. 2003. *Ege Adaları'nın İdarî, Malî ve Sosyal Yapısı*. Ankara: Stratejik Araştırma ve Etüdler Milli Komitesi.

Braudel, Fernand. 1972. *The Mediterranean and the Mediterranean World in the Age of Philip II, vol. 1*. 2 vols. London: Collins.

Çokuğraş, Işıl. 2012. 'Jerusalem Water Supply Systems and Ottoman Fountains'. In İsmail Koyuncu et al. (eds), *IWA WWTAC 201: 3rd IWA Specialized Conference on Water and Wastewater Technologies in Ancient Civilizations March 22–24, 2012 – Istanbul, Turkey*. Istanbul: International Water Association. pp. 612–28.

Constantini, Vera. 2009. *Il sultano e l'isola contesa: Cipro tra eredità veneziana e potere ottoman*. Torino: UTET.

Dinç, Güven and Cemil Çelik. 2012. 'Osmanlı Dönemi Kıbrıs Su Vakıfları (1571–1878)'. *Mediterranean Journal of Humanities* 2 (1): 37–59.

Dündar, Recep. 1998. 'Kıbrıs Beylerbeyliği 1570-1670'. Ph.D. Diss. Malatya: İnönü University.

——. 2010. '18 Mart-14 Haziran 1608 Yılı Kıbrıs Eyaleti Bütçesi'. *Turkish Studies* 5 (4): 1033–48.

Faroqhi, Suraiya. 1977. 'Rural Society in Anatolia and the Balkans during the Sixteenth Century'. *Turcica* 9 (1): 161–95.

151

Water Management Issues in an Ottoman Province

———. 1994. 'Crisis and Change 1590–1699'. In Halil İnalcık and Donald Quataert (eds), *An Economic and Social History of the Ottoman Empire, vol. 2*. 3 vols. Cambridge: Cambridge University Press. pp. 411–636.

———. 1999. 'A Natural Disaster as an Indicator of Agricultural Change: Flooding in the Edirne Area, 1100/1688-89'. In Elizabeth Zachariadou (ed.), *Natural Disasters in the Ottoman Empire: Halcyon Days in Crete III*. Rethymnon: Crete University Press. pp. 251–63.

Gerber, Haim. 1982. 'The Monetary System of the Ottoman Empire'. *Journal of the Economic and Social History of the Orient* 25 (3): 308–24.

Hadjianastasis, Marios. 2004. 'Bishops, Ağas and Dragomans: A Social and Economic History of Ottoman Cyprus, 1640–1704'. Ph.D. Diss. Birmingham: University of Birmingham.

Hadjikyriacou, Antonis. 2011. 'Society and Economy on an Ottoman Island: Cyprus in the Eighteenth Century'. Ph.D. Diss. London: SOAS, University of London.

Hillenbrand, Carole. 2009. 'Gardens beneath which Rivers Flow, The Significance of Water in Classical Islamic Culture'. In Sheila Blair, Jonathan Bloom (eds), *Rivers of Paradise: Water in Islamic Art and Culture*. New Haven: Yale University Press. pp. 27–57.

Hütteroth, Wolf-Dieter. 2006. 'Ecology of the Ottoman Lands'. In Suraiya N. Faroqhi (ed.), *The Cambridge History of Turkey, vol. 3, Late Ottoman Empire, 1603–1839*. Cambridge: Cambridge University Press. pp. 18–43.

İslamoğlu-İnan, Huri. 1987. 'State and Peasants in the Ottoman Empire: A Study of Peasant Economy in North-central Anatolia during the Sixteenth Century'. In Huri İslamoğlu-İnan (ed.), *The Ottoman Empire and the World-Economy*. Cambridge: Cambridge University Press. pp. 101–59.

Jennings, Ronald C. 1990. 'Village Agriculture in Cyprus'. *V. Milletlerarasi Turkiye Sosyal ve İktisat Tarihi Kongresi: Marmara Üniversitesi, Turkiyat Araştırma ve Uygulama Merkezi, İstanbul 21–25 Ağustos, 1989*. Türk Tarih Kurumu, Ankara. pp. 464–76.

———. 1993. *Christians and Muslims in Ottoman Cyprus and the Mediterranean World, 1571–1640*. New York: New York University Press.

———. 1999. 'The Population, Taxation, and Wealth in the Cities and Villages of Cyprus, according to the Detailed Population Survey (Defter-i Mufassal) of 1572'. In Ronald C. Jennings (ed.), *Studies on Ottoman Social History in the Sixteenth and Seventeenth Centuries, Women, Zimmis and Sharia Courts in Kayseri, Cyprus and Trabzon*. Istanbul: Isis Press. pp. 439–62.

Kolovos, Elias. 2006. Η νησιωτική κοινωνία της Άνδρου στο οθωμανικό πλαίσιο: Πρώτη προσέγγιση με βάση τα οθωμανικά έγγραφα της Καϊρείου Βιβλιοθήκης [*H nisiotikí koinonía tis Ándrou sto othomanikó plaísio: Próti proséngisi me vási ta othomaniká éngrafa tis Kaïreíou Vivliothíkis*]. Andros: Kaireios Library of Andros.

———. 2007. 'Insularity and Island Society in the Ottoman Context: The Case of the Aegean Island of Andros (Sixteenth to Eighteenth Centuries)'. *Turcica* 39: 49–122.

———. 2017. ὅπου ἦν κῆπος: Η μεσογειακή νησιωτική οικονομία της Άνδρου σύμφωνα με το οθωμανικό κτηματολόγιο του 1670 [*ópou in kípos: I mesogeiakí nisiotikí oikonomía tis*

Ándrou sýmfona me to othomanikó ktimatológio tou 1670]. Rethymno: Crete University Press; Andros: Kaireios Library.

———. 2018. *Across the Aegean: Islands, Monasteries and Rural Societies in the Ottoman Greek Lands*. Istanbul: Isis Press.

Liata, Eftihia D. 1996. *Φλωρία δεκατέσσερα στένουν γρόσια σαράντα [Floría dekatéssera sténoun grósia saránta]*. Athens: National Hellenic Research Foundation.

Mikhail, Alan. 2014. *The Animal in Ottoman Egypt*. Oxford: Oxford University Press.

Mutafçieva, Vera. 1988. *Agrarian Relations in the Ottoman Empire in the 15th and 16th Centuries*. Boulder: East European Monographs.

Pamuk, Şevket. 2000. *A Monetary History of the Ottoman Empire*. Cambridge: Cambridge University Press.

Panzac, Daniel. 2009. *La marine ottomane: de l'apogée à la chute de l'Empire (1572–1923)*. Paris: CNRS Éditions.

Pieraccini, Paolo. 2013. *The Franciscan Custody on the Holy Land in Cyprus*, Milan: Terra Santa.

Sahillioğlu, Halil. 1964. 'XVII. Asrın İlk Yarısında İstanbulda Tedavüldeki Sikkelerin Râyici'. *Belleten* 1 (1–2): 227–33.

———. 1967. 'Osmanlı İdaresinde Kıbrıs'ın İlk Yılı Bütçesi'. *Belgeler* 4 (7–8): 3–33.

Stournáras, Grigórios I. 2009. 'Η διαχείριση των υδάτινων πόρων στην περιοχή Τρικάλων κατά την Οθωμανική περίοδο [I diacheírisi ton ydátinon póron stin periochí Trikálon katá tin Othomanikí período]'. *Trikaliná* 29: 169–86.

Sunar, İlkay. 1987. 'State and Economy in the Ottoman Empire'. In Huri İslamoğlu-İnan (ed.), *The Ottoman Empire and the World-Economy*. Cambridge: Cambridge University Press. pp. 63–87.

Theocharides, Ioannis P. 1987. 'Στοιχεία από την ιστορία της Κύπρου (μέσα του 17ου αι.) [Stoicheía apó tin istoría tis Kýprou (mesa tou 17ou ai.)]'. *Dodoni* 16 (1): 210–23.

Tvedt, Terje. 2010. '"Water Systems", Environmental History and the Deconstruction of Nature'. *Environment and History* 16 (2): 143–66.

Ursinus, Michael. 1999. 'Natural Disasters and Tevzi: Local Tax Systems of the Post-Classical Era in Response to Flooding, Hail and Thunder'. In *Natural Disasters in the Ottoman Empire: Halcyon Days in Crete III*. Rethymnon: Crete University Press. pp. 265–72.

White, Sam. 2011. *The Climate of Rebellion in the Early Modern Ottoman Empire*. Cambridge: Cambridge University Press.

Yıldız, Netice. 1996. 'Aqueducts in Cyprus'. *Journal for Cypriot Studies* 2 (2): 89–111.

———. 2009. 'The Vakf Institution in Ottoman Cyprus'. In Michalis N. Michael, Matthias Kappler and Eftihios Gavriel (eds), *Ottoman Cyprus (A Collection of Studies on History and Culture)*. Wiesbaden: Harrassowitz Verlag. pp. 117–59.

Zargar, Cyrus Ali. 2014. 'Water'. In John Andrew Morrow (ed.), *Islamic Images and Ideas, Essays on Sacred Symbolism*. Jefferson, NC: McFarland and Company, Inc., Publishers. pp. 112–23.

PART 3

Technologies and Infrastructures

Chapter 7

NATURE'S 'COSMOPOLIS': VILLAGERS, ENGINEERS AND ANIMALS ALONG TERKOS WATERWORKS IN LATE NINETEENTH-CENTURY ISTANBUL

K. Mehmet Kentel

This article is a study of the making of Pera district of Istanbul in the late nineteenth century. But its place of analysis is not the heart of this famous, 'cosmopolitan' urban setting, but rather one of the loci fundamental in its material construction. Through following the course of the waterworks between Terkos and Pera, I examine the environmental impact of Pera's making on Istanbul's wider geographies.

At the northern edge of the metropolitan region, adjacent to the Black Sea shoreline, Terkos shares its name with the biggest lake in the region. Lake Terkos is situated forty kilometres northwest of Istanbul city centre, and separated from the Black Sea by forty- to fifty-metre-high dunes.[1] Now officially called Durusu, literally meaning 'pure water', the lake is a lagoon of 31.7 square kilometres in size[2] and has a maximum depth of around eleven metres. Lake Terkos owes its existence to the tectonic movement of the Black Sea during the third geological age. It collects water from several rivers, mostly coming from the Istranca Mountains, but was historically fed by the salty waters of the Black Sea as well, thanks to a small strait between the lake and the sea. This strait was once named the 'false entrance' by British sailors who mistook it for the entrance of Bosporus and frequently led to shipwrecks in the nineteenth

---

1.   Özgül 2011, pp. 46–7.

2.   Ibid., p. 73.

century.[3] It is now virtually blocked due to siltation,[4] as well as conscious human interventions, which comprise part of the story told in this article.

Two Chimneys

The dunes that stretch westward from Terkos to Bosporus offer occasional sights of 'botanical magic' in the words of the botanist Andrew Byfield, with a wide variety of local flowers blooming in the spring.[5] A short journey from Istanbul proper to Terkos, which takes one through the middle of the Northern Forests, disrupts this magic. The variety of topography and nature is juxtaposed with, or rather ruptured by, the variety of very recent human intervention.[6] One is struck by the mass of concrete and steel imposed over the green spaces, as bridges and highways run over forests, new towns are built over pasture fields

---

3. Great Britain Hydrographic Department 1893, p. 175.

4. Biricik 2013, pp. 18–19.

5. Byfield 2016, p. 71.

6. In the last couple of years, Turkey's Justice and Development Party (*Adalet ve Kalkınma Partisi; AKP)* government has introduced several massive infrastructure projects that have rapidly altered Istanbul's northern periphery (For the infrastructural politics of AKP, see Erensü 2016. İnal mentions the increasing interest of environmental humanities scholars to these policies: see İnal 2018, p. 298.). Long discussed, extremely controversial and hastily constructed, the so-called 'Third Bridge' at the northern Bosporus was opened to the public in 2016, with relentless government propaganda. Further north a third airport, reportedly to be the biggest in Europe, is being constructed as well, with a massive highway that connects the airport to the city and rest of Thrace; and arguably most astonishing of all, a new strait between the Black Sea and Sea of Marmara is planned, amid harsh criticisms by activists and experts, pointing out that these 'mega projects' are in the middle of the city's largest forests, and are endangering the provision of water and clean air to over twenty million residents of metropolitan region, in addition to irreversibly damaging a vital habitat for animal and plant life (For the transformation of the northern regions of Istanbul and present-day water issues, see Gülersoy et al. 2014, Karacor and Korshid 2015, Altınkaya Genel 2016, van Leewuen and Sjerps 2016.).

   What these projects have done, at least for a large part of several generations of *Istanbulites* is not merely the destroying environmental heritage and a vital natural reserve. These projects, while no doubt severely harming the ecology of the metropolitan area of one of the world's largest cities, have put the city's surroundings into the mental map of the urban residents of Istanbul, albeit as zones of imminent danger, devastation and loss. The urban experience of *Istanbulites* was apparently never this much affected by what went on in the periphery, and by the transformation of the country. The northern periphery of the city, one might argue, has been recreated and remapped through its destruction, thanks to infrastructure.

in an apparent 'land rush',[7] and real estate agencies blossom alongside flowers, in the hopes of turning concrete and steel into profit.

There is a chimney in the middle of Terkos village: a short but thick construction, made of bricks, reminiscent of the factories of the late nineteenth century. For the historian of Pera, it is almost an exact replica of one of the silent but significant fragments of the built environment of Istanbul's 'cosmopolitan' district: the chimney of *Tünel*, the world's second oldest subway, the eccentric two-stop funicular that has been operating since 1875 between Galata and Pera.[8] Its lookalike in Terkos belongs to Istanbul's first modern waterworks, which began to operate nine years after the Tünel, with the explicit aim of bringing potable water first and foremost to Pera, to the residences of the district's wealthy members who could afford mains tap water in their new apartment buildings. Contrary to what has been suggested by the urban centre's violent expansion towards the northern rural regions in the last few years, the visual connection between two chimneys, one in Pera and the other one in Terkos, is indicative of the existence of older and arguably more integral links between the epitome of city's urbanity and this northern periphery.

This article introduces the question of environment to the debate on Pera's 'cosmopolitanism'. Istanbul's historical formation, from Byzantine times onward, has been dependent on infrastructural connections between centre and periphery, urban and rural, city and nature.[9] The second half of the nineteenth century marked an especially heightened period of infrastructural activity, the primary target of which was Pera, the 'European district' of the Ottoman capital, as construction of infrastructure was intensified, geographically expanded and materially diversified, while the invested capital and expertise became transnational. Yet the modern historiography has largely ignored these connections and the environmental and material making of Pera in favour of a straightforward narrative of the emergence of modern spaces and a cosmopolitan sociability in isolation.[10] My exploration of the Terkos geography is thus motivated by an

---

7. Lange et al. 2016, p. 5.

8. Engin 2000.

9. For an early exploration of these connections for the Byzantine period, see Mango et al. 1995. In the last couple of decades, environmental historians (Cronon 1991; Klingle 2007) have been joined by the followers of Actor Network Theory, arguing that separating social from material, human from nonhuman, living from nonliving, as well as urban and nature, city and country, obfuscates our understanding of the present and the past (Swyngedouw 2004; Latour 2005).

10. Çelik 1986; Batur 1993; Akın 2011. The works of Eldem (2000), Baruh (2009) and Han (2016), while not necessarily highlighting the environmental connections, provide

uneasiness caused by this isolated treatment of Pera's urban life, as much as it
is driven by the present day transformation of Istanbul's northern regions. This
historical exercise, I hope, will also contribute to the critical study of the current ecological crisis of Istanbul engendered by massive infrastructure projects,
showing that ecological questions involving nonhuman actors have marred the
city's modernisation from the outset. From a larger perspective, I argue, the
insights provided by environmental history and critical geography, attentive to
the production of unequal geographies and nonhuman entanglements in the
process of urbanisation, promise to create a rupture in the study of 'cosmopolitan'
urbanism, especially in the turn-of-the-century Eastern Mediterranean. While
cosmopolitanism has received critical treatment in the last decade, it persists as
an influential framework in the study of late Ottoman port-cities.[11] This critical body of work, moreover, has mostly not benefited from an environmental
and materialist analysis that would locate the environmental entanglements
on which urban spaces and multitudes, framed as 'cosmopolitan', depended.[12]

Selecting water as a node that ties seemingly separate physical geographies and social worlds, as a path to introduce the question of environment
into the heart of the urban, would be fruitful for different periods in history.
But it is essential to note that nineteenth-century urbanisation all around the
world required substantially higher amounts of water than previous periods, for
individual and public consumption in response to developing needs for personal
hygiene, public health and industrial manufacture. A growing literature on the
history of water management documents the varied efforts of public officials,
policy-makers, company representatives, and almost always engineers, to provide
clean and/or potable water for urban residents and industries, not only in the
industrialised West but also in other parts of the world.[13]

---

critical analysis of the production of the spaces of Pera in the nineteenth century.

11. For the larger discussions of the loaded term, see Vertovec and Cohen 2003. For the
Ottoman studies, Kolluoğlu and Toksöz propose to critically approach cosmopolitanism as a 'spatial phenomenon': see Kolluoğlu and Toksöz 2010, p. 8. The term is
marked with colonial nostalgia and thus strongly criticised: see Hanley 2008; Halim
2013. Eldem (2013) offers a nuanced understanding of late Ottoman Istanbul's cosmopolitanism.

12. For an environmental history of the making of late Ottoman Izmir, see İnal 2018.

13. For a general survey, see Tvedt and Oestigaard 2014, pp. 357–686. Within the context
of Ottoman historiography, water has been traditionally under-studied, but there is a
growing interest, especially from environmental historians and historians of technology working mostly on the Arab provinces of the empire. See Çeçen 1984; idem 1999;
Mikhail 2013; Barak 2013; Husain 2014; Low 2015.

Nature's 'Cosmopolis'

In general, however, it is very rarely that the literature concentrating on late Ottoman Istanbul critically delves into the multifaceted relations between the city and the country, urban residents and villagers, modern technology and animals, humans and nonhumans in the stories it chooses to tell. State and/ or company claims and policy justifications are usually taken at face value, and the discourse of modernisation is accepted rather uncritically.[14] But water actually has the potential to provide a critical lens to explore the ways in which modern urban spaces have been shaped with the interaction of a wide variety of human and nonhuman actors, located not only at the heart of urban centres but dispersed along a set of 'uneven geographies'.[15]

Water in Absentia

This larger claim, i.e. the centrality of water for an urban environmental history, should be especially germane to the study of Istanbul, for around the city water is everywhere. From the hills of Istranca to the Bosporus basin, the geomorphological history of the region we now call Istanbul and its environs has been defined with the transformative impact of water on the physical environment, with rivers, lakes, inlets and straits.

Water was everywhere, except that it was not – not in a readily available, easily accessible and safely potable manner. Soon after the Roman Emperor Constantine I (r. 306–337) moved the empire's capital to the Greek city of Byzantium and changed its name to Constantinople in 330 AD, it became obvious that, while the geography seemed to be blessed with water, it was actually so poorly provided with natural freshwater sources that the reign of his successor Constantius II (r. 337–340) was marked by citizens 'dying of thirst'.[16] Such was the observation of Doctor Pardo, the secretary-general of Société Impériale de Médecine de Constantinople, 1,500 years later, in an article that appeared

---

14. See Çeçen 1984, Oğuz 1998; Kazgan and Önal 1999. There are two monographs that deal particularly with Terkos waterworks, from which I have benefited extensively (Dinçkal 2004; Yurdakul 2010). Dinçkal's is an analytical account of water provision of Istanbul between the 1850s to the 1950s, and that is necessarily how it deals with Terkos. It is an institutional history, sensitive to water-usage practices and changing habits of Istanbul inhabitants. The latter is a firm-history of Compagnie des Eaux de Constantinople, which launched the Terkos water project and ran it for decades. While it is very rich in detail and archival material, it fails to problematise the urban and environmental issues that Terkos water aimed to resolve and/or triggered.

15. Harvey 1996; Smith 2008.

16. Mango 1995, p. 5.

in local francophone newspaper *La Turquie* on 7 March 1879. The article compared European cities with the Ottoman capital in terms of their access to water: 'Even in the other capitals which have the advantage of being placed in the vicinity of a river, such as Paris or Vienna, the issue of water is the subject of so much concern … on the part of governments; in Constantinople, where this advantage does not exist, the issue is vital'.[17]

Making water submissive to the needs and desires of the people who chose to reside in/rule over the easternmost corner of the Balkan Peninsula – to clean it, to channel it, to pass it, to surpass it – has constituted one of the most fundamental elements of the region's history over thousands of years.

Pierre de Tchihatcheff (Pyotr Chikhachyov) (1808–1890), one of the founding and most celebrated figures of geology in the nineteenth century had spent several years in Istanbul and in Anatolia and published a few works on the geology of the Ottoman heartlands and the capital. As he wrote in 1864: 'What has been lacking the most in the city of Constantinople since the earliest times was water, and that is the reason why this is the only place where so many monumental works have been built in order to fight the danger [of lack of water]'.[18] Tchihatcheff was right: as Byzantinist James Crow and his team of researchers have shown, the 'long-distance' Thracian water system was indeed the longest such system in the entire Roman-Byzantine geography, longer than the much-celebrated eleven aqueducts of Rome itself. It had its springs in the Istranca Mountains, included several different water sources such as Vize, Danamandıra and Pınarca, and carried water to Istanbul, passing along Terkos and Büyükçekmece lakes, which themselves are nurtured by the catchments of the Istranca water basin.[19]

When the Ottomans took over Constantinople in the second half of the fifteenth century, some of this water infrastructure was repaired, redeveloped and put to use as the city tried to recapture its imperial and urban identity. Their biggest investment, however, was into much closer sources located in and around the Belgrad Forest.[20] Overall, the northern hinterland of the city was essential

---

17. Dr. Pardo, 'Renaissance de La Turquie Au Point de Vue de L'Hygiene', *La Turquie* **54** (7 Mar. 1879): 2 (All translations from French and Ottoman sources are mine). The same comparative line of argumentation was also evident in Gavand, 1869, p. 90.
18. Tchihatchef 2000, p. 20.
19. Crow et al. 2008, pp. 1–24.
20. Magdalino 2015, pp. 3–4.

for its growth and sustainability, but also for the symbolic and commercial power nested by the Ottoman elites into the daily lives of the inhabitants.[21]

Galata and Pera, the district at the other side of the Golden Horn, were even more deprived of local water sources. Before the Genoese semi-autonomous settlement was established in the thirteenth century, this part had a large public bathhouse and several cisterns. The first separate water system built for Galata and Pera, however, came in the 1730s when Sultan Mahmud I (r. 1730–1754) commissioned the construction of the Topuzlu Dam (*bend*) in the Belgrad Forest, whose water was distributed through a reservoir in Pera, giving the area its name: Taksim (partition, distribution).[22]

Benefiting from the resources provided by this new waterworks, Galata and Pera saw rapid growth and urbanisation from the late eighteenth century onwards. As Galata grew around its port and its emergent financial institutions, especially after the Anglo-Ottoman Trade Convention of 1838, Pera's development as a residential and commercial extension of Galata was fuelled by large European embassies, and a service sector catering to the needs and desires of a Western, and Westernised, clientele, with hotels, restaurants, cafés and culture and arts institutions for European genres.[23]

And even though the water of the Valide Dam, built in the late eighteenth century, again in the Belgrad Forest, was completely diverted to the district's use in 1838, this rapid urbanisation put a heavy strain on the city's existing infrastructure. From the late 1840s onwards, the district newspapers, published in almost all languages spoken in the Empire, but most importantly in French and English, featured continuous stories on the water problem in Pera. One of the first and daunting tasks of the 6th District Municipality (*Altıncı Daire-i Belediye*)[24] was to resolve the annual droughts experienced in Pera's hot and dry summers. Changing concerns for public hygiene, largely wooden architecture that was conducive to frequent fires and development of new private spaces in the rising apartment buildings, all necessitated a better access to water. Indeed, the Ottoman state archives abound with official documentation regarding the water problem. In 1845, during a drought that most severely affected Galata

---

21. Hamadeh 2008, pp. 76–109; Karakaş 2013.

22. Çeçen 1999, pp. 252–53.

23. For the overall development of the city in the nineteenth century, see Çelik 1986.

24. With the reform of urban governance in 1857, the Ottoman capital was divided into fourteen municipal districts. Galata and Pera were deemed as the '6th Municipal District', and the first modern municipality of the empire was founded there as a model organisation of local administration. See Neumann 2011.

and Pera, the state even requested 'suitable' individuals to go to Okmeydanı and Kağıthane, Pera's neighbouring regions with large open areas, in order to pray for rain.[25] Even the architectural evidence of northern Bosporus villages' concurrent growth, especially that of Tarabya with the summer residences of European embassies and summer locations of popular establishments of Pera, should be partially understood as a reflection of the physical necessity caused by Pera's hot and dry summers.[26]

Nevertheless, one should also treat this new interest in the newspapers concerning water or its lack as part of a larger phenomenon of writing, reading, documenting and discussing the urban matters. In the nineteenth century, a new discursive space slowly developed around newspapers, which conceptualised urban space and the life in the city as problems to be fixed through constant intervention by policymakers and expert treatments, in a time when practices and institutions of local municipal governance were slowly being established.[27] What is really striking about this discourse was the extent to which it was pursued by experts, writing long reports, historical and technical treatises often on the pages of regular dailies. These experts – mostly, but not exclusively, French engineers – published their takes on the question of water serially.[28] They offered their own reasons for the continuous water problem in the district, typically accompanied with a historical overview of how Byzantines, Genoese and the earlier Ottomans dealt with water shortages, and particular solutions to permanently fix it, trying to make a strong case for their own projects at the expense of others.[29] This expert knowledge, tied to the entrepreneurial and policymaking networks that shaped the urban fabric of nineteenth-century Pera,

---

25. Prime Ministry Ottoman Archives (*Başbakanlık Osmanlı Arşivleri, BOA*), İ.DH. 98/4917 (9 Safer 1261 [17 Feb. 1845]).

26. Girardelli 2014; Tchihatchef 2000, p. 172.

27. Duman 2000, p. 9; Groc and Çağlar 1985, pp. 203–10. For a similar, concurrent, development in Izmir, see Zandi-Sayek 2012, pp. 32–35.

28. For an overview of the reports of these experts, and the full report of Gavand himself, see Gavand 1869.

29. This publishing activity was so commonplace that one engineer who wrote a piece on the urban infrastructure problems in the Ottoman Empire felt the necessity to put a disclaimer that his article was not meant to make it easier for him to receive employment or concessions. See 'Les Travaux en Turquie et son avenir', *La Turquie* **37** (15–16 Feb. 1880): 1–2.

163

Nature's 'Cosmopolis'

was disseminated through these periodicals, and found international audiences as well, through publications in foreign engineering journals.[30]

And within this discursive space, a string of obscure place names in the margins of the Ottoman capital's larger geography were made part of the urban imaginations of the local Pera community. The waters of Bahçeköy, Istranca, Boğazköy, Burgaz, Feriköy, Paşadere, Alibeyköy, Şeytandere, Maslak and Kurudere gained a place in readers' mental maps of larger nineteenth-century Istanbul, just as localities along the northern periphery of present-day Istanbul are being remapped in the minds of its current residents due to the massive projects that have been carried out in recent years.

It was with these series of treatments of the water question in official reports and in the periodicals that the name of Terkos was mapped in the discussions regarding Pera. After Lake Terkos was deemed a suitable alternative for clean water to allocate to Pera in the late 1860s,[31] an engineer, Ternau Bey, teaming up with an Ottoman bureaucrat, Kamil Bey, received the concessions for a waterworks project that aimed to bring water from Terkos to Pera in 1872.[32] The decision was not without controversy, since there were a lot of competing projects on the table, and many opponents of Terkos water had intervened to convince the policymakers and the public that the project was hygienically and financially flawed. In the end, however, rather than endless debates on water quality, it was the Russo-Ottoman War of 1877–78, which put additional financial strains on the already bankrupt treasury,[33] that made it impossible to run an infrastructure project so close to the military zone, as the Terkos–Çatalca axis had been conceived as the last defence line of the Ottoman capital, and the armistice terms allowed the Russian army to pass even beyond this line, approaching to the western fringes of Istanbul.[34]

After the war, water shortage continued to severely affect Pera, including the embassies and consulates populating the district. In some cases the members of foreign legations accused the palace and the rest of the Ottoman elites of exploiting the city's water sources for their own benefit.[35] After the delay caused by the war and financial problems, Ternau brought together an international

30. 'The Water Supply of Constantinople', *The Engineer* (26 Sept. 1873): 202–03; 'The Water Supply of Constantinople', *The Engineer* (7 Nov. 1873): 299.
31. Gavand 1869, p. 23.
32. Pech 1911, pp. 203–06.
33. Yurdakul 2010, p. 27.
34. Baker Pacha 1879, p. 322; Erickson 2003, p. 122.
35. The National Archives of the United Kingdom (TNA), FO 78/3345/103 (4 Jan. 1881).

consortium of investors, including local bankers and real-estate developers, this time under a new company called Compagnie des Eaux de Constantinople or Dersaadet Su Şirketi (Water Company of Istanbul), which was granted a new concession in 1882, for a period of forty years (later extended to 75).[36] A network of local and European elites was now established with the aim of installing a material network of water and steel between Terkos and Pera, gathered for a project that promised lower costs and bigger profits.[37] Even though the medical community was still not satisfied,[38] it was the well-established and connected network backing the project that ended up closing the debate, and laying the foundations of the waterworks that would continue to provide water for the ever-growing Istanbul for another century to come.[39]

'L'élément essentiel à toute vie': Providing Water for 'Cosmopolitan' Gardens

On 2 January 1885, at Jardin des Petits-Champs in Tepebaşı, a high-ranking ceremony celebrated the opening of a water fountain, also marking the arrival of water from Lake Terkos to Pera. Paul Boutan, the chief engineer of the Compagnie des Eaux de Constantinople, finished his speech with the following remark: 'We can easily predict that public support for our work will continue, as we are providing them the essential element to all life!' *(l'élément essentiel à toute vie)*.[40] The invitations were sent to a limited number of people, in order 'for the newly arranged garden not to be spoiled'.[41] This was not extraordinary for the garden, for, although soon after it was opened it became one of the

---

36. Pech 1911, pp. 203–06.

37. The project was financed by the company, which secured the sole rights of using the water sources of Lake Terkos and its vicinities. In 1891, it made a net profit of 334,904 francs, which was almost doubled in less than twenty years. See Ibid., p. 205.

38. Pechedimaldji 1881.

39. As an interim solution, a pump station was established to bring the waters of Kağıthane Creek to Pera in 1882, but the amount of water was not seen as sufficient to meet the needs of the district, and several people were accused of stealing from the water conduits. See Çeçen 1984, p. 147; Compagnie des Eaux de Constantinople 1889, pp. 6–7; 'La Disette d'eau', *La Turquie* **232** (27 Oct. 1882): 1; 'Disette d'eau', *La Turquie* **235** (31 Oct. 1882): 1. Another private company, Compagnie des eaux de Scutari et Kadi-Keui, began its operations in 1893 in the Asian side, and similar companies were granted concessions across the empire, including in Beirut, Salonika and Izmir, between the 1870s and 1890s. Dinçkal 2015, pp. 214–15.

40. BOA, Y.MTV. 17/2 (6 Rebiülahir 1302 [25 Jan. 1885]).

41. BOA, İ.DH. 938/74292 (6 Rebiülevvel 1302 [24 Dec. 1884]).

most important venues for social life in Pera, this life already belonged to a limited coterie. The Jardin, with its entrance fee, theatre hall and expensive dinners in the open air, hosted pashas, beys, the diplomatic corps residing in the city, employees of foreign companies operating in the empire, artists and rich tourists who usually stayed at the hotels surrounding the garden. Thus, the nature of the social circle that participated in the opening event was probably not so different from any other night at the garden. It would not be wrong to assert that this limited elite milieu that consumed the Jardin was a microcosm of the cosmopolitan sociability that was continuously referred to in the history-writing of Pera.

Indeed, this class of people was the project's first and foremost targets. Frederic Briffault, one of the engineers of the project, had elucidated this rather bluntly in a paper he had given at the annual meeting of the Civil Engineers Institute in England:

> Too much reliance must not be placed upon the whole of the native population, amongst a large portion of which great poverty prevails, taking the Water. The Author believes that the Company will have far greater sales of Water in the European than in the native quarter of the Town.[42]

This newly installed infrastructure, then, was underlining and reproducing the already existing inequalities between different parts of the Ottoman capital. Moreover this disparity between different parts was not limited to the two sides of the Golden Horn. Inequalities present within and around the boundaries of the 6th District were represented and reinforced in the operation of Terkos waterworks. A water network plan prepared by the company (Figure 1) provides us with an inside look into the first phase of the project, aimed to distribute water to the northern side of the Golden Horn, and it is a striking representation of how this modern waterscape of the district was planned and distributed.[43]

The Terkos water first reached to the Feriköy Reservoir, and was then channelled, on the one hand to Galata and Pera, and on the other, through an additional reservoir in Şişli, to settlements along the Bosporus. The outer extensions of the network reached to other newly emerging elite neighbourhoods, such as Nişantaşı. Two main conduits merged as they entered to Pera, embodied in a 'monumental fountain' at Taksim. Here was also located the fire brigade of the district. Embassies and consulates were connected to the

42. Qtd in Dinçkal 2008, p. 686.
43. Atatürk Library (*Atatürk Kitaplığı, AK*) Hrt. 5783.

K. Mehmet Kentel

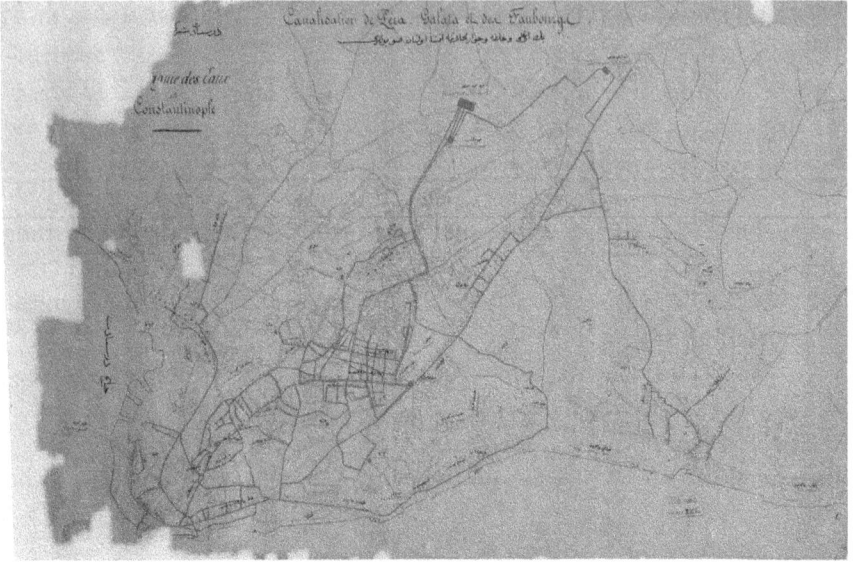

Figure 1. Compagnie des Eaux de Constantinople. Plan de la Canalisation générale de la rive Européenne du Bosphore *[General pipeline plan of the European side of the Bosporus]. Date Unknown. Source: AK, Hrt_5783.*

system, so were schools, hospitals and barracks, which were to be provided with water for free.[44]

From Taksim down to Galata, the water network was much denser, as the point here was not only to make water available in the main arteries and public fountains and buildings, but also to provide apartment buildings with private subscriptions. The upper parts of Grand Rue de Pèra were especially well covered, corresponding to the location of the residences of many wealthy members of the Pera community. In a drastic contrast, the Kasımpaşa region was almost completely deprived of Terkos water. While the contract between Compagnie des Eaux de Constantinople and the Ottoman state necessitated the company to build public fountains, these, at least in this initial phase, were very scattered and in no way sufficient for the densely populated working class neighbourhood of Kasımpaşa. A similar thing could be said for the Tophane area, another adjacent neighbourhood that was within the boundaries of the 6th District. This plan was thus not only a simple outline of the infrastructure

---

44.   BOA, İ.DH. 847/68050 (29 Rebiülahir 1299 [20 Mar. 1882]).

work. It was more importantly a representation of the socio-economic fabric and boundaries of Pera, its inherent inequalities, and how these inequalities were underlined by politics and a physical network of infrastructure that followed the elite networks of the district, rather than aiming to reach a larger public provision. More elites, in turn, followed the waterworks and other municipal services, as noted by Noyan Dinçkal, making centralised water supply a tool for 'social segregation'.[45]

The Terkos water being equally distributed or not, with ninety-kilometre-long subterranean pipes made of steel and cement, with steam-powered pumps fuelled by coal brought from Zonguldak, with monumental fountains at the Tünel Square and in the gardens of Petits-Champs and Taxim, and the company office located at no. 392 of Grand Rue de Pèra – at the cul-de-sac that is still called the Terkos Çıkmazı – the environment of Terkos and the assemblage of Terkos waterworks were finally carved into the material fabric of Pera, following two decades of public controversies and private negotiations, and a construction period of three years.

My intention in the rest of this article is to explore what else was carried between Terkos and Pera along the links established thanks to waterworks. What else did the springs across Thrace that fed Lake Terkos unleash? How did the waterworks transform its environs and the relations of places and things? If cosmopolitan Pera was dependent on the water of Terkos, which it obviously was, what else did this dependency produce? If Terkos gave its water to Pera, what did Pera give back? With these questions in mind, I will now concentrate on how the relations between various humans and animals, as well as various humans and water sources, were reconfigured with the installation of the waterworks.

Old and New Actors in Terkos Fauna

In October 1893, the Ministry of Police (*Zabtiye*) received a request from the Ministry of Foreign Affairs (*Hariciye*) to grant permission for Dr. Franz Steindachner (1834–1919), the famous Austrian zoologist and the director of the zoological collections of the Museum of Natural History of Vienna (*Naturhistorisches Museum*),[46] to visit Lake Terkos, in order to observe its native

---

45. Dinçkal 2015, p. 218.

46. One of the few documents found in the Ottoman state archives concerning this visit prematurely identifies Steindachner ('Doktor Mösyö Firenc Estayn Dahter') as the director of the museum, of which he became the interim director in 1896, and was appointed full director in 1898, a post he held until his death in 1919. See BOA, DH.MKT. 131/11 (1 Rebiülevvel 1311 [12 Sept. 1893]) and BOA, BEO. 280/20955

fish. The Ministry of Police unwillingly accepted the request, but assigned a soldier to escort Steindachner in his observations around the lake, and specifically ordered that this foreign visitor should not be allowed to fish, and rather should be handed samples that were already caught. Even though there is no further account of the type of fish collected by Steindachner from the region of Terkos, we know that this internationally acclaimed expert in ichthyology returned home from his expedition around Istanbul with 68 specimens from forty species. While certainly not constituting a major event in the region's natural or social history, Steindachner's visit marks a period that witnessed the flourishing of new forms of interest in the region's fauna, and hints at the introduction of new actors into the existing relations of humans and animals, partially triggered by the Terkos waterworks.

Situated on a lake basin with several rivers and being close to the Black Sea, the villagers in Terkos were actively engaged in fishing for a long time. Evliya Çelebi (1611–1682), the famous seventeenth-century Ottoman traveller, noted the fishing weirs (*dalyan*) installed in the lake.[47] In the nineteenth century, some of this fishing was done under the auspices of *Bezm-i Alem Valide Sultan Vakfı* (a pious foundation), which owned several land plots around the lake.[48] And perhaps also underlined by Steindachner's visit, the lake was quite rich in fish varieties.[49] Even in the 1940s, reports stated that the lake was home to a panoply of fresh-water fish.[50] The waterworks, however, threw age-old fishing activity in the lake into a controversy. For in 1887, the Ministry of Waqfs accused Compagnie des Eaux of harming the profits the *Bezm-i Alem Vakfı* had made from fishing. The ministry argued that the company's closing of the lake's outlet to the Black Sea in order to increase its water capacity had reduced the amount of fish available to catch.

Indeed, the company's contract with the Ottoman state granted the right to change the course of several rivers, and the topography of the Terkos

---

(1 Rebiülevvel 1311 [24 Sept. 1893]). For Steindachner's biography and bibliography, see Kähsbauer 1959.

47. Evliya Çelebi 2006, p. 285.

48. Yurdakul 2010, p. 56.

49. The British Museum inventories feature a couple of fish varieties collected from Lake Terkos as well, sold to the Museum by Alexander van Millingen, professor at Robert College in Istanbul, famous for his works on the historical topography of the city. See Günther 1864, p. 429.

50. Nirven 1946, p. 196.

lake basin – a right the company used extensively.[51] As part of its topographical transformation, the company hastily completed the millennia-old job of the water flowing from the Balkan Mountains: blocking the narrow strait between Lake Terkos and the Black Sea. The work of the water was of course slow and unintentional; it was a result of materials being carried along and piling up at the edge of the lake. The company's move, on the other hand, was sudden and intended to turn the natural lake into a fresh water reservoir, reducing its saltiness and limiting the loss of water to the tides between the lake and the sea.

The conflict was eventually resolved by an agreement signed between the ministry and the company, as the latter was granted the exclusive rights and concessions to fish in the lake, in return for an annual fee of 200 *kuruş* to be paid to the ministry.[52] This settlement did not satisfy many of the villagers, however, as their individual activities in the lake were restricted by this agreement. Indeed, the archives contain many complaints from the villagers who had previously worked with the pious foundation, which entailed fishing in the lake and then paying taxes, a practice now subjected to restraints and, according to the villagers, excessive fees by the company.[53]

Thus fishing in Terkos became increasingly dependent on the decisions of an international company whose headquarters was situated in Pera, and whose activities were determined by various other concerns than those of the local villagers. Compagnie des Eaux, which invested into the environment of Terkos in order to profit from its inanimate natural resources now expanded its domains into the world of the living, integrating the variety of fish found in the lake into its assemblage of concrete, steel and water.

> After breakfast we shouldered our guns and sallied forth. The weather was still very cold, with a strong, bitter north wind, blowing in from the Black Sea. We walked along the north shore of the lake for about two miles, and then came up to a large patch of open water, and this was literally swarming with wildfowl. There must have been millions of them.[54]

Obstructions put against individual fishing activity by the hands of the company look much more interesting when seen in the light of another concurrent phenomenon concerning the Terkos fauna: the development of leisure hunting. Again from Evliya Çelebi, we know that Terkos was an occasional hunting

51. BOA, İ.DH. 847/68050 (29 Rebiülahir 1299 [20 Mar. 1882]).
52. Yurdakul 2010, p. 117.
53. BOA, DH.MKT. 1764/128 (11 Safer 1308 [26 Sept. 1890]); BOA, BEO 346/25932 (13 Recep 1311 [20 Jan. 1894]).
54. Fitzgerald 1916, p. 65.

ground (*sayd-gah*), especially for various types of ducks, geese and swans; attracting even the attention of Sultan Mehmet II (r. 1444–1446, 1451–1481), who had hunted in the area before the conquest of Constantinople.[55] But despite such precedence, Terkos had never become one of the most popular hunting destinations of the Ottoman elites residing in Istanbul before the late nineteenth century. Even though hunting expeditions into the outskirts of the city were commonplace, small groves (*koru*) used as hunting grounds with specifically built mansions in the much closer vicinity of the city, where the imperial household had the exclusive right to hunt, were the predominant hunting geographies of the Ottoman capital.[56]

However, towards the end of the nineteenth century, I argue, the increasing integration of Terkos into the urban imaginations of the elites, thanks to plans to install waterworks around the region, triggered a new interest in this region as a favourite place for leisure hunting. Terkos, and especially Karaburun, were particularly fruitful grounds for the passage of quail, which had never been a popular game bird for the Ottomans because it was considered too small to hunt, but now attracted new interest as European hunting fashions began to take a root in Istanbul, especially among the elites resident in Pera and Kadıköy.[57] Gradual deforestation due to urbanisation, combined with excessive hunting, resulted in a decrease of the number of local game birds towards the turn of the century, and drew the attention of hunters and enthusiasts to the northern shores of the city, which were the passage grounds of migrant species.[58] With engineers, chemists, physicians and company officials who were in close contact with the foreign legations flowing to Terkos from the 1870s onwards, the region was gradually put on the hunting and leisure map of Istanbul's environs.

In the words of Charles Cooper Penrose Fitzgerald (1841–1921), a British naval officer stationed in Istanbul in 1879–1880, Terkos provided the perfect environment for hunting especially in the harsh winter conditions, when '[each] succeeding shot put up some more birds, and they all [escaped to the Black Sea]; but when they got [there], they apparently found it was too rough for them, for they all came back again … Truly they were between the devil and the deep sea.'[59] While it was the British Consul who recommended him Terkos for hunting escapades, the region was not yet well-known to the resident

---

55. Evliya Çelebi 2006, pp. 220, 236, 316.
56. Artan 2011, p. 95; Yarcı 2009, p. 125; Somçağ 1994, p. 427.
57. Somçağ 1994, pp. 426–29; Tchihatchef 2000, pp. 95–96.
58. Somçağ 1994, p. 427.
59. Fitzgerald 1916, p. 66.

European community of the city, manifested in the troublesome journey of Fitzgerald's party who spent three days covering thirty miles, frequently getting lost on the way. Increased interest in the region due to the activities around Terkos water gradually made it a more familiar destination for visitors looking for recreation; and, once construction began, picnickers thronged the area with the aim of revelling in the spectacles provided not only by nature but by the construction itself, as a manifestation of the wonders of modern technology.[60]

Indeed, after the opening of the waterworks, Ottoman officials began to receive an increasing number of requests from foreign subjects for permission to hunt around Terkos, probably inspired by the accounts of fellow members of their social circles who were commissioned in the region in order to work for the project. The group of people that frequented Terkos, mostly with the intention to hunt, were members of the foreign diplomatic legations resident in Pera. The archives show that German, Swedish and Italian ambassadors, British military attaché, and their entourages, visited, hunted and fished in and around Terkos.[61] Leisure hunting in Terkos became such a feature of the period's elite culture that caricatures in the satirical press ridiculed it.[62]

Another *beastly* link formed between Terkos and Pera was the increasing popularity of live quails, caught in large numbers around Terkos and Karaburun with the help of hunting nets, and sent to Pera's famous Fish Market to be sold in the charcuteries that catered for Pera's 'cosmopolitan' community.[63] And one of the biggest retail stores of the city, Baker Department Store (*ticarethanesi*), located in Galata and selling expensive guns, outfits, gear and accessories imported from various European countries, catered for hunting enthusiasts.[64] Hunting trips to the region were made easier for a larger community of enthusiasts as the Rumeli Railways was launched in 1871, which not only gradually connected the empire to European capitals, but also the Ottoman capital city to its suburbs; and the station of Çatalca, opened in 1872, provided a relatively easy access to Terkos.[65]

---

60. Kazgan and Önal 1999, p. 37.
61. BOA, Y.PRK.ASK. 186/74 (8 Şaban 1320 [10 Nov. 1902]); BOA, Y.PRK.ASK. 222/27 (21 Recep 1322 [1 Oct. 1904]).
62. Reproduced in Kazgan and Önal 1999, p. 94.
63. Somçağ 1994, p. 427.
64. Maison Baker 1908.
65. Engin 1993, p. 108. It was also very common for the (temporary) residents of the European legations and other elites in Tarabya to ride to Terkos through the Belgrad Forest. See, for example, Morgenthau 2004, p. 370.

K. Mehmet Kentel

The congregation of engineers in the region, and the interest of foreigners in Terkos as a leisure space also created a security concern on the part of the Ottoman state about potential imposters who 'pretended to be engineers'. The company engineers were asked to carry with them at all times licenses (*tezkire*), proving that they were in fact engineers commissioned by the company. The same document that ordered the engineers to carry these licenses with them also stated that foreigners who wished to hunt in these environs should get permits from the foreign ministry first.[66] The fact that this same document brought together two seemingly different issues would also suggest that in the minds of the Ottoman authorities, too, the newly gained popularity of hunting was tied to the construction of the waterworks.

The waterworks, in the end, left its mark on the various forms of inter-connections among humans and animals as a new form of dependence was created between the city and its north-western periphery. Animals that were part of a relatively local economy mostly geared towards subsistence were made part of a regional, and even an international, economy of large-scale profit and leisure. While the local villagers' autonomous access to their natural environments was put under increasing control and limitations, Pera's 'cosmopolitan' community became more and more present in the area's food chain, as their interest and contact with the birds, boars and fish of Terkos expanded. The impact of the Terkos waterworks turned out to be crucial for the remaking of the human and animal relations in the region.

This is a reminder that the celebrated diversity and the formation of elite urbanities in the *fin-de-siècle* Pera were not restricted to the *jardins*, but moved between places, and affected larger geographies than the district boundaries. Just as the water of Terkos was a vital resource upon which Pera's elite spaces depended, the rural areas of Terkos provided leisure spaces and animals for newly emerging tastes and hobbies of those elites, as physical and – it must be said – *deadly* manifestations of elite 'cosmopolitanism'. These hunting parties constituted another channel of interdependence between 'cosmopolitan' Pera and 'peripheral, rural, natural' Terkos, challenging the dichotomous position-ing of those geographic and cultural entities, and leaving footprints on the environment. The limited sociability of the *jardins*, in a sense, was exported to

---

66. BOA, Y.A.HUS. 284/67 (10 Cemazeyilevvel 1311 [19 Nov. 1893]) the authorities always tried to control and monitor hunting activity, and carrying licenses for hunt-ing activities was not confined to foreigners. However, in their case, they had to obtain permissions from the Foreign Ministry, and there was a specific sensitivity towards their activities around military zones. See Yarcı 2009, p. 127.

rural Terkos, in exchange for the water that would flow from the taps of private bathrooms, and for birds to be sold in the markets of Pera.

Changing the Flow

With the increasing presence of Pera in Terkos through the material and spatial reconfiguration caused by the waterworks, the villagers living around the lake not only witnessed their access to the animal world being restricted, but their ability to use their domestic water sources, as well as to protect their immediate surroundings from the harmful impacts of water, also diminished. The villagers of Celep and Pınarhisarı (Hisarbeyli), two neighbouring villages close to the southern shores of the Lake Terkos, more directly and acutely felt the severe impact of the newly installed waterworks. A memo sent to the Ministry of Interior Affairs (*Dahiliye Nezareti*) in 1887, only two years after the water of the lake began to be pumped to Pera, informed the bureaucrats of the Ottoman capital that many fields, including farms and meadows of these two villages, were flooded, causing huge material loss. The memo went on to quote the harmed villagers blaming the water company for the floods.[67]

As we have seen, the waterworks had blocked the natural passage between the lake and the Black Sea to make the former a 'natural' reservoir. However, soon after the waterworks began to operate, with heavy rainfalls and melting of the snow in the Balkan Mountains in spring, the excess water flowing into the lake could not find an output, and flooded the nearby villages of Celep and Pınarhisarı. As Stéphane Castonguay notes, in various geographies of the world, villagers in riparian settlements tend to develop mechanisms to cope with recurring floods as 'structural elements of the landscape'. But in many cases, extreme events are 'constructed' through mediation by external forces that alter the landscape, and thus increase the vulnerability of the local human and nonhuman populations.[68] A series of documents in the Ottoman state archives bear witness to the years-long struggle of the villagers, especially of Celep, trying to draw the attention to their newly constructed vulnerability, and to be compensated for the material loss they had to endure because of the company's operations.[69] The Ministry of Interior Affairs and Istanbul Prefecture (*Şehremaneti*) seemed sympathetic to the claims of the villagers; yet the company insisted that it could not be accused of wrongdoing since the

---

67. BOA, DH.MKT. 1448/55 (1 Muharrem 1305 [19 Sept. 1887]).

68. Castonguay 2007, pp. 820–44.

69. BOA, DH.MKT. 1512/56 (4 Şevval 1305 [14 June 1888]).

Figure 2. Çatalca Paftası [Çatalca Plate]. Date Unknown. Source: AK, Hrt_943.

right to change the topography of the lake was given to it by the concession contract of 1882.[70] In 1889, the municipality sent its chief engineer Monsieur Leclerq to the region to craft a report about the situation. His report found the claimants right and suggested that the company should compensate for the damages of the villagers.[71] In the meantime, new petitions kept coming regarding the periodical floods.[72] The archives lose track of the petitioners by 1890, probably suggesting that the company finally sought to compensate the damages caused by the waterworks. However this did not mean its harmful impact on the lake's environs ended; on the contrary, as reports from as late as 1912 and 1913 suggest, yearly floods continued to ruin the surrounding fields, which were turned into swamps when the water fell back in summer, and polluted the lake by bringing waste from the land.[73]

The villagers and their habitat became part of this convoluted story of infrastructural and environmental connections in other ways, too. One such issue was the limitation of their access to several of their traditional water sources, i.e. the local, small torrents that fed Lake Terkos, which were now to be collected by the company in order to reach to the necessary levels of water distribution for the city. In 1888, the inhabitants of Karaca, Ormanlı, Pınarhisarı, Belgrad and Çiftlikköy villages wrote a joint petition to the Ottoman authorities, stating that if the company was to use the entire water of Kuşkaya, a local water source used by these villagers, nine water mills located in the villages would become obsolete, their corn fields and orchards would dry, and their animals would die of thirst.[74] A similar complaint was made by the villagers of Terkos in order to protect their right to use of Karamandere, one of the biggest rivers in the region, which provided for their 'necessities of life' (*havayic-i zaruriye*). Once again, the villagers were told that the concessions agreement had given the company the right to collect the water of these local sources when deemed necessary. Luckily, actual operations on the river were yet to begin, and the company was responsible to provide the necessary reserves for the needs of these villagers.[75]

Whereas the villagers eventually failed to alter the course of the waterworks, they proved themselves to be a force that needed to be dealt with by the state and company authorities. And by their constant petitioning for compensation

70. Yurdakul 2010, p. 44.

71. BOA, DH.MKT. 1603/74 (9 Recep 1306 [11 Mar. 1889]).

72. BOA, DH.MKT. 1612/45 (1 Şaban 1306 [2 Apr. 1889]).

73. Yurdakul 2010, pp. 44–5.

74. Ibid., p. 67.

75. BOA, DH.MKT. 1690/24 (24 Cemaziyelevvel 1307 [16 Jan. 1890]).

for their material loss and access to nearby water sources, they became a much more central part of the company's economic projections and concerns than the poor populations of Pera and its surrounding areas, who, as we have seen, were to a large part completely ignored by the water network installed by the company. Nevertheless, the altered land and waterscapes of Terkos, which limited the villagers' access to their immediate surroundings and curbed their part in the formation of new material assemblages, eventually forced many inhabitants to seek opportunities elsewhere. As Nazım Nirven noted in 1946, the population of the villages around Terkos dropped in the decades after the waterworks began to operate.[76]

Conclusion: Nature's 'Cosmopolis'

Many engineers, integral members of Pera's 'cosmopolitan' community, commissioned to work on various projects in the Ottoman capital in the second half of the nineteenth century, were also asked to prepare reports and craft concrete proposals in order to provide better water supplies for Pera – as the Ottomans loved to 'recycle' the experts they had a temporary hold on. While they offered different solutions and uttered alternative sources, all of them, in their unique ways, offered to connect the peripheral environment to Pera in a better, more efficient and extensive way. During the long years of discussions regarding the water problem of the district, the expert knowledge and material investment put into the making of Pera's urban space attempted to break through its limits. Finally, with the start of the construction of the Terkos waterworks the material relations, expert knowledge, will to modernisation and ideology of progress, which were shaping Pera's urban space, poured into the rural periphery, devouring their 'spatial barriers',[77] following the route opened by the construction of the railways. But this search for a more efficient and integral connection to the periphery resulted in a set of messy and unequal relations between the various human and nonhuman actors involved, from Terkos to Pera.

Not only did the power generated by water meet the basic requirements of the residents of firstly Pera, and then the rest of Istanbul, in unequal ways. What it further generated was connections between urban and rural that contributed to the formation of an elite class, which not only depended on Terkos water as a life necessity, but flourished on its material networks and used it to

76. Nirven 1946, p. 194.
77. Harvey 1996, p. 412.

increase its claim on land, either as part of the 'city' or 'nature', whether through work or through leisure.

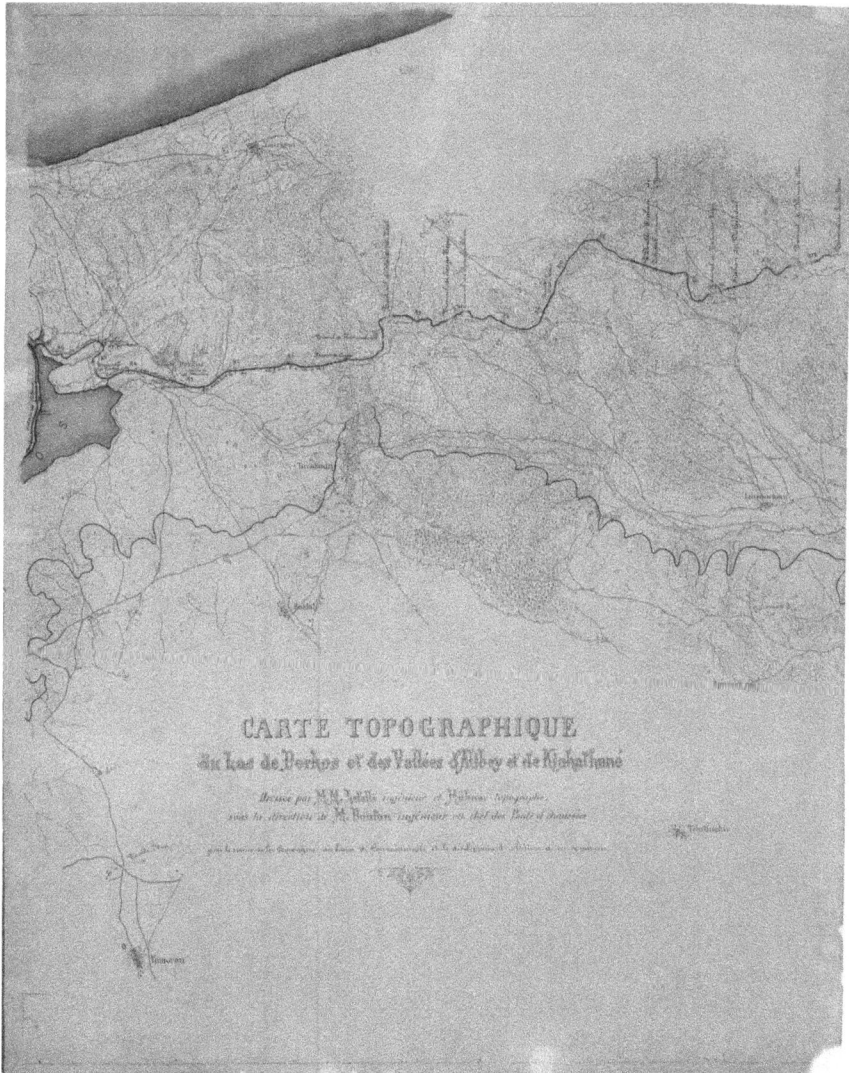

Figure 3. Lefalle, Hübner, Boutan. Carte topographique du Lac de derkos et des Vallées d'Alibey et de Kiahathané *[An excerpt from the Topographic Map of Lake Terkos and the Valleys of Alibey and Kağıthane]. Date unknown. Source: AK, Hrt_Gec_1875/6/7/8.*

Pera historiography, in line with writing on other 'cosmopolitan' urbanities, has been marred by an over-reliance of the sources that exclusively dealt with the urban centre, and an over-attention to the architectural façade of the district. Studying the sources produced outside Pera, with an attentive eye to the peripheral arrangements, situates the district within a wider network of humans and nonhumans. It helps us to appreciate the fact that the fabric of modern, 'cosmopolitan' Pera was woven through the water of Terkos, mud of the riparian villages, fish of the lake and game stock of the surrounding lands, and invites us to explore other forms of diversities that the limited frame of cosmopolitanism not only excludes, but also actively obscures.

It is also crucial, following William Cronon and Timothy Mitchell,[78] to keep in mind that Terkos as a space of 'nature', categorically different from the rest of the region, did not exist before its 'discovery' as a space of vital natural resources, biological diversity and a wondrous terrain for hunting and leisurely promenade. Pera, too, depended upon this world of Terkos, as they co-constituted each other as seemingly distinct entities, even though they were actually part of a larger assemblage of environment, infrastructure and technology. The history of Pera is about any and all actors along this assemblage; it is about the people of Terkos village who struggled for their 'necessities of life', as much as about the attendants of the ceremony at Jardin des Petits-Champs, who celebrated the provision of their district with 'the essential element to all life' – one man's *havayic-i zaruriye* is another man's *l'élément essential.*

ACKNOWLEDGEMENTS

I would like to thank the editors of this volume, and the participants in the Environmental History of the Ottoman Empire and Turkey Workshop 2017 in Hamburg for their helpful suggestions and encouragement. Thanks also to co-panellists, discussants and audiences at conferences and workshops in Istanbul, Berlin and Zagreb, where I presented several papers on the environmental connections between Terkos and Pera. Ayşe Nal kindly gave feedback at short notice. Brian L. McLaren, Selim S. Kuru and the members of the University of Washington (UW) Turkish Studies Circle, especially Esra Bakkalbaşıoğlu and Oscar Aguirre-Mandujano, read and commented on an earlier version of the dissertation chapter this article is partially based upon. I would particularly like to express my gratitude to my advisor Reşat Kasaba, who read several versions and helped me develop my arguments. My dissertation research and writing have been supported by the International Journal for Urban and Regional Research Foundation, Koç University's Research Centre for Anatolian Civilizations, UW Simpson

78.   Cronon 1991, pp. 7–8; Mitchell 2002, p. 35.

Center for Humanities, UW Graduate School and UW Near Eastern Languages and Civilizations Department.

Bibliography

Unpublished Primary Sources

The Atatürk Library (*Atatürk Kitaplığı, AK*), Istanbul
Haritalar (Hrt) 943, 5783
Haritalar (Hrt_Gec) 1875, 1876, 1877, 1878
The Prime Ministry Ottoman Archives (*Başbakanlık Osmanlı Arşivleri, BOA*), Istanbul
Babıâli Evrak Odası Evrakı (BEO) 280/20955, 346/25932
Dâhiliye Nezâreti (DH.) 98/4917
Dâhiliye Nezâreti Mektubî Kalemi Evrakı (DH.MKT) 131/11, 1448/55, 1512/56, 1603/74, 1612/45, 1690/24, 1764/128
İrade Dahiliye (İ.DH) 938/74292, 847/68050
Sadâret Hususî Maruzât (Y.A.HUS) 284/67
Yıldız Mütenevvi Maruzât (Y.MTV) 17/2
Yıldız Perakende Evrakı Askeri Maruzât (Y.PRK.ASK) 186/74, 222/27
The National Archives of the United Kingdom (TNA), London
Foreign Office (FO), 78/3345/103

Published Primary Sources

La Turquie
The Engineer

Baker Pacha, Valentine. 1879. *War in Bulgaria: A Narrative of Personal Experiences, vol. 2.* 2 vols. London: Low, Marston, Searle and Rivington.
Compagnie des Eaux de Constantinople. 1889. *Exposition Universelle de 1889. Sections Étrangéres: Turquie. Compagnie des Eaux de Constantinople. Notice de la Distribution des Eaux de Constantinople.* Paris: Imprimerie J. Semichon & Co.
Evliya Çelebi. 2006. *Evliya Çelebi Seyahatnâmesi 1. Kitap Topkapı Sarayı Kütüphanesi Bağdat 304 numaralı yazmanın transkripsiyonu – dizini* (ed. and trans. by Robert Dankoff, Seyit Ali Kahraman and Yücel Dağlı). Istanbul: Yapı Kredi Yayınları.
Fitzgerald, Charles Cooper Penrose. 1916. *From Sail to Steam, Naval Recollections, 1878–1905.* London: E. Arnold.
Gavand, Eugene Henry 1869. *Projet de distribution d'eau de Galata, de Péra, des Faubourgs et des villages de la côte d'Europe du Bosphore.* Istanbul [Constantinople]: publisher unknown.

Great Britain Hydrographic Department. 1893. *Sailing Directions for the Dardanelles, Sea of Marmara, Bosporus, and Black Sea 4th Edition*. London: The Hydrographic Office, Admirality.

Günther, Albert C.L. 1864. *Catalogue of the Fishes in the British Museum vol. 5*. 8 vols. London: Order of the Trustees.

Maison Baker. 1908. *Catalogue général illustré*. Istanbul [Constantinople]: Imp. du Levant Herald.

Pech, Edgar. 1911. *Manuel des sociétés anonymes fonctionnant en Turquie*. Istanbul [Constantinople]: Gérard.

Pechedimaldji, Dikran S. 1881. *Les eaux du Lac de Derkos et la Société impériale de médecine de Constantinople*. Istanbul [Constantinople]: publisher unknown.

Tchihatcheff (Chikhachyov), Pierre de. 2000 [1864]. *İstanbul ve Boğaziçi [orig. Le Bosphore de Constantinople avec perspectives des pays limitrophes]*. Ed. by Hamdi Can Tuncer, trans. into Turkish by Ali Berktay. Istanbul: Tarih Vakfı Yurt Yayınları.

Secondary Sources

Akın, Nur. 2011. *19. Yüzyılın İkinci Yarısında Galata ve Pera*. Istanbul: Literatür.

Altınkaya Genel, Özlem. 2016. 'Shifting Scales of Urban Transformation: The Emergence of the Marmara Urban Region between 1990 and 2015'. Ph.D. Diss., Harvard University.

Artan, Tülay. 2011. 'Ahmed I's Hunting Parties: Feasting in Adversity, Enhancing the Ordinary'. In Amy Singer (ed.), *Starting with Food: Culinary Approaches to Ottoman History*. Princeton: Markus Wiener Publishers. pp. 93–138.

Barak, On. 2013. *On Time: Technology and Temporality in Modern Egypt*. Berkeley: University of California Press.

Baruh, Lorans İzabel. 2009. 'The Transformation of the "Modern" Axis of Nineteenth-Century İstanbul Property, Investments and Elites from Taksim Square to Sirkeci Station'. Ph.D. Diss, Boğaziçi University.

Batur, Afife. 1993. '19. Yüzyıl İstanbul Mimarlığında Bir Stilistik Karşılaştırma Denemesi: A. Vallaury/R. D'Aronco'. In Zeynep Rona (ed.), *Osman Hamdi Bey ve Dönemi*. Istanbul: Tarih Vakfı Yurt Yayınları. pp. 146–58.

Biricik, Ali Selçuk. 2013. 'İstanbul Şehri ve Su'. *Marmara Coğrafya Dergisi* **2**: 11–32.

Byfield, Andrew. 2006. 'A World beyond the Walls. The Flora of Istanbul'. *Cornucopia* **54**: 64–73.

Castonguay, Stéphane. 2007. 'The Production of Flood as Natural Catastrophe: Extreme Events and the Construction of Vulnerability in the Drainage Basin of the St. Francis River (Quebec), Mid-nineteenth to Mid-twentieth Century'. *Environmental History* **12**: 820–44.

Çeçen, Kâzım. 1984. *İstanbul'da Osmanlı Devrindeki Su Tesisleri*. Istanbul: İstanbul Teknik Üniversitesi.

—— . 1999. *İstanbul'un Osmanlı Dönemi Suyolları*. Istanbul: İSKİ.

Çelik, Zeynep. 1986. *The Remaking of Istanbul: Portrait of an Ottoman City in the Nineteenth Century*. Seattle: University of Washington Press.

Cronon, William. 1991. *Nature's Metropolis: Chicago and the Great West.* New York: W.W. Norton.

Crow, James, et al. 2008. *The Water Supply of Byzantine Constantinople.* London: Society for the Promotion of Roman Studies.

Dinçkal Noyan. 2004. *Istanbul und das Wasser: Zur Geschichte der Wasserversorgung und Abwasserentsorgung von der Mitte des 19. Jahrhunderts bis 1966.* Munich: R. Oldenbourg.

——. 2008. 'Reluctant Modernization: The Cultural Dynamics of Water Supply in Istanbul, 1885–1950'. *Technology and Culture* **49** (3): 675–700.

——. 2015. 'Water as a commodity? Debates and conflicts on the (de)regulation of water infrastuctures in Istanbul, 1885–1937'. In Birte Förster and Martin Bauch (eds), *Wasserinfrastrukturen und Macht von der Antike bis zur Gegenwart.* Munich: De Gruyter Oldenbourg. pp. 206–31.

Duman, Hasan. 2000. *Başlangıcından harf devrimine kadar Osmanlı–Türk süreli yayınlar ve gazeteler bibliyografyası ve toplu kataloğu, 1828–1928.* Ankara: Enformasyon ve Dokümantasyon Hizmetleri Vakfı.

Eldem, Edhem. 2013. 'İstanbul as a cosmopolitan city: myths and realities'. In Ato Quayson and Girish Daswani (eds), *A Companion to Diaspora and Transnationalism.* Oxford: Blackwell. pp. 212–30.

——. 2000. *Bankalar Caddesi: Osmanlı'dan Günümüze Voyvoda Caddesi = Voyvoda Street from Ottoman Times to Today.* Istanbul: Osmanlı Bankası Bankacılık ve Finans Tarihi Araştırma ve Belge Merkezi.

Engin, Vahdettin. 2000. *Tünel.* Istanbul: Simurg.

——. 1993. *Rumeli Demiryolları.* Istanbul: Eren.

Erensü, Sinan. 2016. 'Fragile Energy: Power, Nature, and the Politics of Infrastructure in the "New Turkey"'. Ph.D. Diss., Minneapolis: University of Minnesota.

Erickson, Edward J. 2003. *Defeat in Detail: The Ottoman Army in the Balkans, 1912–1913.* Westport, CT: Praeger.

Gülersoy, Zeren, et al. (eds). 2014. *İstanbul'un Geleceğini Etkileyecek Üç Proje: 3. Köprü, 3. Havalimanı, Kanal İstanbul, Tema Vakfı Uzman Görüşleri.* Istanbul: TEMA.

Girardelli, Paolo. 2014. 'Power or leisure? Remarks on the architecture of the European summer embassies on the Bosphorus shore'. *New Perspectives on Turkey* **50**: 29–58.

Groc, Gérard and İbrahim Çağlar. 1985. *La Presse Française de Turquie de 1795 à nos Jours: Histoire et Catalogue.* Istanbul: Isis Press.

Halim, Hala. 2013. *Alexandrian Cosmopolitanism: An Archive.* New York: Fordham University Press.

Hamadeh, Shirine. 2008. *The City's Pleasures: Istanbul in the Eighteenth Century.* Seattle: University of Washington Press.

Han, Ayhan. 2016. 'İstanbul ve Galata Hendeklerinde Kentsel Toprak Kullanımı'. *Tarih Dergisi* **64** (2): 1–26.

Hanley, Will. 2008. 'Grieving Cosmopolitanism in Middle East Studies'. *History Compass* **6** (5): 1346–67.

K. Mehmet Kentel

Harvey, David. 1996. *Justice, Nature, and the Geography of Difference*. Cambridge: Blackwell Publishers.

Husain, Faisal. 2014. 'In the Bellies of the Marshes: Water and Power in the Countryside of Ottoman Baghdad'. *Environmental History* **19** (4): 638–64.

İnal, Onur. 2018. 'Ottoman and Turkish Environmental History: An Overview of the Field'. *Environment and History* **24**: 297–99.

——. 2018. 'The Making of an Eastern Mediterranean Gateway City: Izmir in the Nineteenth Century'. *Journal of Urban History*: 1–18. doi: 10.1177/0096.

Kähsbauer, Paul. 1959. 'Intendant Dr. Franz Steindachner, sein Leben und Werk'. *Annalen des Naturhistorischen Museums in Wien* **63**: 1–30.

Karacor, Elif Kutay and Dalia Korshid. 2015. 'Projected environmental effects of the third airport in Istanbul'. *Journal of Food, Agriculture and Environment* **13** (2): 223–27.

Karakaş, Deniz. 2013. 'Clay Pipes, Marble Surfaces: The Topographies of Water Supply in Late Seventeenth- and Early Eighteenth-Century Ottoman Istanbul'. Ph.D. Diss., Binghamton: State University of New York.

Kazgan, Haydar and Sami Önal. 1999. *İstanbul'da Suyun Tarihi: İstanbul'un Su Sorununun Tarihsel Kökenleri ve Osmanlı'da Yabancı Su Şirketleri*. Istanbul: İletişim Yayınları.

Klingle, Matthew W. 2007. *Emerald City: An Environmental History of Seattle*. New Haven: Yale University Press.

Kolluoğlu, Biray and Meltem Toksöz. 2010. 'Mapping Out the Eastern Mediterranean: Toward a Cartography of Cities of Commerce'. In Biray Kolluoğlu and Meltem Toksöz (eds), *Cities of the Mediterranean: From the Ottomans to the Present Day*. London; New York: I.B. Tauris. pp. 1–13.

Lange, Katharina, et al. 2016. '(Re)valuing Natural Resources in the Middle East, Africa and Asia'. *ZMO Programmatic Texts* **11**, 1-13.

Latour, Bruno. 2005. *Reassembling the Social: An Introduction to Actor-Network-Theory*. Oxford: Oxford University Press.

Low, Michael Christopher. 2015. 'Ottoman Infrastructures of the Saudi Hydro-State: The Technopolitics of Pilgrimage and Potable Water in the Hijaz'. *Comparative Studies in Society and History* **57** (4): 942–74.

Magdalino, Paul. 2015. 'Introduction'. In Paul Magdalino and Nina Ergin (eds), *Istanbul and Water*. Leuven: Peeters. pp. 1–8.

Mango, Cyril. 1995. 'Introduction'. In Cyril Mango et al. (eds) *Constantinople and Its Hinterland: Papers from the Twenty-seventh Spring Symposium of Byzantine Studies, Oxford, April 1993*. Aldershot: Variorum. pp. 1–8.

Mango, Cyril, et al. (eds). 1995. *Constantinople and Its Hinterland: Papers from the Twenty-seventh Spring Symposium of Byzantine Studies, Oxford, April 1993*. Aldershot: Variorum.

Mikhail, Alan. 2013. *Nature and Empire in Ottoman Egypt: An Environmental History*. Cambridge: Cambridge University Press.

Mitchell, Timothy. 2002. *Rule of Experts: Egypt, Techno-politics, Modernity*. Berkeley: University of California Press.

Morgenthau, Henry. 2004. *United States Diplomacy on the Bosphorus: The Diaries of Ambassador Morgenthau, 1913-1916.* Princeton: Gomidas Institute.

Neumann, Christoph. K. 2011. 'Modernitelerin Çatışması Altıncı Daire-i Belediye, 1857-1912'. In Yavuz Köse (ed.), *İstanbul: İmparatorluk Başkentinden Megakente.* Istanbul: Kitap Yayınevi. pp. 426–53.

Nirven, Saadi Nazım. 1946. *İstanbul Suları.* Istanbul: Halk Basımevi.

Oğuz, Burhan. 1998. *Bizans'tan Günümüze İstanbul Suları.* Istanbul: Simurg

Özgül, Necdet et al. 2011. *İstanbul İl Alanının Jeolojisi Yönetici Özeti.* Istanbul: İstanbul Büyükşehir Belediyesi.

Smith, Neil. 2008 [1984]. *Uneven Development: Nature, Capital, and the Production of Space* 3rd ed. Athens, GA: University of Georgia Press.

Somçağ, Selim. 1994. 'Avcılık'. In *Dünden Bugüne İstanbul Ansiklopedisi vol. 1.* 8 vols. Istanbul: Tarih Vakfı. pp. 426–29.

Swyngedouw, Erik. 2004. *Social Power and the Urbanization of Water: Flows of Power* Oxford; New York: Oxford University Press.

Tvedt, Terje and Terje Oestigaard (eds). 2014. *A History of Water. Series III., vol. 1: Water and Urbanization.* London; New York: I.B. Tauris.

van Leeuwen, Kees and Rosa Sjerps. 2016. 'Istanbul: the Challenges of Integrated Water Resources Management in Europa's Megacity'. *Environment, Development and Sustainability* **18** (1): 1–17.

Vertovec, Steven and Robin Cohen (eds). 2003. *Conceiving Cosmopolitanism: Theory, Context and Practice.* New York: Oxford University Press.

Yarcı, Güler. 2009. 'Osmanlıda Avcılık Yasaları'. *Acta Turcica* **1** (1): 123–52.

Yurdakul, İlhami. 2010. *Aziz Şehre Leziz Su: Dersaadet, İstanbul Su Şirketi, 1873–1933.* Istanbul: Kitabevi.

Zandi-Sayek, Sibel. 2012. *Ottoman Izmir: The Rise of a Cosmopolitan Port 1840–1880.* Minneapolis; London: University of Minnesota Press.

Chapter 8

CESSPOOLS, MOSQUITOES AND FEVER: AN ENVIRONMENTAL HISTORY OF MALARIA PREVENTION IN ISMAILIA AND PORT SAID, 1869–1910

Mohamed Gamal-Eldin

> Unlike many diseases, it is essentially an endemic, a local, malady; and one which unfortunately haunts more especially the fertile, well-watered and luxuriant tracts – precisely those which are of the greatest value to man. There it strikes down, not only the indigenous barbaric population, but, with still greater certainty, the pioneers of civilization, the planter, the trader, the missionary, the soldier.
>
> Ronald Ross, Nobel Lecture (1902)

On 21 August 1882, British forces landed at Ismailia.[1] Thousands of troops secured the Suez Canal and then marched towards the interior and Cairo to meet the revolutionary assemblage of Colonel Ahmad 'Urābī (1841–1911). As a landing point, Ismailia made total sense. It was at this tiny, yet verdant, town that the Fresh Water Canal met the seawater canal. From Ismailia fresh water was supplied to the cities of Port Said and Suez. Walking along the Fresh Water Canal towards Cairo, the British Army, their men and their equipment physically displaced the very earth they trampled upon. The British military project against 'Urābī could not have come at a worse time of year either. Irrigation upkeep and drainage – the clearing by Egyptian farmer peasants (*fellah*) of the numerous canals that splay across the Nile Delta – were delayed in the wake of the British occupation.[2]

---

1. Blunt 1922.
2. Berque 1972.

Cesspools, Mosquitoes and Fever

The almost clockwork-regular yearly flood was to shortly engulf the Delta with fresh levels of Nile water, as well as new layers of sediment and silt carried downstream through to the Mediterranean Sea. As the flood of water and British military might came in August–September 1882, malaria and 'fever' soon followed. British medical journals describe numerous instances of malaria and malarial-type symptoms among soldiers stationed in and around Ismailia.[3] Undrained canals and stagnant water in ponds, sluices, gardens and runoffs across the Delta provided the perfect home for the larvae of the malaria-carrying *Anopheles* mosquitoes to take root.[4] Soon enough malaria would become an unwanted annual visitor to the blushing garden-town of Ismailia, the home of the Suez Canal Company.

In this paper, I will show how an examination of the malaria outbreak and response in Ismailia and Port Said highlights the need for more interdisciplinary work on the convergence of health, environment and the urban in late nineteenth-century colonial Egypt.[5] In addition, by way of the colonial scientists' attempt to fight the mosquitoes and disease, we also get a peek at a history of sewage and wastewater. The cesspools, latrines, garden pots and undrained ponds of water runoff are described in detail, painting a multi-layered and complex portrait of the urban environment. I am heavily influenced by the opening question of Timothy Mitchell's *Rule of Experts*, which asked, 'Can the Mosquito Speak?' As Mitchell argues, and I will show, yes. The project to eradicate malaria and the carrier of the disease gives us a unique chance to learn more about the mosquito in Egypt. Mitchell's correlations between disease (malaria), the new canal and dam projects, agricultural techniques and war are also apparent here.[6] The main sources for this paper are the writings of Ronald Ross (1857–1932), a British scientist stationed in India who then taught at the Liverpool School of Tropical Medicine, and worked on the mosquito eradication programme in the Suez Canal cities. Ross details and maps the towns and the nests of the mosquito larvae, providing us with the mosquito's voice, although silent (it is speechless from an anthropocentric point of view). His research gives us insight into the deep connections between the environmental and the urban.

---

3.   'The Egyptian Expedition', *The British Medical Journal* 2 (1135) (30 Sep. 1882): 646–50.

4.   Cookson-Hills 2013, p. 285.

5.   There is a growing body of literature on the Suez Canal cities. These include, a dissertation looking at the urban and social history of Port Said, Carminati 2018; and an edited volume, Paiton 2016.

6.   Mitchell 2002.

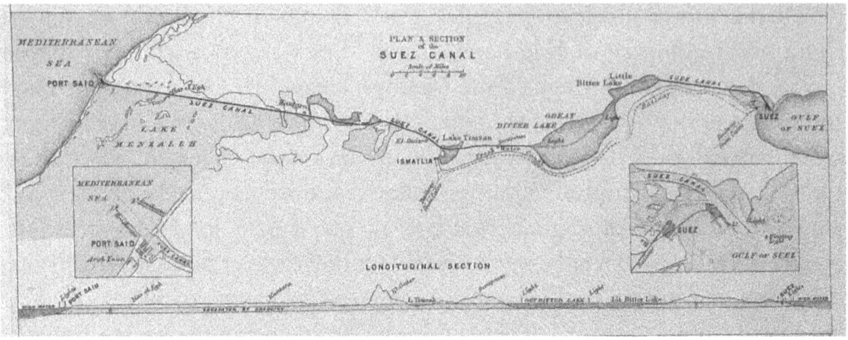

Figure 1. Plan and section of the Suez Canal. Encyclopaedia Britannica, *ninth edition. Author's personal collection.*

Environmental history in Egypt continues to focus on the Nile Valley and Delta. Spaces on the margin remain understudied. The Suez Canal cities lie along a waterway, which before it opened in 1869, did not exist (Figure 1). The lack of research on the impact of urban planning, population growth, and engineering upon the environment in the canal region makes for a significant lacuna within Egyptian historiography.[7] Thus, the case study here on malarial prevention in late Ottoman Egypt is an important addition to environmental history in Egypt. Architects, engineers, urban planners and decision makers have all considered the natural environment prior to the development of new cities.[8] The choice of a former swamp as the location of Mexico City led to concerns about drainage and sub-soil water movement. Topographical features of coastal shorelines determined the positions of port cities. Georges-Eugène Baron Haussmann's (1809–1891) urban renewal plan for nineteenth-century Paris included subterranean sewers, which would carry the city's deleterious elements away from the urban.[9] Historically, the environment has been a backdrop, a space to mould and engineer for the sake of man.[10] As architectural historian Spiro Kostof argues, 'Seen in the aggregate, there is perhaps as widespread a

---

7.   See Ibid.; Mikhail 2011.

8.   Kostof 1991. Kostof studies in detail the various urban forms, typologies of cities throughout history. This great piece of scholarship will help in the analysis of Port Said and Ismailia. He calls concerns for the topography and natural surroundings of the city, the 'organic' pattern. This borrows from the idea of the biological but he is careful to illustrate that it is indeed a pattern decided upon by man's choices.

9.   Gandy 1999, pp. 23–44.

10.   Christensen 1993. See also Bulliet, 2011.

tendency in city-making to *amend* the natural landscape as there is to work with it.'[11] Further, environmental historian Anna Tsing in *The Mushroom at the End of the World* argues for the use of *assemblages*, which link non-human and human actors altogether into an interconnected web.[12] Thus, I hope to show the *assemblages* at work in the two new cities along the canal.

The recent turn to environmental history in modern Egyptian historiography, and more broadly the Middle East, has brought forward the connections and interdependencies of the natural environment and the modernising state.[13] An ecological history of Ismailia and Port Said will highlight the environmental conditions that made the cities ripe for a malaria attack. In addition, the choice of urban form demonstrates the deep interconnections between the natural and physical environment. This work is also an intervention against the heavy historiographical focus on Cairo (as well as Alexandria) and the eliding of other cities and towns across Egypt, which are homogenised as rural. It has created a rural vs. centre (Cairo and Alexandria) dichotomy within Egyptian historiography. Following the research of Zeinab Abu Magd and Hanan Hammad in Egypt and Beshara Doumani in Ottoman Palestine I wish to add to the growing corpus on peripheral cities in the late nineteenth and early twentieth centuries.[14]

Methodologically, travelogues, medical journals and photography provide the evidence to the descriptions of the cities here studied. Additionally, this research intends to further interrogate the ways in which colonial science and technology worked in the field. The case study here of Ismailia and Port Said will demonstrate that decisions on urban development, canalisation projects

---

11.   Kostof 1991, p. 55.

12.   Tsing 2017. We also see this at work in Cronon, 1997. The human-nature and urban-rural dichotomies are broken down and the urban metropolis is examined as part and parcel of nature, and vice versa.

13.   The following works are some of the most cutting edge scholarship on environmental history in the Middle East: Burke and Davis 2011; Burke and Pomeranz 2009; Mikhail 2012; idem 2011; Derr 2011, pp. 136–57; Davis 2007; Dolbee 2017; Gratien 2015; idem 2017, pp. 583–604.

14.   Looking at Mahalla, a city in the Egyptian Delta, *Industrial Sexuality* is an essential examination of labour and the urban in Modern Egyptian history. Hammad 2016; focused on Qena, *Imagined Empires* makes a case for the city as an important node for control of the Egyptian south and trade with the Red Sea and further afield. Abu Magd 2013. This text on Tanta is an important socio-medical intervention within Egyptian urban and social history, Boyle 2013. Doumani 1995 is an important work in the canon that explores the urban history of the provincial city of Nablus in Ottoman Palestine. Reynolds 2017 examines Aswan's development in the 20th century before and after the construction of the High Dam.

and colonialism effected the malarial outbreak in Ismailia that reached epidemic levels post-1882. As such the events of 1882 and the British colonial project will prove to be central to our story, but I will return to that later. What follows is a brief natural history of malaria.

Malaria's Culprit Discovered

Malaria has been around for tens of thousands of years.[15] Prior to the discovery of the mosquito's role in malaria, the miasmatic view of disease held that it came from unsanitary conditions or environmental factors.[16] The idea that the mosquito was the parasite's vector was unknown prior to the nineteenth century. In 1899, Sir Ronald Ross, our eventual protagonist in malaria prevention, would discover while working for the Indian Medical Service in Calcutta that the mosquito was the host of the *Plasmodium* parasite.[17] Specifically, the main transmitter of the disease is the genus *Anopheles* mosquito.[18] Of the 430 species of *Anopheles* in the world only seventy are known to be carriers of the malaria-causing parasite.[19] Some *Anopheles* are zoophilic and prefer the blood of animals, in which the malaria parasite does no harm. Human red-blood cells in the liver are what *Plasmodium* craves.

Principally, the main *anopheles* (or *A. specie*) vectors responsible for malaria in Egypt have been *A. pharoansis* and *A. sergentii*. Yet, during the catastrophic malaria epidemic in Upper Egypt of 1942–44, *A. gambiae* made its way north from the Sudan to Egypt due to environmental changes related to the Aswan Dam and the radical increase in sugarcane production as a cash crop.[20] Ac-

---

15. Although described by the Greek medical historian Hippocrates, the etiology and transmission of the disease was unknown until the turn of the twentieth century.

16. Upton 2008. Upton in this pivotal study demonstrates the ways in which ideas of miasma were used to clean up Philadelphia from the ravages of disease and sickness. The term for the sickness itself carried this connotation with malaria, or *mal-aria* (Italian, 'bad air') used in the English language, highlighting a connection to the belief that diseased winds could bring in the unknown parasite. Above that, the word in French *palusdisme* (*palus*-swamp) linked malaria to swampy and marshy areas of town.

17. Hippocrates 2009. While, Sir Ronald Ross would win the Nobel Prize, Italian scientist Giovanni Grassi, also in 1899, as well as the famous bacteriologist Robert Koch soon after, found the malaria vector. Grassi and his Italian team probably found the mosquito vector first, but Ross the self-promoter took sole credit for the discovery.

18. Burr 1954; Kenawy 1988, p. 2; Kenawy 2015.

19. 'WHO Malaria', WHO, accessed 10 Aug. 2017, http://www.who.int/malaria/en/. In Egypt, there are presently 11 known *anophele* mosquitos. Kenawy 2015.

20. Mitchell 2002.

cording to Ronald Ross, the culprit at the Suez Canal was *A.pharoansis*. Egypt had three environmental factors that influenced the mosquito's lifecycle and reproduction: temperature, humidity and rainfall. While in colder environments, mosquitoes can essentially hibernate during the winter months biding their time for warmer weather. The threat of mosquitoes as a nuisance was understood even by travellers to Egypt. In one *British Medical Journal* article the author details that all insects, but particularly mosquitoes, demanded a 'cleverness of management'.[21] This primarily meant not travelling to Egypt during the hot summers.

The Pathogen Hidden in the Mosquito's Belly

Malaria is not communicable through blood transfer (except in the womb) nor is it an airborne pathogen. The parasite, *Plasmodium*, the wormlike culprit of malaria, before it finds a home in the human liver, seeks out the perfect mosquito to incubate in. As noted in the previous section, not all *Anopheles* mosquitoes are carriers and not all *Plasmodium* are the deadly form of malaria. Unlike cholera and the plague that spread rapidly through urban and rural Egypt in major epidemics of the nineteenth century, the malaria parasite that attacked Ismailia and Port Said did not become a major countrywide epidemic.[22] Most likely this is because it was not one of the two deadly forms of the parasite, which could cause an epidemic, *Plasmodium Vivax* (*P.vivax*) and *P. Falciparum*.[23] Upper Egypt in 1942–44 would find the parasitic culprit to be *P.falciparum*, spread by the malaria loving *A.gambiae*.[24]

    The parasite seeks out female *anopheles* and sets up home inside the mosquito's stomach. It slows down the metabolism of the mosquito to reproduce new parasites within the mosquito before it seeks out human blood. The now swollen and *Plasmodium* filled *anophele* mosquito flies off to inject the parasite into the human body by way of a numbing saliva which masks the

---

21.   Sandwith 1892, 904.

22.   For more on the plague and cholera epidemics and generally on public health in nineteenth-century Egypt, see Kuhnke 1990. In *Lives at Risk* Kuhnke argues that the new institutions of public health took away from the community and indigenous aspects of health and medicine. For a good example of a provincial, or non-core, discussion of health, medicine and cholera, see Boyle 2013. The major malaria epidemic, referenced earlier, of the 1940s and the public health response are tackled here by Gallagher (1990) and Mitchell (2002).

23.   Shah 2011.

24.   Gallagher 1990.

insect's bite. It continues to do this until it is empty. Once inside the new host it seeks out the liver where it attempts to break into red blood cells. To insure the survival of the malaria pathogen once inside the human, new mosquitoes carrying the disease must attack. If enough of the red blood cells are compromised, the human host begins to have a severe fever and chills. Red blood cells provide oxygen to the body and the malaria parasite disrupts this integral process, leading to a lack of oxygen to essential organs.[25] Some less severe forms of the *plasmodium* species can cause fever and chills, then lie dormant until a fresh attack begins. This explains the common incidence among some malaria victims of recurring malaria.

The Ecology of Malaria

One of the more important determinants, besides the right *anopheles*, for the success of *Plasmodium* is climatic conditions. A slight change in sunlight, moisture or temperature can destroy the chances of the malaria parasite in making it to the human. The environmental conditions must remain stable. Cold temperatures are not suitable for mosquito carrying malaria. There are some *anopheles* that carry a weakened form of the malaria parasite, but they are not ideal hosts of the deadly *P.falciparum*. Swampy, moist, wet and tropical natural environments are havens for the larvae of mosquitoes.

These are typically not upset until nature or man disrupt the ecosystem. Torrential rain, flooding, perennial irrigation, canalisation and the felling of forests all upend the mosquitoes' home and increase the landscape available to the *anopheles*. According to the medical historian Sonia Shah, 'The trouble is that the hydrology of puddles, streams, and ponds is one of the more mercurial aspects of the environment, vulnerable to any number of disruptive influences'.[26] As I will illustrate in the next section, the changing environment and re-introduction of Nile River waters to the old eastern Pelusium branch would lead to an influx of fresh water, flooding, new fauna and standing water and a swampy environment.[27] The watering of the desert would lead to new organ-

---

25. Some individuals have developed evolutionary protections against malaria. Those who have the Duffy-negative antigen and haemoglobin S (the sickle cell) are basically immune to the parasite. Shah in *The Fever* calls this an 'immunological fence'.

26. Shah 2011, pp. 60–8. Medical historian Sonia Shah writes about how the Roman Empire was affected by epidemics of the malaria parasite as it grew in strength and changed the natural environment in the Italian peninsula.

27. For more on the historic Pelusiac branches of the Nile River Delta, see Shea 1977, p. 31. Also, see this classical research on the branch: Sneh and Weissbrod 1973, pp. 59–61.

isms and disease growth. The typology, physical design, sewerage network (or lack thereof) and environmental conditions of the new towns of Ismailia, in particular, and Port Said made them suitable spaces for *anopheles*.

Building the Cities of Ismailia and Port Said

The project to build the Suez Canal required the creation of two new cities, Port Said and Ismailia, and new waterways, in addition to the sea-water canal. A freshwater canal was dug manually by tens of thousands Egyptian labourers. The first phase was between April 1861 and December 1863, which extended the Nile waters from the Zagazig Canal at Ras-al-Wadi, all the way to its new outlet, Ismailia, at Lake Timsah and then south to Suez, to provide Suez a continual supply of fresh Nile water for the first time.[28] The direct branch from Ras-al-Wadi to the Nile at Shubra was completed by the Egyptian government in 1865–66. A pipeline supplied Port Said with water until the Abbasiyya Canal was completed in 1896.[29] Before these new supply channels, Port Said, founded in 1859, was provided with drums of water transported from Damietta or by a saltwater distillation plant.[30] Additionally, as part of the gridiron plan for both Port Said and Ismailia, green spaces – central gardens, parks and gardens – were built into the urban space, watered by small water channels.

When Ferdinand de Lesseps (1805–1894), diplomat and founder of the Suez Canal project, made his first exploration of the Isthmus in December–January 1854–55, he remarked upon the land around ancient Pelusium and west of it, where Port Said would be situated, as 'more than muddy, for it has been swamped by the inundation of the Nile'.[31] The marshy and mud inundated home to flamingos, pelicans, and swans would soon house the future

---

28. Some estimates suggest that over a quarter of a million Egyptian labourers worked on the Fresh Water Canal. El Shennawy 2010, is a good text in Arabic on forced labour and the Suez Canal. He estimates that half a million labourers were used on the canal projects. Additionally, animal labour, primarily camel and donkey, was used to move debris, sand, rock, equipment, water and men to and from the construction sites. More work needs to be done to unearth these unique narratives.

29. Michel 2016.

30. Marlowe 1964, p. 173. An article in the *New York Times* in 1891 discusses the scarcity and cost of fresh water in Port Said. In it the city is described as a less than 'desirable' spot for residence, citing the lack of fresh water. 'Water for Port Said', *New York Times* (7 Apr. 1891): 6.

31. De Lesseps 1876, p. 63.

Mediterranean port.[32] On a visit to the Suez Canal works in 1865, the Irish explorer, Thomas Kerr Lynch (1818–1891), described the terrain of Port Said in fabulous detail:

> The soil on which Port Said stands is composed of sand, alluvial mud, and salt; the vast lagune [sic] and dark, oozy plains of Lake Menzaleh, are immediately at the back, in some places covered with an incrustation of salt. So great is the evaporation, it is twice as salty, and generally below the level of the sea, which, when a gale of wind from the north-west assists the slight tide, breaks through these low dunes, and carries with it fresh accessions of that mineral to re-incrustate, for the water soon evaporates, the layer of mud which the Nile yearly deposits over its whole surface.[33]

The triangular piece of land at the edge of Lake Manzala had its main artery, the Quay, follow the line of the canal. The sun-baked earth was etched with a simple gridiron design with large blocks and wide tree-lined streets housing the European Quarter. The grid and blocks got narrower as one went farther northwest from the Quay. The 'native' areas were separated by first an empty plane and then eventually a wide street that ran parallel to the canal all the way to the sandy beach along the Mediterranean; a type of *cordon sanitaire* if you will.

Large piers were the first major infrastructural projects undertaken. This 'muddy' soil would have its shores protected from the Nile's alluvial sediment by the piers that stretched like tentacles into the Mediterranean, both welcoming oncoming vessels and preventing the accumulation of mud in the canal channel. The piers themselves were constructed with lime mined from the southern coast of France and sand and water to form twenty ton apiece barriers against the bothersome and organically-rich silt. The land of the Sinai across from Lake Manzala is primarily made up of loose sand, which would move with the wind, creating an ocean of sand.[34] Both the windswept sand and mud dredged up from the channel would be formed and packed with water and baked in the Egyptian sun to create solid land for the new 'harbour of refuge', Port Said.

Water was the building block to the establishment of what became a major coaling and transit centre on the Mediterranean. Yet, it would remain a constant threat to the stability of the land that Port Said was built upon. As Ross points out in his work *The Prevention of Fever on the Suez Canal*, the sub-soil of the town sat on the former swampy lands of Lake Manzala.[35] Water, both

32. Pudney 1970, p. 95.
33. Lynch 1866, p. 53.
34. Greenwood 1997, p. 27.
35. Ross 1909.

fresh and marshy, would play a part in the urban design of the town. Fresh water from the Ismailia Canal was brought in to green the land on the former lake. The swampy under-layer of the town ensured that the sewage, cesspools, human waste and burials would be a problem that planners and hygiene officials had to work to address. Place de Lesseps in Port Said is a good example of the Suez Canal Company's green initiative. Only two blocks from the Quay and Corniche Street, the square opened to the four major arteries of the city. The avenue from the canal, Rue du Commerce, was the central shopping and trading venue of Port Said. Lined with shops, the street is depicted in photos as a vibrant area filled with businessmen, women tourists and native Egyptians all collected together. From the Quay, those who disembarked could wander to the Place de Lesseps. In the 1870s and 1880s the Corniche resembled a rough dock area of sand and dust. Entering the garden oasis of Place de Lesseps, one first traversed the entry point from the canal along Rue du Commerce. The garden square would become a mainstay on the tourist's shore leave venture through Port Said.

The rich soil, probably because of the sub-soil layer, prompted Lesseps and the Suez Canal Company to erect tree-lined streets and construct ornate French-like verdant central squares. In 1901, another American traveller, Anthony Wilkin (1878–1901), described Port Said as, 'a model of cleanliness, with its well-watered thoroughfares and tram-lines, bordered with trees of uncommon verdancy'.[36] The depiction by Wilkin is challenged by those of others like Ross and Evelyn Waugh (1903–1966).[37] Photographs of Port Said's main square, *Place de Lesseps,* from the nineteenth century give us visual evidence of the verdant nature and richness of Port Said's soil. The central square of Port Said became a symbolic representation of the materiality manipulated and disciplined to green what was once mud and sand.[38] In the centre of the square was a circular water basin that would fill with fresh water and surrounding it in an axial pattern, which resembled new public parks in Paris at the time, were lush gardens of green and flowering plants.

---

36. Wilkin 1901, p. 2.
37. Waugh, who travelled to the Suez Canal city in the 1920s cites examples of individuals exclaiming about the unhygienic conditions of Port Said. Yet, in his travels he said he saw nothing of what others described. Waugh 1974.
38. By disciplined, I am speaking of controlling and managing, as Foucault discusses the disciplining of the body by modernity. The environment I theorise was also disciplined in a very modern fashion by the use of multiple forms of modern and 'pre-modern' technologies.

Photographs demonstrate the traveller's preoccupation with the Water Works of Port Said. Pictures of their towers are collected in postcard form and there are even examples of families enjoying the garden life around the water works. One reads about families during the holidays going to these gardens to get away from the urban. Interestingly, because of the jetties that jutted out into the Mediterranean Sea, sand had begun early on to collect on the Northern coast of Port Said creating a popular sand beach. The use of fresh and sea water in a variety of ways demonstrates the centrality of water to daily life in Port Said.

If Port Said was a sandy-marsh on a spit of land into the Mediterranean, then Ismailia was seen as the polar opposite. Using biblical language, travellers described it as a bountiful Garden of Eden.[39] Ismailia lay adjacent to what was thought to be historical Goshen from the story of Joseph.[40] The French philosopher Jules Barthélemy-Saint-Hilaire (1805–1895), who travelled in 1855 as part of the international commission examining the feasibility of the canal project, commented that the basin of Lake Timsah, filled with 'chirping birds', would be an ideal spot for the primary port along the canal; although this would never come to fruition.[41] Travellers of all sorts described Ismailia as a set of 'pretty gardens and plantations and the view of the blue lake [Timsah] lend the town the appearance of an oasis, with both European and Arabian cultivation'.[42] This man-made oasis rose from the land with the introduction of water (Figure 2).

Prior to the canal dredging, the settlement was small. As in Port Said, fresh water would have had to be imported, although in Ismailia the task was easier. Almost simultaneous to the building of the Suez Canal a fresh water canal was dredged by Egyptian labour through to Zagazig in the Nile Delta. Almost 84.5 miles in length and with a width at the bottom of 45.6 feet, the fresh water canal was shallow but deep enough for small boats to traverse. The channel had to be annually dredged to remove nearly 300,000 cubic metres of silt, soil and sediment from the waterbed.[43] Often it rose over the embank-

---

39. For a similar example of the use of Biblical language as part of the colonial project imaginary, see Davis 2007.

40. Goshen was the richly cultivatable land that the Biblical Joseph was given as his and his people's land by the Pharaoh of Egypt, as told in the *Book of Genesis,* cited in Baedeker 1885, p. 428.

41. Barthélemy-Saint-Hilaire 1857, p. 31. Barthélemy-Saint-Hilaire's observations helped to settle questions about the feasibility of the canal idea. Ismailia, though, would not become the major entry point along the canal.

42. Baedeker 1908, p. 174.

43. Barois 1889, p. 47.

Figure 2. Postcard of Ismailia Public Gardens, year unknown. Author's Personal Collection

ments and inundated the adjacent lands with fresh Nile waters, which ruined the flooded area. Due to the higher Nile level, engineers built locks just outside where the canal met Ismailia, before its journey south to Suez. In theory, these locks were supposed to hold back the excess water; nonetheless it spilled over and created the *birkas* (ponds) outside town. These ponds would become part of the urban form of the city. One pond just west of the town became a swampy wooded zone planted with *casuarina* and eucalyptus trees by the Suez Canal Company's Chief of Waterworks in Ismailia, a Monsieur Cepek, and called *le Forêt* (The Forest).[44]

In town one can recognise a clear cross-axial grid pattern of streets, four superblocks each four blocks by four, meeting at the cross-sections to form picturesque gardens at the centre. Photographs depict tree-lined streets and parks in Ismailia's European sections. This is in stark contrast to the *ville Arabe*. Similar to other colonial cities, the Arab town was to be built using

---

44. 'Sir William MacGregor to Colonial Office', *Sessional Papers no. 9* (London, 1903), p. 29. The *casuarina* tree is not native to Egypt. It was brought in from elsewhere, most likely India or Australia where it is indigenous. We find these trees planted elsewhere along the canal, between Toussam station and Serapeam along the fresh water canal. See also Davis 2007, for French efforts in colonial Morocco to transplant similar trees.

Orientalist conceptions of the Arab/Muslim domestic life.[45] On the European side, the streets of the town, similar to Port Said, were heavily tree-lined. The main artery, Avenue de l'Imperatice, ended with a vista of the train station on the northern side and at the southern termination the fresh water canal, both symbols of modernity. The city was bordered on the south by the fresh water canal, which ran the length of the settlement. It created an isthmus that provided access to Lake Timsah. Additionally, a distributor channel (*Chantier*) sent water in a ring around the northwest of the town. This channel then fed into smaller canals which ran into private and public gardens in town. It was a system that in most places followed the grid of the city. Canals and the railroad would become central parts of the Ismailia urban form. This dictated the growth of the city in the nineteenth and early twentieth centuries. Where the city met the fresh water inlet, towards the west, there developed a marshy environment of new fauna and animal life.[46] Adjacent to the town, water overflow created *birkas* or lagoons of water which became a prime breeding ground of mosquito larvae and other organic/inorganic organisms. As Ross described in 1903, the swamps around Ismailia would be rich real estate for mosquito larvae:

> In some spots near Ismailia, where the surface of the desert sand is much depressed, this sub-soil water produces considerable lakes and ponds; but, owing to the extreme salinity of the sand, most of these pools are brackish, their shores being encrusted with salt, and supporting but little vegetation.[47]

The variety of canal systems proved tough to control. In addition to the overflow, when in the mid-1870s the *canal d'eaux douche* was widened and the new feeder channel opened, large scale flooding became a constant plague on the town. Archival maps show the impact of the deluge. Place Thewfik and the Greek Quarter were almost entirely inundated with water.[48] Due to the flooding, homeowners had to have their properties repaired at the expense of the Suez

---

45. Kostof 1991, p. 63. Kostof cites the Prophet Muhammad's saying that a street should be wide enough for two camels to pass one another, which was carried over into early Islamic city urban planning; but in the nineteenth-century colonial Islamic city the 'native' town reproduced ideas of what an ideal city should look like. The belief was that the 'Islamic City' was some 'organic' urban form. This orientalist view persists even in our contemporary period.
46. Ross 1903, p. 5.
47. Ibid.
48. National Labour Archives (*Archives Nationales du Monde du Travail; ANMT*) 1995 060 4373. Numerous plans on the flooding in Ismailia.

Canal Company. One solution resulted in the creation of drains for the excess water; one drain fed *le Forêt* helping it develop into an expansive plantation.

Visitors to the opening of the canal in 1869, described the town as 'verdant' and full of greenery.[49] Ismailia would in time become the greened landscape wanted by de Lesseps in Port Said. With the proximity of the fresh water canal, tree-lined streets, private and public gardens, and a lush green zone along the former desert, the land demonstrated physically the power to nourish and cultivate. Yet, until Ismailia was cleansed of the 'fever' it would remain in the mind of travellers/residents a *ville morte* (a dead town). In the end, it never lived up to de Lesseps' dream of a capital for the canal because of the sporadic flooding and annual 'fever.' Even so, it attempted to maintain a sense of importance through the design of the picturesque urban.[50]

The waterworks of Ismailia provide a potent symbolism of the meeting of modernity and water management. It was here that the Nile water was filtered and made potable for residents of the town. Simply, like canal and irrigation systems, it represented the power of man to control the movement of water. Secondly, the waterworks was an extravagant lush garden of plant, tree and vegetable life that became a physical manifestation for the Suez Canal Company's greening effort. The land of Ismailia, the waterworks, *le Forêt*, the fresh water canal and her conduits all worked together as a system to bloom the town. Without this organisation of the water, present-day Ismailia would not have a reputation as a verdant oasis. More importantly, the sea water canal would have been hard-pressed to survive on its own without the fresh water canal. Photography from the period demonstrates the lushness of Ismailia compared to the dusty and sandy land of Port Said. Where one was a rough outpost of a town, the city of Ismailia was a picturesque place for residence and rest. Water would green the land of Ismailia and assist in the shape of its urban development into the twentieth century; particularly for the European quarter.

---

49. Badger 1862.

50. While not a circular Garden city plan like that of Ebenezer Howard or the riparian curvilinear suburb of Frank Law Olmsted's Riverside, Illinois, Ismailia demonstrates picturesque town development outside of the West. While the population of the town was small, it deserves to be included in story of nineteenth-century urban/architectural history. The description of a dead town comes from a French guide to Egypt: 'Ismaïlia, ville morte, à demi abandonnée après avoir été prépondérante pendant la période des travaux du canal. Elle apparaîtau loin comme une oasis de verdure au bord des eaux limpides du lac'. Nilsson 1907. http://gallica.bnf.fr/ark:/12148/bpt6k5807878t

Mohamed Gamal-Eldin

Malarial Prevention

In 1902 Prince Auguste d'Arenberg (1837–1924), the president of the Suez Canal Company (1896–1913), invited Sir Ronald Ross to Ismailia in the hopes that he could provide a solution to the malaria and mosquito problem ravaging the town.[51] Ismailia was part of the concession of 1856, which gave the company free land to build the town, as well as cultivable land adjacent to the both canals. In the case of Ismailia, this made malaria prevention work easier because the company could force their employees to comply by fine or termination.[52]

The Mediterranean port was a bit more difficult. Due to the complex web of laws that governed the Capitulations in Egypt, each resident of Port Said would have to give permission for the mosquito prevention brigade to enter homes.[53] The city was home to Greeks, Italians, Maltese, French, English and a number of other nationalities, including Egyptians. To enter the domicile of each would require either individual embassies supporting the project and allowing Ross's teams to enter or a wholesale acceptance by the public of the programme. With the help of Abadi Pasha, the Egyptian Governor of Port Said, and the Suez Canal Company a public event was set up at a town theatre and articles were written in the local newspapers to sell the plan to the public. The formula worked: residents of Port Said got behind the prevention scheme.[54]

Ismailia had been affected by malaria or 'the fever' since the late 1870s when the Fresh Water Canal was widened and new distribution canals flooded parts of the town.[55] But, according to cases recorded by the Suez Canal's medical officer, the malaria fever increased drastically rising from 200–300 cases in

---

51. Ross was joined by Sir William MacGregor, the Governor of Lagos, the small West African British colony plagued by malaria. Ross 1910, p. 500.

52. Ross 1910, p. 4.

53. Capitulations were a series of Ottoman legal agreements that gave Europeans special privileges related to law and taxation. In Egypt, this allowed Europeans to bring civil matters to their own consular court even if it was against an Egyptian national.

54. We hear little about resistance in his writings. Not a surprise. Other sources may help us better understand what residents of the town felt towards mosquito prevention. Did they feel like it was an intrusion? One wonders.

55. This is highlighted by one particularly harsh year in 1877 when large parts of Ismailia were inundated with water and sickness spread. In a census-like map, whole neighbourhoods are documented and the number of sick is almost every resident. ANMT 1995 060 4374.

1876 to an average of 2,000 cases a year by 1882.[56] The upsurge of incidences affected the town's influence and the Egyptian government shuttered its tribunals and moved them to Zagazig and Mansoura.[57] Ismailia became solely a transit point on the journey to Cairo or Port Said. Even so, de Lesseps's garden villa and homes for senior officers and other employees in the company took advantage of the quiet verdant nature and the beautiful lakeside.

The first steps taken by Ross were to ensure that the population understood the work that was about to be done. Next, searching out all the possible places where the mosquito could lay their larvae was essential. Insect eradication was thought the best measure to stop malaria. The search included a home-by-home examination of interiors, gardens, cesspools and latrines for stagnant water and mosquitoes. The maps produced show where major ponds or *birkas* were located and drainage was needed. Maps were also essential in laying out the ground campaign to eradicate all mosquitoes and putrid water.[58] The team led by Ross looked for the culprit and found mosquitoes of the genus *culex* and the malaria vector *anopheles*. Then, as a prophylaxis the company supplied, free of charge, the drug quinine. Quinine in the right dosage worked well to combat malaria, although there were side effects such as taste and ringing in the ears, which turned patients away, especially if taken as a deterrent to the parasite.[59]

The suggested course of action was 1) to continue supplying quinine for free to the entire town; 2) to use petroleum to fill cesspools and to empty jars or objects where water could collect and larvae may breed; 3) weekly inspections to be carried out by a team of malaria health officers to inspect for mosquitoes and stagnant water; 4) to improve the drainage of the various canals, sluices, gardens and ponds that ran around and into town by removing flora which provided protection for larvae and impeded the natural flow; 5) the Ismailia canal would need to be dredged periodically and silt removed. The *anopheles* mosquito was not found in Port Said and most likely malaria was not the cul-

56. ANMT 1995 060 4374. Map and chart highlighting the malaria problem in the city of Ismailia.

57. ANMT 1995 060 4373. In a *Times* article from the 15 Dec. 1877 the sickness is described as affecting the entire town, Europeans and Egyptians. 'Egypt', *Times* (15 Dec. 1877): 4.

58. Hoffman 2016.

59. Shah 2011, ch. 5: 'Pharmacological Failure'.

prit of the yearly fevers. Yet, as part of Ross's project, every and any mosquito, *anopheles* or not, would be eradicated.[60]

Vigilance against standing water, clean or dirty, was the focus of the prevention programme. Teams of three (a European foreman and two 'natives') were to visit each home in Ismailia once every week to search for mosquitoes and add a solution of oil to the cesspools, which lay on the ground floor of every home. In Port Said, five workmen and a foreman were hired to inspect homes. A large oil drum on wheels was purchased as well as buckets for each employee.

> No excess water was allowed to run to waste near the town, but was led into the lake, where it mingled with the sea-water. No water is allowed to remain stagnant in the channels or runnels, and as soon as the ground has been irrigated, the water supplying it is permitted to dry up.[61]

If any evidence of excess water use in the garden or violations related to containers that could collect liquid were found the owners could be punished by way of a fine. Through detailed surveillance and inspection, the towns' citizens were policed. In this way, they tackled the malaria problem 'systematically'.[62] The solution, as laid out above, was simple and similar to work carried out by Egyptians for centuries as part of the annual maintenance of irrigation waterways.[63] The Suez Canal Company had ignored these practices as they considered the urban design of Ismailia. Creating an idyllic garden-town was more important.

Another example of local expertise conquering modernity's supposed 'comforts' follows in the discussion of waste disposal.[64] In both towns the environmental conditions that lurked below the surface of the town in cesspools began to come under the microscope of administrators due to beliefs in

---

60. Today we know that it is only the *anopheles* mosquito that carries malaria. Early on it was still believed that other mosquitos could be vectors as well. This proved to be untrue. Thus, wholesale eradication of the mosquito was thought to be the best manoeuvre.

61. Ross 1903, p. 21.

62. Ibid., p. 501.

63. Mikhail 2011.

64. In Ismailia the sewage system was better organised and the cesspools well-constructed, but, as in Port Said, domestic and *anopheles* mosquitoes were discovered, except in the 'Arab Quarter' of town. Both Ross and the Lagos colonial Governor MacGregor believed this was because the Egyptian residents were disposing of waste in the sand. Thus, rather than gathering moist pools of waste flushed from the house using a cistern system, the Egyptians were using more austere methods which proved successful. MacGregor took this as evidence that he should implement a dry sewage system in the Lagos colony.

the unhygienic nature of these subterranean pits. They were viewed as prime breeding ground for various organisms.[65] Travellers had commented on the smell of the city and questioned its hygiene. This was especially acute during the summer months. Workers of the Suez Canal Company, of all nationalities, took sick days and complained of fever like symptoms. It was not uncommon for classrooms to be empty of pupils due to the sickness, which seemed to float in the air of Port Said. What the inspectors found was described in full detail. Compared to the cesspools of Ismailia, the ones found in Port Said were terrible. As described earlier, the burgeoning city of nearly 50,0000 souls sat on a thin sub-soil of sand, soil and water. Without a standard centralised sewage system, each home held a cesspool in the basement. The cesspools leaked into the marshy sub-soil and collected over time.

The report by Ross paints a vivid picture of the vermin, insects and bacteria living in the cellars of the coastal town. They tell of rats and cockroaches at home in the marshy layer of waste and excrement. In some places, because the high price of land on the narrow spit made renting or owning a home expensive, some were forced to reside in cellars adjacent to the wall which housed the cesspool. The survey of the town found nearly 400 sewage-filled cellars with an estimated water surface area of 7,626 square metres.[66] As a remedy for the cesspool issue, Ross recommended dousing the sitting waste with oil. After the mosquito squads made their rounds and the city began weekly cleaning of standing water and cesspools, residents and visitors noticed a change. The local government also enforced the closing off and cleaning out regularly of cellar cesspools and those in contravention would be fined. As in Ismailia, fines, education and inspection would be the primary bulwark towards mosquito eradication.

Ultimately, the creation of a proper sewage and drainage network would be the solution to removing the waste effectively, but that would come later and in a piecemeal fashion. Through these various methods, the towns of Ismailia and Port Said found that the mosquito population decreased. The health officers of the Suez Canal Company noted by 1909 a significant drop in new malaria cases. It seems that Ross's interventions worked. Ross would head to Cairo afterwards to examine the mosquito problem and to eradicate domestic mosquitoes at the Police Academy. A plan for mosquito eradication had been

---

65.   Similar to the 1896 law in France *'touts l'egouts'* the Suez Canal Company began to systematically organise and build a sewage system for clean water and dirty water. For more on this process see: Gandy 1999, pp. 23–44.

66.   Ross 1903, p. 513.

implemented and carried out in two major Suez Canal cities that changed the hygienic characters of the towns and implemented new rules and regulations to control cesspools and stagnant waters.

Conclusion

As humanity expanded and further impinged on nature, ecologies that were rarely touched were now bent and shaped towards the wishes of man. But wildlife (flora, fauna, animals, and other non-human living organisms) and natural phenomena are a force that fight against people's misguided ideal that they can control the environment. What this paper attempts to show are the possibilities that an interdisciplinary approach between urban and environmental histories could produce. The decision to build two new towns and dig new canals drastically changed the natural environment. Modernity and the idea that the environment could be manipulated, disciplined and controlled went hand in hand. Yet, it also demonstrated the infallibility of humanity's prowess over nature. The increase in water led to the creation of stagnant pools and waterways where new fauna and organisms reproduced in what was a lush eco-system. On top of that, the advent of new colonial populations which followed the occupation of Egypt in 1882, meant a fresh crop of blood for the mosquito and *plasmodium* parasite to attack. As Sonia Shah points out, 'war-making – the digging of trenches, the destruction of dams, the building of road – levels an ecological insult that malaria can often exploit'.[67] While, the environment has been blamed for the rise in malaria, the natural history of the vector and pathogen illustrate the complexity of the disease. The right environmental conditions are not the only part of the story. Movement of new populations and disruptions in nature, the interconnections related to human expansion, greatly increase favourable conditions for the mosquito.[68] New inhabitants also bring with them foreign *anopheles* as stowaways awaiting the right situation to set up home. The occupation of 1882 following the uprising of 'Urābī led to a perfect storm of elements that amplified the probabilities for a malaria breakout. We know that the colonial/imperial machine set change in motion, but we tend to blame environments, germs and parasites for the destruction that they bring and not human actors or political economy.[69]

---

67. Shah 2011, p. 74.
68. Jennifer Derr has made a similar argument by examining another disease case in Egypt. Derr 2018.
69. Cameron, Kelton and Swedlund 2016.

Others have also pointed out the connections between the rise of global travel through the Suez Canal and incidences of cholera.[70] The new populations moving through the cities of Ismailia and Suez after the canal opened in 1869, followed by the occupation of Egypt in 1882 by the British, most certainly played a part in the rise of malaria cases. The natural landscape was ripe for mosquito larvae and the occupiers provided fresh blood-food for the hatchlings of the larvae. Mitchell in *Rule of Experts* showed the ways the mosquito and *plasmodium* offer new interconnections between forces of power in nature, science, technology and public health. This new research into malaria and the Suez Canal cities provides an innovative way to address the environment, urban design and health together. Furthermore, the solutions that Ross specified were not very modern. It was an ancient remedy, one used by *fellah* to disrupt and remove stagnant or sitting water. The Rockefeller Foundation's protocols for mosquito prevention cited by Mitchell in the 1940s, and even today's World Health Organization standards, are eerily like what Ross proposed:[71] creation of teams of workers to sweep the villages and canals for sitting water, larvae and mosquitoes; the distribution of Quinine and the application of oil; what was suggested for the canal cities was used again four decades later to fight against the *P.falciparum* parasite. Further, in 2014 when malaria appeared in Edfu, Upper Egypt, the same methods were once again applied.[72] More than a century later, our ability to fight malaria, let alone eradicate the disease from Earth, remains almost unchanged.[73] What is obvious is that these experts continue to be outmanoeuvred by the *plasmodium* parasites. Disruption of ecologies for development will always lead to a reaction by the environment. The power *plasmodium* demonstrates is at a level greater than that of the anthropoid world.

ACKNOWLEDGEMENTS

Acknowledgements are due to Zeynep Çelik, Peter Gran and Nükhet Varlık who have pushed me towards new avenues of uncovering history. A special gratitude is reserved for Stephanie Boyle who read an earlier draft of this paper and provided valuable feedback. To the organisers at the University of Hamburg, Onur İnal and Yavuz Köse, who put together the conference 'Environmental History of the Ottoman Empire and Turkey' in 2017 and have patiently provided support as editors of this volume. Special

---

70. Kuhnke 1990; Huber 2013.

71. Rockefeller had picked up the anti-malaria campaign in 1915.

72. Kandeel et al. 2016, 274.

73. There have been advancements in medicines, but they are still derivatives of Quinine.

thanks for the speedy assistance of the librarians at the Liverpool School of Tropical Medicine, who in one of the quickest turnarounds of a request, scanned a copy of the original Dr. Edward Ross manuscript and sent it me. I owe them a debt of thanks for their assistance.

Bibliography

Unpublished Primary Sources

National Labour Archives (*Archives Nationales du Monde du Travail, ANMT*), Roubaix (France)

1995 060 4373, 1995 060 4374

The National Archives of the United Kingdom (TNA), London

Foreign Office (FO).

Published Primary Sources

New York Times

The Times (London)

Baedeker, Karl. 1908. *Baedeker's Egypt*, 6th edition. New York: Charles Scribner's Sons.

——. 1885. *Baedeker's Egypt*, 2nd edition. London: Karl Baedeker Publishers.

Badger, George Percy. 1862. *A Visit to the Isthmus of Suez Canal Works*. London.

Barois, Julien Hippolyte Eugène. 1889. *Irrigation in Egypt*, trans. A.M. Miller. Washington DC: Government Printing Office.

Barthélemy-Saint-Hilaire, Jules. 1857. *Egypt and the Great Suez Canal. A Narrative of Travels*. London: R. Bentley

De Lesseps, Ferdinand. 1876. *The Suez Canal: Letters and Documents Descriptive of its Rise and Progress in 1854–1856*. London: Henry S. King and Co.

Lynch, Thomas Kerr. 1866. *Visit to the Suez Canal. With Ten Illustrations*. London: Day and Son.

Nilsson. 1907. *Guide pratique: Alexandrie, Le Caire, Port-Saïd et environs...* Paris: Société de publications égyptiennes.

Ross, Ronald. 1903. *Report on Malaria at Ismailia and Suez*. Liverpool: Williams.

——. 1910. *The Prevention of Malaria*. London: John Murray.

Sandwith, F. M. 1892. 'Notes on Health Resorts: X. – Egypt'. *British Medical Journal* **2** (1660): 904–05.

Wilkin, Anthony. 1901. *On the Nile with a Camera*. New York: New Amsterdam Book Company.

Cesspools, Mosquitoes and Fever

Secondary Sources

Abul-Magd, Zeinab. 2013. *Imagined Empires: A History of Revolt in Egypt*. Berkeley: University of California Press.

Berque, Jacques. 1972. *Egypt: Imperialism & Revolution*. New York: Praeger.

Blunt, Wilfrid Scawen. 1922. *Secret History of the English Occupation of Egypt, Etc.* New York: Alfred A. Knopf.

Boyle, Stephanie Anne. 2013. 'Sickness, Scoundrels and Saints: Tanta in the World and the World in Tanta 1856–1907'. Ph.D. Diss., Boston: Northeastern University.

Bulliet, Richard W. 2011. *Cotton, Climate, and Camels in Early Islamic Iran: a Moment in World History*. New York: Columbia University Press.

Burke, Edmund III and Diana K. Davis (eds). 2011. *Environmental Imaginaries of the Middle East and North Africa*. Athens, OH: Ohio University Press.

Burke, Edmund III and Kenneth Pomeranz (eds). 2009. *The Environment and World History* Berkeley: University of California Press.

Burr, Malcolm. 1954. *The Insect Legion*. London: James Mesbit.

Carminati, Lucia. 2018. 'Empire in an Egyptian and Mediterranean Port-City'. Ph.D. Diss. Tucson: University of Arizona.

Cameron, Catherine M., Paul Kelton and Alan C. Swedlund. 2016. *Beyond Germs: Native Depopulation in North America*. Tucson: University of Arizona Press.

Cookson-Hills, Claire Jean. 2013. 'Engineering the Nile: Irrigation and the British Empire in Egypt, 1882–1914'. Ph.D. Diss. Kingston: Queen's University.

Christensen, Peter. 1993. *The Decline of Iranshahr: Irrigation and Environments in the History of the Middle East, 500 B.C. to A.D. 1500*. Copenhagen: Museum Tusculanum Press.

Cronon, William. 1997. *Nature's Metropolis: Chicago and the Great West*. New York: W.W. Norton.

Davis, Diana K. 2007. *Resurrecting the Granary of Rome: Environmental History and French Colonial Expansion in North Africa*. Athens, OH: Ohio University Press.

Derr, Jennifer. 2011. 'Drafting a Map of Colonial Egypt: The 1902 Aswan Dam, Historical Imagination, and the Production of Agricultural Geography'. In Edmund Burke III and Kenneth Pomeranz (eds), *Environmental Imaginaries of the Middle East and North Africa*. Athens: Ohio University Press. pp. 136–57.

——. 2018. 'Labor-Time: Ecological Bodies and Agricultural Labor in 19th-and early 20th-century Egypt'. *International Journal of Middle East Studies* 50 (2): 195–212.

Dolbee, Samuel. 2017. 'The Locust and the Starling: People, Insects, and Disease in the Late Ottoman Jazira and After, 1860–1940'. Ph.D. Diss. New York: New York University.

Doumani, Beshara. 1995. *Rediscovering Palestine: Merchants and Peasants in Jabal Nablus, 1700–1900*. Berkeley: University of California Press.

El Shennawy, Abdel Aziz Mohamed. 2010. *Al-Sukhr fī Hifr Qanāt al-Sūways*. Cairo: Egyptian General Book Organization.

Gallagher, Nancy Elizabeth. 1990. *Egypt's Other Wars: Epidemics and the Politics of Public Health*. Syracuse: Syracuse University Press.

Mohamed Gamal-Eldin

Gandy, Matthew. 1999. 'The Paris Sewers and the Rationalization of Urban Space', *Transactions of the Institute of British Geographers* **24** (1): 23–44.

Gratien, Chris. 2015. 'The Mountains are Ours: Ecology and Settlement and Early Republican Cilia, 1856–1956'. Ph.D. Diss. Washington DC: Georgetown University.

——. 2017. 'The Ottoman Quagmire: Malaria, Swamps, and Settlement in the Late Ottoman Mediterranean'. *International Journal of Middle East Studies* **49** (4): 583–604.

Greenwood, New. 1997. *The Sinai: A Physical Geography*. Austin: University of Texas Press.

Hammad, Hanan. 2016. *Industrial Sexuality. Gender, Urbanization, and Social Transformation in Egypt*. Austin: University of Texas Press.

Hippocrates. 2009. [original date unknown], trans. Francis Adams. *On Airs, Waters and Places*. Dodo Press.

Hoffman, Monica. 2016. 'Malaria, Mosquitos, and Maps: Practices and Articulations of Malaria Control in British India and WWII'. Ph.D. Diss., San Diego: University of California.

Huber, Valeska. 2013. *Channelling Mobilities: Migration and Globalisation in the Suez Canal Region and Beyond, 1869–1914*. Cambridge: Cambridge University Press.

Kandeel, A. et al. 2016. 'Control of Malaria Outbreak due to Plasmodium Vivax in Aswan Governorate, Egypt/Lutte Contre Une Flambee de Paludisme a Plasmodium Vivax Dans Le Gouvernorat d'Assouan (Egypte)'. *Eastern Mediterranean Health Journal* **22** (4): 274–79.

Kenawy, Mohamed A. 1988. 'Anopheline Mosquitoes (Diptera: Culicidae) as Malaria Carriers in AR Egypt' History and Present Status'. *Journal of the Egyptian Public Health Association* **63** (1): 67–85.

——. 2015. 'Review of *Anopheles* Mosquitoes and Malaria in Ancient and Modern Egypt'. *Journal of Mosquito Research* **5**: 4. doi: 10.5376/jmr.2015.05.0004

Kostof, Spiro. 1991. *The City Shaped: Urban Patterns and Meanings through History*. Boston: Little, Brown.

Kuhnke, LaVerne. 1990. *Lives at Risk: Public Health in Nineteenth-Century Egypt*. Berkeley: University of California Press.

Marlowe, John. 1964. *World Ditch; the Making of the Suez Canal*. New York: Macmillan.

Michel, Nicolas. 2016. 'La Compagnie du canal de Suez et l'eau du Nil (1854–1896)'. In Claudine Piaton (ed.), *L'isthme et l'Égypte au temps de la Compagnie universelle du canal maritime de Suez (1858–1956)*. Cairo: Institut français d'archéologie orientale. pp. 273–302.

Mikhail, Alan. 2011. *Nature and Empire in Ottoman Egypt: An Environmental History*. Cambridge: Cambridge University Press.

—— (ed.). 2012. *Water on Sand: Environmental Histories of the Middle East and North Africa*. New York: Oxford University Press.

Mitchell, Timothy. 2002. *Rule of Experts: Egypt, Techno-Politics, Modernity*. Berkeley: University of California Press.

Piaton, Claudine (ed.). 2016. *L'isthme et l'Égypte au temps de la Compagnie universelle du canal maritime de Suez (1858–1956)*. Cairo: Institut français d'archéologie orientale.

Pudney, John. 1970. *Suez; De Lesseps' Canal.* New York: Praeger.

Reynolds, Nancy. 2017. 'City of the High Dam: Aswan and the Promise of Postcolonialism in Egypt', *City & Society* **29** (1): 213–35.

Ross, Edward Halford. 1909. *The Prevention of Fever on the Suez Canal.* Cairo.

Shah, Sonia. 2011. *The Fever: How Malaria Has Ruled Humankind for 500,000 Years.* New York: Picador.

Shea, William H. 1977. 'A Date for the Recently Discovered Eastern Canal of Egypt'. *Bulletin of the American Schools of Oriental Research* **226**: 31–8.

Sneh, Amihai and Tuvia Weissbrod. 1973. 'Nile Delta: The Defunct Pelusiac Branch Identified'. *Science* **180** (4081): 59–61.

Tsing, Anna Lowenhaupt. 2017. *The Mushroom at the End of the World: On the Possibility of Life in Capitalist Ruins.* Princeton: Princeton University Press.

Upton, Dell. 2008. *Another City: Urban Life and Urban Spaces in the New American Republic.* New Haven: Yale University Press.

Waugh, Evelyn. 1974. *Labels: A Mediterranean Journal.* London: Duckworth.

PART 4

Ideas and Actors

Chapter 9

THE RICE DEBATES:
POLITICAL ECOLOGY IN THE OTTOMAN
PARLIAMENT

Chris Gratien

In July 1908, Sultan Abdülhamid II (r. 1876–1909) capitulated to a rebellion within the ranks of the Ottoman military and reinstated the Ottoman constitution that had enjoyed a brief debut during the 1870s. The constitution brought parliamentary elections and, that autumn, candidates throughout the empire vied for 288 seats in the lower house of the parliament called the Chamber of Deputies (*Meclis-i Mebusan*). Over subsequent years, parliamentarians representing the different political factions, religious communities, ethnolinguistic groups and varied geographies of the Ottoman Empire gathered to debate new laws that, for the first time in the empire's history, would be legislated through a multi-vocal, representative governing body. The period of parliamentary government, while a brief moment in the history of a long-lived empire, has represented an important facet of the study of how communities of the Middle East engaged with ascendant notions of citizenship, nationhood and modernity.[1] The parliament itself brought together some of the most influential figures in the history of the late Ottoman Empire: lifetime bureaucrats, clerics, military officers, lawyers, doctors and provincial notables who would become fixtures of the post-World War I political landscape of the Middle East. And for a few lengthy sessions in late winter 1910, these notable personages gathered in vociferous debate about rice cultivation and its purported relationship to the spread of malaria.

The Chamber of Deputies did not spend hours debating about rice because it was necessarily a central concern of the empire or even one of its most

---

1.   See Brummett 2000; Kayalı 1997; Watenpaugh 2006; Campos 2011; Sohrabi 2014; Der Matossian 2014.

important agricultural products. It was the complex questions contained within the issue of rice cultivation that animated the rice debates. On the surface, they reflected an exploration of managing what environmental historians often refer to as 'second nature', i.e. an anthropogenic environment with pervasive impacts on human life.[2] Both the critics and defenders of rice invoked arguments about nature and science, variously seeking to cast rice paddies as sources of pollution that could negatively impact public health or harmless and economically beneficial spaces that should be nurtured for the good of the empire. In the process, the deputies traced the interplay of agriculture, water, climate, trees, birds, rural villages and malaria – a blood-borne parasite transmitted between human beings by the bite of the anopheles mosquito.[3]

As an earnest attempt by the Ottoman Empire's new representative government to address a significant public health issue in light of emergent scientific understandings of nature, the rice debates embodied the fullest manifestation of modern legislation in the Ottoman Empire with its attendant pluralism, rivalry and occasional absurdity. But they amounted to much more than discussions about the vagaries of rice cultivation. In the background of these involved conversations about the ecology of the rice paddy was a much larger political struggle to determine who would manage rural environments of the provinces and who both the government and economy were meant to serve. The question of rice and malaria was a matter of political ecology.[4] Individuals representing different interests within the parliament and within the ruling Committee of Union and Progress (CUP; *İttihad ve Terakki Cemiyeti*) itself chose the rice paddy as an ideological battlefield for two competing visions of progress: one in which the government served to uplift and protect every citizen and another in which its role was to facilitate agricultural prosperity and economic growth.

The rice debates resulted in the creation of the Rice Cultivation Law (*Pirinç Ziraatı Kanunnamesi*) of 1910, which stipulated how precisely rice should be safely produced under the supervision of the Ministry of Agriculture in order to reduce the impact of malaria. In this regard, they were the precursor to further attempts made at curtailing malaria through government

2.   See Judd 2014; Cronon 1991.
3.   On malaria, see also the contribution of Mohamed Gamal-Eldin in the volume.
4.   See Perreault et al. 2015. For research on colonialism and political ecology in the Middle East, see Davis 2007; Tvedt 2004; Mitchell 2002. Also Mikhail 2013; Davis and Burke III 2013.

regulations in the Republic of Turkey.[5] They are evidence of a successful legislative compromise on an important and multi-faceted issue confronted by the Ottoman government during the constitutional period. Yet the history of the Rice Cultivation Law also serves as a window onto rival political programmes during a particularly volatile period in Ottoman politics. Through the lens of the Ottoman parliament and the laws created by ministries concerned with the environment and public health, one may examine how political battles played out in the realm of ecology within the framework of a representative governing body. In this article, I study the creation of the Rice Cultivation Law of 1910 by comparing the final law as passed with the proposed versions contained within the published minutes of the Ottoman parliament and the arguments made in support of those versions. These debates reveal that agriculture was not merely the target of state regulation but also a field of political contention. In tracing its political ecology, I explore how rice prompted reflection on the differentiation and organisation of imperial, provincial and agricultural space as well as on the Ottoman government's responsibilities towards its citizens in the era of constitutionalism.

Malaria and the Rice Cultivation Law

Rice was widely cultivated in many parts of the Ottoman Empire at the time of its earliest expansion and the specific forms of land use its production entailed were long part of the Ottoman administrative apparatus. The area of rice cultivation, referred to as *çeltik*, was subject to specific forms of taxation and there were a number of ways in which landowners could apply to the Ottoman government to open a rice paddy of their own on state or vacant land. By the early twentieth century, rice was most widely cultivated in the Tigris and Euphrates basins – that is, Iraq and Eastern Anatolia – as well as other parts of Anatolia, the Black Sea coast and sections of the Balkans. Perhaps with the exception of certain regions of modern-day Iraq (more below), rice was generally cultivated in a manner involving large landholders who employed local peasants on their land. Like cotton, tobacco or poppies, rice was a commercial crop.[6]

---

5.   On the history of malaria in the Ottoman Empire and Turkey, see Kurt and Yaşayanlar 2017; Köse et al 2017; Günergun and Etker 2013; Evered and Evered 2012; Tuğluoğlu 2008; Tekeli and İlkin 1999.

6.   Over the course of the empire's last century, some areas of dense rice cultivation in the Balkans, such as the Plovdiv region that long supplied the imperial kitchen, were severed from the Ottoman Empire in successive conflicts. For an overview of rice in the Ottoman Empire, see İnalcık 1982.

Rice was not vital to the empire but was important in select regions and to the commercial interests of certain individuals. Data from Ottoman Ministry of Agriculture demonstrate that rice was relatively insignificant in numerical terms. Even in major rice-growing regions, much more land overall was devoted to wheat production. For example, the Province of Diyarbakir was one of the most important rice-growing areas, yet out of its more than three million *dönüm*s of cultivated land, no more than a few hundred thousand were recorded as being planted with rice.[7] In comparison with staple crops, rice cultivation was extremely localised. The distribution of land devoted to rice shows that the crop was absent in entire provinces of the empire while intensely concentrated in certain local districts or *kaza*s.[8] The list below further suggests that most rice-growing regions were peripheral districts of their respective provinces. For example, almost all the rice in the *sancak* of Kastamonu was grown in the *kaza* of Tosya; almost all the rice grown in the *sancak* of Skopje was grown in the *kaza* of Kočani. Table 1 lists regions of the Ottoman Empire and their total area cultivated with rice, according to pre-war government statistics. Baghdad and Basra were not included in the data, although they are attested as major areas of rice cultivation.

Ottoman officials did not regulate rice and spend so much time thinking about the regulation of rice because it was an indispensable crop. Rather, it was due to the specific questions of political economy and public health that arose out of the conditions of rice production. The creation of a Ministry of Agriculture and Public Works (*Nezaret-i Ziraat ve Nafia*) during the nineteenth century empowered the Ottoman government to become more involved in

---

7.   Estimates of cultivated area from *1325 senesi* 1911–12.

8.   During the period in question, *vilayet* refers to the largest administrative unit, the province, whereas *sancak* refers to the subdivision of the province (and sometimes smaller provinces not attached to a *vilayet*). *Kaza* is in turn the subdivision of a *sancak*, generally centred on a single large town with an administrative centre and court. County or district may be considered an approximate equivalent of *kaza*. The term *nahiye* applied to the subsequent subdivisions of a *kaza*. The size of these administrative units could vary greatly depending on the region but, by way of examples from this article: According to *1325 senesi Asya ve Afrika-yı Osmani Zıraat İstatistiği*, in 1909, Ankara *vilayeti* was approximately 75,000 square kilometres, about 7.6 per cent of its land was registered as cultivated, and it contained 25 *kazas*; Diyarbakır *vilayeti* was approximately 47,000 square kilometres, about 6.5 per cent of its land was registered as cultivated and it contained 15 *kazas*; Mosul *vilayeti* was about 90,000 square kilometres, about 2.5 per cent of its land was registered as cultivated, and it contained 15 *kazas*. These three examples suggest that there were 100–300 square kilometres of cultivated land per *kaza*. A square kilometre contained roughly 1,100 dönüms.

The Rice Debates

Table 1. Areas of rice cultivation in the Ottoman Empire.

Ottoman Asia, 1913		Ottoman Europe, 1907		*Kazas* (with corresponding *Sancaks*) with most rice cultivation	
Sancak	Dönüms	Sancak	Dönüms	Maden (Ergani)	50,000
Kirkuk	59,000	Skopje	10,392	Kirkuk (Kirkuk)	50,000
Mosul	50,610	Serres	4,550	Siverek (Siverek)	45,000
Ergani	50,000	Salonica	4,130	Amedi (Mosul)	30,000
Siverek	46,000	Preveze	3,300	Tosya (Kastamonu)	25,000
Ankara	43,050	Drama	3,000	Diyarbakır (Diyarbakır)	24,230
Diyarbakır	28,340	Berat	2,050	Akre (Mosul)	20,000
Kastamonu	28,000	Janina	2,000	Nallıhan (Ankara)	19,000
Sulaymaniyah	25,213	Ergiri	200	Baziyan (Sulaymaniyah)	15,000
Maraş	24,000			Ayaş (Ankara)	13,750
Sinop	6,000			Maraş (Maraş)	13,000
Bolu	4,670			Pazarcık (Maraş)	11,000
Bursa	4,550			Gülanber (Sulaymaniyah)	10,000
Amasya	4,000			Kočani (Skopje)	9,570
All Others	26,081			Boyabad (Sinop)	6,000

Source: *1323 Senesi Avrupa-yı Osmani Zıraat İstatistiği*, (Istanbul: Mahmud Bey Matbaası, 1326/1910); *Memalik-i Osmanlye'nin 1329 Senesine Mahsus Zıraat İstatistiği*, (Istanbul: Ticaret ve Zıraat Nezareti, 1330/1914).
Note: Data not available for Baghdad and Basra provinces

agrarian production through regulation and the deployment of experts trained in technical agricultural methods.[9] In May 1910, the Ottoman government passed a series of laws (*kanunname*) concerning the cultivation of rice, aimed at standardising the definition of proper rice cultivation throughout the empire. The Ministry of Forests, Mines and Agriculture (*Orman ve Maadin ve Ziraat Nezareti*) also published a short manual on proper rice cultivation.[10] While these regulations and guidelines focused on a number of points regarding the management of rice fields, the central issue was the link between rice cultivation and elevated rates of malaria infection. Over the course of the late nineteenth century, medical discoveries concerning malaria lent coherence to longstanding

9.   For recent research on the subject, see Williams 2015.

10.   *Pirinç Ziraatı* 1910.

conventional wisdom about the hazards of swamps: stagnant water contributed to the proliferation of malaria, not due to its nature as such, but because it provided ideal breeding ground for mosquitoes, the vector that transmits the malaria parasite between humans.

This discovery rendered the observed link between wet lowlands and malaria more legible and gave impetus to target certain agricultural activities for regulation. Agriculture in general was usually cast as an *antidote* to malaria. Feyzullah İzmidi (1845–1923), who led the late Ottoman battle with malaria stated in his university lectures that 'malaria likes unworked lands and desolate, empty countryside. It cannot hold up in the face of civilisation and the efforts of mankind'.[11] But rice was different. Its cultivation required more water than common grains such as wheat or barley and commercial crops like cotton and tobacco. Generally speaking, rice paddies were maintained through the creation of irrigation channels that would pool water into large wet tracts of land where rice was sown in the spring. Thus, well-watered regions with large rivers, lakes or swamps were most conducive to growing rice. The anthropogenic environment created by rice differed markedly from that resulting from most crops; while the Ottoman government promoted the clearing of wetlands by encouraging cultivation of many crops, rice cultivation effectively entailed the *creation and maintenance* of wetlands for an economic purpose. This practice was at odds with the Ottoman government's growing concern about the public health impacts of swamps and especially about malaria, which was spread between humans by the mosquitoes that bred in stagnant water. With all swamps slated for elimination by the end of the Ottoman period, rice became a unique ecological conundrum.[12]

The 1910 Rice Cultivation Law treated rice as a source of illness or a form of pollution and charged cultivators with certain responsibilities vis-à-vis maintaining a healthy ecological equilibrium in the countryside. By 1910, Ottoman ministries concerned with regulating both agriculture and public health had already been in operation for decades. The Ottoman technocratic state had grown considerably during the *Tanzimat* period and the reign of Abdülhamid II. What made the law particularly unique was that it was to be legislated by the newly-reinstated Ottoman parliament, a representative governing body charged with the reformulation of Ottoman rule in accordance with the constitution and the collection of interests and ideals embodied by the

---

11. 'Sıtma işlenmemiş araziyi tenha hali memleketleri sever. Medeniyet önünde ve mesai-i beşer karşısında dikiş tutturamaz. Mahvolur'. İzmidi 1911, p. 17.

12. This issue is addressed at greater length in Gratien 2017.

1908 Revolution. While influenced by recommendations from the Ottoman agricultural officials, the language and articles of the law were carefully and painstakingly reviewed in the Chamber of Deputies, which was comprised of representatives elected at the provincial level. Thanks to the thorough records of the chamber minutes, we have nearly complete transcripts of the arguments and debates that ensued.[13]

Competing Visions of Progress and the Nature of Rice Cultivation

The Chamber of Deputies deliberated at considerable length on the articles in the regulation concerning rice cultivation on four occasions in 1910: 1, 4 and 8 February and 8 March. Over the course of those many hours, articles and amendments to the rice law were discussed one by one. During the deliberations, more than fifty deputies representing a wide variety of districts and backgrounds participated to lesser or greater degrees. Some participated in all four conversations but most were only partially present for the entire debate. In each session, the statements lasted for hours. The relationship between malaria and rice remained central to the discussion and creation of the law. But in attempting to reconcile how rice could be properly produced without exacerbating the presence of malaria, the law opened up complicated questions about not only epidemiology but also pollution, property, social and economic priorities and the obligations of the state towards its citizens concerning health and wellbeing.

While the law would eventually be enacted despite lack of consensus, the deputies were in general agreement that a regulation concerning rice cultivation would be passed. When dissenters pushed too hard against the premise of the

---

13. All references to the parliamentary proceedings are taken from the minutes of the Ottoman parliament, published by the Press of the Grand National Assembly of Turkey (*Türkiye Büyük Millet Meclisi; TBMM*) in 1985 and available through the TBMM website. See https://www.tbmm.gov.tr/kutuphane/tutanak_sorgu.html. The TBMM transliteration differs in some cases from standard spelling and transliteration practices in modern Turkish, and the original transliterations have been modified to conform to the style guidelines of this volume. Translations of the minutes are my own. The following four sessions concern the question of rice and malaria: *Meclis-i Mebusan Zabıt Ceridesi (MMZC)*, Devre 1, Cilt 2, Sene 2, 33. İnikad (19 Kanunisani 1325 [1 Feb. 1910]), pp. 57–88; *MMZC*, Devre 1, Cilt 2, Sene 2, 35. İnikad (23 Kanunisani 1325 [5 Feb. 1910]), pp. 117–48; *MMZC*, Devre 1, Cilt 2, Sene 2, 38. İnikad (27 Kanunisani [9 Feb. 1910]), pp. 215–50; *MMZC*, Devre 1, Cilt 2, Sene 2, 50. İnikad (23 Şubat 1325 [8 Mar. 1910]), pp. 597–637. For published Rice Cultivation Law, see *Pirinç Ziraatı Kânûnnâmesi*, (Istanbul: Matbaa-yı Amire, 1328/1910-11]).

regulations, the chamber settled the matter with relative civility or recommended that the issue be reconsidered by the core committee charged with formulating the law.[14] The final version of the law was much changed through the debate. Because of the diversity of vantage points from which the Ottoman deputies approached the Rice Cultivation Law, it is mistaken to present the entirety of the proceedings as a neatly polarised dichotomy. However, these proceedings demonstrate that there were two main camps – which I refer to here as the 'technocrats' and the 'liberals' – who furthered rather different visions of the Ottoman government's role in regulating agriculture.

The initial framing of the restrictions on rice cultivation was conceived from a technocratic vantage point within the Ministry of Agriculture; a number of prominent parliamentarians, some of whom were associated with the ministry, advocated the general point that agricultural experts and officials should manage how cultivation was to take place. Rıza Paşa of Afyonkarahisar was the main representative of the ministry on the committee that formulated the law. In addition, İstrati Efendi, identified in the minutes as the Chief of Agriculture (*Ziraat Müdürü*), as well as other figures involved in policy concerning agriculture and public works such as Aristidi Paşa (1862–1938), an influential Rum physician and politician elected on the CUP ticket, weighed in heavily. The most outspoken proponent of strict prohibitions on rice cultivation was Nazaret Dagavaryan (1862–1915), an Armenian physician representing the Province of Sivas and one of the founders of the Armenian General Benevolent Union (AGBU). Though not monolithic, this technocratic camp consistently defended both prescriptive and proscriptive clauses in the regulation that would not only protect against the potential impacts of malaria but also delineate the parameters of acceptable rice cultivation, and its larger ecological context within the Ottoman countryside, in accordance with modern agriculture methods or what was consistently invoked as 'science' (*fen*).

The Ministry of Agriculture's official stance was that the Rice Cultivation Law should not be mistaken for an anti-rice law. It would facilitate the increased production of rice while also improving public health. Rıza Paşa emphasised that the Ottoman government was an 'agricultural government' (*zirai bir hükümet*), citing statistics indicating that Japan had five times the overall rice production of the Ottoman Empire, despite the fact that it was only the size of a 'cow's tongue' (*sığır dili*) and comparable to just 'one of our provinces' (*bir*

---

14. The minutes reveal boredom as a productive influence in the discussions. There are instances in the minutes wherein some deputies begin calling out 'enough' in apparent exasperation during particularly drawn-out arguments.

vilayetimiz). He speculated that, with new irrigation works, Konya or Bursa alone could equal Japan's production and stressed the strategic value of agriculture as well, saying 'the Japanese lived on rice alone during the Russo-Japanese War'.[15] Istirati Efendi confirmed that rice should be subjected to supervision of the Ministry of Agriculture, saying that 'if not done in accordance with scientific methods, rice cultivation does not give [good] yields'. Rıza Bey of Drama, also part of the agriculture committee, seconded this statement.[16] In other words, the technocratic camp believed that science would *both improve cultivation and eliminate malaria* if cultivation were subject to sound regulation.

By contrast, the deputies who might be broadly labelled as members of the 'liberal' camp were generally opposed to the law and advocated minimised restrictions on economic activity. These voices presented government oversight as *inherently at odds with the interests of cultivators* and the broader economic goals of the empire. As one deputy put it, the law would 'create nothing but problems for the people'.[17] Many of these deputies were in fact wealthy provincial notables with some commercial and landed interests. The most vocal among them was Feyzi Bey of Diyarbakır, himself a wealthy land owner whose family name of 'Pirinççizade' essentially translates as 'Rice-Man', referring to specialisation in the cultivation and trade of rice. Pirinççizade Feyzi Bey (1878–1933) derived much of his wealth and position from rice grown on his family's vast landholdings – over thirty villages according to Uğur Ümit Üngör – in the Province of Diyarbakır.[18] Statistics from Table 1 indicate that the Diyarbakır-Ergani-Severek triangle was one of the most concentrated regions of rice production in the empire. Ali Cenani Bey (1872–1934), a notable and major landholder from the Aintab region (where rice was cultivated near Kilis) also echoed generally anti-regulation opinions.[19] Both men would play a prominent role in shaping economic policy not only as dictated by the Ottoman Chamber of Deputies but also in the early Republic of Turkey.

Whereas the 1910 Rice Cultivation Law was buttressed by the scientific expertise of agronomists and doctors, these opponents of the law claimed to represent a commercial perspective. Feyzi Bey positioned himself as the bearer of practical knowledge concerning profitable rice cultivation, advocating the

---

15. 'Japonlar, Japonya-Rusya muharebesinde yalnız pirinç ile tagaddi ettiler'. *MMZC*, Devre 1, Cilt 2, Sene 2, 33. İnikad (19 Kanunisani 1325 [1 Feb. 1910]), p. 62.

16. 'Fenne muvafık olmayarak yapılacak olursa mahsul vermez'. Ibid., p. 64.

17. 'Halkı tamamen müşkilâta uğratıyor'. Ibid., pp. 63–64.

18. Üngör 2012, p. 273.

19. On Ali Cenani Bey, see Kurt 2018; Şavkılı 2008.

privatisation of resources such as streams used for irrigation and opposing to any environmental aspects of the regulation that stood in the way of his conception of efficient agriculture. His potential conflicts of interest were not obscure or subtextual within the chamber's meetings. At one point, Abdülaziz Mecdi [Tolun] Efendi (1865–1941) of Karesi called out Feyzi Bey in defense of the technocratic camp, saying 'I'd like to speak against our Pirinççizade brother. As can be understood by his title, because he is entirely occupied with rice business, he wants to leave it completely free of responsibility. To leave rice cultivators this unsupervised is not right'.[20] However, Feyzi argued that his voice should count more than the other deputies' due to the relevance of rice to the Diyarbakır region and his personal livelihood. At one point in the meetings he became indignant, declaring that 'since more [rice] comes out of our parts than any other region, I have a specialty in this'.[21]

It is notable that with regard to the rice debates, a reasonably representative selection of the multi-ethnic and multi-confessional Ottoman Empire's diverse communities had their say. This is not only due to the fact that non-Muslims had some mandated representation in the parliament but also that the question of rice and its regulation was relevant to a large mix of different interest groups. Non-Muslims figured prominently among the doctors and Ministry of Agriculture officials who commented on technical matters; Arab and Kurdish deputies of Eastern Anatolia, Syria and Iraq meanwhile tended to side with the camp representing the interests of local landed elite. Of course, the group most immediately affected by the law – the men and women who provided agricultural labour and lived in the immediate vicinity of rice-growing areas – had no real voice in the chamber. They were ultimately the ones who both had to grapple with impact of malaria on rural communities and to bear the brunt of the impacts that regulation or promotion of rice might have on the political economy of the provinces. Interestingly, both the main camps claimed at various moments, as would be expected in a representative governing body, that their views represented the interests of the rural masses. While the technocrats claimed to protect ordinary people from the impacts that rice had on public health, the liberals stressed that their understanding of proper rice cultivation was most attuned to what farmhands actually practised.

---

20. 'Pirinççizâde biraderimize karşı söyleyeceğim. Unvanından dahi anlaşıldığına göre, bütün pirinç işi ile meşgül olduğu için pirinççileri suret-i kat'iyede haliü'l-izar olarak bırakmak istiyor. Pirinççileri bu kadar başıboş salıvermek doğru değildir'. *MMZC*, Devre 1, Cilt 2, Sene 2, 38. İnikad (27 Kanunisani 1325 [9 Feb. 1910]), p. 232.

21. 'Her memleketten fazla bizim taraflarda çıktığından, onun için bunda ihtisasım vardır. Paşa hazretleri iyi takdir buyurmuyorlar'. Ibid., p. 229.

The Rice Debates

The minutes reveal a fascinating conversation about ecology that, while referring to expert and common knowledge about rice cultivation, did not reflect the latest understandings of malaria epidemiology that inspired the creation of the law. In the chamber, rice paddies were debated as sources of pollution that negatively impacted public health. Rice cultivation did in fact exacerbate the pervasive impact of malaria in many provinces of the Ottoman Empire, because the irrigation canals and stagnant water of rice paddies created suitable aquatic environments that, when coupled with the warm and humid lowland climates of the regions that specialised in rice production, supported the proliferation of larvae of anopheles mosquitoes in great numbers. This link was already known to the Ottoman medical establishment. Alongside the university lectures of Feyzullah İzmidi, which reflected up-to-date knowledge about malaria within the Ottoman medical establishment, the prominent CUP figure Tevfik Rüştü (1883–1972) wrote a pamphlet about the causes and prevention of malaria in his capacity as health inspector of Salonica, a rice-producing region.[22] Trained physicians in the Chamber of Deputies such as Arif İsmet and Nazaret Dagavaryan were key figures in the rice debates; yet, even they framed rice cultivation as an activity that vaguely 'disrupts the air' (*havayı ihlal eder*), thereby causing malaria.

This 'miasmatic' conception of malaria being caused by 'bad air' likely served as common ground with the ecological imaginaries of staunch sceptics. One such sceptic outright denied findings that rice cultivation did potentially support the spread of malaria, remarking that if it had been the case, 'nobody would be left in our Ottoman lands'.[23] As a result, much of the debate centred on defining the ecology of rice cultivation and explaining under which conditions it was a hazard to public health. A proposed stipulation that cultivators plant eucalyptus alongside their paddies and irrigation ditches spiralled into over an hour of debate about trees and their impact on agriculture. The Ottoman Ministry of Agriculture promoted the cultivation of eucalyptus, sometimes called the 'malaria tree' (*sıtma ağacı*), and eucalyptus was widely regarded at the time as an antidote to malaria (and other environmental issues) in the Ottoman Empire and throughout the world.[24] But opponents of regulation cited the

22. Rüştü 1910; İzmidi 1911. See also Ersoy 1998.

23. 'Dagavaryan Efendinin sözüne intibak ediliyor ve onun hakikaten aslı olursa, bizim Memalik-i Osmaniyye'de şimdiye kadar hiç kimse kalmamalı idi'. *MMZC*, Devre 1, Cilt 2, Sene 2, 50. İnikad (23 Şubat 1325 [8 Mar. 1910]), p. 614.

24. *Orman ve Maden ve Ziraat Mecmuası*, no. 10 (Aug. 1894); Prime Ministry Ottoman Archives (*Başbakanlık Osmanlı Arşivleri; BOA*), Y.PRK.UM. 1/86 (23 Rebiülevvel 1297 [5 Mar. 1880]); BOA, Y.A.HUS. 290/21 (5 Şaban 1311 [11 Feb. 1894]); BOA,

various problems trees would bring: their shade impedes the development of crops, they attract birds that will eat the seed, and care for trees was an unfair burden upon cultivators.[25] As I demonstrate further below, quibbling about the birds and the trees was critical to the political issue at hand not primarily for the sake of arriving at a scientifically-accurate understanding of the relationship between malaria and rice but rather because delineating the nature of rice involved the careful definition of the rice paddy and how it should be governed as well as who would bear the responsibility and cost of its regulation and whom the law was to protect.

Geographies of Rice

The considerations of geography and climate in the Rice Cultivation Law reveal how the space of the rice paddy and the jurisdiction of regulation were imagined and, in turn, the extent to which standardised practice for rice cultivation could be implemented throughout the empire. A number of deputies took umbrage at the very first words in the very first sentence of the first article of the original draft of the law, which stated that the law would apply to rice paddies being formed 'in the places with a suitable climate' (*iklimi müsait olan yerlerde*). This phrasing was removed from an amended version of Article 1 of the 1910 Rice Cultivation Law and replaced with 'in the locations that are fertile, have enough water, and the soil of which is conducive to rice cultivation'.[26] Neither appeared in the final version enacted in May 1910.[27]

At first glance, the above phrases might seem merely superfluous, but in fact, it was the implicit power of jurisdiction granted to Ministry of Agriculture by this wording that bothered some deputies. As Ali Cenani Bey explained, either phrase would give local agriculture officials the power to refuse permits for rice cultivation merely on the basis that the land was not deemed suitable. On behalf of the committee, Rıza Paşa agreed to lift the phrase, but then ob-

---

DH.İD. 44–2/1 (22 Cemaziyülahir 1329 [21 May 1911]); BOA, DH.MKT. 2801/55 (13 Rebiülahir 1327 [2 July 1909]). On global context, see Davis 2016; Farmer 2013.

25. *MMZC*, Devre 1, Cilt 2, Sene 2, 38. İnikad (27 Kanunisani 1325 [9 Feb. 1910]), pp. 222–26.

26. '… arazisi pirinç ziraatına kabiliyetli ve suları kâfi ve elverişli olan mahallerde …' *MMZC*, Devre 1, Cilt 2, Sene 2, 33. İnikad (19 Kanunisani 1325 [1 Feb. 1910]), p. 67.

27. *Pirinç Ziraatı Kanunnamesi*, p. 3.

jections poured in from both sides of the argument.[28] Artas Yorgaki Efendi of Salonica sought to restore the original wording of 'in the places with a suitable climate' on the basis that such a consideration was necessary to evaluate the potential impacts of cultivation for public health. Mehmet Vâsıf Efendi of Manastır concurred, adding:

> ... it is not good to leave the population unrestricted in all matters ... Since [they] do not know agriculture in its entirety, they could plant rice in a place that is not conducive and end up confused and disappointed at the needless loss of a whole year's work. If this is done under the examination of a technical officer, it will be more beneficial in any event.[29]

These arguments positioned the technically-trained employees of the ministry before local cultivators in terms of understanding the specificities of agricultural land. But other deputies would remain resistant to this notion throughout the proceedings. Abdülhamid Zöhravi Efendi (1855–1916), a journalist and religious notable from Homs who represented Hama in the parliament, argued that the conditions of rice cultivation in the law were already sufficiently described and that referring to climate or suitability of the land was counterproductive.[30] Then, at the very end of the session, Hacı Hasan Fehmi, a representative from Maraş, submitted a proposal that would virtually negate Article 1 altogether. His motion stated that the phrase '"in the locations that are fertile, have enough water, and the soil of which is conducive to rice cultivation" could bring about nothing but upsetting and troubling the cultivators, because it is impossible to imagine land that is not suitable for rice cultivation'. He then proceeded to suggest the deletion of most of the rest of the article.[31] It is easy to see why Hacı Hasan Fehmi adopted this optimistic position regarding the environmental conditions suitable for the cultivation of rice. He represented one of the most important rice-growing districts in the Ottoman Empire, and much akin to Pirinççizade Feyzi Bey of Diyarbakır, he was at the head of Maraş's foremost

28. *MMZC*, Devre 1, Cilt 2, Sene 2, 33. İnikad (19 Kanunisani 1325 [1 Feb. 1910]), p. 67.
29. 'Ziraatte, bendenizce ahaliyi her hususta mutlak bırakmak iyi değildir ... Çünki ahali tamamiyle bu ziraatı bilmediği için, kabiliyeti olmayan yerde pirinç eker, bütün sene emeği beyhude hâ'ib ve hâsir olur. Bunları bir fen memurunun tetkiki tahtında yaparsa, her halde daha nafi olur'. Ibid., p. 67.
30. Ibid., pp. 68–69.
31. 'Birinci maddenin 'arazisi pirinç ziraatine kabiliyetli, suları kâfi ve elverişli olan mahallerde' kaydı zürrâi üzmekten ve yormaktan başka bir şeye sebep olamaz. Çünkü pirinç ziraatına kabiliyeti olmadık bir toprak tasavvur edilemez'. Ibid., p. 69.

rice-cultivating dynasty: the Kadızade family.[32] His motion was struck down by the chamber.

The final version of the first paragraph in Article 1 read as follows:

> Rice cultivation is unrestricted on the condition that the water used to establish rice paddies is not left in a stagnant state, conveyed by proper canals, made to flow out of the paddy, and the discharged waters does not accumulate any-where so that they do not become fetid; it is discharged in a manner that does not harm the locations through which it passes or the land and water sources belonging the people of the villages and towns in the vicinity and in the event it does harm it is indemnified; and it is at least four metres from paved roads, along with the conditions written in the articles below.[33]

This version of the article stipulated that rice should be cultivated in a manner that does not affect public health or negatively impact others in the vicinity. Absent from the final version of the law was the proposed language to the effect that particular regions or land could be deemed suitable for rice cultivation, with the Ministry of Agriculture claiming implicit right to arbitrate. In this way, the law constrained the capacity of Ministry of Agriculture personnel to dictate where which crops would be cultivated, *limiting them to statements as to how.*

Yet geography and climate continued to play a role in the debates, due to rice cultivation's different forms and manners in different regions. Much of the debate in the Chamber of Deputies concerned how the law could be drafted in such a way as to account for the variety of contexts of rice cultivation, with some deputies pushing against certain regulations on the basis that their universal application would undermine cultivation. Early on in the sessions, the chamber fielded an inquiry from the government concerning what was to be done about rice cultivation in the Bursa plain. The countryside of the Bursa region in north-western Anatolia had undergone considerable transformation due to the spread of commercial agriculture and immigration from the Balkans

---

32.   Göl 2006, p. 45.

33.   'İhdas olunacak çeltik kıtaaları iskâ olunmak üzere istimal olunacak sular taaffün etmemek için râkid bir halde bırakılmayıp muntazam harklarla sevk ve kıtaalardan cereyan ettirmek ve akıttırılacak sular dahi hiç bir yerde teraküm etmemek ve geç-tikleri mahallerde veyahut o mahaller civarındaki köy veya kasaba ahalisine ait araziye ve çeşmelere ve su yollarında mazarrat vermeyecek surette akıttırılmak ve mazarrat verdiği halde tazmin etmek ve şoselerden dört metre uzak bulunak şartıyla ve mevvad-ı âtide muharrer şeraitle pirinç ziraatı serbesttir. Kıtaat henüz teşekkül etmeyen veyahut teşekkül edip de işbu kıtaat haricinde kalan yerlerde hususi pirinçlikler ihdas etmek isteyenler de şerait-i mesrude ve âtiyeye tabi olacaklardır'. *Pirinç Ziraatı Kânünnamesi*, pp. 3–4.

and the Caucasus.[34] Amid the many developments and points of contention that emerged in the countryside, there was an attempt to completely forbid rice cultivation in the Bursa plain. Rıza Paşa's description of the controversy is instructive in multiple senses. It demonstrates on one hand the complex intertwining of private interests and the local administrations and, on the other, showcases the types of evidence and documentation introduced during the debates in the Ottoman parliament.

Rıza Paşa had recently visited Bursa to survey the situation. He stated that the confusion started about twenty years prior when a woman named Zeynep Hanım obtained a decree from the Ottoman government declaring that rice cultivation was not permissible in the Bursa plain. However, during the late Ottoman period, immigrants from Dagestan and the Balkans settled in the plains region and began to cultivate rice. This cultivation was highly lucrative and those who owned rice paddies soon became wealthy, to the consternation of some of the other landowners of the Bursa region, who served on the local administrative council. They tried to use the prior decree to break up the rice paddies. But when the Ministry of Agriculture inspected the region, rice cultivation was found to be carried out in a proper manner. Then, in 1909, a health inspector in Bursa determined that rice was to blame for the observed rise in malaria, once again threatening to end rice cultivation in the plain. Rıza Paşa visited Bursa and inquired with the governor, who attested that even he was suffering the effects of the spiking malaria. Yet when Rıza Paşa spoke with the health inspector who had made the determination, he found that the inspector had not actually toured the plain. According to Rıza, the judgment against rice in the region was motivated by the fact that the inspector had a relative in the renowned baths and hot springs of Çekirge. They did not want rice to be cultivated in the Bursa plain because they thought it would deter visitors.

Rıza Paşa sought to overturn this ruling by citing the study of an Ottoman doctor who wrote about the rise in malaria cases throughout the Province of Bursa. What that study showed was indeed a marked rise in malaria rates in the Bursa plain, but even more accelerated spread of malaria in other parts of the province where there was no rice cultivation to speak of. In this particular case, a direct relationship between malaria and rice had not been substantiated. The chief explanation that this doctor gave for the rise in malaria was that drought had diminished the flow of small bodies of water, resulting in stagnation throughout the province. Leaving aside the veracity of this assessment, what Rıza Paşa attempted to demonstrate through the case of Bursa was in fact that

---

34. Terzibaşoğlu 2003.

there was no proven correlation between malaria and rice cultivation where properly practised. The description of his experience in Bursa also revealed the complex political dynamics in the provinces, which influenced the way in which regulations were implemented.[35]

What worked in Bursa did not necessarily work everywhere. At the other end of the empire, in Iraq, rice cultivation was an old business with local particularities. Mehmet Şevket Paşa, a deputy from Baghdad's fertile Divaniye district that bordered the Province of Basra described a form of rice cultivation very different to that practised in the provinces surrounding the Ottoman capital. He noted that certain districts of Iraq such as Şamiye were crossed by the Euphrates River and so well-endowed with water that they could be cultivated with rice indefinitely, whereas other regions might need to have fallow periods. In such regions, villagers resided very close to the paddies. Therefore, a ban on cultivation in proximity to settlements would completely destroy the rice economy of Iraq. 'They have even planted rice in the garden of the government building of Şamiye', Mehmet Şevket marvelled, declaring that he had stayed there for four months and 'I did not even get a headache, and there is no malaria or anything'.[36] In a later session, he reiterated his point that regulation would ruin rice cultivation in Iraq. Hızır Efendi, who represented the Muntafig region in the Province of Basra claimed that, in many of their districts, rice was the only thing grown and that they planted three times per year.[37] Indeed, many of the marsh communities in the Province of Basra specialised in rice cultivation and lived directly within the very wetlands that, by the end of the Ottoman period, were designated as sources of malaria slated for possible drainage (Map 1).[38]

---

35. *MMZC*, Devre 1, Cilt 2, Sene 2, 33. İnikad (19 Kanunisani 1325 [1 Feb. 1910]), p. 75.

36. 'Hattâ Şamiye Hükümet konağının bahçesinde bile çeltik ziraat etmişlerdir… Bendeniz çeltik, zer'olunduğu mevsimde Hükümet konağının önü bile zer'olunduğu halde gittim, binnefs dört ay orada oturdum. Katiyen başım bile ağrımadı ve oralarda sıtma falan yoktur'. Ibid., p. 85.

37. *MMZC*, Devre 1, Cilt 2, Sene 2, 35. İnikad (23 Kanunisani 1325 [5 Feb. 1910]), p. 122.

38. A late Ottoman map indicating 'swamps to be drained' (*kurutulacak bataklıklar*) shows extensive tracts of swamps in Iraq, which were theoretically slated for elimination, though no such mass drainage project was undertaken in Iraq during the Ottoman period. See BOA, HRT.h 372 (29 Zilhicce 1341 [12 Aug. 1923]).

The Rice Debates

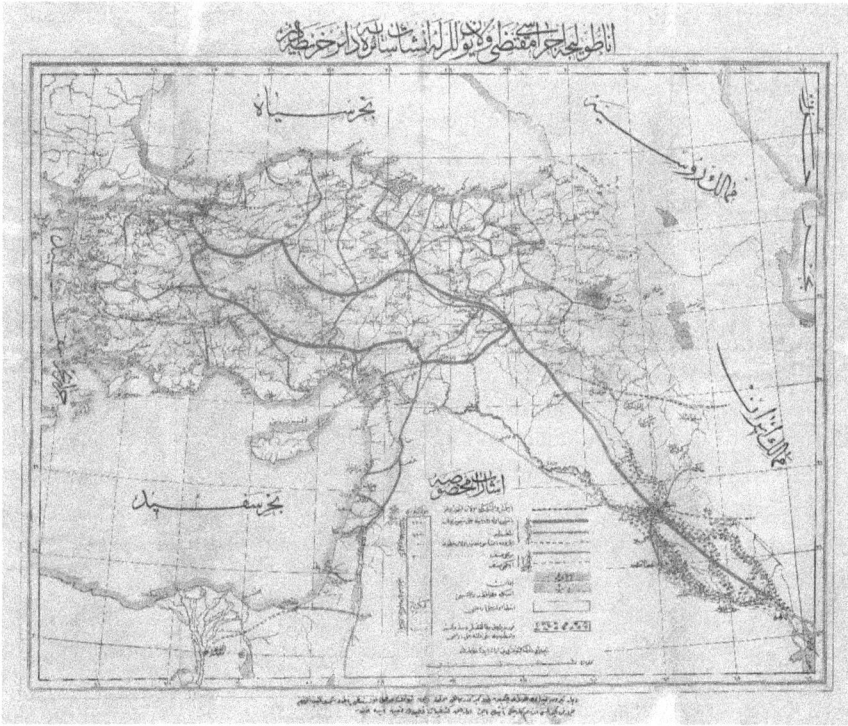

*Map 1. Late Ottoman map displaying infrastructure projects such as railways, ports, and 'swamps to be drained' (*kurutulacak bataklıklar*), ca. 1914. Source. BOA, HRT.h 372.*

Article 3 of the Rice Cultivation Law contained a curious exception regarding Iraq that attracted considerable debate. It stipulated that rice cultivation should take place at a certain distance from significant settlements. Specifically, it stated that rice should be planted at least three kilometres from the limits of any settlement of greater than 500 people. However, this clause would not apply to Baghdad, Basra and Mosul, which instead would be governed by longstanding conventions regarding cultivation and water usage. While the case was rightly made that Iraq's environment and agrarian economy were markedly different from most other parts of the empire, the issue of exception raised objections from both camps. For the technocrats, why would Iraq be exempted from this regulation and the population potentially left unprotected from malaria? For the liberals, why would it be that only Iraq would be free of regulations? Why not other regions of longstanding rice cultivation as well? Particularly given the fact that Iraq was the most important rice cultivating

Chris Gratien

centre, what would be the value of a law that did not apply there? In seeking to answer these questions and further define where rice should be cultivated, the deputies also opened the question of who would bear the financial burden of regulation and ultimately whom the government was principally meant to serve: the provincial elite who made rice cultivation possible or the Ottoman citizens the law was meant to protect?

Responsibility and Scepticism

The underlying principle of the Rice Cultivation Law, stating that scientific knowledge and practice should govern agricultural activity, was at the core of the rice debates, but the implications of scientific knowledge about the links between malaria and rice and how it should be applied highlighted a further distinction regarding the Ottoman government's responsibility towards its subjects. The deputies who advocated a liberal approach to rice cultivation consistently pushed back against the involvement of the Ministry of Agriculture, but it was at the points in which red tape could impact the bottom line that the Ministry's claim to scientific expertise was most vigorously challenged. For example, on the issue of requiring the plantation of trees to offset the environmental impact of rice, the liberal deputies argued that the law was ultimately counterproductive and 'futile' due to the way in which it would undermine the profitability of rice cultivation.[39] The Ministry acknowledged that regulation would entail a cost for the cultivators. Mehmet Vasıf Efendi of Manastır (a province with no significant rice cultivation) noted, 'It is obvious that it damages the rice, but it is necessary for the rice cultivators to receive this damage, because they are the ones who are planting the rice. I object to choosing to harm others in order to protect the rice cultivators from harm.'[40]

The deputy most concerned with the harm rice cultivation might bring to others was Nazaret Dagavaryan. He was a latecomer to the conversation, having apparently been away for prior sessions while investigating the relationship between rice and malaria in other regions, but was deeply invested in its outcome as a member of the committee that drafted the law. He was himself a doctor, agronomist and founding member of the AGBU, a charity

39. *MMZC*, Devre 1, Cilt 2, Sene 2, 38. İnikad (27 Kanunisani 1325 [9 Feb. 1910]), p. 222.

40. 'Bu kuşlar pirinçlere zarar iras etmez demedik. Pirinçlere zararı müsellemdir. Fakat bu zarar pirinççilere ait olmak lazım gelir. Çünkü pirinci eken onlardır. Pirinçcilerin zararını vikayeten diğerinin zararını tercih ettiğinden dolayı itiraz ediyorum'. Ibid., p. 223.

organisation that got its start by providing agricultural equipment and materials to Armenians in the Ottoman Empire.[41] In other words, he was a major proponent of agricultural 'modernisation' but also wedded to a political project that focused on uplifting the peasantry and Anatolian Armenians in particular. Dagavaryan sought to push the limits of the debate by questioning the definition of a settlement and the law's apparent lack of protection for settlements with less than 500 inhabitants. He argued that allowing rice to be cultivated in close proximity to settlements of less than 500 individuals would be to the extreme detriment of the people in those small villages, who represented a large percentage of the Ottoman population. Instead, he proposed that rice be kept at least two kilometres from all villages (irrespective of size) and a whopping ten kilometres from large cities.[42]

This suggestion resonated with the spirit of the Constitutional Revolution, which foregrounded notions of citizenship and equality. Mehmet Vehbi of Konya, who had expressed concerns that the law was going to generate problems for cultivators, agreed with Dagavaryan on principle. He invoked the ascendant notion of humanity, saying, 'if the size of villages and towns is being taken into consideration, then the people in villages of populations that are less than 500 are not being considered important, as if they have no human worth'.[43] Yorgi Honeus Efendi of Salonica would express a similar sentiment in support of the suggestion that, in smaller villages, rice cultivation still be kept at least 500 metres from the end of the settlement. He added,

I think the people who live there are still human beings. Our National Council is also responsible for preserving their lives just as it preserves the rest. Especially in our country the majority of the people have farms. Our homeland is an agricultural country and the population of most of the villages, I think, does not reach 500. If we leave the article like this, we will have left thousands of our cultivators exposed to this danger.[44]

---

41. See AGBU 1948. The AGBU was founded in Cairo by Boghos Nubar Pasha. During and after World War One, its primary focus shifted towards care for refugees and orphans. Many of its records are housed at the Nubarian Library in Paris.

42. *MMZC*, Devre 1, Cilt 2, Sene 2, 50. İnikad (23 Şubat 1325 [8 Mar. 1910]), p. 614.

43. 'Kura ve kasabâtın büyüklüğüne itibar olunuyorsa da beş yüz nüfustan akal ahalisi olan köylerdeki insanların, gûyâ kıymeti insâniyyesi yokmuş gibi, nazarı itibara alınmıyor'. Ibid.

44. 'Zannedersem, orada ikamet edenler de insandır. Onların hayatını da Meclisi Millîmiz sairlerinin hayatını muhafaza etmiş olduğu gibi muhafazaya vazifedardır. Bahusus memleketimizde halkın ekserisi çiftlik sahibidirler. Vatanımız ziraat memleketidir ve ekseri

While some of the deputies made compelling cases for the defence of every Ottoman life, such provisions would ultimately be deemed too impractical with regard to regulating rice. In the final version of the law, the provision stating that rice cultivation was to occur at a distance of three kilometres from settlements with populations larger than 500 was upheld. Yet, by raising the question of whether rice was truly a threat to every person in the empire, Nazaret Dagavaryan unleased a tidal wave of dissent that struck at the fundamental premise of the law by calling into question the very understanding of nature upon which it was founded. He used catastrophic language when citing the impacts of rice on public health in other settings, claiming that malaria killed so many people in Portugal that rice could no longer be grown there. He made a similar claim about the French-controlled Comoros, where rice had to be banned after spurring epidemics immediately after its introduction. He referred to towns in Italy, a region overrun by malaria, which had suffered dramatic population decline due to the introduction of rice. He even cited an article from a medical publication in Turin stating that '16 hectometres of rice harvests [equalled] the destruction of one human body', in other words insinuating that for every grain of rice harvested there would be a human cost.[45]

Numerous deputies objected to Dagavaryan's claims. Pirinççizade Feyzi Bey retorted that

> Egypt and Alexandria are nearby; most of our colleagues have gone there. In the towns near Alexandria, rice is grown. If the water in the rice paddies does not circulate and festers, disease arises. But if it was this much as you have said, exaggeratedly, then there would be nobody left on the planet. Everywhere it has been established through experience that only if the water festers and the water is not removed after the rice is harvested, then disease arises. But if attention is paid to these issues and it is not left in a swampy state, no disease emerges. Our villages do not drink from that water anyway. The people of places where it is planted know this quite well. Therefore, these theories should not be considered at all.[46]

---

karyelerin nüfusu, zannedersem, beşyüze varmaz. Eğer bu maddeyi böyle bırakacak olursak, binlerce zürrâımızı bu tehlikeye maruz bırakmış olacağız'. Ibid., p. 615.

45. 'Onaltı hektometre pirinç hâsılatı, bir insanın vücudunu mahvetmekte imiş'. Ibid., p. 614.

46. 'Efendim, bendeniz Dagavaryan Efendinin pirinç fikrine iştirak edemem. Mısır ve İskenderiyye'ye yakındır, ekser rüfekamız oralara gitmiştir. İskenderiyye'ye civar kasabalarda pirinç ekiliyor. Pirinçliklerde sular cereyan etmeyip taaffün ederse hastalık tevellüt eder. Fakat böyle, buyurdukları gibi, mübâlağa-kârâne olsa idi o zaman Kürre-i Arzda hiç insan kalmaz idi. Her yerde tecrübeyle sabit olmuştur ki, yalnız sular taaffün ederse, pirinç hâsılatı alındıktan sonra suları alınmazsa, o vakit hastalık tevellüt eder.

Of course, medical knowledge of the time clearly refuted any link between drinking polluted waters and the spread of malaria, and Dagavaryan's anecdotal evidence was likewise difficult to substantiate. But with the doors of doubt open, the debate intensified. Hacı Bayram Efendi, who represented İçel in the Eastern Mediterranean, stated that in some villages of his region, rice is planted a half hour from the villages without any disease occurring as a result, declaring that 'therefore, it does not corrupt the air there. If we are going to put this condition, there must be an exception for places where the water accumulates, stagnates and becomes swamp and does not corrupt the air'.[47] This assertion was met with scorn. Dagavaryan quipped that 'it corrupts the air everywhere, sir'.[48] Honeus Efendi concurred adding that 'it is only to prevent the harm caused by [rice cultivation] that this law is being created [in the first place]'.[49]

Here, the main representatives of the committee that drafted the law sided against Honeus Efendi and Dagavaryan. Rıza Paşa issued a long rebuttal to Dagavaryan, prompting the latter to exclaim 'for goodness sake!' (*aman efendim aman*) in the middle of the proceedings. Rıza took a personal shot by calling Dagavaryan's knowledge into question saying, 'if Dagavaryan Efendi can explain to me what the operations of ten *dönüm*s of rice are, how it is planted, and what [mosquito] larva are, then he too will understand that rice cultivation is truly in no way unhealthy'.[50] He claimed that he and Dagavaryan had recently visited Plovdiv and, even though there is rice cultivated in the entire countryside surrounding the city, malaria was down by 75 per cent. Rıza's only concern was that, if rice were shown to cause malaria in a certain region, the paddy should be removed, saying he would 'pay the cost himself'. Dagavaryan fired back saying 'and will you also bring the people who have been wiped out

Fakat bunlara dikkat edilirse, bataklık halinde bırakılmazsa hiçbir hastalık tevellüt etmez. Zaten köylülerimiz de o sudan içmezler. Ekin ekilen yerler ahalisi de bunu pekâlâ bilirler. Binaenaleyh bu nazariyeler hiçbir vakit nazarı dikkate alınmamalı'. Ibid.

47. 'Bu şartı koyacak isek, sular toplanıp da, teraküm edip de bataklık hâsıl olarak havayı ihlâl etmeyen yerleri istisna etmeli'. Ibid.

48. 'Her yerde havayı ihlâl eder efendim'. Ibid.

49. 'Yalnız bundan tevellüt edecek mazarratın önü alınması için bu kânūn vaz' ediliyor'. Ibid., p. 615.

50. 'Evvel emirde, müsaadenizle, Dagavaryan Efendi bana on dönüm pirinç ziraatı ameliyatı nedir ve nasıl ekilir, sürfeleri nedir? Bunları izah ederse ondan sonra hıfzıssıhha nokta-i nazarından kendisi de anlayacaktır ki pirinç ziraatı kat'iyyen ve hakikaten mihllüssıhha değildir'. Ibid.

back to life, Paşa?'[51] Dagavaryan's acerbic retorts appear to have then derailed Rıza Paşa, causing him to launch into a long rant that went on to the point that other deputies began to cry out 'we've gotten off topic' (*sadetten çıktık*), and the Chamber of Deputies President Ahmet Rıza repeatedly commanded Rıza Paşa to adhere to the questions at hand.[52]

Nazaret Dagavaryan had the last word in the heated exchange with Rıza Paşa:

> That rice cultivation is unhealthy is something accepted throughout the world. To speak to the contrary is to speak against reality. I will not discuss this at all. When I showed this many examples of rice cultivation causing deaths, I did not say let's completely remove rice cultivation from our country. Let it be three kilometres from the cities and at least two kilometres from the villages. I mean, if someone lives in a village comprising 400 people, is their life not a life? It's known that a 20–25 year old youngster's life is worth 5,000 lira and I showed that a person's life is in danger for sixteen hectolitres of rice. All I wanted to say is let's increase the distances a little. Whether a village is made up of 300 people or 500 people, let the rice fields be 1.5 km away. This is what I said. This is also something accepted by science.[53]

It is telling that the most acrimonious moment in the Ottoman rice debates occurred when Nazaret Dagavaryan, a member of the agriculture committee, broke ranks and advocated a significantly different account of extant knowledge concerning rice and malaria from what was supported by the Ministry of Agriculture. The efficacy of the law and authority of the ministry was contingent upon a compromise between the interests of highly influential rice cultivators, who would naturally put profits first, and the imperative to protect the public's wellbeing from the potential ill-effects of economic activity. When Dagavaryan

---

51. 'Ya mahvolan insanlara da can verecek misiniz Paşa?' Ibid.

52. Ibid., p. 616.

53. 'Pirinç ziraatının muzırr-ı sıhhat olduğu dünyada kabul olunmuş bir şeydir. Buna karşılık söz söylemek hakikate karşı söylemektir. Bundan hiç bahsetmeyeceğim. Bendeniz pirinç ziraatının bu kadar telefat gösterdiği misalleri gösterdiğimde, pirinç ziraatını bütün bütün memleketimizden kaldıralım demedim. Şehirlerden üç kilometre, hiç değilse köylerden de iki kilometre uzak olsun. Yani, eğer bir kimse dört yüz nüfustan ibaret olan bir köyde yaşarsa, onun ömrü ömür değil midir? Bi'l-hesap malumdur ki, yirmi, yirmi beş yaşına gelen bir delikanlı hayatı beş bin lira değer ve hesapça da gösterdim ki on altı hektolitre pirinç hâsılatı için bir insanın ömrü tehlikede bulunur. Yalnız bendenizin söylediğim şudur ki, mesafeleri az artıralım. Bir köy üç yüz nüfustan da ibaret olsa, beş yüz nüfustan da ibaret olsa, pirinç tarlaları bir buçuk kilometre uzak olsun. Bendenizin söylediği budur. Bu da fen tarafından kabul olunmuş bir şeydir'. Ibid., pp. 616–17.

challenged the ministry on its own turf – that is, the realm of scientific know-ledge – in the interest of advocating tighter regulation, Rıza Paşa moved closer to the side of cultivators in order to maintain his position as arbiter in this compromise. But, in pressing the issue, Dagavaryan had revealed that Rıza Paşa and the Ministry of Agriculture were perhaps more concerned with laying claim to jurisdiction over and expertise in the cultivation of rice than with using the law to aid in the medical establishment's struggle with malaria.

Conclusion

The final version of the Rice Cultivation Law was an important precedent for the Ministry of Agriculture that was palatable to rice cultivators like Pirinççi-zade Feyzi Bey. In the end, Nazaret Dagavaryan's more hard-line stance on rice cultivation might have been more prudent with regard to curtailing malaria, which remained widespread in Anatolia long after the collapse of the Otto-man Empire. Prohibitions on rice cultivation would become a concern of the early Republic of Turkey, especially during the 1930s, as the national struggle with malaria faltered. As Kyle and Emine Evered have shown, Dr Şerif Korkut condemned the ascendant capitalism in the countryside of modern Turkey during the 1940s in a work entitled *Malaria and Rice* [*Isıtma ve Çeltik*], which used public health as a means to formulate a critique of Anatolia's political economy.[54] That critique, which resembled those brought to the Ottoman parliament by doctors like Nazaret Dagavaryan some decades prior, pointed to both an intellectual and ecological continuity between the late Ottoman period and the very different world of post-WWII Turkey, forged by liberal economics.

Applying scientific knowledge about malaria to regulate the cultivation of rice in the late Ottoman Empire was not a straightforward matter. Positions on the subject within the Ottoman parliament ranged from those of wealthy cultivators, who all but denied the link between malaria and rice, to physicians who viewed rice cultivation as an absolute menace to public health. Amid the discussion between the two camps and many other deputies who worked on the redrafting of the Rice Cultivation Law in late winter 1910, there were numerous pieces of commentary that reflected the collective thinking of a newly-formed government attempting to work through an incredibly complex ecological question using the full varieties of logic and argumentation avail-able to an early twentieth-century person. The debates drew on a wide body of knowledge ranging from local wisdom to recent scientific discourses imported

---

54.   Evered and Evered 2016; Korkut 1950.

from the west and global comparisons. On some level, they represented debates about ecology and the impacts of human activity on the environment. Yet to read these arguments and the economic or environmental worldviews they espoused under the heading of 'Ottoman debates about nature' or the global circulation of ideas during the long nineteenth century, as extricable from the vested interests represented in the parliament, is to deny the political essence of the ecological issues in question. The Rice Cultivation Law was drafted through the tense reconciliation of rival political imaginaries that not only extended into the realm of ecology but were also linked to political questions well beyond the realm of rice and malaria.

Scholarship on the late Ottoman period increasingly demonstrates the ways in which different communities and political factions embraced and mobilised the various discourses of modernity for specific and often competing goals. Recently, Bedross Der Matossian has shown how different non-dominant groups enthusiastically supported and embraced the 1908 Constitutional Revolution for various reasons, even though it ultimately empowered political elements who would prove hostile to the interests of non-Muslims in the empire.[55] As the example of the rice debates shows, political ecology offers an alternative way of looking at politics in the empire that prompts us to rethink confessional boundaries as the primary framework for thinking about late Ottoman politics.

Yet the paradox of this claim is that the two polar figures in the rice de-bate – Nazaret Dagavaryan and Pirinççizade Feyzi Bey – were also on opposite sides of a political issue more well-studied and more consequential than the regulation of malaria. Dagavaryan was one of many Armenian notables who would be arrested and deported from Istanbul on 24 April 1915 in connec-tion with involvement in Armenian political organisations. He was allegedly assassinated by the Special Organisation (*Teşkilat-ı Mahsusa*) en route to face court martial in Diyarbakır.[56] Meanwhile, Pirinççizade Feyzi Bey became an anti-Armenian voice in Diyarbakır and a key functionary of the CUP during the war.[57] Though unrelated to the rice debates, this subsequent context de-mands mention. Yet another figure, Agop Hırlakyan, an Armenian Catholic who represented Maraş in the *Meclis-i Mebusan*, complicates a fixation on the confessionalisation of all matters within late Ottoman politics. As one of the major rice cultivators of Maraş he and his Muslim business partners lobbied the Ottoman government successfully to obtain an exception from the 1910 Rice

---

55. Der Matossian 2014.
56. Kévorkian 2011, p. 524.
57. Jongerden 2012, pp. 66–67; Üngör 2012, p. 274.

The Rice Debates

Cultivation Law.[58] Though he too was Armenian – indeed playing a leading role in Armenian politics of Cilicia during the French occupation period – when it came to the crucial debate over regulation of rice, Hırlakyan had much more in common with Pirinççizade than the likes of Nazaret Dagavaryan.

It is no great claim to argue that rival discourses about socio-political organisation, progress and modernity in the Ottoman Empire were linked to various political agendas that clashed, overlapped with or complemented one another. This article has above all made the simple case that the study of environment in late Ottoman society is not outside the study of politics. In evaluating the framing and impact of state policies concerning ecology, an understanding of the state that accounts for the ways in which it contained competing and conflicting interests is essential. I have employed the detailed and relatively transparent minutes of the Ottoman Chamber of Deputies to show that environmental discourses were not only between the lines of Ottoman politics. Environmental questions in the empire were highly political and politicised. To study them is not to deny the importance of other political debates; it is to enrich our view of these debates and explore their ignored facets.

ACKNOWLEDGEMENTS

A prior version of this research was published in Turkish translation as 'Pilavdan Dönen İmparatorluk: Meclis-i Mebusan'da Sıtma ve Çeltik Tartışmaları' (trans. by Burcu Kurt) in *Osmanlı'dan Cumhuriyet'e Salgın Hastalıklar ve Kamu Sağlığı* (Tarih Vakfı, 2017) ed. by Burcu Kurt and İsmail Yaşayanlar. However, despite many identical passages and quotations, this version differs from that text. This article was developed through presentations at the 'Harvard University Political Ecology Working Group' and the 'Beyond Circulation' workshop at Columbia University. Special thanks to Burcu Kurt, İsmail Yaşayanlar, John Chen, Angela Giordani, Vanessa Ogle, Marwa Elshakry, Ümit Kurt, Eda Çakmakçı, Sam Dolbee, Seçil Yılmaz and Ajantha Subramanian.

Bibliography

Unpublished Primary Sources

Prime Ministry Ottoman Archives (*Başbakanlık Osmanlı Arşivi, BOA*), Istanbul

    Dâhiliye Nezâreti İdare Evrakı (DH.İD) 44–2/1

    Dâhiliye Nezâreti Mektubî Kalemi Evrakı (DH.MKT) 2801/55

    Dâhiliye Nezâreti İdare-i Umumiye Evrakı (DH.İ.UM) 79/62

---

58.   BOA, DH.İ.UM. 79/62, no. 1 (1 Kanunisani 1331 [14 Jan. 1916]).

236

Chris Gratien

Haritalar (HRT.h) 372
Yıldız Perakende Evrakı Askeri Maruzât (Y.PRK.ASK)
Yıldız Perakende Evrakı Umum Vilayetler Tahrirâtı (Y.PRK.UM) 1/86
Yıldız Sadâret Hususî Maruzât Evrakı (Y.A.HUS) 290/21

Published Primary Sources

Orman ve Maden ve Ziraat Mecmuası

İzmidi, Feyzullah. 1911. *Maraz-ı Merzagi: Sıtma*. Istanbul: Tanin.
Orman, Maden ve Zıraat Nezareti. 1326/1910. *Pirinç Ziraatı*. Istanbul: Matbaa-ı Amire.
——. 1326/1910. *Pirinç Ziraatı Kanunnamesi*. Istanbul: Matbaa-ı Amire.
——. 1326/1910-11. *1323 senesi Avrupa-yi Osmani ziraat istatistiği*. Istanbul: Mahmut Bey Matbaası.
——. 1327/1911-12. *1325 senesi Asya ve Afrika-yi Osmani ziraat istatistiki*. Istanbul: Matbaa-ı Osmaniye.
Rüştü, Tevfik. 1326/1910. *Sıtma'ya Karşı Muharebe*. Selanik: Rumeli Matbaası.
Ticaret ve Zıraat Nezareti. 1914. *Memalik-i Osmaniye'nin 1329 Senesine Mahsus Zıraat İstatistiği*. Istanbul: Ticaret ve Zıraat Nezareti.
Türkiye Büyük Millet Meclisi. 1985. *Meclis-i Mebusan Zabıt Ceridesi*. Ankara, TBMM. https://www.tbmm.gov.tr/kutuphane/tutanak_sorgu.html.

Secondary Sources

Armenian General Benevolent Union Central Committee of America.1948. *Armenian General Benevolent Union: Historic Outline, 1906–1946*. New York: Gotchnag Press.
Brummett, Palmira. 2000. *Image and Imperialism in the Ottoman Revolutionary Press, 1908–1911*. Albany: State University of New York Press.
Campos, Michelle. 2011. *Ottoman Brothers: Muslims, Christians, and Jews in Early Twentieth-century Palestine*. Stanford: Stanford University Press.
Cronon, William. 1991. *Nature's Metropolis: Chicago and the Great West*. New York: W.W. Norton.
Davis, Diana K. 2007. *Resurrecting the Granary of Rome: Environmental History and French Colonial Expansion in North Africa*. Athens, OH: Ohio University Press.
——. 2016. *The Arid Lands: History, Power, Knowledge*. Cambridge: MIT Press.
Davis, Diana K. and Edmund Burke III. 2013. *Environmental Imaginaries of the Middle East and North Africa*. Athens, OH: Ohio University Press.
Der Matossian, Bedross. 2014. *Shattered Dreams of Revolution: From Liberty to Violence in the late Ottoman Empire*. Stanford: Stanford University Press.
Ersoy, Nermin. 1998. *Doktor Feyzullah İzmidi*. Kocaeli: self published.

Evered, Kyle and Emine Evered. 2012. 'State, Peasant, Mosquito: The Biopolitics of Public Health Education and Malaria in Early Republican Turkey'. *Political Geography* **31**: 311–23.

——. 2016. 'A Conquest of Rice: Agricultural Expansion, Impoverishment, and Malaria in Turkey'. *Historia Agraria* **68**: 143–78.

Farmer, Jared. 2013. *Trees in Paradise: A California History*. New York: W.W. Norton.

Göl, Ercan. 2006. 'Cumhuriyet Döneminde (1923–1950) Maraş'ın Sosyo-Ekonomik Yapısı ve Gelişimi'. MA Thesis, Kahramanmaraş: Sütçü İmam University.

Gratien, Chris. 2017. 'The Ottoman Quagmire: Malaria, Swamps, and Settlement in the Late Ottoman Mediterranean'. *International Journal of Middle East Studies* **49**: 583–604.

Günergun, Feza and Etker, Şeref. 2013. 'From Quinaquina to "Quinine Law": A Bitter Chapter in the Westernization of Turkish Medicine'. *Osmanlı Bilim Araştırmaları* **14**: 41–68.

İnalcık, Halil. 1982. 'Rice Cultivation and the Çeltükci-re'âyâ System in the Ottoman Empire'. *Turcica* **14**: 69–141.

Jongerden, Joost. 2012. "Elite Encounters of a Violent Kind: Milli İbrahim Paşa, Ziya Gökalp and Political Struggle in Diyarbakır at the Turn of the 20th Century'. In Joost Jongerden and Jelle Verheij (eds), *Social Relations in Ottoman Diyarbekir, 1870–1915*. Leiden: Brill. pp. 55–84.

Judd, Richard. 2014. *Second Nature: An Environmental History of New England*. Amherst: University of Massachusetts Press.

Kayalı, Hasan. 1997. *Arabs and Young Turks: Ottomanism, Arabism and Islamism in the Ottoman Empire, 1908–1918*. Berkeley: University of California Press.

Kévorkian, Raymond. 2011. *The Armenian Genocide: A Complete History*. London, I.B. Tauris.

Korkut, M. Şerif. 1950. *Isıtma ve Çeltik*. Ankara: Yeni Matbaa.

Köse, Şükran et al. 2017. *Tarihsel Süreçte Anadolu'da Sıtma*. Istanbul: Gece Kitaplığı.

Kurt, Burcu and İsmail Yaşayanlar (eds). 2017. *Osmanlı'dan Cumhuriyet'e Salgın Hastalıklar ve Kamu Sağlığı*. Istanbul, Tarih Vakfı.

Kurt, Ümit. 2018. 'The Curious Case of Ali Cenani Bey: The Story of a Génocidaire during and after the 1915 Armenian Genocide'. *Patterns of Prejudice* **52**: 58–77.

Mikhail, Alan. 2013. *Water on Sand: Environmental Histories of the Middle East and North Africa*. Oxford: Oxford University Press.

Mitchell, Timothy. 2002. *Rule of Experts: Egypt, Techno-politics, Modernity*. Berkeley: University of California Press.

Perreault, Thomas Albert, Gavin Bridge and James McCarthy. 2015. *The Routledge Handbook of Political Ecology*. London: Routledge.

Şavkılı, Cengiz. 2008. 'Birinci Dönem Türkiye Büyük Millet Meclisi'nde Antep Milletvekili Mehmet Ali Cenani Bey ve Faaliyetleri'. *Gaziantep Üniversitesi Sosyal Bilimler Dergisi* **7**: 405–25.

Sohrabi, Nader. 2011. *Revolution and Constitutionalism in the Ottoman Empire and Iran, 1902–1910*. Cambridge: Cambridge University Press.

Tekeli, İlhan and Selim İlkin. 1999. 'Türkiye›de Sıtma Mücadelesinin Tarihi'. In Gül E. Kundakçı (ed.), *70. Yılında Ulusal ve Uluslararası Boyutlarıyla Atatürk'ün Büyük Nutuk'u ve Dönemi.* Ankara, Orta Doğu Teknik Üniversitesi.

Terzibaşoğlu, Yücel. 2003. 'Landlords, Nomads and Refugees: Struggles over Land and Population Movements in North-western Anatolia [1877–1914]'. Ph.D. Diss., London: University of London.

Tuğluoğlu Fatih. 2008. 'Türkiye'de Sıtma Mücadelesi (1924–1950)'. *Turkiye Parazitolojii Dergisi* **32**: 351–59.

Tvedt, Terje. 2004. *The River Nile in the Age of the British: Political Ecology and the Quest for Economic Power.* London: I.B. Tauris.

Üngör, Uğur Ümit. 2012. 'Armenians and Kurds in the Young Turk Era, 1915–25'. In Joost Jongerden and Jelle Verheij (eds), *Social Relations in Ottoman Diyarbekir, 1870–1915.* Leiden: Brill. pp. 267–95.

Watenpaugh, Keith D. 2006. *Being Modern in the Middle East.* Princeton: Princeton University Press.

Williams, Elizabeth Rachel. 2015. 'Cultivating Empires: Environment, Expertise, and Scientific Agriculture in Late Ottoman and French Mandate Syria'. Ph.D. Diss., Washington DC: Georgetown University.

Chapter 10

DISCOVERING THE NATURE OF THE NEW HOMELAND: ALEXANDER VON HUMBOLDT (1769–1859) IN THE OTTOMAN EMPIRE AND IN EARLY REPUBLICAN TURKEY

Yavuz Köse

On 14 September 1869 Alexander von Humboldt's centennial was celebrated literally across the world. In several cities across Europe, Africa, Australia as well as the Americas tens of thousands of people were out on the streets to celebrate this famous man whom the Prussian King Wilhelm IV (r. 1840–1861) had characterised as 'the greatest man since the Deluge'.[1]

To give an impression of how outstandingly esteemed Humboldt was, just a few numbers: 8,000 people celebrated in Cleveland, 15,000 in Syracuse and another 10,000 attended with President Ulysses Grant the Humboldt celebration in Pittsburgh. In New York more than 25,000 people gathered in Central Park. Yet, by far the greatest celebrations took place in Humboldt's hometown of Berlin, where – despite heavy rain – 80,000 people joined the festivities.[2] And finally, even in the *de jure* still Ottoman city of Alexandria, of course on a much smaller scale, the German community celebrated Humboldt's anniversary 'under palms'. According to the German journal *Die Gartenlaube*, representatives of all resident consulates accepted the invitation of the organisers. The city's governor Hurşid Pasha[3] was unable to attend due to illness, but he was represented by a pasha, six *bey*s and their entourage.[4] Clearly, ten years after

---

1. Wulf 2015, p. 282.
2. Ibid., pp. 6–7.
3. Sāmī 2009, vol. 4, p. 781. For this reference I would like to thank Serena Tolino.
4. 'Eine Humboldt-Feier unter Palmen', *Die Gartenlaube* 43 (1869): 689–90.

his death, Humboldt or, as Charles Darwin called him, 'the greatest scientific traveller who ever lived' was still a kind of pop star of science.[5]

So, it seemed obvious to ask how Humboldt and these global festivities honouring him were perceived within the Ottoman lands, which he never visited. Surprisingly, though, a preliminary examination of Ottoman journals and dailies did not yield any results regarding the festivities of 14 September 1869. They failed to notice this remarkable event.

Still, Humboldt had been quite influential for people who travelled to the Ottoman Empire. He had correspondence with the founder of Ottoman studies, the Austrian diplomat and historian Josef von Hammer-Purgstall (1776–1856), whom he met in Paris.[6] Additionally, Humboldt encouraged painters, like his friend Eduard Hildebrandt (1818–1868), to visit the 'Orient' in order to paint the landscapes and nature. Hildebrandt travelled in 1851 to the Ottoman Empire, paying visits to and painting in, among others, Egypt, Palestine, Damascus, Izmir and Istanbul.[7] Finally, between 1849 and 1854, Humboldt's great admirer George Perkins Marsh (1801–1882), an American diplomat, philologist and pioneering environmentalist, stayed in Istanbul as American envoy and undertook several extended journeys within the Ottoman realm.[8]

Without doubt Humboldt had been influential for generations of travellers, geographers and environmentalists all over the world.[9] But to what extent he had been acclaimed as scientist or significant in the Ottoman Empire or early Republican Turkey has hitherto remained unclear. This paper aims to unearth the imprint of Humboldt in the Ottoman Empire and the Turkish Republic, its major successor. For this purpose, it explores how Humboldt and his work were perceived in the late nineteenth and early twentieth centuries. At first sight it seems that Humboldt found his way into the Ottoman realm through encyclopaedic entries. It was only in 1932 that a short biography of him was published in Turkish.[10] Since this will be the main source to be discussed, the scope of this study extends into the early Republican period. The author of Humboldt's first biography in Turkish, Mustafa Niyazi [Erenbilge]

5.   Wulf 2015, p. 282.
6.   Höflechner and Wagner 2011, pp. 956, 966. The book is accessible online: http://gams.uni-graz.at/hp/pdf/24_Briefe1811.pdf (accessed 4 Mar. 2018).
7.   Rhein 2003, pp. 63, 68, 227.
8.   Wulf 2015, pp. 283–90.
9.   Ibid., chs 4 and 5.
10.   Mustafa Niyazi 1932.

(1887/1888–1947),[11] had witnessed the last years of the crumbling empire as a soldier and a teacher of geography. He was also the author of *Anadolu*, probably the first geography publication focusing on Anatolia, which appeared during the years of the Turkish War of Independence (1919–1922). This paper, by examining Mustafa Niyazi's perception of Humboldt and analysing his *oeuvre*, will give an insight into the transition process from empire to nation-state. Geography curricula – as in the late Ottoman period – had a central role to play within the nationalist education policy of the newly founded Turkish Republic.

Mustafa Niyazi's biography of Alexander von Humboldt shows that the latter figured as a role model for the Turkish youth. Mustafa Niyazi prescribed the young to follow Humboldt's footsteps and try to be explorers, discoverers and scientists like him, and thus fulfil their real objective: by exploring and discovering the new homeland – Anatolia – and nation to become loyal and exemplary citizens. Mustafa Niyazi's Humboldt biography is clearly embedded in the socio-political realities of his time.[12] Thus, *his* Humboldt sought to fashion a new youth that was 'Turkish by nature' thereby support the development of a homogenous nation state. Ironically, it was the cosmopolitan and 'proto-environmentalist'[13] Humboldt who, according to Jürgen Osterhammel, 'had never heard the term "environmental history", but in essence … was, quite incidentally its founder',[14] whom Mustafa Niyazi admired so much. Mustafa Niyazi certainly was intuitively aware of the historical relationship between humans and the environment; yet, for him, nature was first and foremost 'the basis of national unity'.[15]

Before presenting and discussing the content of Humboldt's biography, I will give a brief outline of the transformation process that the Ottoman state and society was undergoing during the late nineteenth century. I will then provide a short overview of the development of geography and its institutional expansion within the Ottoman and early Republican education system, before presenting some preliminary findings of descriptions concerning Humboldt from the late Ottoman and early Republican period. Finally, I will investigate Mustafa Niyazi's short biography on Humboldt and compare it with his earlier geographical publication on Anatolia.

---

11. On 21 June 1934, the Turkish Surname Law (*Soyadı Kanunu*) was adopted. The law required every Turkish citizen to use a hereditary family name.
12. For an environmentalist perspective on the early Republican period, see Dursun 2017.
13. The term was coined by Aaron Sachs. See Sachs 2007, p. 5.
14. Original in Osterhammel 1999, p. 131, English quote from Rupke 2005, p. 185.
15. Dursun 2017, p. 119.

Yavuz Köse

The Transformation of Late Ottoman State and Society

The year 1869 was a memorable one for the Ottomans too, and one may infer that the still young Ottoman press had other things to report than the celebration of Humboldt's anniversary.[16] A few weeks after the birthday celebration, on 17 November, the Suez Canal was inaugurated with a grandiose event.[17] The same month, the Balian Brothers, Ottoman-Armenian architects, began the construction work for the last imperial mosque, Pertevniyal Valide Sultan Mosque;[18] and the concession for the Chemins de fer Orientaux (Oriental Railway), which would connect Istanbul and Vienna, was given to the Bavarian-born financier Maurice de Hirsch.[19] Furthermore, the largest ever number of state orphanages (*ıslahhane*), a total of nine, was established throughout the empire in the same year.[20] Simultaneously, the Ottoman state enacted the Law of Citizenship (*Tabiyet-i Osmaniye Kanunu*), guaranteeing the equal status of Ottoman subjects regardless of their religious affiliation, and thereby promoting 'Ottomanism' in order to create an overarching identity for its multi-ethnic and multi-religious citizens. And finally, the Public Education Regulation (*Maarif-i Umumiye Nizamnamesi*) passed, aiming to transform the educational system since it was considered 'clear that the reason why nations belonging to the civilised world get their share from the treasures of the world's wealth is their access to the most perfect means of human education', as the introduction to the regulation has it.[21] All these events took place during the peak stage of the so-called *Tanzimat* period (1839–1876) and highlight the Western-oriented reform process that the troubled Ottoman state underwent in order to avert the danger of total disintegration. The Ottoman state was running out of time, since, simultaneously with the implementation of these adjustments, it was confronted not only with a series of uprisings within the Ottoman realm but constant losses of territory, above all in the Balkans.[22]

---

16. On the Ottoman press, see Ahmed Emin 1914.
17. Konrad 2009, pp. 403–11.
18. Yerasimos 2002, p. 373.
19. Christensen 2017, p. 12.
20. Maksudyan 2014, p. 79.
21. Yalçınkaya 2015, p. 80.
22. The suppression of upheavals with massive violence – especially under Abdülhamid II (r. 1876–1909), then under the Young Turk regime – shows the Ottoman state's inability to solve the increasing inter-communal tensions among its non-Muslim and Muslim subjects. This was aggravated by a steady influx of Muslim refugees from the Balkans (*muhacir*), the state's 'demographic engineering' – a settlement policy that

Discovering the Nature of the New Homeland

Adapting to European models of education and science – under the centralising efforts of the state, and its promotion of Ottomanism, i.e. Ottoman patriotism – was deemed the most promising approach in order to achieve this goal because it was 'science and useful learning that [had] steered European nations to the highest summit of civilisation and power'.[23] Consequently, the Ottoman state established the required infrastructure by opening new schools and the *Darülfünun* (university) in Istanbul. From the beginning, this project was carried out from above, that is by the state and its elite. As in late nineteenth-century Germany, the school system in the Ottoman Empire was essential since 'it was used to translate and transfer the concepts, meaning and consciousness of *imperial* [national] unity "down" to the people'.[24]

Geography and Its Institutional Development

Among the various disciplines considered crucial was geography, a field of study that built on the pioneering work of Alexander von Humboldt on the natural world and quickly expanded and developed a variety of sub-disciplines in Europe.[25] It seems a fortunate coincidence that it was also in the year 1869 that geography became a subject in the *Darülfünun*.[26]

Alper Yalçınkaya stressed that the debates on science within the late Ottoman society were characterised and guided by 'ethicopolitical rather than epistemological matters'. He further stated that the discourses surrounded 'different ways of defining and practicing the right and the good'[27] – that is, morality – instead of different epistemological approaches. Correspondingly, scientific knowledge was also closely linked with patriotism, the former's dissemination considered as essential for building up a 'population of learned patriots'.[28]

---

aimed at creating a homogenous Muslim population in strategic regions – and the fact that, beginning in 1911, the Ottomans were in a permanent state of war. For instance, see Erol 2016; Zürcher 2009; and Hanioğlu 2008.

23. Quote from Halil Şeref Pasha, Ottoman ambassador to St. Petersburg in 1861 cited by Yalçınkaya 2015, p. 81.

24. Sandner 1994, p. 72. For the Ottoman case the author inserted 'imperial' instead of 'national'.

25. Christensen 2017, p. 2.

26. Kreiser 2001, pp. 71–87.

27. Yalçınkaya 2015, pp. 220–21.

28. Ibid., p. 222.

The discipline of geography was particularly suitable for creating a sense of homeland (*vatan*) among students but also state servants, and legitimising the sultan's power as well the empire's spatial policies.[29] Within this concept of 'empire patriotism', geography had to be sided with history, with both together deemed able to create Ottoman patriotism, as the director of the School of Education, Sati Bey underlines in a conference given in 1913:

> Geography is a crucial science to teach the body and the physical characteristics of *vatan*. History as a science is important to teach the spirit of *vatan*. These two sciences are the most important tools for the education of patriotism … Teaching of these two sciences should be restructured to engender the love of *vatan* in the hearts of people.[30]

Besides the *Darülfünun*, geography courses were offered in other institutions and schools like the School of Administration (*Mekteb-i Mülkiye*), School of Civil Engineering (*Hendese-i Mülkiye*) and School of Education (*Darülmuallimin*). In *rüşdiye*s (high schools) geography lessons became compulsory, and of course geography was likewise on the curriculum of all sorts of military schools.[31]

A correspondingly large number of geographical publications, above all geography textbooks, were published in the late nineteenth century. Besides school books, several multi-volume geographical dictionaries as well as translations of Western geographical texts appeared by the end of the nineteenth century. Whereas early publications appeared to be neutral, and did not seek to promote patriotic loyalty, from the Hamidian period (1876–1909) onward most of the schoolbooks were aiming at patriotism by presenting on a textual basis and with maps fixed borders of the empire so as to enable the students to visualise a unified homeland.[32] According to Behlül Özkan, not only the content, but also the titles of textbooks changed dramatically after the 1908 Revolution. The Young Turk regime also began to use geography as a 'central instrument for patriotic education', for propagating Ottoman patriotism, in other words.[33] After 1912, with the total loss of the Balkan territories, geography textbooks put a special emphasis on Anatolia as homeland of the Turks.[34]

29. Özgen 2016, p. 132. For other examples other than the Ottoman Empire, see Hooson 1994; Durgun 2012.
30. Quoted from Özkan 2014, p. 457. For original quote see Satı' Bey 1913, pp. 36–37, 46–48.
31. Kreiser 2001, p. 71. See also Özkan 2012, pp. 108–11.
32. Akpınar 2010; Özgen 2016, p. 132 referring to Durgun 2012.
33. Özkan 2012, pp. 112–14; idem, 2014, pp. 462–63.
34. Özkan 2012, p. 117.

Discovering the Nature of the New Homeland

The term *Anadolu* entered dictionaries in the late nineteenth century. Whereas Ahmed Rifat Efendi (d. 1895) in his 1881-published *Lügat-ı tarihiye ve coğrafiye* needed only twelve lines for the description of the term, Ali Cevad in his *Memalik-i osmaniyenin tarih ve coğrafya lügatı* of 1895 devoted five pages to it. And, the ten pages in the 1898 geographical dictionary by Şemseddin Sami [Frashëri] (1850–1904) represent not only by far the most extended description of *Anadolu* but also the most systematic one in geographical terms.[35] However, unlike in publications after 1912, in these dictionary entries 'Anatolia' is not identified as the 'homeland of the Turks'.[36] Likewise, the emphasis on Turks belonging to the Turanic race is to be found only in publications after 1912.

The development of geography as a modern science in academia also gained momentum after 1908.[37] But it was only in 1915 that the geography department in the *Darülfünun* opened.[38] Until 1918 the German geographer Erich Obst (1886–1981) chaired this department; and Walter Penck became head of the department for geology in 1915. Despite strong German influence on the development of the academic geography, the French school – represented by Ottoman geographers like Faik Sabrik [Duran] (1882–1943), Ali Macid [Arda] (1885–1967) and Selim Mansur – never lost its influence. İbrahim Hakkı [Akyol] (1888–1950) who studied in Lausanne and Berlin became professor of geography in 1923.[39] From 1923 on, French professors such as Théodore Lefebvre (1889–1943) and Ernest Chaput (1882–1943) were appointed. In 1933, the *Darülfünun* became Istanbul University. The pioneers of Turkish geography in the following years, such as Besim Darkot (1903–1990), Ali Tevfik Tanoğlu (1904–1978), Ahmet Ardel (1902–1978) and Cemal Arif Alagöz (1902–1991), received their degrees from French universities.[40]

Alexander von Humboldt in Ottoman and Turkish Sources

As mentioned, I was not able to find any report concerning his death or festivities honouring him in 1869. Likewise, my random checks in Ottoman geography textbooks have not thus far been successful. Only in Şemseddin

---

35. Ahmet Rifat Efendi 1881, p. 267; Ali Cevad 1885, pp. 28–32; Şemseddin Sami 1889, pp. 389–99.
36. Özkan 2012, p. 117.
37. Ibid., p. 114.
38. Gümüşçü and Özür 2016, p. 132.
39. Kreiser 2001, p. 80.
40. Ibid., p. 81.

Sami's *Kamusü'l-alam. Tarih ve coğrafya lügatı*, dated 1898, do we find a short entry for Alexander von Humboldt.[41] Şemseddin Sami's description is based on the entry to be found in the famous dictionary *Dictionnaire Universel d'Histoire et de Géographie*, known also as *Le Dictionnaire Bouillet*, published by Marie-Nicolas Bouillet. Faik Sabri, who also belonged to the first generation of Turkish geographers,[42] does mention Humboldt in his book on the economic geography of the Ottoman Empire (*Osmanlı coğrafya-yı tabii ve iktisadisi*, 1915) as the 'founder of geography', without going further into detail.[43] In an article from 1916 outlining the scientific methods of geography he points to the important role Alexander von Humboldt and Carl Ritter (1779–1859) played in the development and establishment of geography as a scientific discipline. Thanks to them, Faik Sabri asserts, the 'old and invalid geography' (*ihtiyar ve alil*) founded centuries ago by Aristotle, Eratosthenes and Ptolemy became 'a young and very new science'. For the first time, these two masters (*üstad*) regarded geography as a rational explanation (*akli bir izah*).[44]

Another sixteen years would pass before Mustafa Niyazi published the first Turkish biography of Humboldt in 1932. And it was only in 1959 that Ahmet Ardel, a professor of history, dedicated a short biography of three pages to Alexander von Humboldt on the 100th anniversary of his death.[45] In 1982, the Turkish geographer Selman Uslu published an article of no less than 26 pages in the *Orman Fakültesi Dergisi* (of Istanbul University) on the occasion of the founding of the Humboldt Grant Foundation in Turkey (*Türkiye Humboldt Bursiyerler Derneği*). Therein, Uslu addresses the history of the Humboldt foundation and its Turkish grant holders and also gives an overview of Humboldt's life, travels and work.[46] And finally, in 1994, İlhami Kızıroğlu dedicated to Humboldt a brief biography of 32 pages: *Alexander Von Humboldt: büyük bir doğa bilimcinin kısa bir biyografisi*.[47] The number of publications on Humboldt is small. It seems that Humboldt and his *oeuvre* hardly had a substantial impact on Ottoman and Turkish geographers besides reminiscences about his distinctive form of natural inquiry – what Susan Cannon labelled as

41.   Şemseddin Sami 1889, pp. 4773–74.

42.   '… première génération de géographes turcs …'. See Ginsburger 2014, pp. 255–56.

43.   Faik Sabri 1915, pp. 12–13.

44.   Idem 1916, pp. 170–71.

45.   Ardel 1960, pp. 111–15. This short text was also published in German. Idem 1960, pp. 70–73.

46.   Uslu 1982, pp. 31–56.

47.   Kızıroğlu 1994.

Discovering the Nature of the New Homeland

'Humboldtian science' and described as a 'synthetic, empirical, quantitative' method.[48] Yet, it was Carl Ritter and his followers who set the standards for the future development of the academic discipline(s) of geography. It was their scientific work that was also followed by the Ottoman/Turkish academics. It is therefore not surprising that none of Alexander von Humboldt's works has ever been translated into Turkish. Consequently, as will be exemplified in the following, in the early Republican period Humboldt was above all admired and propagated as scientific traveller, explorer and discoverer, serving as an example for all young Turks.[49]

The First Turkish Biography on Alexander von Humboldt: In Search of Turkish Identity[50]

The short biography by Mustafa Niyazi on Humboldt deserves a closer look. Mustafa Niyazi's booklet has around forty pages, plus a foreword of sixteen pages. For sure, this is far from the quantity of Andrea Wulf's recently published, almost hagiographic, biography of Humboldt, *The Invention of Nature: Alexander von Humboldt's New World*,[51] a study that allows readers to follow Humboldt's travels, research and ideas as well as the way he saw the world.[52] Nevertheless, despite the small number of pages, for Mustafa Niyazi too, Alexander von Humboldt was the most important scientist related to the study of geography – actually he was deemed to be the founder of the discipline and worth praising for this more than any other person. Mustafa Niyazi's *Alexander von Humboldt ın* [sic] *Hayat ve Asarı* was published in 1932 by Tefeyyüz Kitaphanesi, a leading publishing house established in 1887. We learn from the title page that the author has dedicated his work to his son and his students: 'Oğluma ve talebelrime' [sic]. The very same page informs us that Mustafa

---

48. Nicolson 1987, pp. 167–94.

49. Since the 1950s a considerable number of Turkish scientists have been granted a Humboldt grant. Since 2015, due to the political situation in Turkey, many Turkish researchers have lost their jobs and / or are threatened. Some of them have been able to leave the country with the support of the Philipp Schwartz Initiative of the Alexander von Humboldt Foundation.

50. The quote 'in search of Turkish identity' is derived from the title of Gerhard Sandner's article 'In Search of Identity: German Nationalism and Geography'. See Sandner 1994.

51. For a critical review, see Glaubrecht 2016.

52. In 2017, a Turkish translation of Andrea Wulf's book on Alexander von Humboldt was published under the title *Doğanın Keşfi: Alexander von Humboldt'un Yeni Dünyası*.

Niyazi was a teacher of geography at the Military High School (*Kuleli Askeri Lisesi*) in Istanbul.

The small booklet is full of mistakes, starting with wrong pagination, and typographically of poor quality, likewise the illustrations.[53] It seems as if Mustafa Niyazi had delivered an Ottoman manuscript (with Arabic script) that was transferred into Latin script in a careless manner. The high number of spelling errors is striking but not an uncommon phenomenon in the publications of the early 1930s,[54] although Turkish officials had provided spellers to simplify the change. Undoubtedly, the early Republican printing houses not only had technical difficulties but also lacked qualified staff. Turkey, in addition to its limited economic capabilities in the 1920s, was further severely hit by the 1929 global economic crisis, an event that profoundly affected the printing market among many other sectors in the country.[55] Yet, despite the low quality of layout, typography and pictures, the text is literarily elaborate. Mustafa Niyazi was undoubtedly a skilled writer. This is confirmed by the fact that he published at least thirteen books and almost thirty articles between 1922 and 1943, most of which were dedicated to geographical topics (see also below).[56]

The introduction of Mustafa Niyazi's biography of Humboldt gives a good idea of what he had in mind in offering sketches of Humboldt's life and scientific achievements. Similarly to late Ottoman 'learned patriots', Mustafa Niyazi stressed particularly the importance of science for development and progress and continued: 'everybody knows the outstanding position geography has among the civilised nations'.[57] In this regard, it is without doubt that he considered Germany the leading nation, which successfully became the 'homeland of geography' ('*Coğrafyanın vatanı*'):

> Alexander von Humboldt, Karl Ritter, Oskar Peschel, Friedrich Ratzel, Alfred Kirchoff, Ferdinand von Richthofen, Albrecht Penck, Alfred Hpilippson [sic, Philippson], Alfred Hettner, Alexander Supan, Passarge, E. Obst …. are …

---

53. Mustafa Niyazi 1932, pp. 22, 33, 42, 45.

54. 'The alphabet reform took getting used to' is the image caption of a picture showing the front of a shop with correct spelling of its name in Ottoman script but an incorrect version in Latin. See Findley 2010, p. 254.

55. Kabacalı 2000, pp. 169–77.

56. Among them are titles such as *Osmanlı Türklerinde coğrafya* (Istanbul 1936), *Avrupa memleketleri coğrafyası* (Istanbul 1940), *Büyük devletler coğrafyası* (Istanbul 1934), *Eski zamanda Türklerin coğrafyaya hizmetleri* (Istanbul 1933). He also translated a chapter of Obst 1933.

57. 'Coğrafyanın medenî memleketlerde nekadar mümtaz bir mevki ihraz ettiği her kesçe malûm bir keyfiyettir'. Mustafa Niyazi 1932, p. 3.

Discovering the Nature of the New Homeland

godlike great geographers (*ilah gibi büyük*) who in the course of the last two centuries were educated in this country, [moreover] these unique scientists honoured not only Germany but probably the whole science world.[58]

Additionally, the introduction and the main text show that Mustafa Niyazi was well-read. The geographers he mentions and geographical works he quotes suggests that he had a broad knowledge of Ottoman but even more of foreign geographical literature. He must have mastered at least German, French and most probably Italian. Among the authors he directly cites are, for instance, the geographer Ewald Banse (1883–1953),[59] whom he possibly knew personally (he calls him 'my dear friend' – 'aziz dostum'); poet and novelist Otto Ernst (1862–1926); geographer Franz Schnaß (1889–1957); pedagogue Ernst von Sallwürk (1839–1926);[60] Siegfried Passarge (1866–1958), geographer, geologist, palaeontologist;[61] and the Italian geographer Stefano Grande. Mustafa Niyazi even quoted from Johann Wolfgang von Goethe's (1749–1802) *Wanderjahre* [Willhelm Meister's Journeyman Years].

The main aim of the book's introduction is to discuss the importance of geography as a discipline among the civilised countries and the need to develop its teaching in Turkey. According to Mustafa Niyazi, Turkey needed a contemporary geography education. In order to achieve that goal, he names nine major factors that he considers to be central:

1. A good teacher
2. Good textbook on geography
3. Well-equipped classrooms
4. Regular study trips in Turkey and neighbouring countries
5. Visiting exhibitions, museums, factories and observatories
6. Use of maps and illustrations in classes
7. Projections and school cinemas

---

58. Mustafa Niyazi 1932, p. 4. Most of the named geographers held chairs at German universities. See Sandner 1994, p. 73.

59. For Ewald Banse, see Lammers 2015, pp. 165–84.

60. *Die Schule des Willens als Grundlage der gesamten Erziehung* published in 1915, (Mustafa Niyazi 1932, p. 12).

61. Quoting probably from his *Vergleichende Landschaftskunde* (Mustafa Niyazi 1932, pp. 12–13).

8. Founding of a geographical society[62]
9. Reading of geographical journals

Books on leading geographers would, in particular, be of great importance and example for young students. Mustafa Niyazi names, among others, the Swedish geographer and explorer Sven Hedin (1865–1952); the Norwegian scientist, explorer and diplomat Fridtjof Nansen (1861–1930); the Norwegian explorer of polar regions Roald Amundsen (1872–1928); the British polar explorer Ernest Shackleton (1874–1922); and the American explorer Robert Edwin Peary (1856–1920). Learning of the adventures and works of these famous travellers and discoverers would motivate the children to model themselves on these men.

Consequently, besides the biography of Humboldt, Mustafa Niyazi published a number of books and translations about other explorers and scientists, such as Fridtjof Nansen, Sven Hedin, John Franklin (1786–1847), the Finnish and Swedish explorer scientist Adolf Erik Nordenskiöld (1832–1901) and the American explorer George W. DeLong (1844–1881).[63] Additionally, between 1936 and 1943, Mustafa Niyazi was the editor of the monthly geographical journal *Bilgi yurdu*[64] in which most of his articles were published.[65]

---

62. The founding of a geographical society was a long-lasting matter of debate that goes back to the late Ottoman period. See for instance Faik Sabri 1328/1912, pp. 24–26 or Osman İzzet 1329/1914, pp. 35–37. But it was only in 1941 that the Turkish Geographical Society (*Türk Coğrafya Kurumu*) was founded.

63. *Franklin in* [sic] *kutup seyahati* (1933), probably this is a translation from a German version; *Sven Hedin Ortaasyada* (1933), translation from German (*Die geographisch-wissenschaftlichen Ergebnisse meiner Reisen in Zentralasien 1894–97*. Supplementary volume 28 to Petermanns Mitteilungen. Gotha 1900). *Nordenskiold, de Long, Fridtjof Nansen* (1936), which is, I suppose, a partial translation of *The White North with Nordenskiold, De Long, and Nansen* by M. Douglas published in 1899. In 1933 he published a book on famous discoverers *Meşhur kaşifler* (Istanbul). Besides him there were other Ottoman authors who translated the adventurous travels of famous explorers. See Türkay 1958, pp. 60–89.

64. The second issue of *Bilgi Yurdu* was announced in the daily newspaper *Cumhuriyet* (12 Dec. 1936): 4.

65. Most of the articles are concerned with regions in Turkey; a few examine other regions and countries like Gibraltar, Sicily, Japan, Italy or Siberia. One article from 1939 is entitled 'How many Jews are there in the world?' (*Bilgi Yurdu* 10: 677–83). Other articles appeared in the journals *Konya: Halkevi tarafından aydabir çıkarılır* (1936/37–1950) and *Gündüz: her ayın onbeşinde çıkar san'at ve fikir mecmuası* (1936–1940). Apparently Erenbilge was also giving public lectures in *halkevleri* (people's houses), which were established in 1932 by Atatürk as an educational project to gain support for his reforms. For an announcement of Erenbilge's lecture see *Cumhuriyet* (26 Mar. 1936): 10.

Discovering the Nature of the New Homeland

In the introduction to Humboldt's biography, Mustafa Niyazi addresses the students as follows:

> Youth! The heroes of geography are not less outstanding than the heroes of history. The former – by being very creative – were just regarded as less prestigious than the latter. But, by conquering nature and exhibiting it they crowned humanity. Are people like *Roald Amundsen, Peary*, the lieutenant *Shackleton* and *Nansen* less strong personalities than *Napoleon* or *Alexander* and *Caesar*?[66]

Mustafa Niyazi summons students to read the adventures of these men and aspire to become like them, so that their 'character would [be] hardened, their intelligence and their sense for creativity awakened'. And then he follows:

> So that today's and tomorrow's generations of the sublime Turkish nation, which has been honouring each page of six thousand years of history a thousand and one times, shall compete with other civilised nations and even achieve a degree of perfection in order to outstrip them on the ground and in the air. As his ghazi highness [*gazi hazretleri*, that is, Atatürk], the greatest among the heroes the centuries bring forth so rarely, has commanded, we shall not expect less than that from the Turkish children whose high aspiration we trust in.[67]

Given this highly ambitious task, it appears quite natural that Mustafa Niyazi chose Alexander von Humboldt – the (almost) conqueror of Chimborazo – as a role model for his students. Mustafa Niyazi's approach neatly fits into the Republican vision of modernisation along European lines and its strong emphasis on the education of children. This vision appears to be an updated – that is, nationalistic – version of the late Ottoman approach mentioned above. And likewise, geography was considered one of the most important topics to be taught, since it was a source of identification with and loyalty to the new homeland of the Turkish nation. Mustafa Niyazi was clearly a man of his time, a Turkish Republican nationalist, who considered the Turks to be the first civilisation

---

66. 'Gençler! Coğrafyanın kaharamanları tarihin kahramanlarından daha az değildir. Ancak bu çok yüksek yaradılışlı insanlar tarih ilâhları kadar perestiş edilmiyor. Halbuki tabiati fetih ve teshir ederek beşeriyetin alnını ebedî ve hakiki zafer ve şeref çelenkleri ile süsleyen bir *Roald Amundsen*, bir *Peary* bir mülâzim *Shackleton* ve bir *Nansen* acaba bir *Napoleon* yahut bir İskender ve *Sezar*'dan daha az kuvvetli şahsiyetler midir?' Mustafa Niyazi 1932, p. 13.

67. 'Taki altı bin yıldanberi tarihin her sayfasına bin bir şeref kazandıran ulu Türk milletinin bugünkü ve yarınki nesilleri ilim ve fen sahasında da diğer medenî milletlere boy ölçüşecek ve hattâ yerde ve gökte onlare [sic] galebe çalacak bir mertebei kemale yükselsin! Asırların nadiren doğurabildiği kahramanların en büyüğü olan Gazi Hazretlerinin buyurdukları gibi yüksek hasretlerine emniyetle baktığımız türk [sic] çocuklarından biz daha az şey istemeyiz'. Mustafa Niyazi 1932, p. 13.

on earth – in line with the 'Turkish Thesis of History' (*Türk Tarih Tezi*) that was officially propagated from 1930 onwards (*Türk Tarihinin Ana Hatları*).[68] As a teacher of geography, he was at the forefront of the 'pedagogy of space'.[69]

Mustafa Niyazi, like Mustafa Kemal Atatürk (1881–1938), was born in 1887/88 in Salonica;[70] firstly he served as an officer in the military, and from 1926 onwards he worked as a teacher of geography and history. He retired in 1943 due to health problems and was inducted to a military post in the regional air defence until 1946.[71] His earliest geographical booklet entitled *Anadolu* was first published probably in August 1922 in Istanbul.[72] The small booklet has only sixteen pages. According to the bibliography of Seyfettin Özege there is another book entitled *Anadolu* by Mustafa Niyazi, published in 1923 in Cairo: with 48 pages, it may be an extended version of the first issue.[73]

Mustafa Niyazi's *Anadolu* was firstly discussed by Osman Gümüşçü and Tahir Kodal in 2008. They consider the text to be the very first geographical work on Anatolia and a kind of scientific support ('geographical manifesto') for the war of independence that aimed to introduce Anatolia and endear it to the supposedly Turkish reader, thus generating a territorial identity. Because, they go on, 'just as men only love those whom they know well, to love one's homeland one must get to know it'.[74] By presenting themselves in line with the (official) nationalist position the authors fail to discuss the depiction of non-Muslim minorities in Mustafa Niyazi's text.

The first part of the booklet is a classical geographical description of Anatolia, in a scientific and yet literarily elaborate style. A few sections also offer an environmental perspective by considering the historical relationship

68. Copeaux 1997.

69. Özkan 2012 (Ch. 3: From Geography to Vatan).

70. More than a third of the 'small band of men who made up the leadership of the republic' came from the Ottoman Balkans, and Salonika was well represented. See Zürcher 2005, pp. 379–94.

71. Yiğit and Tunçel 2017, pp. 25–26.

72. Niyazi, *Anadolu*. Istanbul: Balıkcıyan Matbaası, without publication date. See Gümüşçü and Kodal 2008, pp. 137–82.

73. Entry: Özege Nr. 24000. See http://www.oncu.com/eskiharflikitaplar-wordpress/index.php/2011/06/16/anadolu-40927/ (accessed 1 Mar. 2018).

74. '[E]serin hedefi ana hatlarıyla okuyucuya Anadolu'yu tanıtarak sevdirmektir…nasıl ki insanlar ancak iyi tanıdıkları kişileri sevebiliyorlarsa vatanın sevilebilmesi için de iyi bilinmesi gereklidir'. Gümüşçü and Kodal, 2008, p. 142.

between inhabitants and the Anatolian environment.[75] But, when Mustafa Niyazi comes to the non-Muslim inhabitants of Anatolia, his style changes dramatically; and the descriptions of Greeks, Armenians and their history turn out to be harsh examples of 'othering'.[76]

For the legitimisation of Anatolia as homeland of the Turks, Mustafa Niyazi firstly defines the internal enemy: Greeks and Armenians. For the mass murder of Armenians, it is the Armenians who are to be blamed: if they had not betrayed the Turks, they would not have suffered this degree of serious loss (*vahim zayiat*). But who, Mustafa Niyazi asks, could change the course of history? He finishes his chapter with: as you sow, so you reap ('*el ceza-u min cinsü'l-'amel*').[77]

This conforms to the increased interest in Anatolia that could be discerned from 1908, much more so from 1912.[78] And, according to Erik-Jan Zürcher, the 'feeling that Anatolia was the "Turk's last stand", the homeland that had to be secured at all cost', directly led to the attempts of the Young Turks and their Kemalist successors to homogenise the population of Anatolia and turn it into a land for Turks only.[79] Zürcher further posited: 'This process started in 1914, with the expulsion of over 150,000 Greek Orthodox from the Aegean seaboard in retaliation for the expulsion of thousands of Muslims from the Balkans and culminated in the Armenian Genocide of 1915–1916'.[80]

A second argument for legitimising Anatolia exclusively as a homeland for the Turks is the claim that Anatolia was populated by the Turks from the beginning, from ancient times, long before all other groups appeared on the scene. Mustafa Niyazi argues this by referring to American archaeologists who had found out that even before the Hittites the *akvam-ı turan* (that is the Turanic tribes) had been active in the region (without giving a clear reference).[81]

---

75. For instance, see Gümüşçü and Kodal, 2008, pp. 148, 158–61 (original text, pp. 1, 6–9).

76. Ibid., p. 162 and following pages (section 'Anadolu Halkı' – Anatolian people, original text, p. 9 and following).

77. Ibid., p. 169 (original text, p. 13).

78. Zürcher 2005, 388.

79. Doğan Gürpınar shows that the 'Roumelian-born elite in exile had to domesticate and familiarise Anatolia as their new patrie (*vatan*). To complicate matters, their opinion of Anatolia was highly unfavourable'. Gürpınar 2012, p. 904.

80. Zürcher 2005, p. 388.

81. Gümüşçü and Kodal 2008, p. 162 (original text, p. 9).

Yavuz Köse

For Mustafa Niyazi it is clear: 'Anatolia is the homeland of the Turks. If the source of the prosperous and sacred Turkish blood is Turan, Anatolia is its honour'. There is no doubt for him: 'Anatolia lives with Turks and it dies with Turks'. Anatolian Turks are everything that the 'others' are not: they are truthful and hate hypocrisy, they are free, brave and of course pious/religious – that is, Muslims. And probably the most important: they are not infected by the 'poison of cosmopolitanism' (*kozmopolit zehri*).[82]

A New Enviro-Political Landscape: Anatolia Becomes Turkey

It is somehow ironic that Mustafa Niyazi ten years after his *Anadolu* chose Alexander von Humboldt as example for his students. Who, if not Humboldt, was a 'cosmopolitan environmentalist'[83] one may wonder? Of course, in his biography, Mustafa Niyazi refrains from discussing these sort of topics. In 1922, in his *Anadolu* he urges his readers to be sure that the fight for the homeland will be victorious and that on the horizon of Anatolia the new Turkish culture and civilisation will be rising.[84] Ten years later, Anatolia would become Turkey in Mustafa Niyazi's Humboldt biography. Not even once does he mention the term 'Anadolu' in this publication. Likewise, not a single word is to be found considering non-Turkish ethnic groups in Turkey. In this case, he is in line with geography textbooks published after 1930 – in almost all of them the names of non-Turkish minority groups were omitted completely.[85]

It is not Humboldt the cosmopolitan environmentalist but Humboldt the scientific traveller and discoverer who serves as a good role model and argues for the importance of geography in school education. The driving force was to support the students in getting to know and love the new homeland. And according to Mustafa Niyazi, Humboldt himself stressed the utmost importance of inquiry into the natural conditions of the fatherland (*ana vatan*).[86]

---

82. Idem, p. 163–64 (original text p. 10). As stated by Behlül Özkan 'one of the earliest articulations of the Turkification of Anatolia was İsmet İnönü's speech at the Turkish Hearth in 1925'. See Özkan 2012, p. 104. For earlier examples on the Turkishness of Anatolia see Gürpınar 2012, pp. 907–08.

83. Zimmerer 2006, p. 456.

84. See Gümüşçü and Kodal 2008, p. 175 (original text p. 16).

85. Özkan 2012, p. 144.

86. Mustafa Niyazi 1932, p. 66.

Discovering the Nature of the New Homeland

Given the volume of his publications dedicated to great scientist travellers and discoverers, we may assume that Niyazi, who died in 1947,[87] really admired personalities like Humboldt. Certainly, Niyazi tried to portray nature as masterfully as Humboldt did. Yet, like geography, Humboldt and other discoverers (*kaşif*) seem to have served altogether one goal: 'to create a 'natural' link between the national homeland and its people'.[88]

And finally, not only was Alexander von Humboldt cosmopolitan, an attitude that began to be viewed with suspicion among Ottomans, as mentioned earlier. His views on nature were more or less pulverised at the latest with the publication of Charles Darwin's ground-breaking *On the Origin of Species*, just six months after Humboldt's death. Since, as we know, Darwin's view gained momentum with the rise of the Young Turks,[89] Humboldt must have appeared rather out-dated in times of the growing influence of nationalism. Perhaps that is one reason he did not get the attention in the Ottoman Empire/ Turkey that he deserved.

Bibliography

Published Primary Sources

Ahmet Rifat Efendi. 1881. *Lügat-ı tarihiye ve coğrafiye*. Istanbul: Mahmud Bey Matbaası.

Ali Cevad. 1885. *Memalik-i osmaniyenin tarih ve coğrafya lügatı*. Istanbul: Mahmud Bey Matbaası.

Anonymous. 1869. 'Eine Humboldt-Feier unter Palmen'. *Die Gartenlaube* 43, 689–690. Url: https://digipress.digitale-sammlungen.de/view/bsb10498421_00263_u001/1 (accessed 27 Feb. 2018).

Anonymous. 'Bilgi Yurdu'. *Cumhuriyet* (12 Dec. 1936), p. 4.

Anonymous. 'Konferans'. *Cumhuriyet* (26 Mar. 1936), p. 10.

Anonymous. 'M. Niyazi Erenbilge'. *Cumhuriyet* (1 May 1947), p. 3.

Erenbilge, M. Niyazi. 1936. *Nordenskiold, de Long, Fridtjof Nansen*. Istanbul: Tefeyyüz Kitaphanesi.

——. 1936. *Osmanlı Türklerinde coğrafya*. Istanbul: Akşam Matbaası.

——. 1940. *Avrupa memleketleri coğrafyası*. Istanbul: İnkılâp Kitabevi.

[Erenbilge], M. Niyazi. n.d. [1922] *Anadolu*. Istanbul: Balıkcıyan Matbaası.

——. 1932. *Alexander von Humboldt ın* [sic] *Hayat ve Asarı*. Istanbul: Tefeyyüz Kitaphanesi.

---

87. On 1 May 1947 (p. 3) the newspaper *Cumhuriyet* published an obituary notice with a picture of M. Niyazi Erenbilge.

88. Özkan 2012, p. 105.

89. See for instance Doğan 2006.

——. 1933. *Eski zamanda Türklerin coğrafyaya hizmetleri*. Istanbul: Başvekalet Müdevvenat Matbaası.

——. 1933. *Coğrafya Seyahat Kitapları (birinci kitap)*. Istanbul: Tefeyyüz Kitaphanesi.

——. 1933. *Franklin in* [sic] *kutup seyahati*. Istanbul Necmi-i İstikbal Matbaası.

——. 1933. *Sven Hedin Ortaasyada*. Istanbul: Tefeyyüz Kitaphanesi.

——. 1933. *Meşhur kaşifler*. Istanbul: Tefeyyüz Kitaphanesi.

[Erenbilge], M. Niyazi. 1934. *Büyük devletler coğrafyası*. Istanbul: Publisher unknown.

Faik Sabri. 1328/1912. 'Coğrafya Cemiyetleri'. *Resimli Kitap* **8** (43): 24–26.

——. 1332/1916. 'Coğrafyanın İlmi Usulleri / Eski Coğrafyanın Yeni Maksat Ve Gayeleri – Humboldt ve Ritter'den Sonra Coğrafya – Vahdet-i Arziyye Kanunu – Mazinin Haldeki İntibaatı – Eski Tesirler, Yeni İzler'. *Darülfünun Edebiyat Fakültesi Mecmuası* **1** (2): 170–78.

——. 1915. *Osmanlı coğrafya-yı tabii ve iktisadisi*. Istanbul: Kanaat Matbaası.

Höflechner, Wallter and Alexandra Wagner (eds). 2011. *Joseph von Hammer-Purgstall. Erinnerungen und Briefe*. Version 1 201107: Briefe von 1790–bis Ende 1819. Graz 2011. Url: http://gams.uni-graz.at/hp/pdf/10_BriefeVorbemerkungen.pdf (accessed 27 June 2018)

Osman İzzet. 1329/1914. 'Milli İhtiyacımız Coğrafya Cemiyeti'. *Cihad* **1** (9): 35–37.

Satı' Bey. 1913. *Vatan İçin Beş Konferans*. Dersaadet: Kader Matbaası.

Şemseddin Sami. 1889. *Kamusü'l-alam. Tarih ve coğrafya lügatı. Dictionnaire Universel D'Histoire et de Géographie*. Istanbul: Mihran Matbaası.

Secondary Sources

Ahmed Emin. 1914. *The Development of Modern Turkey as Measured by its Press*. New York: Columbia University Press.

Akpınar, Özkan. 2010. 'Geographical Imagination in School Geography during the Late Ottoman Period, 1876–1908'. MA Thesis, Istanbul: Bosphorus University.

Ardel, Ahmet. 1960. 'Alexander Von Humboldt'. *Istanbul University Institute of Geography Review* **6**: 70–3.

——. 1960. 'Alexander von Humboldt (Ölümünün Yıldönümünün Münasebetiyle'. *İstanbul Üniversitesi Coğrafya Enstitüsü Dergisi* **6** (11): 111–15.

Christensen, Peter H. 2017. *Germany and the Ottoman Railways. Art, Empire, and Infrastructure*. New Haven: Yale University Press.

Copeaux, Étienne. 1997. *Espaces et temps de la nation turque analyse d'une historiographie nationaliste, 1931–1993*. Paris: CNRS Editions.

Doğan, Atilla. 2006. *Osmanlı Aydınları ve Sosyal Darwinizm*. Istanbul: Küre Yayınları.

Durgun, Ö. Sezgi. 2012. 'Yer Bilgisinden Ulusal Coğrafya'ya'. In S. Gülden Ayman (ed.), *Mekân, Kimlik, Güç ve Dış Politika*. Istanbul: Yalın Yayıncılık. pp. 7–13.

Discovering the Nature of the New Homeland

Dursun, Selçuk, 2017. 'The History of Environmental Movements and the Development of Environmental Thought in Turkey, 1850–1980'. In Hrvoje Petrić and Ivana Žebec Šilj (eds), *Environmentalism in Central and Southeastern Europe: Historical Perspectives*. Lanham, Maryland: Lexington Books. pp. 111–32.

Erol, Emre. 2016. *The Ottoman Crisis in Western Anatolia. Turkey's Belle Époque and the Transition to a Modern Nation State*. London: I.B. Tauris.

Findley, Carter Vaughn. 2010. *Turkey, Islam, Nationalism, and Modernity. A History, 1789–2007*. New Haven and London: Yale University Press.

Ginsburger, Nicolas. 2014. 'Influences Européennes et création de l'école Turque de géographie'. In Güneş Işıksel and Emmanuel Szurek (eds), *Turcs et Français. Une histoire culturelle 1860–1960*. Rennes: Presses Universitaires de Rennes. pp. 251–70.

Glaubrecht, Matthias. 2016. 'Überschätzter Universalgelehrter'. *Der Tagesspiegel* (28 Dec.). Url: https://www.tagesspiegel.de/wissen/alexander-von-humboldt-ueberschaetzter-universalgelehrter/19181812.html (accessed 1 Mar. 2018).

Gümüşçü, Osman and Nazan Özür. 2016. 'Türkiye'de Modern Coğrafyanın Kuruluşu ve Örgütlenmesi 1915–1941)'. *Atatürk Araştırma Merkezi Dergisi* 93: 105–47. Url: http://www.atam.gov.tr/wp-content/uploads/003-Osman-gumuscu.pdf (accessed 1 Mar. 2018).

Gümüşçü, Osman and Tahir Kodal. 2008. 'Millî Mücadeleye Destekleyen ve Bilinmeyan Bir Çoğrafya Eseri: Anadolu'. *Erdem* 52: 137–82.

Gürpınar, Doğan. 2012. 'From the Bare and Arid Hills to Anatolia, the Loveable and Beautiful: Kemalist Project of "National Modernity" in Anatolian Countryside'. *Middle Eastern Studies* 48 (6): 903–26.

Hanioğlu, Şükrü. 2008. *A Brief History of the Late Ottoman Empire*. Princeton: Princeton University Press.

Hooson, David (ed.). 1994. *Geography and National Identity*. Oxford; UK: Blackwell.

Kabacalı, Alpay. 2000. *Başlangıcından Günümüze Türkiye'de Matbaa Basın ve Yayın*. İstanbul: Literatür Yayıncılık.

Kızıroğlu, İlhami. 1994. *Alexander von Humboldt: büyük bir doğabilimcinin kısa biyografisi*. Ankara: Desen Ofset.

Konrad, Felix 2009. *Der Hof der Khediven von Ägypten: Herrscherhaushalt, Hofgesellschaft und Hofhaltung 1840–1880*. Würzburg: Ergon Verlag.

Kreiser, Klaus. 2001. 'Geographie und Patriotismus. Zur Lage der Geowissenschaften am Dârülfünûn unter dem Jungtürkischen Regime (1908–1918)'. In Daniel Balland (ed.), *Hommes et terres d'Islam. Mélanges offerts à Xavier de Planhol, vol. 1*. 2 vols. Leuven: Institut de recherche en Iran. pp. 71–87.

Lammers, Uwe. 2015. *Sieben Leben: Wissenschaftlerbiografien an der kulturwissenschaftlichen Abteilung der Technischen Hochschule Braunschweig im Nationalsozialismus*. Braunschweig. Url: https://publikationsserver.tu-braunschweig.de/receive/dbbs_mods_00058531 (accessed 1 Mar. 2018).

Maksudyan, Nazan. 2014. *Orphans and Destitute Children in the Late Ottoman Empire*. Syracuse: Syracuse University Press.

Nicolson, Malcolm. 1987. 'Alexander von Humboldt, Humboldtian Science and the Origins of the Study of Vegetation'. *History of Science* 25: 167–94.

258

Yavuz Köse

Obst, Erich. 1933. *Boğazlar: İstanbul-Çanakkale mıntıkası iklimi*. Istanbul: Necmi-i İstikbal Matbaası.

Osterhammel, Jürgen. 1999. 'Alexander von Humboldt. Historiker der Gesellschaft, Historiker der Natur'. *Archiv für Kulturgeschichte* **81**: 105–31.

Özgen, Nurettin. 2016. 'A Critical Approach to Discipline of Human Geography as an Apparatus for State Hegemony in Turkey'. *Journal of Geography in Higher Education* **40** (1): 131–53.

Özkan, Behlül. 2012. *From the Abode of Islam to the Turkish Vatan: The Making of a National Homeland in Turkey*. New Haven: Yale University Press.

——. 2014. 'Making a National *Vatan* in Turkey: Geography Education in the Late Ottoman and Early Republican Periods'. *Middle Eastern Studies* **50** (3): 457–81.

Rhein, Karin. 2003. *Deutsche Orientmalerei in der zweiten Hälfte des 19. Jahrhunderts: Entwicklung und Charakteristika*. Berlin: Tanea Verlag.

Rupke, Nicolaas A. 2005. *Alexander von Humboldt. A Metabiography*. Frankfurt am Main et.al.: Peter Lang.

Sachs, Aaron. 2006. *The Humboldt Current: A European Explorer and His American Disciples*. Oxford: Oxford University Press.

Sāmī, Amīn. 2009. *Taqwīm an-Nīl, vol. 4*. 6 vols. Cairo: al-Hay'a al-ʿĀmma li-quṣūr al-ṯaqāfa.

Sandner, Gerhard. 1994. 'In Search of Identity: German Nationalism and Geography, 1871–1910'. In David Hooson (ed.), *Geography and National Identity*. Oxford: Blackwell. pp. 71–91.

Türkay, Cevdet. 1958. *İstanbul Kütüphanelerinde Osmanlı'lar Devrine aid Türkçe – Arapça – Farsça Yazma ve Basma Coğrafya Eserleri Bibliografyası*. Istanbul: Maarif Basımevi.

Uslu, Selman. 1982. 'Alexander von Humboldt (1769–1859). Türkiye Humboldt Bursiyerleri Derneğinin Kuruluşu Nedeniyle, 1982'. *İstanbul Üniversitesi Orman Fakültesi Dergisi*, Seri B **33** (1): 31–56. Url: http://dergipark.gov.tr/download/article-file/175693 (accessed 25 June 2018).

Wulf, Andrea. 2015. *The Invention of Nature. Alexander von Humboldt's New World*. Trans. by Emrullah Ataseven. New York: Alfred A. Knopf.

——. 2017. *Doğanın Keşfi: Alexander von Humboldt'un Yeni Dünyası*. Istanbul: Ayrıntı Yayınları.

Yalçınkaya, M. Alper. 2015. *Learned Patriots. Debating Science, State, and Society in the Nineteenth-Century Ottoman Empire*. Chicago: University of Chicago Press.

Yerasimos, Stéphane. 2002. *Konstantinopel. Istanbuls historisches Erbe* [orig. *Constantinople. De Byzance à Istanbul*, 2000]. Cologne: Könemann.

Yiğit, Ali and Harun Tunçel. 2017. *100. Yılında Türkiye'de Coğrafyacılar. Türkiye Coğrafyacı Biyografileri (1915–2015)*. Bilecik: Türk Coğrafya Kurumu Derneği.

Zimmerer, Karl S. 2006. 'Humboldt and the History of Environmental Thought'. *Geographical Review* **96** (3): 456–58.

Zürcher Erik-Jan. 2005. 'How Europeans Adopted Anatolia and Created Turkey'. *European Review* **13** (3): 379–94.

Discovering the Nature of the New Homeland

—— . 2009. 'The Late Ottoman Empire as Laboratory of Demographic Engineering' *Il mestiere di storico* I (1): 1–12. Url: https://www.torrossa.com/resources/an/2411979 (accessed 2 Mar. 2018)

Chapter 11

DISPOSSESSION BY CONCESSION: FOREST COMMONS IN THE OTTOMAN EMPIRE AND EARLY TURKISH REPUBLIC

Selçuk Dursun

The legal status of forests and the property regime in the late Ottoman and early Republican periods have been the subject of a number of previous studies.[1] On the other hand, the number of studies that analyse forest commons is very few.[2] This article examines the various ways in which people benefited from forest commons and their resources and the legal process of dispossession from the Ottoman Empire to the early Turkish Republic. It is not surprising that this type of forests were not subject to the property regime from the outset, since the conception of property in them was originally different in nature from private property. For this reason, the crucial point that needs to be emphasised is the changing attitude of the state towards common forests, including open access, through time. The restriction of usufruct rights of peasants by giving them concessions at certain moments in history constituted one of the main axes of forest history in the Ottoman Empire and later in the early Turkish Republic.

While the concept of '*orman*' (forest) used to refer to the areas covered with trees in the pre-industrial period, though less frequently than *koru* (piece of meadow or forest land, being enclosed, or supposed to be enclosed, kept for private use), *odunluk* (woodland) or *baltalık* (coppice), its modern meaning, which underlines the new opportunities of using wood and timber resources for monetary purposes, emerged in the nineteenth century as a result of new

---

1.   Köprülü 1948; idem 1949; idem 1950; Tunçsiper 1957; idem 1964; Cin 1981; Çağlar 1992; Sönmez 1998; Koç 1999; idem 2005.

2.   The concept 'forest commons' refers both to the *cibal-i mubaha* (unenclosed forests on the mountains) and *baltalık*s (village coppices). For a sophisticated legal analysis of the *cibal-i mubaha*, see Köprülü 1949. For a patchwork compilation of what the concept means in selected legal texts, see Birben 2009.

accumulation practices. The history of this transformation enables us to understand how the state came to monopolise the management of forests during the second half of the nineteenth century. During this period, we see a gradual appropriation and expropriation[3] by the state of forests in the waste and unoccupied lands, the *cibal-i mubaha* (unenclosed forests on the mountains), the *baltalık*s and a part of the waqf (pious foundations) and private forests, of which the ownership were blurred. Subsequently, local use rights, such as the clearing of forests for agricultural purposes, grazing and fuel, were restricted and prohibited, due to the aims of commercialisation and exploitation.

The state, says David Harvey, 'with its monopoly of violence and definitions of legality', supports and enforces these accumulation practices. He defines such practices as:

> the commodification and privatization of land and the forceful expulsion of peasant populations ... conversion of various forms of property rights (common, collective, state, etc.) into exclusive private property rights ... suppression of rights to the commons; commodification of labour power and the suppression of alternative (indigenous) forms of production and consumption; colonial, neocolonial, and imperial processes of appropriation of assets (including natural resources); monetization of exchange and taxation, particularly of land; ... and usury, the national debt and, most devastating of all, the use of the credit system as a radical means of *accumulation by dispossession* [emphasis mine].[4]

Attracted by the definition of Harvey's 'accumulation by dispossession', I would like to label this transformation process as 'dispossession by concession'. In this way, the early Republican governments managed to finalise the project of establishing state property rights on forests begun during the Ottoman Empire, not mainly by using its monopoly of violence, but by its definitions of legality and by giving concessions.

Commons in Brief

Economists incorrectly define 'commons' as resources that belong to nobody. Since they do not belong to anybody, human beings like to use them as they want, eventually causing them to be ruined because they belong to everybody. This formula forces us to confront Garrett Hardin's famous 'tragedy of the commons',[5] that is, natural resources are rarely restored by beneficiaries, or

---

3.   For the definitions of these terms, see Foster and Clark 2018.

4.   Harvey 2005, p. 159.

5.   Hardin 1968, p. 537.

abandoned to regenerate themselves. On the contrary, they are consumed and wasted.[6] The solution Hardin finds to prevent this 'tragedy' is that commons should either be privatised or undergo state control. According to William Ophuls, one of Hardin's followers, the state is exemplified by the symbol of the powerful and invincible Leviathan à la Hobbes.[7] From this point of view, from the mid-eighteenth century to the present day, exclusive property rights have prevented excessive use of resources and encouraged the owner to find the most appropriate investment for accumulating wealth. Thus, it becomes possible to overcome the 'tragedy of the commons'.[8]

However, the story was not quite like the one told by the Hardinians. As Elinor Ostrom has shown, there was no such great tragedy at all. On the contrary, commons have suffered more due to their withdrawal from the hands of indigenous communities, who have traditionally benefitted from them, and due to the disappearance of the local experience and knowledge of these communities. Local users usually have a long-term perspective and affect each other by instituting behavioural rules, also known as 'working rules', rules that are acknowledged, monitored and enforced by the members of the community.[9] Ostrom shows us that there are social control mechanisms that can regulate the use of commons without resorting to private property.[10] Traditionally, indigenous people are part of the ecosystem they live in; thus they need the forest and its resources for their subsistence needs and therefore develop ethical rules for using and protecting the forests around themselves.

According to its first meaning, the common denotes the 'common wealth of the material world, like air, water, fruits of the soil, and all the generous gifts of nature, which is the legacy of all humanity that must be shared by all'.[11] In Hardt and Negri's path-breaking book *Commonwealth*, we are invited to reconsider that we do not need to accept this theological perspective of the gift of God, while thinking about 'the commons'.[12] Thus, the common is not a divine gift, or even a natural given, but both a condition and a result of human activity in any society, both 'common resources' and 'common products'.[13]

---

6.   Rose 1991, p. 3.
7.   Ophuls 1977.
8.   Rose 2003, p. 90.
9.   Ostrom 1990; idem 1999; Ostrom et al. 1999; Ostrom and Gardner 1993.
10. Cited in Walljasper 2014, p. 41.
11. Dardot and Laval 2018, p. 171.
12. Hardt and Negri 2009, *passim*; Dardot and Laval 2018, p. 171.
13. Dardot and Laval 2018, p. 171.

Dispossession by Concession

As Massimo De Angelis rightly observes, though Ostrom decoupled open access and commons, she did conceptualise commons as social systems. However, he argues that Ostrom's decoupling of open access and commons 'may not indicate an analytical and categorical *mutual exclusion*, rather a type of possible, although non-inevitable, *interrelation*: a commons is a system, and free access can be one of its subsystems'.[14] He further claims:

> in order for this free access to (re)produce, ... it has to be part of a commons, and has to be taken care of and governed by a specific bunch of commoners, the maximum number of which could be all the users of the free access space. So, commons and free access are not always opposed, as Ostrom indicated in her enlightening critique of Hardin.[15]

I argue that De Angelis's reformulation of the relationship between open access and commons – that is, free access resources as a subset of a commons system – was also true for the Ottoman Empire.[16] Before getting into the details of my argument, I would like to refer to some concepts from Roman law to better understand open access forest resources and commons in the Ottoman Empire.

While doing this, I have mainly employed certain non-exclusive property categories of Roman law. These are *res nullius* (things that do not belong to anyone), *res communis* (things that belong to all), *res publicae* (properties that belong to the public and are open to all through law-state property), and *res universitatis* (properties that belong to a general organisation in terms of common capacity, joint ownership).[17] Among them, *res nullius* and *res communis* are the two of the most important concepts of Roman law, with great significance in many of the imperial laws related to land, sea, underground water and game.[18]

Res communis is something that is owned or used commonly by all, like seas, underground water and many other natural resources. On the other hand, *res nullius* means any object, or thing, which is an ownerless property and is usually free to be owned, like wild animals, abandoned property and many other natural resources, like the products of rivers, lakes, seas, oceans and forests. In short, *res communis* means belonging to all, and *res nullius* means belonging to no one. Put another way, *res nullius* is open access resources and *res communis* is common property. The Romans defined *res nullius* as 'an object that belonged

---

14. De Angelis 2017, p. 145.
15. Ibid., p. 146.
16. For a brief discussion of commons and open access, see ibid., pp. 144–49.
17. Buckland 1921, p. 184; Rose 2003, pp. 92–105.
18. On *res nullius* in early modern writings, see Benton and Straumann 2010.

to no one and was therefore free for occupation by everyone'.[19] According to the capitalist mind, which expected substantial returns from investments of any kind, everything that is priceless and non-marketable is considered to be valueless. For the imperial mind, barren and unproductive territories, tradition-ally seen as *res nullius*, were regarded as 'not valuable' and 'free for the taking'.[20] This last statement also says something very important about the colonial expropriations that went hand in hand with the declensionist narratives of the colonialists.[21] Thus, it was not expected that something with no price or market value would be subject to ownership. Things that belong to the category of *res nullius* comprise things that are by their nature non-monopolistic and have not yet become the property of anyone.[22]

These Roman law concepts are useful to understand what open access and commons means and to trace the process of dispossession in the Ottoman Empire. Although the influence of both Roman and Jewish law on Islamic law needs further study, there is a certain similarity between Roman and Islamic legal conceptualisations with respect to 'things', some of which consisted of land, game, water, forest and certain rights over them.[23] One of the most im-portant categories of forests in the pre-industrial era was *cibal-i mubaha*, which corresponds to *res nullius* in Roman law. On the other hand, there were also the *baltalık*s belonging to certain villages and towns, which are an equivalent of *res communis*.

In Ottoman and even Islamic law, there are certain things, like forests and fisheries, which resemble the *res nullius* concept of the Roman law. The jurists considered there to be no private property right over these and them to be jointly owned by all: as such, they are considered as a type of corporation. The *Mecelle* (Ottoman Civil Code) calls such corporations *şirket-i ibaha*.[24] The fourth paragraph of article 1045 of the *Mecelle* stated that *şirket-i ibaha* means of equality among all, all the real and legal persons, including the state itself, in owning *mubah* things that have no owner. Yet, as emphasised by one of the most important Ottoman jurists, Hoca Eminefendizade Ali Haydar

---

19. Roselaar 2010, p. 89.
20. Weston and Bollier 2013, p. 10.
21. Davis 2007.
22. Rose 2003, p. 92.
23. In this context, the similarity between the terms 'occupatio', '*istila*' and '*ihraz*' is worth mentioning. See Schmidt 1910. For a general discussion of legal influences between Roman and Islamic law, see Crone 1987. For a critique of Crone, see Hallaq 1990.
24. Onar 1944, p. 504.

(1852–1918), this corporation is different from ordinary corporations, for the subject of partnership is not a thing, but 'the meaning, that comprises the right to use and own'.[25] Similarly, naturally growing trees in mountains that are in nobody's ownership and the fruits of trees in un-owned lands are all *mubah*. Peasants use labour to turn them into property and thus remove them from the category of *mubah*. Because these *mubah* things could become property by use of labour, they are like *res nullius* and nobody can be denied the right to benefit from them.[26] According to Sıddık Sami Onar, a pre-eminent professor of administrative law, 'the individual's ownership of common property and his right to make it his own is not subject to a permission or grace of the ruler, but is a right directly tied to his self; the ruler and government can only issue rules regarding the form of the exercise of that right'.[27]

Forest Ownership and Forms of Use in the Pre-industrial Period

To understand the basics of forest property regime, land access and control in the pre-Republican period, we need to understand the Ottoman land tenure system. There were five basic types of land in the Ottoman land regime: 1) *arazi-i memluke* (private land), 2) *araza-i miriyye* (state/public land), 3) *arazi-i mevkufe* (land belonging to pious foundations) 4) *arazi-i metruke* (abandoned land) and 5) *arazi-i mevat* (dead land). Some jurists classified abandoned land as land belonging to the treasury, thus making it state, or public, land.[28]

The relationship between land access and control is to be understood in terms of struggle among different groups and institutions. Thus, the land tenure, or 'resource tenure' would be a better expression, relations and the structure of land ownership in a specific historical context have many facets. 'Resource tenure' also covers the relationship between different groups in land, forest, mining and water resources. It refers to the economic aspects of revenue extraction from these resources, whether in terms of rent, produce or taxation. Here, my aim is not to establish a polarisation between traditional and modern 'resource tenure', but to follow up the continuity and change and to pinpoint the ruptures. While doing this, it will be possible to differentiate the nature of ownership and usufruct rights, and to understand how forest resources had been utilised in the past.

25. Ali Haydar 1330/1914, p. 224, quoted in Onar 1944, p. 504.
26. Onar 1944, p. 505.
27. Ibid., pp. 505–6.
28. Ali Haydar 1330/1914.

In the pre-industrial period, it was very common to open fields for agriculture from forests within the *tımar* lands (lands granted in return for military service). After these lands were cleared, they were considered to be *miri* (public) land and a *resm-i tapu* (official land tax) was due to compensate the usufruct rights of the cleared tract. However, the *rakabe* (eminent domain) of these lands still belonged to the state. Furthermore, in a law dating from the sixteenth century, there was an injunction stipulating that villagers, once they had cleared a forest by axe and opened a field with the permission of the *sahib-i arz* (land captain), would only be obliged to pay him the *öşür* (tithe) of their produce. Therefore, the *sahib-i arz* could not demand another tax. Yet, in a *fetva* (legal opinion issued by a mufti), it was stipulated that the villagers would be obliged to pay the same amount of *resm-i tapu* for a field that they had cleared as that due at the time when it was a forest.[29] Once forest was cleared for agricultural purposes, the *sahib-i arz* could reallocate the usufruct rights to someone else if there had been no agricultural activity within three years.[30] On the other hand, if two subjects had joint usufruct rights to a forest and one of them turned part of the forest to agricultural land by clearing away the forest by axe, his shareholder had joint usufruct rights over the field as well.[31] Here we see that joint usufruct rights had priority over the labour deployed. Furthermore, third persons were inhibited from cutting wood in such lands.[32] These acts can be seen as 'absolute disorder' arising out of the conception of land as an income-bringing commodity, as distinct from the forests.

However, when evaluating forests in the category of *cibal-i mubaha*, it is imperative that we consider them as part of a commons system. Everybody could take benefit from naturally grown trees in *cibal-i mubaha*,[33] which makes them very similar to open access resources. The transformation of *mubah* into 'property' occupies an important place in Islamic law. Ömer Nasuhi Bilmen has stated that it was possible for unclaimed things to be turned into property by way of invasion, or *ihraz* (appropriation), so long as it was in the name of the same person. Starting cultivation of an empty land is such a means of obtaining property.[34] However, the critical issue regarding *cibal-i mubaha* forests is not whose property they were, but rather whether the trees were naturally grown

---

29. Kutluk 1948, p. 27.
30. Barkan 1943, pp. 232–34.
31. Kutluk 1948, p. 23.
32. Ibid., p. 28.
33. Bilmen 1970, p. 186.
34. Ibid., p. 185.

or not. Since their use was not subject to any usufruct rights, the trees were the true subjects of property. It would be helpful to appeal to certain *fetva*s and *kanuname*s (lawbooks) to understand the issue of '*mubah*' with regard to forests.

According to the lawbooks dating from the sixteenth century, it was *mubah* to cut wood from the mountains. For example, in one of these lawbooks from the time of Süleyman I, the 'Lawgiver' (*Kanuni*) (r. 1520–1566), it was stated:

> the naturally grown wood and grass and fruits that sprout in mountains and forests are true *mubah*. They belong to whoever gathers them. If protected, occupied and planted, only the one who has the lawful usufruct rights can gather, if not, they should not be appropriated.[35]

Moreover, if we look into the local implementation of provincial lawbooks (*liva kanunameleri*), we see decisions taken in favour of persons who cut wood from '*mubah*' mountains for household needs, on the grounds that the sums taken from them were against 'law and tradition'.[36] The newer laws regarding the exploitation of *cibal-i mubaha* also refer to old laws. For example, the following is recorded in the lawbook of the Lesbos Island:

> Since it was written in the old-book that the villagers should not be prevented from cutting as usual from mountains that lie within the borders of their village where the wood and bushes that have existed since time immemorial and until now have been *mubah* to all, the same is written in the new book as explained.[37]

Again, according to the ancient law from the time of the Lawgiver, the *sahib-i arz* cannot claim tithe or any tax in kind from a villager who cuts trees and sells timber from *mubah* mountains.[38] There were often vicious struggles among neighbouring villagers and between villagers and local notables regarding the issue of cutting from *cibal-i mubaha* forests. It was not possible for one village to prevent other villagers' right to benefit from *cibal-i mubaha* on the ground of relative proximity.[39]

Woodlands where villagers have been cutting wood since time immemorial were not supposed to be given by title deeds to anyone. On the other hand, cutting wood from a mountain that lay within *sahib-i arz*'s *tımar* land

---

35. Kutluk 1948, p. 26.

36. Barkan 1943, p. 37.

37. Ibid., pp. 332–38.

38. Kutluk 1948, p. 23.

39. Ibid., p. 24. Prime Ministry Ottoman Archives (*Başbakanlık Osmanlı Arşivleri; BOA*), A.MKT.UM 48/22 (3 Rebiülevvel 1267 [5 Feb. 1851]; BOA, A.MKT.DV 142/44 (13 Safer 1276 [11 Sept. 1859]).

and was not categorised as *cibal-i mubaha*, was subject to the permission of the *sahib-i arz*. According to an early eighteenth century *fetva* journal, the use of woodland is stated under the heading '*Der-beyan-ı Kanun-ı Odunluk*' (The Law of Woodland) as follows:

> Woodlands (*odunluk*) are not given by deed, and even if they are, they are still judged as woodlands. Even when some people claim that they procured a deed from the land captain over a forest that happens to lie on the border of a land captain's *tımar*, such woodland does not become property or claimed by a deed. It is law that even when people have been cutting wood from a woodland and then procured a deed to turn the woodland into *mülk* (freehold), the woodland should still be taken from their hands and be opened to all people.[40]

In the same vein:

> When the *reaya* of a land captain's village have abandoned their homeland, is the land captain allowed to charge anything from someone who cut wood from the village's woodland? Answer: No he cannot. The land is *mubah*. Wood that grows on its own and has not been planted is common to all and cannot become anybody's property and thus anyone can meet their need without having to pay any compensation.[41]

This practice continued until the nineteenth century when *cibal-i mubaha* forests were exported to the category of state forests. For example, in December 1851, in the Tikveş district of Manastır, a petition was sent to the *mutasarrıf* (district governor) of Rumelia regarding someone named Süleyman Ağa, who had 'unlawfully occupied' a *cibal-i mubaha* that was being used by eight nearby villages with the claim that 'he had usufruct rights to this forest that he had inherited from his father' and had rented the 'naturally growing' grass in the forest at the rate of twenty piastre per sheep to villagers who had been grazing their animals there; and moreover, that he had been selling substantial amount of wood from the forest and unjustly harmed the villagers. The appeal of the villagers was so that they would be relieved of this difficulty arising from Süleyman Ağa's seizure of the aforesaid *cibal-i mubaha* forest without an official document verifying his claim. In the reply addressing the Rumelia *mutasarrıf* (district governor) and written from the Grand Vizierate, dated 24 December 1851, it was ordered that this usufruct claim did not rest on any deed and that the district council should ensure that no one would dare to confiscate *cibal-i*

---

40. Kutluk 1948, p. 27.

41. Ibid., p. 28.

mubaha that is 'contrary to the just rule'.[42] Apart from the articles in the legal documents, such struggles over *cibal-i mubaha* forests also inform us about the usufruct rights over open access and commons.

Despite all these circumstances, how did it come about that the Ottoman government included *cibal-i mubaha* forests in the category of *miri* (state) forests with the 1870 Forest Regulation? The factors that enable involuntary loss of common property rights are related to rules and regulations. For example, Liz Alden Wily argues that laws generally leave

> customary owned common properties most vulnerable to reallocation by governments to non-traditional holders and investors. This is generally because all customarily held lands are considered to have no more than permissive occupancy and use rights on national or government lands. On these grounds, government may lawfully appropriate these lands for purposes it considers more important.[43]

Thus, the lack of formal property rights, and the failure to recognise customary lands as commons, is why 'people's common lands are frequently deemed to be unowned or unownable, vacant, or unutilized, and therefore available for reallocation'.[44]

However, some early Republican forest experts, who retrospectively impose their twentieth century classifications and conceptions regarding forests back on the pre-industrial era, claim that this category of forests were cut down in an uncontrolled manner and call this pre-industrial forest regime, where multiple property categories often transposed on one another a 'period of unlimited exploitation'.[45] Taking the 1930s state property ownership as the norm, they claim that any kind of property category different from that norm leads to deforestation and corruption. These experts largely disregarded the role of the state in the dispossession of peasants and townspeople, who once benefitted from mountain forests, as the government appropriated the *cibal-i mubaha* forests. Furthermore, the idea of 'rational forest administration' that emerged in Prussia in the second half of the eighteenth century under the influence of cameralism, after spreading to other continental European countries, was often used as the basic justification for safeguarding the 'public good'.[46]

---

42. BOA, A.MKT.DV 49/27 (2 Safer 1268 [24 Dec. 1851]).

43. Wily 2011, p. ix.

44. Ibid.

45. Acun 1945, pp. 1–4.

46. Diker 1947, p. 27.

Selçuk Dursun

An excerpt from the 1928 *Türk Yılı* (Turkish Year) compilation of the Undersecretary of Agriculture (*Tarım Müsteşarlığı*) clearly shows how the Republican governments began this construct:

> Everybody had the right to use and exploit these forests called *cibal-i mubaha*. People living close to and far from such forests could cut trees as they liked, clear parts that they deemed appropriate for cultivation and turn them into fields or farms. When taxes were allocated, the despots and influential people could take over wide swathes of land from *cibal-i mubaha* forests if they deemed them appropriate for cultivation and call them *mera* (pasture) or *koru*).
>
> Moreover, military or administrative men who owned *tımar*s, like the *sipahi*, *zaim*, or *mütesellim*, and men of influence and village chiefs, *kadı*s and *müftü*s, would sell off forests as *mera* and *koru* and issue *temessük*s and *hüccet*s.[47]

While some observations in these statements might be valid, it is not appropriate for Republican governments to have identified *cibal-i mubaha* status as the culprit. For in the archival documents, one example of which we had seen above, we often see peasants waging struggles against such influential or despotic persons of local power in order not to lose their time-honoured rights in *cibal-i mubaha* forests.[48]

In sum, up until now, sources on pre-Tanzimat Ottoman forestry define *cibal-i mubaha* forests as forests which everybody takes advantage of in an unlimited manner.[49] Such a definition means putting *cibal-i mubaha* forests in the same category as the 'unregulated' open access resources, which Hardin has wrongly formulated as 'the tragedy of the commons'; and, consequently, it has led to the completely inaccurate description of pre-Tanzimat forestry as 'the absolutely unregulated period'.[50] Furthermore, Louis Bricogne (1825–1906), a prominent member of the French forest mission and one of the forest engineers invited from France in order to reorganise Ottoman forest administration in a modern and rational manner, has claimed that the means deployed to administer forests were those of 'absolute free management' with no control whatsoever, despite the fact that there was no solid assessment of the extent of Ottoman forest resources besides some travel narratives and reports by local officials.[51] In the reports he prepared after seven- to eight-month-long explorations during 1866–67, he repeatedly said that people would soon face

---

47.   Akçuraoğlu 1928, p. 163.
48.   BOA, TFR.I.A 4/399 (26 Kanun-ı Sani 1318 [8 Feb. 1903]).
49.   Diker 1947; Çağlar 1992; Günay 2003.
50.   Diker 1947, p. 23.
51.   Bricogne 1877; idem 1940, p. 4.

shortages due to the continuing destruction in the forests and that the state treasury would consequently be harmed. Claiming the existence of a 'rooted destructive mentality' among the people, his reports predicted that the commercial organisation was in a very bad state and that Turkey's existing forestry wealth would soon be exhausted.[52]

As I have discussed above, it was possible for everyone to use the *cibal-i mubaha* forests according to pre-industrial era rules and regulations and articles of the Land Code and the *Mecelle*. However, the curtailing of peasants' right to usufruct from these forests, first with the relevant article of the Land Code and second with the fifth article in the Forest Regulation dated 14 January 1870,[53] can justifiably be called an important turning point, a point which signalled a new era that began in the nineteenth century and continued into the early Republican period. In fact, the fifth article of the Forest Regulation has a significant similarity with the 104th of the Land Code:[54]

The residents of villages will be able to cut wood for free from state forests for building or repairing their houses, depots or stables, to make carts or agricultural tools and to make as much charcoal as they need, but they will have to pay the value of the wood they cut for trade, the value of which will be determined by the administration and will be liable to the same regulations as traders. The wood and coal that each village transports to its own market place with its own carts and animals is independent from this and will be regulated with its special directive.[55]

In general, this article appeared to include important concessions safeguarding the needs of the villagers but, actually, it meant a restriction of their ancient

---

52. Idem 1940, p. 4.

53. With this legal document, certain measures having to do with 'scientific forestry' attained binding power. Broadly, this Regulation stipulated bans having to do with the forests and the rights and privileges of the local people, traders and entrepreneurs; as well as the needs of the imperial artillery and arsenal and punishments for animal grazing and forest crimes.

54. Article 104 of the 1858 Land Code had stipulated that villagers would have the right to cut wood from *cibal-i mubaha* mountains to repair or rebuild their houses, depots or stables, to make carriages or agricultural tools, or to make charcoal solely for the needs of their household, so long as those forests had not been *korus* or forests allocated to anyone. While taking advantage of these rights nobody could interfere with another. Ali Haydar 1905, p. 452.

55. This article 5 of the Regulation and the directive that followed were rescinded with the *Baltalık Kanunu* (Coppice Law) dated 7 Mart 1337 (7 Mar. 1921). This law was again rescinded with the law no. 484, dated 15 Nisan 1340 (15 Apr. 1924) that again regulated the use of state forests by villages.

rights. In terms of protection of forests, the idea was to allocate woodlands to villagers in order to prevent them from cutting wood from public forests without paying anything.

This last stipulation concerning peasants' rights to use forests aroused criticism among some forest experts. For example, Bricogne argued that, if the Ottoman government aimed to make use of its natural resources, the administration should immediately modify this article, which, in his opinion, could be interpreted wrongly. This article, he noted, would cause the peasants to control the local trade in forest products. In his report to the government, Bricogne advised interpreting the concessions given to local people by this article as a 'privilege', not a 'right'.[56] The same issue led to a debate among the British officials in India in the 1860s. The British debate ended with a decision that 'the right of conquest is the strongest of all rights – it is a right which there is no appeal'. From that time onward, the customary use of forests was based on 'privilege' rather than 'right' in India.[57]

In fact, Ottoman codifiers probably did not consider this stipulation as a 'right' given to the local people, since it was, in reality, a limitation of a traditional 'right', which had its roots in customs, even in *shari'a* (religious law). In this regulation there were similar articles limiting the so-called 'rights' of other actors, such as owners of private forests and beneficiaries of pastures.

The 1858 Land Code and the 1870 Forest Regulation

In order to understand the fundamental legal framework with regard to forests in the Ottoman era, it is imperative to have an idea of certain articles of the 1858 Land Code having to do with forests and grazing lands. Even before the Land Code, the imperial edict of 24 August 1857 declared that *yaylak*s (summer pastures), *kışlak*s (winter pastures) and *mera*s (grazing lands) with indeterminate status were to henceforth include in *miri* land. From 1847 onwards, *Defterhane-i Amire* (Imperial Land Registry) had been responsible for issuing deeds for *miri* lands. The records used in this process were the land surveys extant in the Land Registry. Since the newest of these registers dated from the mid-seventeenth century and as no land surveys had been conducted since then, many winter and summer pastures or groves had no record. The government then declared that all such lands, whether they had a record or not, were to be treated as state property when it was not clear how they had come into existence, in order to

---

56.   Bricogne 1940, p. 27.

57.   Guha 2000, p. 38.

prevent existing or possible disputes arising from this situation. That is, this imperial edict broadened the extent of public land to the benefit of the state by accepting the principle that all winter and summer pastures and *koru*s not recorded in the Land Registry belonged to the state unless usufruct rights were proven with a document.[58] The aforementioned process, already begun with the *Tapu Nizamnamesi* (Title Deed Regulation) on 21 May 1847, continued with land surveys conducted between 1848 and 1872. The records named *arazi-i atik* (old lands) were created in these years. Scrutinising this process reveals that the state was trying to transfer summer and winter pastures and forests on abandoned land, village and town coppices on uncultivated lands, pastures and *cibal-i mubaha* forests all into the category of *miri* land.

Even state policies toward creating free market for forest resources sought to establish private property rights over *cibal-i mubaha* forests in 1866. For example, in a document sent to the Danubian provinces and the Ministry of Public Works, we learn that the government enquired about the current status of *cibal-i mubaha* forests and reports of damages resulting from corrupt practices of wood collection, protection measures and administration. The plan was to divide these forests into various categories according to their substance and value, other than the ones reserved for the Imperial Shipyard and Arsenal, and to sell them to private individuals, who were to be Ottoman subjects exclusively, in return for reasonable prices, as the treasury would benefit from the amount to be received.[59]

Interestingly enough, the document classified the forests in the Ottoman Empire in three categories, different from the Land Code: 1) forest that belongs to its owner by title deeds, or forests attached to a pious foundation or a *mukataa* (tax farm); 2) the *baltalık* used individually or jointly by towns and villages and 3) the *cibal-i mubaha*.[60] The document does not mention anything about the first and second categories. The main issue of the government was to transform the *cibal-i mubaha* forests into marketable goods. Although Article 104 of the Land Code states that not even a part of the *cibal-i mubaha* could be divided into parcels and owned independently or jointly, the document states that the postulates of such laws and the provisions in force could be corrected in accordance with the exigencies of time by the order of the Sultan.[61] The conclusion to be taken from what I have described so far is that *cibal-i mubaha*

---

58.   Barkan 1980, p. 328.

59.   BOA, A.MKT.MHM 360/26 (28 Safer 1283 [12 July 1866]).

60.   BOA, A.MKT.MHM 360/26 (28 Safer 1283 [12 July 1866]).

61.   BOA, A.MKT.MHM 360/26 (28 Safer 1283 [12 July 1866]).

forests were to be imported into the *miri* category before being transferred to private individuals.

In the nineteenth century, the category of *miri* represented the central governments' exclusive right to revenues from land.[62] At the same time, by overseeing the institution of individual property rights, the state was linking these to the practices of a modern state by such means as issuing title deeds.[63] After the Forest Regulation of 1870, the measures followed by the state regarding forests on state land took a different direction. Even though they were called state forests before the Regulation, it was only after the Regulation that the state began denying recognition to any rights acquired by deed or via rent contracts. Therefore, following the Regulation, many issues came up regarding title deeds contrary to fact or deemed invalid. This situation also applied to private forests upon which property rights were claimed on the basis of title deeds with indeterminate borders.

The common pastures and woodlands belonging to villages and towns were put in the category of *arazi-i metruke* (abandoned land). In reality, these were *miri* land, but their usufruct had been given to towns and villages since time immemorial as common property. These forests were now deemed public property and public good was considered to reign supreme over all other rights. Moreover, forests in this category could not become subject to private property claims.

Forest Ownership in the Aftermath of the Second Constitution

One of the first draft laws of Second Constitutional period was the *Orman ve Mer'a Kanununun Esbab-ı Mucibe Layihası* (Memorandum on the Justification for the Forest and Pasture Law). In this draft prepared by the pioneering Turkish forester Hoca Ali Rıza Efendi (1843-1925), the categories of the 1870 Regulation were maintained. Yet the forests belonging to *vakıf*s (pious foundations) were included in the section on private forests and differentiated into various parts. Moreover, there were also measures stipulating the allocation of woodlands to villages near forests in proportion to their population, if they did not already have one, while woodlands allocated to villages in the past were to be limited based on the assessment of the actual needs of the villages. In this draft law, forest officials were given wide-ranging oversight and control

---

62. Islamoğlu 2000, p. 28.
63. Ibid., pp. 27–29.

rights over village coppices 'to protect the interests of the relevant parties and the rule of science'.[64]

The first objective of this proposal to give a coppice for felling to peasants who did not have any was to abolish the fifth article of the Forest Regulation and to ban people from cutting trees from state forests without paying dues. The second objective was to grow self-sufficient coppices by protecting one fourth of the coppice each time. Moreover, it was also envisioned to ban the construction technique called *çatma* (stave houses) used in villages close to state forests, for it was deemed to waste too many trees.[65]

We know that the privileges given to villagers with the fifth article of the Forest Regulation also fed merchants and timber contractors. The merchants made contracts with villagers who, in return for the payment of tithes, were allowed to cut wood from forests for sale, instead of attending the state auctions for buying timber from forests. There was no article, either in the Regulation or in the directives that came in its wake, that could prevent this inconvenience. In the justification prepared by the *Şura-yı Devlet* (Council of State) during the preparation of the Regulation, the legislators recognised that villagers who cut wood from forest for trade were to pay the value of the timber and were liable to the articles of the Forest Regulation like merchants and contractors.[66]

According to Hoca Ali Rıza Efendi, the Land Code, allowing individuals to open *korus* and forests to make agricultural land, not only caused the destruction of forests and *korus* on rocky or arid lands, but was counterproductive as these lands would often turn out to be too unproductive to yield sustainable produce, despite the labour invested. He recommended these articles of the Land Code should be abolished.[67] In brief, the main solution introduced with this draft law was allocation of coppices from state forests to villagers, supplying them with the necessary and sufficient means to prevent them from cutting trees from state forests without payment.

The Constitutional period created an 'ancient régime' by abolishing the Hamidian regime – the period of Sultan Abdülhamid II (r. 1876-1909) – at once, which attracted criticism from opponents of the Committee of Union and Progress (CUP; *İttihad ve Terakki Cemiyeti*).[68] Many politically and economically structural (embedded) problems were now recast as remnants of the 'old' regime.

---

64. İsmail Hakkı 1328/1912, p. 180.
65. Ali Rıza 1328/1912.
66. Ibid.
67. Ibid.
68. Hanioğlu 2001, p. 6.

Hoca Ali Rıza Efendi also claimed that forests were destroyed during the 'age of Hamid' due to insufficient attention being paid to scientific management and administration of forests with the prioritisation of increasing revenue; and that this destruction came to an end with the 'age of Constitution', but that necessary measures needed to be immediately taken for the 're-invigoration and continuing prosperity of these forests'.[69]

While the draft touched on important points regarding forests and foresting, sufficient capital could not be procured until the outbreak of the Balkan Wars in 1912 for the management of important forests. Between 1912 and 1922, the consecutive wars again precluded forest administration from working properly. Until 1922, when the parliamentary government revisited the question of the forest resources of the country, the only measure to do with forests was the 1917 *Ormanların Usul-i İdare-i Fenniyyeleri Hakkındaki Kanun* (Law on the Scientific Management of Forests), which opened the way for the working of forests within the framework of management plans. However, the articles of this law only applied to state forests and the forests belonging to individuals or villages were still left within the jurisdiction of the Land Code.[70] In describing the forestry of this period, Mazhar Diker has claimed that the constitutional regime hardly differed from the previous periods and failed to effect fundamental change since it could not liberate itself from the precepts of Islamic law and Mecelle regarding *cibal-i mubaha*.[71] One of the most important judicial decisions of this period is the appeal decision from 1914 that stated that all forest would be considered *miri* forest until proven otherwise.[72]

Forest Property Ownership and Usufruct in the Early Republican Period

According to Diker, forests had to be 'liberated from the yoke of *cibal-i mubaha* and turned into a source of revenue'. Thus, resting on article 27 of the Mecelle, which said that 'in order to alleviate general harm, personal harm is preferred', and article 1254, which said 'everyone can benefit from *mubah*, but it is necessary not to harm anyone', it was reasoned that forests were actually public property and had to be taken under registration in order to be protected from being destroyed; and so the Regulation was issued.[73] Yet, again according to Diker,

---

69. Ali Rıza 1328/1912.
70. Diker 1947, p. 24; Eraslan 1957; idem 1973.
71. Diker 1947, pp. 26–27.
72. Günay 2003, p. 57.
73. Diker 1947, p. 25.

the issue of *mubah*-ness, which had been continuing for ages, had important repercussions just when it was thought to have been resolved:

> The Ottoman Empire, which considered it a fundamental principle to rest on Islamic law and jurisprudence in all its articles of law, had to materially benefit from the forests that the Islamic law and jurisprudence called *cibal-i mubaha*. Thus, it called the revenues to be taken from them the forest due, meaning the right of the state for protecting the forests, and thus thought to resolve the issue with a legal trick. Yet in return for the small revenue accrued to the treasury, an unsubstantial and unwarranted right was recognised that was to bring lasting harm to the country, rendering a major trouble to the forestry of the country.[74]

According to Diker, the Ottoman Empire found two ways to deal with the 'forest issue'. One was to give woodlands for cutting to villagers and the other was to allow them to use the *miri* (state/public) forests in a regulated and free manner.[75] Declaring *cibal-i mubaha* forests to be state forests was perhaps the most important step taken in changing the immemorial order. An initial period can be identified between 1920 and 1924 when forest policy was determined in accordance with the Coppice Law (*Baltalık Kanunu*) no. 29, issued on 7 March 1921.[76]

The first article of this law stipulated the allocation of a maximum of eighteen old *dönüm*s (one *dönüm* is about 919 square metres) of coppice per house in villages located at a maximum distance of twenty kilometres from large state forests. The existing coppices were to be expanded to reach the same proportion and were to be distributed without deeds to villages. The oversight of and responsibility for the protection of these coppices and the regulation of the villagers' access was devolved to village eldermen's councils. Interestingly, already in 1917, a decree presented to the government by the *Orman İdaresi* (Forest Administration) had already considered the 'protection and maintenance' of village coppices and forests belonging to individuals, as well as those of state forests. To that end, it was advised that villages without coppices should be allocated ten old *dönüm* per house from nearby forests and that the village council should be responsible for protection and management. By this measure, the government aimed to prevent individuals from cutting trees from state forests, again without payment. With regard to forests and groves in private hands, the goal was to prevent the cutting and removing of trees from places that were unsuitable for cultivation. The interesting part is that the eighteen old *dönüm*

---

74. Ibid., pp. 25–26.
75. Ibid., p. 22.
76. See footnote 55 above.

per household envisioned in the law was perceived as two hectares of woodland per household by many commentators.[77] The amount actually amounted to 16.5 *dönüm*s, and thus was nowhere near two hectares.

Article 2 of the Coppice Law stipulated that, if it proved impossible to set aside the amount of coppice prescribed in article 1 due to the forests near the village being in the hands of individuals, a commission of three (comprising two people chosen by villagers and the forest owner, and a neutral third person that both sides agreed on, or elected by the forest official if there was no agreement) was to determine an approximate value for the necessary amount of forest, the cost was to be paid by the village upfront and the woodland was to be registered in the name of the village. If the village was able to come up with the price, they were to be extended credit from the *Ziraat Bankası* (Agricultural Bank) with the backing of the Ministry of Economy. If the sides could not agree on the price, they could go to the court to either increase or decrease it but such an appeal was not sufficient to forestall the decision to sell. Another important article of the Coppice Law was article 4, which decreed that villagers could not enter state forests for any reason without an official document, issued by the forest administration, or graze their animals therein.

As shown, the Coppice Law revisited the old concerns and, besides preventing cutting of trees for free from state forests, also tried to prevent unpermitted animal grazing. There are opinions to the effect that this law constituted a concession to villagers to ensure their continuing support and backing for the Turkish National Struggle (19 May 1919–24 July 1923), or that it was a form of support for a populace that got increasingly poor due to continuing wars.[78] Yet, according to article 7 of this Law, timber, wood or charcoal procured by villagers in their own coppice were exempted from all kinds of dues. This alone suffices to explain how the villagers ended up cutting the coppices allocated to them and selling them at market, turning the cleared coppices into agricultural land.

With the 1937 Law of Forests, all forests in Turkey were nationalised. Even before being taken into the category of state forests, most private forests and forests owned by *tüzel kişiler* (corporate bodies) as well as by waqfs were already facing destruction. Once they became nationalised, they were considered 'ownerless' for a time and, with the previous protection measures eliminated and the state's forest organisation not yet having sufficient power, were exploited in an uncontrolled manner by opportunists. According to Friedrich

---

77.   Ibid., p. 29.
78.   Diker 1947, p. 28; Küçük 1978, p. 19.

Zednik, who conducted research on Turkish forests in the 1950s, the best way to prevent such infringements and to protect forests was to reintroduce the idea of 'public forests'.[79]

The Forest Regulation stayed in force with certain revisions and additions until the 1937 Forest Law, number 3116. The 1937 Law abolished villagers' right to freely use state forests, while allowing villagers living within a distance of five kilometres to cut wood at one fourth the price. The extent of these rights was further expanded with the 1938 law number 3444, and the distance for villages allowed to make use of the products of state forests was increased to ten kilometres, while the price was reduced to one tenth. With the 1945 Forest Law, forests in Turkey were completely nationalised. The articles that primarily aimed to curtail the use of state forests for free were retained in the Forest Law no 6831 that came into effect in 1956.[80]

In Lieu of Conclusion

When the government shifted the category of *cibal-i mubaha* forests, originally covering extensive lands, probably not less than half of the whole forests of the empire, a critical phase in the dispossession of the commons was completed in the Ottoman Empire. The dispossession was made possible by the appropriation of commons and communal resources for so-called public benefit and to meet the state's financial needs In the Ottoman Empire, this process happened through the state's ability to present formerly used rights as if they were being given back to the villagers and townspeople by the Regulation. The dispossession of villagers from their traditional rights resulted in an increase in rural poverty for those villagers who provided their livelihood from forest-related products. It seems that the source of livelihood for villagers became the source of revenue for the state. Due to this social transformation, the traditional beneficiaries of forest commons increasingly depended on selling their labour to the local forest administrations.

The state ownership of *cibal-i mubaha* forests precipitated the 'privatisation' of forests by removing them from common use or joint usufruct. Local and central government commercialised these forests in favour of economic interest and against the interest of poor peasants. At this point the state protected and prioritised the commercial interest, the local notables and timber traders. In this process there were some setbacks, struggles and negotiations, and plenty

79. Zednik 1963, p. 5.
80. Çağlar 1992; idem 2012; Özdönmez et al. 1989.

of legislation that was incommensurate with the desired outcome. Before the nineteenth century, it mattered that forests should be converted into agricultural land for subsistence production, and there were already administrative and legal regulations serving that end. In that perspective, there were some safeguards protecting the individual rights of poor peasants but, overall, these rights were considered secondary to the basic objective of increasing the production of grain. In the nineteenth century, with the forest becoming a commodity in its own right, the privatisation of forest use eventually entailed an absolute loss of poor peasants' right to use state forests.

The main issue was whether peasants could still meet their basic needs from *cibal-i mubaha* forests once the dispossessing of forests had been carried out. At least in theory, the people had equal rights to make use of these forests. Léon Duguit, who played a founding role in the development of administrative law in Turkey, has claimed that state forests are also public property, as 'properties that are allocated to free and direct use by the people'.[81] Based on the analogy of the *cibal-i mubaha* forests, allocated to the free use of the people and treated as common property outside of the private and state property regime, with state forests, the 1870 Forest Regulation had consecrated them as state forests. Thus, references to the destructive acts and mentalities of peasants in the *cibal-i mubaha* promoted a legal and administrative rhetoric that justified the dispossession of commons.

From the mid-nineteenth century to the twentieth century the main thrust of the history of forestry was the institution of the state property rights and the concomitant curtailment of the certain privileges initially granted to those who had traditional usufruct rights over forests. Naturally, this process, and the implementation of the legislations and principles it brought about, witnessed struggles and negotiations especially between the forest administration and other state institutions, villagers and local power holders. In the end, due to the discrepancies emerging from the implementation of rules and regulations regarding forest and agricultural land, especially from the 1870s onwards, private individuals claimed large tracts of forest and, in return, the state nationalised all forests. The people who had traditionally made use of forests were thus deprived of their ancient rights to benefit from open access and commons.

---

81.   Onar 1944, p. 488.

Dispossession by Concession

Bibliography

Unpublished Primary Sources

The Prime Ministry Ottoman Archives (*Başbakanlık Osmanlı Arşivleri, BOA*), Istanbul
Sadâret Mektubî Kalemi Deâvî (A.MKT.DV), 49/27, 142/44
Sadâret Mektubî Kalemi Mühimme Kalemi (A.MKT.MHM), 360/26
Sadâret Mektubî Kalemi Umûm Vilâyât (A.MKT.UM), 48/22
Rumeli Müfettişliği Defterleri (TFR.I.A), 4/399

Published Primary Sources

Akçuraoğlu, Yusuf (ed.) 1928. *Türk Yılı*. Istanbul: Yeni Matbaa.

Ali Haydar. 1321/1905. *Şerh-i Cedîdi'l-Kânûni'l-Arazî*. Istanbul: A. Asaduryan Matbaası.

———. 1330/1914. *Dürerü'l-Hükkâm Şerh-i Mecelleti'l-Ahkâm: Hacr ve İkrâh ve Şüf'a, Şirket, Vekâlet Mesâilini Hâvîdir, vol. 3*. 4 vols. Istanbul: Matbaa-i Hukuk and Matbaa-i Tevsi-i Tıbaat.

Ali Rıza. 1328/1912. *Orman ve Mer'a Kanununun Esbab-ı Mucibe Layihası*. Istanbul: Mahmud Bey Matbaası.

Bricogne, Louis [Adolphe Ambroise]. 1877. 'Les fôrets de l'Empire ottoman'. *Revue des eaux et fôrêts* 16: 273–289 and 321–335.

———. 1940 [1877]. *Türkiyede Ormancılık Heyeti*. Ankara: TC Ziraat Vekâleti.

İsmail Hakkı. 1328/1912 *Hukuk-ı İdare*. Istanbul: Edeb Matbaası.

Kutluk, Halil (ed.) 1948. *Türkiye Ormancılığı ile ilgili Tarihî Vesikalar, 893–1339 (1487–1923)*, TC Tarım Bakanlığı Orman Genel Müdürlüğü Yayını, No: 56. Istanbul: Osmanbey Matbaası.

Secondary Sources

Acun, Niyazi. 1945. *Ormanlarımız ve Cumhuriyet Hükümeti'nin Orman Davası*. Ankara: Recep Ulusoğlu Basımevi.

Barkan, Ömer Lütfi. 1980. 'Türk Toprak Hukuku Tarihinde Tanzimat ve 1274 (1858) Tarihli Arazi Kanunnamesi'. In *Türkiye'de Toprak Meselesi*. Istanbul: Gözlem Yayınları. pp. 291–375.

———. 1943. *XV-XVI inci Asırlarda Osmanlı İmparatorluğunda Ziraî Ekonominin Hukukî ve Malî Esasları*. Istanbul: Istanbul Üniversitesi Yayınları.

Benton, Lauren and Benjamin Straumann. 2010. 'Acquiring Empire by Law: From Roman Doctrine to Early Modern European Practice'. *Law and History Review* 28 (1): 1–38.

Bilmen, Ömer Nasuhi. 1970. *Hukuk-ı İslâmiyye ve Istılahat-ı Fıkhiyye Kamusu, vol. 7*. 8 vols. Istanbul: Bilmen Yayınevi.

Birben, Üstüner. 2009. 'Cibal-i Mübaha'. In Ahmet Tolunay, Mehmet Korkmaz and Hasan Alkan (eds), *II. Ormancılıkta Sosyo-Ekonomik Sorunlar Kongresi*. Isparta: Süleyman Demirel Üniversitesi. pp. 395–404.

Buckland, William Warwick. 1921. *A Text-Book of Roman Law from Augustus to Justinian.* Cambridge: Cambridge University Press.

Çağlar, Yücel. 1992. *Türkiye'de Orman ve Ormancılık.* Istanbul: İletişim.

——. 2012. *Türkiye Ormancılık Tarihi.* Ankara: ODTÜ Geliştirme Vakfı.

Cin, Halil. 1981. 'Tanzimattan Sonra Türkiye'de Ormanların Hukuki Rejimi.' *Ankara Üniversitesi Hukuk Fakültesi Dergisi* 35 (1–4): 311–79.

Crone, Patricia. 1987. *Roman, Provincial and Islamic Law: The Origins of the Islamic Patronate.* Cambridge: Cambridge University Press.

Dardot, Pierre and Christian Laval. 2018. *Müşterek: 21. Yüzyılda Devrim Üzerine Deneme.* Trans. Emine Sarıkartal and Ferhat Taylan. Istanbul: Bilgi Universitesi Yayınları. Original edition: *Commun: essai sur la révolution au XXIe siècle* [2014].

Davis, Diana K. 2007. *Resurrecting the Granary of Rome: Environmental History and French Colonial Expansion in North Africa.* Athens: Ohio University Press.

De Angelis, Massimo. 2017. *Omnia Sunt Communia: On the Commons and the Transformation to Postcapitalism.* London: Zed Books.

Diker, Mazhar. 1947. *Türkiyede Ormancılık: Dün-Bugün-Yarın.* Ankara: TC Tarım Bakanlığı.

Eraslan, İsmail. 1957. 'Türkiye'de Silvikültür ve Amenajman Münasebetlerinin 100 Yıllık Tarihî İnkişafı'. In Halil Kutluk and Hasan Asmaz (eds), *Türk Ormancılığı Yüzüncü Tedris Yılına Girerken, 1857–1957.* Ankara: Türkiye Ormancılar Cemiyeti. pp. 62–67.

——. 1973. 'Türkiye'de Orman Amenajmanının Gelişimi ve Yeni Yönelimleri'. *İ.Ü. Orman Fakültesi Dergisi* 23–24: 1–12.

Foster, John Bellamy and Brett Clark. 2018. 'The Expropriation of Nature'. *Monthly Review* 69 (10): 1–27.

Guha, Ramachandra. 2000. *The Unquiet Woods: Ecological Change and Peasant Resistance in the Himalaya.* Berkeley: University of California Press.

Günay, Turhan. 2003. *Ormancılığımızın Tarihçesine Kısa Bir Bakış.* Ankara: Tarım Orkam-Sen.

Hallaq, Wael B. 1990. 'The Use and Abuse of Evidence: The Question of Provincial and Roman Influences on Early Islamic Law'. *Journal of the American Oriental Society* 110 (1): 79–91.

Hanioğlu, M. Şükrü. 2001. *Preparation for a Revolution: The Young Turks, 1902–1908.* Oxford: Oxford University Press.

Hardin, Garrett. 1968. 'The Tragedy of the Commons'. *Science* 162: 1243–48.

Hardt, Michael and Antonio Negri. 2009. *Commonwealth.* Cambridge, MA: Belknap Press of Harvard University Press.

Harvey, David. 2005. *A Brief History of Neoliberalism.* Oxford and New York: Oxford University Press.

Islamoğlu, Huri. 2000. 'Property as a Contested Domain: A Reevalution of the Ottoman Land Code of 1858'. In Roger Owen (ed.), *New Perspectives on Property and Land in the Middle East.* Cambridge, MA and London: Harvard University Press. pp. 3–61.

Koç, Bekir. 1999. 'Osmanlı Devletiḥdeki Orman ve Koruların Tasarruf Yöntemleri ve İdarelerine İlişkin Bir Araştırma'. *Ankara Üniversitesi, Osmanlı Tarihi Araştırma ve Uygulama Merkezi (OTAM) Dergisi* 10: 139–58.

——. 2005. '1870 Orman Nizamnamesi'nin Osmanlı Ormancılığına Katkısı Üzerine Bazı Notlar'. *A.Ü. DTCF Tarih Araştırmaları Dergisi* 24 (37): 231–57.

Köprülü, Bülent. 1948. 'Türk Hukukunda Orman Mülkiyeti'. *İ. Ü. Hukuk Fakültesi Mecmuası* 14 (3–4): 700–54.

——. 1949. 'Cibal-i Mubaha ve Sahih Vakıflara Ait Ormanlarla Baltalıkların H.1274 Tarihli Arazi Kanunnamesine Nazaran Hukukî Durumları'. *İ. Ü. Hukuk Fakültesi Mecmuası* 15 (2–3): 703–26.

——. 1950. '11 Şevval H. 1286 Tarihli Orman Nizamnamesinin Getirdiği Yenilikler'. *İ. Ü. Hukuk Fakültesi Mecmuası* 16 (1–2): 237–71.

Küçük, Yalçın. 1978. *Türkiye Üzerine Tezler, 1908-1978*. Istanbul: Tekin Yayınevi.

Onar, Sıddık Sami. 1944. 'Türk Hukukunda Âmme Emlâki Teorisi'. In *Ebül'ula Mardin'e Armağan*. Istanbul: Kenan Matbaası. pp. 479–535.

Ophuls, William. 1977. *Ecology and the Politics of Scarcity: Prologue to a Political Theory of the Steady State*. San Francisco: W.H. Freeman.

Ostrom, Elinor. 1990. *Governing the Commons: The Evolution of Institutions for Collective Action*. Cambridge and New York: Cambridge University Press.

——. 1999. 'Coping with Tragedies of the Commons'. *Annual Review of Political Science* 2 (1): 493–535.

Ostrom, Elinor, Joanna Burger, Christopher B. Field, Richard B. Norgaard and David Policansky. 1999. 'Revisiting the Commons: Local Lessons, Global Challenges'. *Science* 284: 278–82.

Ostrom, Elinor and Roy Gardner. 1993. 'Coping with Asymmetries in the Commons: Self-Governing Irrigation Systems Can Work'. *The Journal of Economic Perspectives* 7 (4): 93–112.

Özdönmez, Metin, Turhan İstanbullu and Aytuğ Akesen. 1989. *Ormancılık Politikası*. Istanbul: Taş Matbaası.

Rose, Carol M. 1991. 'Rethinking Environmental Controls: Management Strategies for Common Resources'. *Duke Law Journal* 40 (1) : 1–38.

——. 2003. 'Romans, Roads, and Romantic Creators: Traditions of Public Property in the Information Age'. *Law and Contemporary Problems* 66 (91): 89–110.

Roselaar, Saskia T. 2010. *Public Land in the Roman Republic: A Social and Economic History of Ager Publicus in Italy, 396–89 B.C.* Oxford: Oxford University Press.

Schmidt, Franz Frederik. 1910. 'Die occupatio im islamischen Recht'. *Der Islam. Journal of the History and Culture of the Middle East* 1 (3–4): 300–53.

Sönmez, M. Tului. 1998. *Osmanlıdan Günümüze Toprak Mülkiyeti: Açıklamalı Sözlük*. 2nd ed. Ankara: Yayımevi.

Tunçsiper, Nedim. 1957. 'Tarih Boyunca Ormancılık Politikamız'. In Halil Kutluk and Hasan Asmaz (eds), *Türk Ormancılığı Yüzüncü Tedris Yılına Girerken, 1857-1957*. Ankara: Türkiye Ormancılar Cemiyeti. pp. 316–23.

——. 1964. *Türk Hukuk Tarihi, İdare Hukuku ve Medeni Hukukumuz Muvacehesinde Orman Mevzuatımız İle İlgili Araştırmalar*. Ankara: Orman Genel Müdürlüğü.

Walljasper, Jay. 2014. *Müştereklerimiz: Paylaştığımız Her Şey*. Istanbul: Metis.

Weston, Burns H. and David Bollier. 2013. *Green Governance: Ecological Survival, Human Rights, and the Law of the Commons*. Cambridge and New York: Cambridge University Press.

Wily, Liz Alden. 2011. *The Tragedy of Public Lands: The Fate of the Commons under Global Commercial Pressure*. Rome: CIRAD and International Land Coalition.

Zednik, Friedrich. 1963. *Türkiye Ormanları, Bugüne Kadar Tatbik Edilen ve Gelecekte Tatbiki Tavsiye Edilen Silvikültürel Muameleler*. Trans. Hasan Selçuk. Ankara: Güzel Istanbul Matbaası.

INDEX

Index

Index

Index

Index

Index

U

V

W

Index

www.ingramcontent.com/pod-product-compliance
Lightning Source LLC
Chambersburg PA
CBHW022302280326
41932CB00010B/951